A MUCH MISUNDERSTOOD MAN

A MUCH MISUNDERSTOOD MAN

SELECTED LETTERS OF AMBROSE BIERCE

Edited by S. T. Joshi and David E. Schultz

THE OHIO STATE UNIVERSITY PRESS
Columbus

Copyright © 2003 by The Ohio State University Press
All rights reserved.

Library of Congress Cataloging-in-Publication Data

Bierce, Ambrose, 1842–1914?
  A much misunderstood man : selected letters of Ambrose Bierce / Edited by S. T. Joshi and David E. Schultz.
     p. cm.
Includes bibliographical references and index.
ISBN: 978-0-8142-5332-8
  1. Bierce, Ambrose, 1842-1914?—Correspondence. 2. Authors, American—19th century—Correspondence. 3. Journalists—United States—Correspondence. I. Joshi, S. T. (Sunand Tryambak), 1958– II. Schultz, David E., 1952– III. Title.
  PS1097.Z5 A4 2003
  813'.4—dc21

2002154626.

Cover design by Dan O'Dair

The paper used in this publication meets the minimum requirements of the American National Standard for Information Sciences—Permanence of Paper for Printed Library Materials. ANSI Z39.48-1992.

9 8 7 6 5 4 3 2 1

To Lawrence I. Berkove

CONTENTS

List of Abbreviations	xiii
Introduction	xv
A Note on This Edition	xxv

Selected Letters
1. To Clara Wright (8 June 1864) — 1
2. To Bret Harte [December 1870] — 3
3. To John H. Carmany [February 1871?] — 4
4. To John H. Carmany (15 March 1871) — 5
5. To Timothy H. Rearden (8 January 1872) — 6
6. To Charles Warren Stoddard (29 December 1872) — 7
7. To Charles Warren Stoddard (16 March 1873) — 8
8. To Charles Warren Stoddard (28 September 1873) — 10
9. To Charles Warren Stoddard [22 November 1873] — 11
10. To Charles Warren Stoddard [January 1874?] — 12
11. To Charles Warren Stoddard (26 April 1874) — 13
12. To Charles Warren Stoddard (4 July 1874) — 14
13. To Charles Warren Stoddard (2 June 1875) — 15
14. To Laura Bierce (13 February 1876) — 16
15. To Laura Bierce (30 April 1876) — 17
16. To E. L. G. Steele (25 February [1884]) — 17
17. To Helen Bierce (2 April 1885) — 18
18. To John H. Boalt (16 April 1885) — 19
19. To Sergt. Abe Dills (13 August 1887) — 20
20. To Helen Bierce [September 1890?] — 21
21. To Ella Sterling Cummins (13 March 1892) — 22
22. To Blanche Partington (31 July 1892) — 23
23. To Blanche Partington (15 August 1892) — 24
24. To Blanche Partington (17 August 1892) — 26
25. To Blanche Partington (28 September 1892) — 28
26. To Blanche Partington (25 December 1892) — 29
27. To Blanche Partington (9 January 1893) — 30
28. To Gustav Adolphe Danziger (1 February 1893) — 31
29. To Blanche Partington (5 February 1893) — 33
30. To Gustav Adolphe Danziger (11 February 1893) — 34
31. To James Tufts (16 April 1893) — 35
32. To Percival Pollard (22 April 1893) — 36
33. To Blanche Partington (26 April 1893) — 37
34. To Percival Pollard (20 July 1893) — 38
35. To Stone & Kimball (7 November 1893) — 39
36. To Stone & Kimball (4 December 1893) — 40

37.	To Mrs. E. L. G. Steele [3 July 1894?]	41
38.	To Warring Wilkinson (18 June 1895)	41
39.	To Carroll Carrington (26 June 1895)	42
40.	To Ray Frank (13 July 1895)	42
41.	To Herman Scheffauer [12 August 1895]	43
42.	To Ray Frank (5 September 1895)	45
43.	To Warring Wilkinson (24 September 1895)	45
44.	To Lily Walsh (13 October 1895)	47
45.	To C. W. Doyle (21 October 1895)	47
46.	To C. W. Doyle (22 November 1895)	48
47.	To C. W. Doyle (22 December 1895)	49
48.	To Myles Walsh (16 February 1896)	50
49.	To C. W. Doyle (22 March 1896)	51
50.	To C. W. Doyle (25 May 1896)	52
51.	To Ray Frank (13 July 1896)	52
52.	To Ray Frank (30 October 1896)	53
53.	To C. W. Doyle (8 February 1897)	54
54.	To Edwin Markham (19 May 1897)	55
55.	To Harriet Hershberg (11 July 1897)	55
56.	To Ray Frank (3 October 1897)	56
57.	To Percival Pollard (12 October 1897)	58
58.	To Myles Walsh (14 November 1897)	58
59.	To C. W. Doyle (26 December 1897)	59
60.	To Jean Hazen (16 March 1898)	60
61.	To C. W. Doyle (8 May 1898)	60
62.	To Percival Pollard (8 January 1899)	62
63.	To Eleanor Vore (27 January 1899)	63
64.	To Edwin Markham (14 March 1899)	64
65.	To Edmund Clarence Stedman (19 March 1899)	65
66.	To S. O. Howes (4 May 1899)	67
67.	To Edmund Clarence Stedman (4 May 1899)	67
68.	To S. G. Blythe (27 November 1899)	68
69.	To S. O. Howes (29 November 1899)	68
70.	To Herman Scheffauer (8 June 1900)	69
71.	To Gustav Adolphe Danziger (21 August 1900)	70
72.	To Herman Scheffauer (1 December 1900)	72
73.	To Gustav Adolphe Danziger [late December 1900?]	74
74.	To C. W. Doyle (23 January 1901)	75
75.	To Herman Scheffauer (29 March 1901)	77
76.	To Herman Scheffauer (2 April 1901)	78
77.	To George Sterling (22 May 1901)	78
78.	To Myles Walsh (7 September 1901)	79
79.	To Herman Scheffauer (17 October 1901)	79
80.	To George Sterling (16 December 1901)	80

81.	To George Sterling (15 March 1902)	82
82.	To Robert H. Davis [summer 1902?]	86
83.	To Herman Scheffauer (2 July 1902)	86
84.	To George Sterling (10 July 1902)	87
85.	To Herman Scheffauer (2 August 1902)	88
86.	To Herman Scheffauer [September 1902?]	90
87.	To Herman Scheffauer (5 October 1902)	92
88.	To Herman Scheffauer (23 October 1902)	94
89.	To Herman Scheffauer (5 February 1903)	98
90.	To George Sterling (1 March 1903)	99
91.	To Herman Scheffauer (27 March 1903)	100
92.	To Herman Scheffauer [6 May 1903?]	103
93.	To George Sterling (13 June 1903)	104
94.	To Herman Scheffauer [July 1903]	106
95.	To Herman Scheffauer (4 August 1903)	109
96.	To George Sterling (12 September 1903)	110
97.	To Herman Scheffauer (27 September 1903)	111
98.	To Herman Scheffauer (12 October 1903)	113
99.	To Herman Scheffauer (11 November 1903)	114
100.	To George Sterling (8 January 1904)	115
101.	To George Sterling (31 January 1904)	117
102.	To Herman Scheffauer (12 February 1904)	118
103.	To George Sterling (29 February 1904)	120
104.	To Herman Scheffauer (20 March 1904)	122
105.	To George Sterling (11 May 1904)	123
106.	To Herman Scheffauer (17 July 1904)	124
107.	To George Sterling (4 August 1904)	125
108.	To George Sterling (5 October 1904)	126
109.	To Robert H. Davis (12 October 1904)	128
110.	To Herman Scheffauer (4 & 5 November 1904)	129
111.	To George Sterling (18 February 1905)	131
112.	To Herman Scheffauer (10 April 1905)	132
113.	To George Sterling (16 May 1905)	135
114.	To Myles Walsh (6 June 1905)	136
115.	To George Sterling (16 June 1905)	137
116.	To S. O. Howes (17 September 1905)	140
117.	To S. O. Howes (4 November 1905)	141
118.	To John O'Hara Cosgrave (19 November 1905)	142
119.	To George Harvey (19 November 1905)	144
120.	To George Sterling (3 December 1905)	145
121.	To George Sterling (3 February 1906)	146
122.	To George Sterling (12 March 1906)	147
123.	To George Sterling (20 April 1906)	149
124.	To George H. Casamajor (22 April 1906)	149

125.	To George Sterling (6 May 1906)	150
126.	To S. O. Howes (9 June 1906)	152
127.	To George Sterling (11 June 1906)	153
128.	To William Randolph Hearst (12 October 1906)	155
129.	To Perriton Maxwell (23 November 1906)	156
130.	To S. O. Howes (19 February 1907)	157
131.	To George Sterling (21 February 1907)	158
132.	To George Sterling (11 June 1907)	159
133.	To William Randolph Hearst (8 July 1907)	160
134.	To William Randolph Hearst (13 July 1907)	161
135.	To George Sterling (17 August 1907)	162
136.	To George Sterling (7 September 1907)	164
137.	To Herman Scheffauer (30 September 1907)	165
138.	To W. C. Morrow (9 October 1907)	166
139.	To Robert H. Davis (13 October 1907)	167
140.	To James D. Blake [29 October 1907?]	169
141.	To Helen (Bierce) Cowden (14 November 1907)	170
142.	To S. O. Howes (30 November 1907 / 1 December 1907)	171
143.	To George Sterling (28 December 1907)	171
144.	To S. S. Chamberlain (22 March 1908)	172
145.	To S. O. Howes (24 March 1908)	173
146.	To William Randolph Hearst (30 March 1908)	174
147.	To Herman Scheffauer (31 March 1908)	175
148.	To Walter Neale (28 April 1908)	178
149.	To George Sterling (8 May 1908)	179
150.	To William Randolph Hearst (18 May 1908)	180
151.	To William Randolph Hearst (23 May 1908)	182
152.	To Walter Neale (7 June 1908)	183
153.	To George Sterling (11 July 1908)	185
154.	To George Sterling (14 August 1908)	187
155.	To George Sterling (6 November 1908)	189
156.	To Herman Scheffauer (10 January 1909)	190
157.	To William Randolph Hearst (7 March 1909)	191
158.	To George d'Utassy (23 March 1909)	193
159.	To S. O. Howes (27 July 1909)	193
160.	To Harry Cowden (8 August 1909)	194
161.	To S. O. Howes (6 September 1909)	196
162.	To George Sterling (29 January 1910)	198
163.	To S. O. Howes (7 March 1910)	199
164.	To George Sterling (7 March 1910)	201
165.	To Walter Neale (24 May 1910)	202
166.	To Walter Neale (15 July 1910)	203
167.	To George Sterling (1 September 1910)	204
168.	To William E. Connelley (4 October 1910)	205

169.	To Helen (Bierce) Cowden (4 November 1910)	205
170.	To Lora Bierce (29 November 1910)	206
171.	To George Sterling (15 February 1911)	207
172.	To Ruth Robertson (1 March 1911)	209
173.	To Colonel Archibald Gracie (9 March 1911)	210
174.	To Walter Neale (22 March 1911)	212
175.	To Samuel Loveman (28 May 1911)	213
176.	To George Sterling (31 July 1911)	214
177.	To S. O. Howes (17 September 1911)	215
178.	To Charles Dexter Allen (27 September 1911)	215
179.	To George Sterling (29 September 1911)	216
180.	To Walter Neale (21 October 1911)	217
181.	To George Sterling (16 November 1911)	218
182.	To Mrs. Percival Pollard (17 December 1911)	219
183.	To Walter Neale (3 January 1912)	220
184.	To Eleanor (Vore) Sickler (10 January 1912)	220
185.	To George Sterling [25 April 1912]	221
186.	To Walter Neale (22 May 1912)	222
187.	To S. O. Howes (14 June 1912)	223
188.	To Walter Neale (2 July 1912)	224
189.	To the Editor of *Town Talk* (6 August [1912])	225
190.	To George Sterling (9 September 1912)	226
191.	To Helen (Bierce) Cowden (6 November [1912])	226
192.	To Blanche Partington (8 November 1912)	227
193.	To Walter Neale (8 January 1913)	228
194.	To Walter Neale (23 January 1913)	232
195.	To Helen (Bierce) Cowden (27 January 1913)	234
196.	To H. L. Mencken (21 April 1913)	235
197.	To Willard Huntington Wright (9 May 1913)	236
198.	To H. L. Mencken [May 1913]	236
199.	To Amy L. Wells (13 June 1913)	237
200.	To Amy L. Wells (10 July 1913)	238
201.	To Amy L. Wells (5 August 1913)	239
202.	To Helen (Bierce) Cowden (10 September 1913)	240
203.	To the Neale Publishing Co. (19 September 1913)	240
204.	To Eleanor (Vore) Sickler (21 September 1913)	241
205.	To Amy L. Wells (21 September 1913)	242
206.	To Lora Bierce (1 October 1913)	243
207.	To Helen (Bierce) Cowden (30 October 1913)	243
208.	To Helen (Bierce) Cowden (4 November 1913)	244
209.	To Blanche Partington (26 December 1913)	244

Bibliography	247
Index	249

LIST OF ABBREVIATIONS

AB	Ambrose Bierce
AJHS	American Jewish Historical Society (Worcester, Mass.)
ALS	autograph letter, signed
BL	Bancroft Library, University of California (Berkeley)
CC	Colorado College (Colorado Springs)
CHS	California Historical Society (San Francisco)
CU	Columbia University (New York, N.Y.)
CW	*Collected Works* (Neale Publishing Co., 1909–12; 12 vols.)
EPFL	Enoch Pratt Free Library (Baltimore, Md.)
GS	George Sterling
HL	Huntington Library and Art Gallery (San Marino, Calif.)
HU	Harvard University (Cambridge, Mass.)
LC	Library of Congress (Washington, D.C.)
MEG	Mary Elizabeth Grenander Papers, State University of New York at Albany
NYJ	*New York Journal*
NYPL	New York Public Library (New York, N.Y.)
PU	Princeton University (Princeton, N.J.)
SC	Scripps College (Claremont, Calif.)
SC	*Shapes of Clay* (1903)
SF	*San Francisco Examiner*
SFPL	San Francisco Public Library (San Francisco, Calif.)
TLS	typed letter, signed
UC	University of Cincinnati (Cincinnati, Ohio)
UL	University of Louisville (Louisville, Ky.)
UP	University of Pennsylvania (Philadelphia)
USC	University of Southern California (Los Angeles)
VA	University of Virginia (Charlottesville)
WC	Wagner College (Staten Island, N.Y.)
YU	Yale University (New Haven, Conn.)

INTRODUCTION

In response to a friend's suggestion in 1895 that he write his memoirs, Ambrose Bierce derisively suggested *The Autobiography of a Much Misunderstood Man* as one of several preposterous titles for a work that he thought would be supernumerary and self-promotional. Anticipating the New Critics by a generation, Bierce felt that a writer's work was entirely sufficient for purposes of literary evaluation, and that his life, opinions, and character served only to "darken counsel." Accordingly, despite a literary *oeuvre* well exceeding five million words in a forty-two-year career as journalist and author, and nearly 500,000 words of surviving correspondence, Bierce remains—by design—a man of mystery in American letters. His disappearance into Mexico in late 1913 was a fittingly enigmatic conclusion to the life of a man who, both as writer and as human being, always played his hand close to the vest. Yet Bierce's mock title for that unwritten autobiography is apt for more than one reason, and it is precisely because his correspondence—which alone of the many facets of his writings comes closest to revealing the "true" Bierce—has not been widely available that misunderstandings of his life, work, and character abound. Bierce the cynic; Bierce the misanthrope; Bierce the chillingly emotionless chronicler of horror and death: all these characterizations have a kernel of truth, but they are too crude and unnuanced to be anything but dismissive putdowns.

The standard conception of Bierce is perhaps best summed in Clifton Fadiman's well-known screed:

> Bierce's nihilism is as brutal and simple as a blow, and, by the same token, not too convincing. It has no base in philosophy and, being quite bare of shading or qualification, becomes, if taken in overdoses, a trifle tedious. Except for the skeleton grin that creeps over the face when he has devised in his fiction some peculiarly grotesque death, Bierce never deviates into cheerfulness. His rage is unselective. The great skeptics view human nature without admiration but also without ire. Bierce's misanthropy is too systematic. He is a pessimism-machine. He is a Swift minus true intellectual power, Rochefoucauld with a bludgeon, Voltaire with stomach ulcers.[1]

Like many of his predecessors and successors, Fadiman sought to infer Bierce's personality from those stories and apparently from little other evidence. However, as Bierce's letters reveal, Fadiman's commentary is wildly at variance with the truth. The letters reveal a man whose sensitivity to the fragility of beings faced with the cold indifference of an unfeeling universe was so pronounced, whose moral code of unflinching honesty and rectitude so unwavering, and whose expectations of moral uprightness in his friends so resolute, that he was prepared to face a hostile world—that "unknown destination" of his final letter—alone but unbroken.

Of Bierce's early life and upbringing we know little. He was born on 24 June 1842, in Meigs County, Ohio, the tenth of thirteen children of Marcus Aurelius and Laura (Sherwood) Bierce and the youngest to survive to adulthood. By 1857 he had left his family and moved to Elkhart, Indiana, where he worked as a printer's apprentice on the *Northern Indianan,* an abolitionist newspaper. In a late letter to William E. Connolley, Bierce confessed "I am reprehensibly ignorant of family matters, having lived apart from my relations from an early age" (letter 168). Of his multitude of siblings, he remained close only to his older brother Albert and, later, to Albert's son Carleton (a surrogate, perhaps, for the two sons he lost to early deaths) and his wife Lora.

Bierce joined the Ninth Indiana Volunteers almost immediately upon the outbreak of the Civil War in April 1861. He served nearly four years, seeing action in some of the bloodiest battles of the war—Shiloh, Chickamauga, Pickett's Mill, Missionary Ridge, and others. Nearly a half-century later, writing to the Southern revisionist historian Archibald Gracie, Bierce still recalled many of the smallest particulars of the Battle of Chickamauga. Although he wrote no formal memoir, the several sketches he collectively called "Bits of Autobiography" (in the first volume of his *Collected Works*) contain several strikingly vivid accounts of his military service, written, for the most part, twenty and more years after the fact. We are fortunate to have one letter written from a camp in Atlanta in 1864 to Clara Wright, the sister of Bierce's fiancée Fatima. His engagement did not last, but the letter has.

It is a common assertion that Bierce developed his "pessimism," "misanthropy," and "cynicism" as a result of his war experiences. To be sure, it took Bierce decades to digest the hard lessons of the Civil War, but the result of his cogitations was far from simple or straightforward.[2] The war might have shattered Bierce's idealism, rendering him bitter and disenchanted—bitter over the folly of some of his commanding officers, over the tragic and oftentimes needless waste of young life, and perhaps over the moral and political ramifications of the war's outcome—but such a reaction was common among the men and women of his generation. Evidence suggests that Bierce found army life exhilarating and that he prided himself on being a war-tested soldier. He was, after all, one of the few active participants of the Civil War to become a distinguished literary figure.

By 1867, after a brief stint as an aide in the Treasury Department, Bierce established himself as a writer in San Francisco. His earliest publications date to that time, mostly in the *San Francisco News Letter and California Advertiser,* of which he became editor in December 1868. For the next three years Bierce wrote the weekly "Town Crier" column and other miscellaneous work. His letters for this period are sparse, consisting only of some brief messages to Bret Harte and others concerning his contributions to Harte's pioneering magazine, the *Overland Monthly.* Bierce's marriage to Mary Ellen ("Mollie") Day on Christmas 1871 passes without mention in his surviving correspondence.

By the spring of 1872 Bierce had decided to seek his fortune in England, as had fellow Californians Mark Twain, Joaquin Miller, and Charles Warren Stoddard. Since

Twain was chiefly a lecturer and Bierce an overworked journalist on Grub Street, their contacts were few. Later in life Bierce admitted that he and Twain were frequently mistaken for each other, especially when they both gained a shock of strikingly white hair and eyebrows. Bierce's British stay is made extraordinarily vivid by his letters to Stoddard, whose grotesquely misspelled replies also survive.[3]

Bierce probably expected his stay in England to be permanent, but it lasted only three years. Mollie had borne their two sons, Day in December 1872 and Leigh in April 1874. Homesick and pregnant with their third child, she returned to her family in San Francisco in April 1875. Bierce followed in September, and their daughter Helen was born in October. His wry comment upon Leigh's birth—"As to myself, I have another boy. He is, I believe ['here insert the age of the child']" (letter 11)—was no doubt a bit of whimsy intended to amuse the bachelor Stoddard, but it also betrays a lack of paternal responsibility that the facts of his subsequent life do much to reinforce. Bierce was not a particularly attentive husband or father, and his separation from Mollie in the winter of 1888–89 is not mentioned in the very few letters of that date. Bierce manifestly enjoyed the company of a wide circle of women, but he clearly had no inclination to be a either a full-time husband or parent, although his affection for his children is evident in his later letters, especially those to Helen.

For the period 1875–86 the epistolary record is virtually barren but striking for the existence of two poignant letters to his mother from 1876, reacting to his father's illness and death. Whether they were written only to console Laura Bierce is unclear. Her death two years later is passed over in silence as there are no surviving letters at all from 1876 to 1880. It was at this time that Bierce resumed his journalistic career, working for two weekly San Francisco papers, the *Argonaut* (1877–79) and the *Wasp* (1881–86). During a brief hiatus from journalism, he engaged in an extraordinary attempt to mine gold in the Black Hills of South Dakota. This venture—which occupied much of 1880—is chronicled voluminously in surviving letters to various officials of the Black Hills Placer Mining Company. The matters under discussion are so technical and abstruse that it would be unfeasible to present any of this correspondence without exhaustive annotation, so none is included here. Readers interested in this exasperating episode in Bierce's life are referred to Paul Fatout's monograph on the subject.[4]

Bierce's letters become substantial only around 1892, a full five years after William Randolph Hearst chose him as chief editorial writer for his *San Francisco Examiner*. Not surprisingly, the only previous major selection of Bierce's letters—*The Letters of Ambrose Bierce* (1922), nominally edited by Bertha Clark Pope, but for all practical purposes edited by Bierce's disciple George Sterling—begins at this date. Bierce was now a towering literary figure in San Francisco, not so much for his fiction (his *Tales of Soldiers and Civilians*, although dated 1891, was released only in early 1892) but for his newspaper work. He became the most respected—and, perhaps, most feared—journalist on the West Coast, whose praise or censure could make or break the reputation of any local writer, politician, or social figure. Bierce's long-running column, "Prattle," certainly contains abundant invective, but invective written with such verve and stylistic pyrotechnics that it remains vibrant to this day. Does Bierce's satire contain a strain of misanthropy? Such a conclusion is unjust from a number of perspectives, not the least of which is the tacit assumption that misanthropy of any sort is always morally censurable. To perceive Bierce's scorn as uniform or indiscriminate is simply to ignore the evidence. Bierce himself, in his last surviving letter, made the pointed remark: "Evidently you share the current notion that because I don't like fools and rogues I am a kind of monster—a misanthrope without sentiment and without heart." The "fools and rogues" he chose to pillory in his columns—talentless but drearily prolific poetasters; scheming politicians, many of them in the pockets of the Southern Pacific Railroad; and countless others who chose to make their folly and roguery a matter of public record—seem eminently to have deserved scourging. There is no reason to doubt Bierce's claim, in a letter to Blanche Partington, that "I like many things in this world and a few persons" (letter 22).

In the 1890s, a band of disciples began to gather around Bierce who would help to perpetuate his fame long after his death. Among them was the redoubtable Gustav Adolphe Danziger, a sycophant and charlatan who caused Bierce no end of financial and personal trouble. Having collaborated on the translation of Richard Voss's *The Monk and the Hangman's Daughter*, the two quarreled ceaselessly about the proceeds from that work and from the Western Authors Publishing Company, the firm they jointly established. Yet even under these trying circumstances, Bierce's humanity is evident. In late 1900, when he heard that Danziger had a serious illness, Bierce immediately wrote him a long and sympathetic letter, offering comfort and material assistance.

Other disciples were somewhat more respectable: the critic Percival Pollard (who wrote perspicaciously about Bierce in *Their Day in Court*, 1909); the fiction writers C. W. Doyle, W. C. Morrow, and Emma Frances Dawson; and a number of California journalists, notably Carroll Carrington and Edward H. Clough, who spread Bierce's fame in articles for various local newspapers. Perhaps the most surprising of Bierce's colleagues of this period is Ray Frank, an American Jewish writer and lecturer who—as Bierce's women correspondents tended to do—inspired some of his warmest letters. Nor can we forget the poignant story of Lily Walsh, the deaf-mute whom Bierce took under his wing during her tragically short life, and whose grave he dutifully tended for years after her death. Certainly, she was one of those "few persons" in this world whom Bierce liked.

A potentially more significant disciple, Herman Scheffauer, came upon the horizon in 1895. Bierce at once recognized the merit of Scheffauer's verse, and for the next decade he tirelessly tutored the hot-headed youth in matters of poetry, philosophy, and life. When Scheffauer, vaunting his German ancestry, revealed an ugly strain of nationalism and racism in his letters, Bierce warned him earnestly to shed his "tribal instincts and patriotic prejudices" (letter 110), apparently to no avail. Bierce also was mentor to Edwin Markham, until the latter revealed a strain of propagandistic didacticism with "The Man with the Hoe" (1899) and other poems. Bierce began searching for a poet more to his liking to vaunt as a counterweight to Markham, and in 1899 he discovered such a poet: George Sterling, a transplant from Long Island who had long been acquainted with Albert and Carleton Bierce and also Joaquin Miller, and whose devotion to "pure poetry" suited Bierce's temperament exactly. Bierce's letters to Sterling and Scheffauer are probably the most substantial in his epistolary corpus. Bierce lashed Sterling, then inclined toward a kind of sentimental socialism, with his unflinching realism in regard to social and political affairs. While Sterling sympathized with the "poor" against the "rich," Bierce ruefully admitted: "Both 'classes,' when you come to that, are about equally disgusting and unworthy—there's not a pin's moral difference between them" (letter 81). To Scheffauer, when he and Sterling sought to publish Bierce's poetry collection *Shapes of Clay* (1903), Bierce cogently and penetratingly elucidated his theory of literary and poetic satire. He also admitted at this time that he is not a poet but a wit—a comment that reminds us of H. L. Mencken's claim that Bierce is the "one genuine wit" that America has produced.[5]

It is disappointing how infrequently Bierce discusses his fiction in his letters. *Can Such Things Be?*, his landmark collection of supernatural tales, appeared in 1893, and *Tales of Soldiers and Civilians* was reprinted on several occasions in his lifetime, most notably in an augmented Putnam's edition of 1898, under the title *In the Midst of Life*. Although Bierce attained celebrity with his Civil War tales, he published relatively few in magazines after the 1890s. Firstly, he felt a loyalty to Hearst because Hearst paid him a regular salary—amounting, toward the end, to $100 per week—regardless of the amount of material he wrote for Hearst's newspapers. Secondly, he professed a disdain for the standard American magazines of the day, with their penchant for formulaic stories with happy endings in contrast to the grim "tragic" burden of his own tales. In 1907 Bierce strongly censured Bob Davis of *Munsey's* for soliciting, then rejecting, one of his Civil War stories—possibly on the grounds (although this is only an inference, since it is not known which tale was rejected) that the story in question combined a Civil War background with overt supernaturalism. Bierce became content to allow his later tales to appear in *Cosmopolitan* after Hearst acquired it in 1905.

The final decade of Bierce's career was in some senses the most frustrating of his life. Although 1896 saw his greatest triumph—when he was sent to Washington, D.C., and wrote dozens of articles that led to the defeat of the railroad baron C. P. Huntington's attempt to ram a bill favorable to his railroad through Congress—the situation thereafter rapidly deteriorated. As early as 1897 Bierce tendered the first of numerous short-lived resignations from Hearst's employ, chiefly on the grounds that the newspaper editors (especially those on the *New York Journal*) tampered with his work. He always allowed himself to be persuaded back to work, and one gains the impression from Bierce's numerous letters to Hearst (Hearst's letters to Bierce do not survive) that Hearst felt considerable loyalty to the first and best of his editorialists. Bierce moved to Washington in late 1899 largely for health reasons (his chronic asthma made living in the San Francisco area a daily torture), but difficulties with Hearst's editorial staff persisted. When Hearst acquired *Cosmopolitan*, Bierce saw an opportunity to rid himself of the onus of newspaper work (which in a literary sense he considered transitory and ephemeral) and to write work of greater substance. But his plans came to naught: either from the malice (as he suggests) or indifference of the *Cosmopolitan* editors, his work appeared sporadically and without fanfare, and his attempt to write a column of topical commentary ("The Passing Show") for a monthly magazine proved a failure. Bierce's letters to Hearst from 1906 to 1909 keenly depict his frustration and sense of indignity: he rightly regarded himself as a writer far superior to those "beboomed" in the pages of *Cosmopolitan,* and it becomes clear that Hearst, among his many other activities (including, at this time, pursuit of high political office), simply did not have the time or inclination to come consistently to Bierce's aid. Bierce did not help his cause by refusing to fight Hearst's battles with journalistic rival Joseph Pulitzer. It was a principled decision, but one not likely to be favored by the partisan Hearst.

In the spring of 1909 Bierce resigned permanently, after working for Hearst for twenty-two years. But retirement did not bring about languid idleness. A year earlier, his friend and publisher Walter Neale proposed to issue his *Collected Works* in ten (later twelve) volumes. It was a monumental undertaking, and the task of assembling, revising, and proofreading nearly 5,000 pages of his life's work proved tedious and exhausting. Matters were not made easier by Neale's typesetters, whose slovenliness inspired several stern yet amicable letters on the fine points of typographical accuracy that reveal Bierce's acute concern with the smallest nuances of style, diction, and punctuation.

During his post-newspaper career, Bierce attracted new colleagues and disciples whose association would bear interesting fruit. The most surprising association was with Ezra Pound, whose father had sent Bierce several of Pound's poems, including "The Ballade of the Goodly Fere," in late 1909. Pound cannot be considered a colleague, much less a disciple, of Bierce; but the mere fact that Bierce had praise for some of Pound's poetry, given his conservatism regarding poetic form and meter, may make us reassess his own claim that he was not a literary critic. By this time Bierce's two earlier poetic disciples, Scheffauer and Sterling, had begun to alienate him; his letters to Scheffauer in particular seem censorious in the extreme, but the evidence suggests that they are not unjust. Bierce's years-long attempt to secure the publication of Sterling's remarkable excursion into poetic fantasy, "A Wine of Wizardry," bore mixed fruit when the poem appeared in *Cosmopolitan* in September 1907. The subsequent uproar over the poem and Bierce's lavish praise of it was fueled and abetted by Hearst's newspaper editors into a nine-days' wonder, with the result that both Bierce and Sterling were roundly abused and ridiculed. Bierce responded with one of his most delightfully vitriolic excursions into personal polemic ("An Insurrection of the Peasantry," *Cosmopolitan,* December 1907), but thereafter his relations with Sterling deteriorated, so that by the end of 1912 Bierce had washed his hands of him. Whether it was because Sterling continued to adhere to socialism, or because his flagrant womanizing offended the morally scrupulous Bierce, it is difficult to say; but whatever the case, Sterling was dropped. Indeed, being friends with Bierce could be a difficult proposition. As he explained:

To hold my regard one must fulfil hard conditions—hard if one is not what one should be; easy if one is. I have, indeed, a habit of calmly considering the character of a man with whom I have fallen into any intimacy and, whether I have any grievance against him or not, informing him by letter that I no longer desire his acquaintance. This I do after deciding that he is not truthful, candid, without conceit, and so forth—in brief, honorable. If any one is conscious that he is not in all respects worthy of my friendship he would better not cultivate it, for assuredly no one can long conceal his true character from an observant student of it. Yes, my friendship is a precarious possession. It grows more so the longer I live, and the less I feel the need of a multitude of friends. (letter 147)

Is this really too much to ask of a friend? H. L. Mencken did not think so. His relations with Bierce were, indeed, fleeting—they had attended the funeral of Percival Pollard in 1911[6] and exchanged a half-dozen letters in 1913[7]—but the subsequent course of Mencken's work makes it evident that he was Bierce's twentieth-century disciple, both as journalist and as satirist.

So what of the caricatures of Bierce cited earlier? His entire life and correspondence underscore the truth of his own dictum, in a letter to the unduly sensitive Ray Frank: "It is not worth while to hate anybody, nor to assume that anybody is taking much trouble to be malignant and vengeful. Men and women have as slack a diligence in doing evil that profits them nothing as in nearly all else" (letter 56). Bierce, to be sure, gained more than his share of enemies over a long career as a polemical journalist; but his public joustings with his opponents are starkly contrasted with the unfailing courtesy and propriety of his dealings with his friends, acquaintances, and correspondents—except when they crossed certain clearly demarcated lines in matters of morals and conduct. And yet, Bierce was sensitive to the issue of his own correspondents' misinterpretation of his letters: perhaps paying too much attention to his public persona as the lasher of fools and rogues, some of his associates read unwarranted satire or sarcasm into his missives. William Randolph Hearst was one of these, and Bierce was forced to admit: "You are not alone in this error however, I have had to drop many good friends because they persisted in finding in my letters some of the qualities that distinguish some of my public work" (letter 151).

To the charge made by some of his own closest colleagues that he was nothing but the blandly unemotional chronicler of death and tragedy, Bierce was again forceful in rebuttal. Consider this gauntlet thrown down to Scheffauer as their bitter parting loomed ahead:

Maybe, as you say, my work lacks "soul," but my life does not, and a man's life is the man. Personally, I hold that sentiment has a place in the world, and that loyalty to a friend is not inferior as a characteristic to correctness of literary judgment. If there is a heaven I think it is more valued there. . . . And let me tell you that if you are going through life as a mere thinking machine, ignoring the generous promptings of the heart, sacrificing it to the brain, you will have a hard row to hoe, and the outcome, when you survey it from the vantage ground of age, will not please you. (letter 147)

Even Sterling accused Bierce of advising young authors to "leave all heart and sentiment out of their work," to which Bierce responded: "If I did the context would probably show that it was because their time might better be given to perfect themselves in form, against the day when their hearts would be less wild and their sentiments truer. You know it has always been my belief that one cannot be trusted to feel until one has learned to think—and few youngsters have learned to do that" (letter 196).

No further testimonials to Bierce's humanity are needed than the poignant letters recording the deaths of family members (especially his son Leigh, whose untimely passing left him "a bit broken in body and mind" [letter 76]) and friends like C. W. Doyle. When Doyle, in his last letter to Bierce before his suicide, wrote: "God bless you, dear Bierce,—you have helped me so much—more, more than you know," Bierce commented with simple eloquence: "I shall never be able to read that with dry eyes; and I don't want to" (letter 92).

A very different sort of sentiment permeates Bierce's many letters to female correspondents, most of whom were society women in San Francisco who had struck his acquaintance in the 1890s as he traversed the Bay Area in search of a locale that would help ease his recurrent asthma. These letters are unfailingly, if harmlessly, coy and flirtatious, to such a degree that several of his correspondents misunderstood their import and wondered whether he had something more serious in mind. Bierce himself acknowledged the difficulty when he wrote: "*My* besetting sin has been in writing to my girl friends as if they were sweet-hearts" (letter 94).

Bierce professed to find in letters merely a kind of adjunct to, or replacement for, conversation. Unlike H. P. Lovecraft, whose enormously long and complex letters tell all one might need or want to know about his life, his work, and his constantly developing thoughts on metaphysics, religion, politics, society, and literature, Bierce claimed to eschew such discussion in correspondence:

> I don't feel "called" to settle weighty matters of morals, sociology or ethics, and do not think you and I could do it in correspondence, anyhow. . . . I simply don't write letters on such subjects, nor care to get them; and if you want formal, conventional letters from me you should write me formal and conventional letters. From a rather extensive correspondence with men and women of brains I know that in writing to one another they are as little given to "etiquette" as to discussion of "problems" in Thisorthatology. The imparting and eliciting of wisdom is not among the purposes of cor-

respondence, as they understand the matter, judging from their practice. They talk shop to the public only. (AB to Ella Sterling Cummins, 16 May 1892; ALS, CHS)

Still, it is difficult to deny the intellectual substance of a number of Bierce's letters, revealing as they do a view of the world far more nuanced than the laconic tag "Nothing matters" that he frequently claimed to sum up his outlook. Consider his scorn of didacticism in literature in letters to Blanche Partington (letters 22 and 23); his rebuke of C. W. Doyle for finding obscenity in one of W. C. Morrow's novels (letter 74); the moral relativism he urges on Scheffauer (letter 97); and many others that could be cited. It does appear, however, that in his last years he became somewhat dogmatic and rigid, especially in regard to political philosophy: his detestation of socialists was long standing but was exacerbated when friends like George Sterling and even his own niece-in-law, Lora Bierce, ventured into the enemy's camp. He huffily declared to his daughter that his chief reason for refusing to visit California after 1912 was the omnipresence of "socialists, suffragists [and] anarchists," stating: "You see I have a pretty good opinion of myself as a thinker, take myself pretty seriously, and can have no pleasure in the society of persons who think their fool leaders wiser than I. So I shall not go where they are" (letter 191).

Blanche Partington was the last of the many friends and associates whom Bierce dismissed in old age, as if closing the door to one era as he opened the door to another. Can we trust him in his contention that he only wished to observe the Mexican Civil War, then in progress, while continuing on to South America? Was the now famous utterance made in October 1913—"To be a Gringo in Mexico—ah, that is euthanasia!" (letter 206)—a grisly jest or prediction of some scarcely concealed death-wish? The evidence of his late letters is ambiguous on this critical point; but it is fitting that the bland but chilling postscript of his final missive—"As for me, I leave here tomorrow for an unknown destination"—comprises the last words we have from Ambrose Bierce.

It would be naïve to believe that Bierce's letters are in any way open windows into his soul. There is a certain stiffness about them, a certain labored propriety—what Lovecraft, in reference to his stories, somewhat unjustly termed "prosaic angularity"[8]—that makes one wonder whether Bierce ever truly let his hair down even to his closest associates. Nevertheless, the insights we gain into Bierce the man, the writer, and the thinker from his correspondence should go far in producing a broader, more detailed picture of him than can be gained merely from reading his macabre tales, his newspaper invective, or his versified lampoons.

Perhaps Mencken came closest to the truth. Reviewing Carey McWilliams's biography—the first to use any significant number of Bierce's letters—Mencken wrote: "The man who emerges is far more interesting and charming than the old fee-faw-fum. He was not, it appears, the appalling cynic that trembling young reporters used to admire. On the contrary, he was 'one of the most idealistic men that his generation produced in America'—in fact, 'a great moral force, ... for he would not lie, and truth alone mattered to him. It came to mean more than beauty; ... it came to be the paramount value of his life.'" Bierce's integrity, Mencken added, "was never betrayed by compromise. Right or wrong, Bierce always stuck to the truth as he saw it. He was magnificently decent. It cost him something, but he never wavered."[9]

S. T. Joshi
David E. Schultz

NOTES

1. Clifton P. Fadiman, "Portrait of a Misanthrope," *Saturday Review* (12 October 1946): 12. Later used, with revisions, as the introduction to *The Collected Writings of Ambrose Bierce* (New York: Citadel Press, 1946).

2. See Lawrence I. Berkove, *A Prescription for Adversity: The Moral Art of Ambrose Bierce* (Columbus: Ohio State University Press, 2002), esp. chapter 2.

3. See M. E. Grenander, "Ambrose Bierce and Charles Warren Stoddard: Some Unpublished Correspondence," *Huntington Library Quarterly* 23 (May 1960): 261–92.

4. Paul Fatout, *Ambrose Bierce and the Black Hills* (Norman: University of Oklahoma Press, 1956).

5. H. L. Mencken, "The Literature of a Moral Republic," *Smart Set* 47, no. 2 (October 1915): 152.

6. See H. L. Mencken, "Ambrose Bierce," in *Prejudices: Sixth Series* (New York: Knopf, 1927), 259–65.

7. Mencken's side has been published as "H. L. Mencken to Ambrose Bierce," *Book Club of California Quarterly News Letter* 22 (Winter 1956): 5–10.

8. "Supernatural Horror in Literature" (1927), in *The Annotated Supernatural Horror in Literature,* ed. S. T. Joshi (New York: Hippocampus Press, 2000), 52.

9. H. L. Mencken, "Bierce Emerges from the Shadows," *American Mercury* 19, no. 2 (February 1930): 252.

A NOTE ON THIS EDITION

In this volume we have sought to present judiciously edited texts of the letters for a general, non-specialist audience. The texts have been derived, where possible, from manuscript sources. Most letters are printed without abridgement, although space considerations have necessitated some excisions of repetitious or inconsequential matter. Such excisions are indicated by ellipses within brackets; all other ellipses are Bierce's. Any other editorial additions (e.g., to supply a word evidently omitted by Bierce) are enclosed within brackets. Brackets are also used to supply addresses found on printed stationery used by Bierce. In a few instances we have silently corrected apparent slips of the pen (e.g., the occasional omission of the apostrophe in contractions: "dont," "wont," etc.), although other idiosyncratic usages have been preserved.

In some cases, manuscripts of the letters are unavailable. Many of the extant letters to Herman Scheffauer and C. W. Doyle exist only in transcripts made at some unspecified date (probably in the early twentieth century) by an unknown hand. Our text for Bierce's letter to Clara Wright (8 June 1864) is taken from an article by Bierce's biographer, Carey McWilliams, entitled, "Ambrose Bierce and His First Love" (*Bookman*, June–July 1932).

An important source in our work has been the Mary Elizabeth Grenander Papers at the State University of New York at Albany. Professor Grenander had been working since at least 1960 on an edition of Bierce's complete correspondence but regrettably died before her work could be completed. Although we secured most of Bierce's letters independently of Grenander (including several not known to her), her research unearthed some letters otherwise unobtainable. Some of these letters exist only in transcripts made by Grenander. In a few instances, we have been compelled to employ texts obtained from published sources, primarily *The Letters of Ambrose Bierce* (1922) and Adolphe de Castro's *Portrait of Ambrose Bierce* (1929). The manuscripts of these letters probably no longer exist. There may be a question as to the textual soundness of the letters printed by de Castro (Gustav Adolphe Danziger); but comparison of the texts of other letters in his book with surviving manuscripts suggests that he has transcribed the texts with tolerable accuracy and has not made any deliberate alterations.

The locations of manuscripts of Bierce's letters are given in brackets following the name of the recipient at the head of each letter. Abbreviations used to designate institutions are given below.

Explanatory notes elucidating references to persons, historical events, works by Bierce and others, and other such matters are printed following respective letters. In the preparation of these notes we have followed the conventional scholarly procedure of not annotating matters that can be looked up easily in encyclopedias or other reference works, but have largely focused on points where specialized expertise is required. Citations of Bierce's own works are usually abbreviated, and reference is generally made to convenient modern editions rather than first editions now difficult to locate. For full bibliographical information on all works by Bierce, see our volume,

Ambrose Bierce: A Bibliography of Primary Sources (Westport, Conn.: Greenwood Press, 1999). Bierce habitually quoted lines of poetry in his letters; we have attempted to identify these where possible. Citations to poems by standard authors are much abbreviated, giving only the title of the poem, the date, and the line(s); in most cases the poem can be found in any comprehensive edition of the poet in question, so no specific edition is cited. Our bibliography lists only those publications (chiefly editions of Bierce's letters in book form or in scholarly journals, as well as other biographical and critical works) that were consulted in preparing this edition.

We are grateful to the following institutions for permission to print Bierce's letters in their possession: Bancroft Library, University of California (Berkeley); Scripps College (Claremont, Calif.); Specialized Libraries and Archival Collections, University of Southern California (Los Angeles); California Historical Society, North Baker Research Library Manuscript Collection (San Francisco); James D. Phelan California Authors Collection, San Francisco Public Library (San Francisco); The Huntington Library (San Marino, Calif.); Special Collections, Tutt Library, Colorado College (Colorado Springs); Beinecke Rare Book and Manuscript Library, Yale University (New Haven, Conn.); Manuscripts Division, Library of Congress (Washington, D.C.); Special Collections: Rare Books, University of Louisville (Louisville, Ky.); Houghton Library, Harvard University (Cambridge, Mass.); Enoch Pratt Free Library (Baltimore, Md.); Manuscripts Division, Department of Rare Books & Special Collections, Princeton University Library (Princeton, N.J.); M. E. Grenander Papers, University Archives, M. E. Grenander Department of Special Collections and Archives, University Libraries, University at Albany, SUNY (Albany, N.Y.); Edmund Clarence Stedman Papers, Rare Book and Manuscripts Library, Columbia University (New York, N.Y.); Robert H. Davis Papers and H. L. Mencken Papers, Manuscripts and Archives Division, The New York Public Library, Astor, Lenox and Tilden Foundations (New York, N.Y.); Berg Collection of English and American Literature, The New York Public Library, Astor, Lenox and Tilden Foundations (New York, N.Y.); Horrmann Library, Wagner College (Staten Island, N.Y.); Archives and Rare Books Department, University of Cincinnati (Cincinnati, Ohio); Rare Book and Manuscript Library, University of Pennsylvania (Philadelphia); Ambrose Bierce Collection (#5992), Clifton Waller Barrett Library, The Albert and Shirley Small Special Collections Library, University of Virginia (Charlottesville). We are also grateful to Lawrence I. Berkove, Scott Connors, Robert Gale, and Alan Gullette for their assistance in preparing this volume and for their general support of our work on Bierce.

THE SELECTED LETTERS

[1]   To Clara Wright[1]
                    Hd. Qrs. 2nd Brig. 3d Div. 4th A.C.
                    Ackworth, Ga., June 8th, 1864.[2]
My Dear Clare:
              Will you be very much displeased to hear from me by letter?
If I thought so I would never touch pen again. 'Tis true you never asked me to write to you, but the knowledge that I still live cannot be unwelcome to one who professed to regard me as a *friend*. I don't know Clare what the word *friend* means to you who have so many, but to *me* friendship has a meaning deeper than the definition of Webster or Worcester.[3] And my friendship for you is a feeling which no language can define. Do you call this flattery? If so you do not know me and I forgive you.

I have not written to you before, but my neglect was not caused by indifference. I knew Tima[4] would sometimes mention my name to you. But I want to hear from you very much; not because you will tell me of Tima, but of yourself. You always seemed to think, Clare, that I never cared for you except as Tima's sister—a sort of necessary evil. (*Vide*—our carriage ride by Eagle lake.) Is it necessary for me to say you were unjust to me? No, Clare, except our sweet Tima, I love you better than any one on this earth.

Perhaps this is not right;—perhaps my mother and sister should be first in my affections,—but so it is.

I am getting very tired of my present life and weary of the profession of arms. Not because of its horrors or dangers; not because its hardships affect me, but because I wish to be with you and my darling. The pleasant weeks with you, so like a dream, have nearly spoiled the soldier to make the—pensive individual.

Ask Tima why I get no more letters from her. Have I offended her? I may have written something as heartless and cruel as I used to say to her. If I have I hope she will forgive me. Her last letter was dated May 11th.

Do you think that there is a probability of my letters getting into other hands than hers? Please tell me for the thought troubles me very much. Oh, if I could be with you both again my measure of happiness would be full. I do not see how I could have been so unhappy as I sometimes was when with you.

But I ought rather to be thankful for being allowed so much happiness with you—so much more than I deserved—than to repine at the fate which withholds more. I hardly expect ever to see you again, and perhaps it is better so. Every day some one is struck down who is so much better than I. Since leaving Cleveland Tenn. my brigade has lost nearly one third its numbers killed and wounded.[5]

Among these were so many good men who could ill be spared from the army and the world. And yet *I* am left. But my turn will come in time. Oh, how pleasant would death be were it for you and Tima, instead of for my country—for a cause which may be right and may be wrong. Do you think I lack patriotism for talking this way? Perhaps so. Soldiers are not troubled with that sort of stuff.

May I talk to you about D———? Do you love him yet? or think you do?

Is that a blunt question? You know you told me you did once. Please answer it.

Oh, I wish I could help you. You who have been so good to me. But my hands are tied. I can only warn you. There is a metal among the rocks here which viewed at a distance has all the appearances of gold. A close inspection shows it to be the basest dross. You are an admirer of pebbles I believe.

Do tell me all about yourself and Tima. What books you read, what society you have, and if you have lots of fun. Capt. Webster desired to be remembered to you and Tima if I ever wrote you. By the way is Jo Williams at W.? The less you have to do with him the better you will please me. If you require reasons I will give them. Do you know my mother yet, and does Tima call on her as she promised me? How is Lyde C.?

Now Clare if you don't write to me at once I shall take it as proof that you don't wish to hear from me again.

Give my kindest regards to 'Slissa and the girls.

Take my darling in your arms, and kiss her a thousand times for me.

With more love than I can tell, I am

    Your friend

        A. G. Bierce

P.S. Do you hear from Ol?[6] I can get no word from him.

        B———

It is raining very hard and I am very lonely. In looking over my valise just now I found tucked away snugly a little embroidered handkerchief. Do you remember it? Then there were also some little pebbles; common looking things enough, but each one is transparent, and looking into it I see two tiny figures with skirts just *slightly* elevated, showing such delicate little—feet, stepping along the soft sand, and picking up these little nothings for me. What delicate little tracks they leave behind them. But these tracks will all be erased by the next rain. Not so the impressions left on the hard and stony soil of my heart. Every examination shows me how some mischievous persons have crept into the garden of my soul, and tracked it up worse than a melon patch by school-boys.

But not one of the little tracks shall be blotted out by the rude gardener Time. The amount of it all is, Clare, that I love you and Tima so I can't find language to tell it.

I just wish I could pass my whole life with you both, and have nothing to do but give myself up to the delicious intoxication of your society. For that, I would renounce the whole world and all the ties of kindred; throw away every ambition or aim in life, and make a fool of myself in the most approved style generally.

        Brady.[7]

1. Clara Wright, the sister of AB's girlfriend, Fatima, both of Warsaw, Indiana. This letter, one of two letters to survive from AB's days in the Civil War, was published in Carey McWilliams, "Ambrose Bierce and His First Love," *Bookman* (June–July 1932).
2. At the time, AB was serving in a brigade commanded by General William B. Hazen, part of William Tecumseh Sherman's Southern march. On 10 June several skirmishes in Ackworth, Lost Mountain, and other points occurred. On 27 June AB suffered a serious gunshot wound in the head at the Battle of Kennesaw Mountain, but he returned to Hazen's brigade in September.
3. AB refers to two American lexicographers. Noah Webster (1758–1843) compiled his first dictionary in 1806. His *American Dictionary of the English Language* was first published in 1828. In the next year Joseph Emerson Worcester (1784–1865), a compiler of geographical dictionaries and gazeteers, produced an abridgment of Webster's dictionary and subsequently produced dictionaries rivalling Webster's.
4. Fatima Wright (later Mrs. W. J. Fleming). See Carey McWilliams, "Ambrose Bierce and His First Love," for AB's untitled poem "Fatima, should an angel come from heaven," and his acrostic poem to her. AB and Fatima were engaged in December 1863, but by September 1864 the engagement was broken for unknown reasons.
5. Cleveland, Tennessee, is 26 miles northeast of Chattanooga. AB refers to the Battle of Missionary Ridge (23–25 November 1863), fought near Cleveland.
6. "Ol" is Oliver Wright, brother to Fatima and Clara. Like AB, he enlisted in the 9th Indiana Volunteers.
7. "Brady" was a nickname given to AB by his schoolmates.

[2]   To Bret Harte[1] [ALS, YU]

Sunday [Dec. 1870]

My Dear Harte; Upon reading again the stuff I showed you first, I am quite convinced it is as good as I can make—good in itself and for the mag. So I have *re*-written it (this is the fourth time, 'pon honor) and have made some more things, also. Now, if you think the first things are not suitable, don't use 'em. I have marked the margin of the others with a pencil. These are, in my opinion, suitable for a regular department; if all go in together make 'em a department or series of papers as you think best. In fact, I must leave the whole matter to your better judgment. Of course when one batch is published it will be easy to go on in that vein; but I must say I have bothered my pate about this d——d thing more than a little, trying to avoid, on the one hand, the Scylla of Bret-Hartism and on the other, the Charybdis of the Town Crier.[2] I think I have preserved an originality of style, but suitable subjects were the devil. Of course you'll cut out anything which is too frivolous in subject to be redeemed by treatment, and *vice versa*. Cut out *anything*. If you wish, I'll make some more things to replace what you reject, as soon as the proofs shall indicate your taste in the matter. You must Christen the thing.

   Thine
      Bierce

And—please—*don't* let the beast of a printer stick a handful of comma's into every sentence. It would kill me with vexation.

I stick to "Ursus";³ it is just the name for us.

    1. [Francis] Bret Harte (1836–1902), the first prominent literary figure in the history of California, helped to found the *Overland Monthly* in 1868 to promote the literature of the region. In this letter AB refers to his series of "Grizzly Papers," published in five installments in the *Overland Monthly* (January, February, March, April, and June 1871).

    2. At this time, AB was writing a column called "The Town Crier" for the weekly paper, the *San Francisco News Letter and California Advertiser*.

    3. Ursus (Latin for "bear") was AB's pen name for "Grizzly Papers."

[3]   To John H. Carmany¹ [Transcript (MEG)]

Tuesday [Feb. 1871?]

My dear Mr. Carmany:—

    I don't think we quite understand one another. Mr. Harte, while editor of the "Overland," repeatedly urged me to write for the mag., and I as repeatedly declined unless paid $50 for *anything* I might write. I would not write ten lines for any magazine for less, and I think I so informed you. Any one who has passed the ABC of his art would be a goose to accept less, unless necessity compelled him. It does *not* compel me. I gave an order on you for my money, and the bearer was told that the amount due was $28.00! Permit me in all kind of courtesy to ask if, and why, you think I would accept any such sum from *any* one. If the sketch was not good it should not have been accepted—if good such a sum is baldly ridiculous. If it is *not* worth $50, it is worth nothing, and you will confer a favor by accepting it gratis,—and I will return the obligation by abstaining from bothering you with anything more. How you can conduct a first-class magazine by paying less than half the usual rates to contributors, it is not my business to inquire; I can only pray that you may permanently succeed. Twenty-eight dollars! Excuse me but I do not deal in a commodity that can be purchased by measure—and at $4.00 per page.

    I am respectfully

        A. G. Bierce

    1. Carmany had purchased the *Overland Monthly* from its owner, Anton Roman, in the summer of 1869. When Harte left San Francisco on 2 February 1871 to write for the *Atlantic Monthly*, AB's relations with the magazine deteriorated.

[4]   To John H. Carmany [ALS, LC]
                                              Wednesday, March 15, 1871

Mr. Carmany—Dear Sir; If the "proofs" I had yesterday represent the amount of my copy which is accepted, I think I will quit. Everything I send you is constructed with the utmost care; most of it being written three times over, and all of it twice. This involves too much labor to be undertaken without some reasonable hope that it will not be wasted. You told me the character of the mag. was not to be changed when Harte left. Harte never suppressed, nor altered, a line of my composition—nor, I may say, did anybody else ever do so, to any great extent. Of course I cannot hope to remain *incog.;* some of the Eastern papers are even now publishing the "Grizzlies" over my real name. I cannot therefore concede the right of any editor to make any alterations or excisions in what he accepts—it is unfair and unprofessional. Whatever a writer (if he is known—especially if he have already some reputation) is permitted to say, he should be allowed to say in his own way. I have myself some editorial experience, and this rule I never dared to disregard. The suppression of entire articles is perfectly proper, but has in my case been carried too far to be endurable. Besides it changes the *tone* of the papers as a series—a tone which I carefully decided upon giving them, and in accordance with which each separate article or paragraph is written. But I cannot complain of the *principle* of suppression—only its excessive application.

I do not know Mr. Bartlett,[1] and I assure you I am very far from claiming a judgment superior to his; simply our tastes are irreconcilable. I would prefer that you would not speak to him of this, for he might not be pleased and—however, do as you like.

If my immediate withdrawal would inconvenience you, I will do the "Papers" as usual till you can supply my place. Of course I would prefer to continue, but I cannot as things go now, and there's an end. This scissors business is quite unprecedented, and I don't like it.

Very cheerfully yours
A. G. Bierce.

---

1. William C. Bartlett (1839–1908), longtime editorial writer for the *San Francisco Bulletin* and assistant editor at the *Overland Monthly*.

[5]   To Timothy H. Rearden[1] [ALS, BL]

San Rafael,
Jan. 8th, 1872.

My Dear Tim,

If Mollie[2] is the "instrument of Divine Vengeance", as you ungraciously state, I think Divine V. is being shamefully swindled; for she couldn't be nicer if she tried. She's too good for anything. She commissions me to say all manner of grateful nothings, the matter and purport of which I but indifferently apprehend, but which have some occult reference to a certain silvern thing with which she absurdly professes to be much pleased and to set great store by. It *was* thoughtful of you, certainly, Dear Tim, [to] come and spend an evening with us. There! I know you won't for that you are a brute—a broot beest! You probably think it would be an "intrusion". I happen at this moment to remember certain talk of yours anent the altered relations between friends consequent upon one taking a woman to wife. Go on in this error, as you will, but you will thereby do grievous injustice and deprive yourself of the society of all good and true men. For I hold the mob of rascals, among whom there is neither marrying nor giving in marriage, in deathless contempt, as being neither good nor true.

We are living very c[omfortably?][3] up here, and are, of course, happy in our delusion. Nor do we anticipate any present awakening. Who does?

My regards to Jack, Whit and the rest of your horde of unmarried barbarians—poor devils, ribless like a famishing cur!

Thine own in all true sincerity Dear Old Tim,

A. G. Bierce.

her mark

---

1. Timothy H. Rearden (1839–1892), judge, classical scholar, and poet. See AB's tribute, "A Man of Letters," *SF* (15 May 1892): 6 (unsigned); rpt. (as "Timothy H. Rearden") in CW 9 and in Rearden's *Petrarch and Other Essays* (San Francisco: Doxey, 1893).

2. Mary Ellen ("Mollie") Day, who became AB's wife on 25 December 1871.

3. The ms. is torn here.

[6]   To Charles Warren Stoddard[1] [ALS, HL]
[drawing of insect]
Bristol, England.
Dec. 29th, 1872.

My Dear Charles,

    Just before leaving London, last September, Tom Hood[2] and you had some "think" of making another book; and perhaps I could find a publisher for it. I was then concerned with Hotten about a screed of my own, and at my last interview I spoke to him of you. He did not give me any encouragement, affected to know little of you, etc. etc. I am confident he knows all about you, and it is probable he would give something for your book. He bought one very bad thing of mine, which I compiled at his request from old newspaper paragraphs,[3] but he shows no disposition to do anything more than advertise it, at present—which suits me. He is not a nice publisher to deal with, and I shall probably give him nothing else. But as Tom has since called my attention to the matter, I write this to say that if you have your things prepared, and will send them to him (Tom) I will try Hotten with them, and try hard. If he won't give you money down it would be better to give them to some other house. And I am very sure I can get some good house to take them, provided you don't insist on money down, but will take your chance on percentages. (They can't have my things that way, but I don't care to publish) Perhaps you do. If so please state what you ought to get, and what you are willing to take; I will stick for a sum so near the former as it is possible to obtain.

 All this when I return to London, which may be in two weeks, maybe not so soon, possibly in a month or two. It will be no trouble to me, and I will do a great deal more for your book than I would for my own; for I am comparatively independent of publishers as yet. If I can't get anyone to take it at your lowest terms, I will return it to you. As I am *not* Bret Harte, I think you can rely upon my doing my best for you.

 Should like to see you, old boy. I have had a very pleasant time in England, and so would you have.

 I am at Bristol because I fear the London fogs, and because my boy so far forgot himself as to be born while I was on a tour.[4] He swears he won't travel fast yet.

 Tell me all about everybody, won't you, and about your last voyage. Did you fall in love with another nigger boy.[5] Stanley's "Kalends" would charm you.

 Address me, "London, Poste Restante"; or "Care Tom Hood, 80 Fleet st. E. C."

 Haven't time this evening for much of a letter. Wife, who is in excellent health since coming across the seas, sends affectionate regards; and baby—well, baby has his finger in his eye.

 I am, Charles, very truly yours,
    A. G. Bierce.

1. Charles Warren Stoddard (1843–1909) was an important literary figure in San Francisco for forty years and a coeditor of the *Overland Monthly*. His works include *Poems* (1867), *South-Sea Idyls* (1873), and *The Lepers of Molokai* (1886).
2. Thomas Hood the Younger (1835–1874), son of the comic poet Thomas Hood (1799–1845) and a prolific writer, editor, and illustrator. He was the editor of *Fun*, to which AB contributed voluminously during his entire English stay, and *Tom Hood's Comic Annual*, to which AB also contributed.
3. John Camden Hotten (1832–1873) published AB's first book, *The Fiend's Delight* (as by "Dod Grile"; London: John Camden Hotten, [July 1873]; New York: A. L. Luyster, 1873), "against my protest" (letter to James D. Blake, 22 October 1907; ALS, SFPL). The book is culled primarily from writings in the *San Francisco News Letter and California Advertiser* and the *Overland Monthly*.
4. AB's first son, Day, was born earlier in December.
5. Stoddard was homosexual. See his novel, *For the Pleasure of His Company* (1903; rpt. San Francisco: Gay Sunshine Press, 1987).

[7] To Charles Warren Stoddard [ALS, HL]

Bath, Eng., March 16th, '73.

My Dear Charles;

Your very agreeable letter was read with much pleasure. I am particularly glad to know you have found a publisher. It is much better for you to "come out" in America than here, all other things being equal. I don't know what I could do with your things in London, but would do my best. I have some things a-publishing there,[1] but my atrocities afford no criterion as to the sale of your better wares. I should have burnt all mine if I could have afforded that luxury.

I am doing just work enough over here to pay my current expenses at this somewhat expensive place. It does not require much of my time either. Have not attempted to get any permanent work, and don't suppose I shall; as my object in coming was to loaf and see something of the country—or as Walt Whitman expressed it when the paralysis had, as yet, invaded only his brain, to "Loaf and invite my soul."[2]

Have been to London but once since I wrote you; stayed a fortnight and came away sick. The London Winter is nasty.

Tom Hood's wife is dead, poor girl, and he is much depressed in spirit. Intends going to America soon. Hope you will see him. I saw Joaquin once or twice when I was in London. He looks well and likes England.[3]

We—wife and I and the lad—have been in Bath about a month. It is the most charming of all imaginable places. Every street has its history, every foot of the lovely country its tradition. Old Roman, and even Druidic, remains are plenty as green pease. You are aware that Bath was the stamping ground of Pope, Fielding, Smollet, Warburton, Malthus, Beau Nash, Ralph Allen—who "did good by stealth and blushed to find it fame"[4]—and a lot of worthies whose haunts I frequent, or whose graves I shed judicious drops above, and try to fancy myself like them. I don't succeed. The place is good for a dozen long magazine articles if I were not too lazy to write 'em.[5]

My love to the Bohemian Club collectively, and individually to Newcomb, Bowman, and other good fellows.[6]

I am undecided when, or whether, to return to London. Shall try to get on to the Continent before I go to 'Frisco, if I can manage the expense.

I have not seen Mulford[7] at all, but met Harry Jackson some weeks ago, which was some small comfort. Come over and see us. I will give you a dose of Bath waters that shall make your hair curl—like that l.[8]

Wife sends regards, and I am very truly yours,

A. G. Bierce.

---

1. At this time, AB was publishing regularly in *Fun* and *Figaro*, and his second book, *Nuggets and Dust Panned Out in California* (London: Chatto & Windus, 1873) was in preparation.

2. Walt Whitman (1819–1892), "Song of Myself" (1855), l. 4. In 1872, Whitman began suffering dizzy spells, which ended in paralysis in 1873. AB's opinion of Whitman's poetry was not favorable; see *The Unabridged Devil's Dictionary*, ed. David E. Schultz and S. T. Joshi (Athens: University of Georgia Press, 2000): "INCOMPOSSIBLE, *adj*. Unable to exist if something else exists. Two things are incompossible when the world of being has scope enough for one of them, but not enough for both—as Walt Whitman's poetry and God's mercy to man" ("The Devil's Dictionary," *Wasp*, 26 September 1885: 3).

3. Cincinnatus Hiner (Joaquin) Miller (1837–1913), California poet and longtime friend of AB, who was visiting England at this time. He had attained spectacular fame in England upon the publication of his *Songs of the Sierras* (1871).

4. Alexander Pope (1688–1744), "Epilogue to the Satires" (1738), Dialogue I, l. 136: "Do good by stealth, and blush to find it fame."

5. AB had earlier written a series of letters for the *Alta California* (6 July–6 December 1872; rpt in highly truncated form in *Nuggets and Dust*, and also in *A Sole Survivor: Bits of Autobiography*, ed. S. T. Joshi and David E. Schultz [Knoxville: University of Tennessee Press, 1998]) recording his initial impressions of the people, topography, and political and social conditions of what he believed would become his adopted homeland. So far as is known, he wrote no further articles of this kind.

6. The Bohemian Club was (and is) an exclusive club for writers, politicians, and prominent businessmen in San Francisco. AB probably refers to the journalist James Pearson Newcomb (1837–1907), who edited the San Jose *Tribune*, started San Jose *Times*, and later edited the *American Flag* in San Francisco, before editing various papers in Texas. The journalist James F. Bowman (d. 1882), with the help of AB and others, founded the club around 1872; AB served as its secretary in 1876–77 but later resigned because he felt the club was too sycophantic to royal and noble visitors from overseas.

7. Prentice Mulford (1834–1891), another of AB's friends, wrote for the *Golden Era* and was known for his "compressed novels"—e.g., *Barney McBriar the Shootist*—and is still known for his "New Thought" essays and books. Like AB, he went to England in the early 1870s and sent back amusing travel letters (his to the *San Francisco Bulletin*). In late years he contributed voluminously to the *San Francisco Chronicle*.

8. The *l* in "curl" was exaggeratedly curled.

[8]   To Charles Warren Stoddard [ALS, HL]

Private &
Confidential   Hampstead, Sept. 28, 1873.

Dear Charly;
         I am unexpectedly called away to Paris for a month, and you must try to forgive me for causing you the annoyance of coming out here. (If you have not dismissed your cab yet, don't pay the driver more than 3 shillings for driving you from the Station out here.) I wanted to see you badly, to tell you how to live, whom to know, whom *not* to know and how to get on generally. I daresay Miller can tell you better than I, however, if you and he are still friends, as I hope you are. His address when I last saw him was 11 Museum-st.

I have told Tom Hood to look after you. Now mark this: Tom is one of the very dearest fellows in the world, and an awful good friend to me. *But* he has the worst lot of associates I ever saw—men who (with one or two noble exceptions, whom you cannot readily pick out) are not worthy to untie his shoe latchet. He will introduce you to them *all*. Treat them well, of course, but (1) don't gush over them; (2) don't let them gush over you; (3) don't accept invitations from them; (4) don't get drunk with them; (5) don't let them in any way monopolise you; (6) don't let them shine by your reflected light. I have done all these things, and it is not a good plan, "for at the last it biteth like a serpent and stingeth like an adder."[1] *I* don't mind biting and stinging, but you would—particularly if done in the dark.

Remember this: London—literary London—is divided into innumerable cliques, which it will require some time [to] get the run of. Remember, also, that if you fall into the hands of one clique, all the others will give you the cold shoulder. Remember, also, that everybody will profess the most unbounded admiration for you, and not one of them can tell a line you have written. They will be very good, but upon the implied understanding that you are not to compete with them in their pitiful struggle for bread. The moment you do, God help you, if you are sensitive.

I speak, so far, only of the obscure journalistic nobodies—men with a merely local reputation or none at all. Let them alone. Make friends, if friends you must make—amongst the men whose work has delighted you in America; remembering, however, that an American reputation is easily made by a third rate Englishman. But the men at the top of the profession are at least above the necessity of being meanly jealous.

You will, by the way, be under a microscope here; your lightest word and most careless action noted down, and commented on by men who cannot understand how a person of individuality in thought or conduct can be other than a very bad man. Lord! how I have laid myself out inventing preposterous speech and demeanor just to set their silly tongues wagging. It is good fun for me—it would ruin you. Walk, therefore, circumspectly, keep your own counsel, don't make speeches at Clubs, avoid any appearance of eccentricity, don't admire anything, and don't disparage anything; don't eat mustard on mutton!

I know all this will make you laugh. There is no reason why you should not laugh; but you just "bet your boots", old man, I know these fellows, and their ways. They think they know *me*, but they don't. I am hand-in-glove with some hundreds of them, and they think they are my intimate friends. If any man says so, or acts as if he were, avoid him; he is an impostor. When I come back, I'll tell you the fellows you can tie to.

You will like the English when you get to know them; I do. I have not an enemy in London. There are a lot of fellows who would like to be my enemies, but I won't permit it; I am cordial as a summer noon to them—the puppies. But, generally speaking, the English are good fellows, the Scotch are better, and the Irish are a bad lot. You'll find this so; see if you don't.

You may take as much of this advice as you like; it is no trouble to write it. But this letter is *strictly confidential,* and when I come back I shall ask you to hand it to me.

Don't know what will be my address in Paris; Tom will have it, and I beg you will write me at once.

Believe me very truly yours,
A. G. Bierce.

You will probably go to the Fun Office first, so I have thought best to address you there. I intended at first to leave this letter for you at my lodgings in Hampstead. But you are *sure* to get it at the *Fun.*

Bierce.

1. Proverbs 23:32.

[9] To Charles Warren Stoddard [ALS, HL]

Hampstead, Saturday.
[November 22, 1873]

My Dear Stoddard;

I shall go on Tuesday next; naturally I have very little time at my command. But if Monday evening will be convenient I shall be very glad to dine with you and Clemens,[1] as per kind invitation, but shall have to leave early. I am particularly anxious to see you, to clean up a little social misunderstanding between you and Sampson[2]—who thinks you have not treated him with proper courtesy. Don't mention that I have spoken to you of it, if you see him, but correct the matter by your manner, if (as I presume) his grievance is imaginary. You owe a good deal to Sampson, by the way. But this matter will keep till I see you.

My friendly regards to Mark.

I am very truly yours

A. G. Bierce.

On the top of my hat—Strand

P. S.

Mark will receive from Chatto—who hopes he does not inherit Hotten's feuds—a little book which I am authorized to say is intended as a peace-offering.[3] (Happy thought—to go into the peace-making business regularly!)

A. G. B.

---

1. Samuel L. Clemens [Mark Twain] (1835–1910), the American lecturer and humorist, and friend of Stoddard. At the time, Clemens was in London to lecture and to attend to the publication of *The Gilded Age* (1873), written in collaboration with Charles Dudley Warner.
2. Henry Sampson (1841–1891), owner of *Fun* from 1874 to 1878.
3. Chatto & Windus, successor to John Camden Hotten, published *Nuggets and Dust*.

---

[10] To Charles Warren Stoddard [ALS, HL]

6 Sydney Buildings, Bath.
[January 1874?]

My Dear Charles;

I trust the fog has by this time purged you of homesickness. When is the book to come out?[1] I grow impatient of delay.

It gives me much pleasure to know that Mark's new lecture is successful, as I learn from the papers it is. Why don't *you* lecture? Seriously, Mark might put you up to the trick of it, and there are things in the Idylls that would "take" wonderfully from the tongue. Have you any 'Frisco news? Did you know Algernon Smith was dead? Did Chatto hand you the News Letter critique of your book which I sent him for you? I wanted *him* to see it, and feared you would be too modest [to] show it him.

I am pleased that Mark likes my Fables,[2] but your idea—that they ought to create a "furor"—I think that is the word—amuses me. I don't create furors. The book in question has never, I believe, been sent to a single journal for review, is not published in anybody's list, and is not even advertised. If there were any furor it would necessarily be the roar of very few indeed.

[. . .]
If I had one of Mark's cocktails I would finish this letter; as it is I have not the spirit to get through it, and if anything else strikes me I'll telegraph.
    Very truly yours,
        A. G. Bierce.

Oh! have you seen Sampson?

  1. Charles Warren Stoddard, *Summer Cruising in the South Seas* (London: Chatto & Windus, 1874), an illustrated British edition of *South-Sea Idyls*.
  2. AB's "The Fables of Zambri, the Parsee" appeared in *Fun* (13 July 1872–8 March 1873) and were later reprinted in *Cobwebs from an Empty Skull* (London: Routledge, 1874).

[11] To Charles Warren Stoddard [ALS, HL]
                      20 South Parade,
                            Leamington, Warwickshire,
                                    April 26th, 1874.

My Dear Charles;
                I ought to have written you long ago, if only to let you know that I have left Bath. We have been here (of course you know the place) for several weeks, and are very pleasantly situated indeed. When are you coming home? that is, to London, for I hope you begin to look on England as your home. I was sorry to leave Bath, for I wanted to show you the place this summer. But of course you will want to see Kenilworth, Warwick, and Stratford-on-Avon again.[1] You have no notion of the beauty of the country now, when it is green. So I shall hope to see you here in June or July. (This in your ear. My wife is expecting to be confined about the middle of May,[2] so I can't see anyone before then with satisfaction. At least she *won't* see any one.) Mrs. Day[3] is with us, but will sail for New York when the event alluded to has duly occurred.
[. . .]
Mrs. B. and Mrs. D. wish to be remembered.
    Very truly yours,
        A. G. Bierce.

  1. AB had written about each of these places in his *Alta California* letters of 1872 (see *A Sole Survivor* 112–22).
  2. AB's second son, Leigh, was born on 29 April.
  3. AB's mother-in-law, who also was staying in England.

[12] To Charles Warren Stoddard [ALS, HL]

20 South Parade, Leamington.
July 4th 1874.

My Dear Charles;
I am a beast not [to] have answered your other letter. But I have had a deal of worry of my own. Let me see. I don't know when I *did* write you. I do know that I am extremely sorry for your accident, and wish you were here in Leamington; though what with my having more work than I can do, and Mrs. B. having two babies and a nursemaid to look after, I fear it would be agreeable only as change,—to you, that is; to us it would be not comparatively but absolutely agreeable. You must come up anyhow when you are again in the island. Did I tell you the letter you sent me to Bath is received? Mrs. B. thanks you for the "fine herbs" nourished with poet-juices.

As to the book "Cruisings," I know nothing further than that Chatto wrote me last Winter, or in the early Spring,—since which I have not heard from him—that it was selling as well as he expected it would. Being a publisher he would probably not confess as much to you. There is, I find, only one way to do in matters of this kind: make up your book ready for the printer, then submit it. Believe me the "relations" between author and publisher have no other basis than a purely commercial one, and the more briefly business-like they are the better. When you have anything to sell put it in shape and sell it to the highest bidder. I can think of no reason why you should not write to Chatto telling him what you propose, but I am very sure he'll answer to the same effect that I have done, namely, that he'll be happy to look at what you've got. But perhaps you have none on hand, and won't have till you get them in American print—in which case you would have no English copyright. If that is the case I am quite unable to advise you, as I don't know if *any* course would give you property in them here. Chatto would tell you—and I think quite honestly—about that.

I hear nothing from London—don't know what's going on—don't wish to. Tom writes me three lines of nothing occasionally—Mortimer[1] three sheets (in the wind) of business—and Sampson has written me once, I believe, since I've been here. Therefore I have not had the happiness to hear Miller's character defamed, and don't know what you allude to. Don't tell me. I *did* hear, now that I think of it, that he had acted "like a hog"—not very definite that—about "Josie", and that she was married to Prentice Mulford. I did not ask for particulars, and had quite forgotten both pieces of information. If you see Miller give him my love.

[...]

As to myself, I have another boy. He is, I believe ["here insert the age of the child".] It is either six weeks, two months, or something like it; I swear I do not know, and Mrs. B. is not within call. He has had a hard struggle for life, and we have only just begun to entertain hopes of saving him. Mrs. Day left for home a couple of weeks or so ago.

Do you know Belle Thomas² of San Francisco? She is in Paris, "training to howl". She just spent a couple of weeks with us. Then, too, I have been, and am, up to my ears in work—grinding stuff for five publications: one semi-weekly, two weekly, one monthly, and one "occasional"—a *pizen* thing of which I write every line.³ If some of these don't die of me I shall die of them. Perhaps *now* you'll forgive, or excuse, my neglect of your letter, though *I* can't.

I should like to see London, but with "ties" like these how can I break away? London is the "thief of time."⁴

Love to you, and luck to the arm. Have you tried oiling it?

A. G. Bierce.

1. James Mortimer (d. 1911) was an American journalist and editor of *Figaro*, for which AB did much writing from 1872 to 1875. At the time, the paper was being published twice a week, on Wednesday and Saturday.
2. Belle Thomas later married AB's friend, Captain Nichols, a miner.
3. The semi-weekly is *Figaro*, one weekly is *Fun*, the monthly is the *London Sketch-Book,* and the "occasional" is the *Lantern*, two issues of which came out in May and July 1874, every word of which was written by AB. The second weekly has not been identified.
4. Edward Young (1683–1765), *Night Thoughts* (1742–45), 1.392: "Procrastination is the thief of time."

[13] To Charles Warren Stoddard [ALS, HL]
20 South Parade, Leamington,
June 2d, 1875.

My Dear Charles;

Awfully glad you are back, and want to see you very much, for I am lonely, of course, without the wife and babies. The wife, by the way, told me before leaving that if you came back I'd better have you down here for a while. Perhaps she thought you would keep me out of mischief. That's all very well, but I wouldn't have you here for the world, although I have a whole house to myself. First, I have no time to talk to you for I'm struggling with more work than I can manage, and that is partly what has made me ill—for I am ill, though I keep pegging away, somehow. Second, I live precariously and abominably. There is only one decent place in the town to get a meal—a hotel which lives by swindling Americans, and which, having once swindled me, I do not enter. I am not a good housekeeper, and my landlady, though honest for a wonder, has not the advantage of knowing anything. So as soon as I feel well enough to travel I'm coming to London till Mrs. B. returns, when I shall take a house somewhere in the scruburbs.

I have heard nothing from Mrs. B. since she left New York, but am expecting a letter every day from Salt Lake. She is probably at Pioche before this time.

Do you know Fred Whymper[1] is in Town? 30 Essex-st., Strand, is his address, I think—I'm too lazy to look up his letter to verify it.

I thank you very much for the kind interest you take in my health, but I am not so ill as you suppose. It is only a cursed sort of semi-lunacy, I think, from lack of sleep, hard work, and unchristian evoking. I shall throw over some of the work, take opiates, and come to London.

Hope you won't go to Ireland—or is it Iceland?—or will soon return, for I want to see you often. Give my love to Miller and believe me very truly
    Your friend,
        A. G. Bierce.

How *dare* you spell study with two d's?

1. Frederick Whymper (1837?–1901), British travel writer and artist, and brother of the explorer Edward Whymper. From 1870 to 1875, he worked for the *Alta California*.

[14] To Laura Bierce[1] [Transcript (MEG)]

                                San Francisco, Cal.,
                                February 13, 1876.
My Dear Mother,

    Al[2] has shown me your letter of the fourth, and I can not tell you how deeply it has grieved me to learn that my poor Father[3] is so low. Of course I had long expected some such news, but had, I think, never fully realized how dreadful it would be. There is nothing I can [do] to comfort you, Mother; I need comfort myself. If Father is still living when you receive this I beg you to tell him how deeply I feel for him, how sorry I am for all the sorrow and trouble I have ever caused him, and ask him [to] forgive me for the sake of the love I have always borne him. Mrs. Bierce is, I think, almost as much pained as I at the thought of losing one whom she had learned to love, and whom she hoped to meet on this side of the grave.

My poor Mother, I cannot write as I feel; you know what I would say; you know how dreadful is this affliction to me, who have not even the consolation of having been a good son to so good a father. It is very hard for us all, but there is nothing for us to do but endure whatever it may please a superior power to inflict upon our helpless hearts. Of us all, you, my poor Mother, are the only one to whom the consciousness of having always performed your every duty with unswerving patience, gentleness and grace will come to temper the bitterness of grief.

I can write no more for I am blind with tears.
                          Ambrose.

1. Laura (Sherwood) Bierce married Marcus Aurelius Bierce in 1822 and subsequently bore him thirteen children, each of them given a name beginning with A. At this time she was living in Elkhart, Indiana. She died in May 1878.
2. Albert Bierce, AB's elder brother and the only one of his siblings to whom he felt an attachment.
3. Marcus Aurelius Bierce died before month's end.

[15] To Laura Bierce [Transcript (MEG)]

San Francisco, Cal.,
April 30, 1876.

My Dear Mother,

    I have delayed writing you for so long since receiving your sad account of the great grief which has fallen upon us all, only because I felt it too keenly for me to trust myself to write of it. I had, and have now, no consolation to offer you, and it seems worse than useless to revive a sorrow so great, without some attempt to alleviate it. Be assured that I deeply sympathize with you in [a] loss which is only less to me than to you.

    I hope you will not for the present remain in Elkhart, but will go to your girls for at least a few months. But on this point Al has already written you giving his views and mine. He knows better than I, and in all things I defer to his superior judgement. Whatever he recommends I most cordially approve and will endeavor to assist in accomplishing. It seems to me you need a change of scene associations to better enable you to bear the great loss of which everything in your Elkhart house must constantly remind you.

    Mollie wishes me to tell you how deeply she feels for you in your bereavement, and I know she is sincere from the way she feels for me in mine.

    Write to me, Mother, whenever it may give you relief to do so.

              Ambrose.

[16] To E. L. G. Steele[1] [ALS, VA]

Auburn, Feby 25. [1884]

My Dear Steele,

    [...]

    I have been turning your other flattering proposition[2] over in my mind a good deal. I thought that civility demanded its hospitable entertainment for a long time before I "sped the parting guest."[3] Well, even with the intelligent prompting of my self-interest—to which accommodating quality I am much obliged for the assistance—I am unable to figure out of the project any profit or hope of profit—for you.

    The instances you mention of "provincial" journals that have paid are not accurately in point. Springfield, Mass., and Louisville, Ky., are not country towns but cities, and large cities—lively cities, in dense populations—news centers. The papers that thrive there are daily papers. A daily paper at Sacramento would be comparable with them in several points, but no editorial talent could make even that a parallel case in respect of pecuniary value. However, having decided not to accept your kind offer I need [not] attempt any elaborate justification. That would have been demanded by acceptance.

[. . .]

  Aloha![4]

    A. G. Bierce.

Come up.

 1. AB's friend E. L. G. Steele (d. 1894), a wealthy San Francisco businessman, head of C. Adolphe Low and Company, Importers, published *Tales of Soldiers and Civilians* in 1891. In a prefatory note to that volume AB wrote: "Denied existence by the chief publishing houses of this country, this book owes itself to Mr. E. L. G. Steele, merchant, of this city. In attesting Mr. Steele's faith in his judgment and his friend, it will serve the author's main and best ambition."
 2. Steele was proposing to found a newspaper of which AB would be the editor.
 3. From Alexander Pope's translation of the *Odyssey*, 15.84 ("speed" in Pope).
 4. AB presumably acknowledges that Steele was a Knight of the Hawaiian Order of Oceania.

[17] To Helen Bierce[1] [ALS, BL]

                  Auburn, Apr. 2, '85.

My Dear Baby,

    I suppose I must stop calling you Baby pretty soon, for you are becoming a young woman. But you will always seem to me to be a baby, and I like to think of you that way. So I think I will just call you Baby as long as you sign your letters that way. When you don't any longer then I will know that you don't wish me to call you so any more.

 I suppose you had a nice time while your Mama and brothers were in Nicasio, but I should have thought you would have wanted to go there too, for you must get very tired of San Francisco, and Nicasio is such a pretty place. I wish I could live there and not be sick, then I could see you so often. I want to see you all the time, and sometimes I feel that I must see you or I will be ill, I like you so much. I'm sure no other man has such a good daughter as you are. When you are as old as I am now, and I am gone, you will know how much I loved you, but you can't know it now.

 You may tell Leigh that I shall write to him in a day or two; and tell Day that I am waiting for him to write me and send me some drawings that I told him to make for me. It rained last night, and there was lightning and it thundered like the sound of

cannon. Did you ever hear a lot of cannon all firing at once? It was just like that. The country is very beautiful now. Write to me often. I would like to kiss you ten thousand times on the mouth.
Your father,
A. G. Bierce

1. At this time, AB's daughter was nine years old.

[18] To John H. Boalt[1] [ALS, VA]

Auburn, Cal'a.
April 16 1885.

My Dear Boalt,
I want your legal advice and assistance, if the matter is not too small a one for you. If it is, please tell me whom to employ.

In the summer of 1880 I was the General Agent of the Black Hills Placer Mining Company of New York. The First National Bank of Deadwood was my banker and paid out a good deal of money on my checks. Finally, my remittance from New York came to another bank, and the First National, seeing it had lost our business, stopped out of my account the sum of $3,500—an old claim that it had against the company for an alleged overdraft by my defaulting predecessor. (If it is necessary for you to know the circumstances more in detail, see enclosed Exhibit B—rough notes of a deposition made by me in September, 1881, in San Francisco—especially under Answer 14. The questions I have no memorandum of.)

Through the Company's attorneys, M‹Laughlin & Steele, I brought a suit to recover, in the District Court of Laurence County, Territory of Dakota. The attorneys advised that it be brought in my name—"Ambrose G. Bierce *vs.* the First National Bank of Deadwood." Before it came to trial I had left the Territory and the Company's service, having distinctly refused to stay and prosecute this suit and others. I never had a cents worth of interest in it, and was not a stockholder in the Company, which I have heard nothing from since, and believe to be no longer in existence, though I don't know.

McLaughlin & Steele, depending on the recovery of this money for their pay for legal services of various kinds, to the Company, pushed the suit, and I assisted as shown in Exhibits A, B and C, enclosed. (I don't think it will be necessary for you to study these—get a general idea of them and go on to Exhibits D to J. These will show you what has been done.) They, McL & S., won and both the Company and I assigned them all our claims to the judgment—though the Company, according to the testimony of its officers, never had any claim to assign; according to mine, I hadn't!

I supposed that ended the whole interesting matter, with which I have all along been disgusted and worried. The lawyers, McLaughlin & Steele, you understand, are working for themselves. I never liked them, but good naturedly acquiesced in their use of my paw to pull out their chestnuts, and trusted that they would not get me into any worse litigation nor put me to any expense.

Now read Exhibits K and L, enclosed, and you have the story to date.

They have not replied. What shall I do?

Yours very truly,

A. G. Bierce.

1. Judge John H. Boalt counseled AB on litigation relating to AB's involvement with the Black Hills Placer Mining Company. The matter is addressed in detail in Paul Fatout, *Ambrose Bierce and the Black Hills* (Norman: University of Oklahoma Press, 1956).

[19] To Sergt. Abe Dills[1]

Oakland, Cal., Aug. 13, 1887.

My Dear Dills.—It was very good of you to remember to send me an invitation to the reunion, and although unable to attend I am grateful for the invitation. I saw a report of the first reunion—Hazen[2] sent it to me—but have heard nothing since. It would give me great pleasure to meet the members of the old Ninth, for some of whom I retain the tenderest regard, after all this lapse of years, and I hope to be able to do so some day. This year it is quite impossible.

How can I obtain reports of all the meetings? I should greatly like to have them, and will remit to the proper person any sum necessary to procure them. Please inform me.

I was greatly pleased to find in the report I had (I think the first) a complimentary mention of me in connection with Boothroyd,[3] the Ninth's first martyr, killed at Bealington in the three months' service. But my name was spelled "Bruce." If these things are ever published in a volume, I hope the error will be corrected, for I am vain enough to be rather proud of the incident related.

Your letter has called up all manner of memories—men and things that had not for years been in my mind. I recollect you with special kindness as a good soldier and good fellow. I hope you have prospered as you merit.

I should be pleased to have you mention me to such of our old comrades as you think would care to hear of me—there are, I hope, too many to specify. A member of the Ninth lives in San Francisco, Henry Healy, brother to the captain. He is one of the three or four whom I have seen since coming to California.

Good bye for the present, Abe, let me hear from you again. Very truly your friend.

A. G. Bierce.

1. The letter was published in *Fourth Reunion of the 9th Regiment Indiana Vet. Vol. Infantry Association* ([Delphi, Ind.:] Watskeka Republican Book Print, 1887), 66–67.

2. Brigadier General (USV) William Babcock Hazen (1830–1887) was perhaps AB's closest associate during the Civil War. AB joined his staff as a topographical engineer, or mapmaker, in the spring of 1863. Hazen commanded the 2nd Brigade, 2nd Division, XXI Corps at Chickamauga.

3. The *Indianapolis Journal* (27 July 1861) reported: "Privates A. J. [sic] Bierce . . . and [Dyson] Boothroyd . . . Ninth Indiana Volunteers, advanced up the hill to within fifteen paces of the enemy's breastworks when Boothroyd was wounded in the neck by a rifle ball paralyzing him. Bierce, in open view of the enemy, carried poor Boothroyd and his gun without other assistance, fully twenty rods, balls falling around him like hail." Quoted in Paul Fatout, *Ambrose Bierce: The Devil's Lexicographer* (Norman: University of Oklahoma Press, 1951), 39–40. AB's heroism probably had much to do with his rapid promotion.

[20] To Helen Bierce [ALS, UP]

Suñol

Sunday.

[September 1890?]

Dear Bibsy,

I have just written to Leigh. You are like a dainty tidbit which one lays aside to eat last. I wish I had time and talent to write as long and interesting a letter as you did. It was interesting more, probably, because of its subject—*you*—than for any other reason.

I was able to go to San Francisco yesterday, and as I walked along the streets I kept seeing you, with your back to me. But you would not remain *you*,—you always turned out to be another girl. This always occurs to me in the city, and it is very disappointing. I wish you would not do it.

Of course if you visit me here I shall be delighted, but you must let me know as long as possible beforehand, so that I can arrange to see you. And you must not come late in the week, nor expect to stay long, for you could hardly amuse yourself alone, and I would have to work.

[. . .]

No, I am not writing "a *new* book," though some of it will be new to you. I have only collected some of my stories. But I hope the book will be worthy of the father of so clever a young woman as you.[1]

[. . .]

Your Father.

1. *Tales of Soldiers and Civilians* (1891).

[21] To Ella Sterling Cummins [ALS, CHS]

Angwin, Cal'a,
March 13, 1892.

It is very good of you, dear Mrs. Cummins, to undertake the project which you outline, but whether the best service that you can render to California's literature is to direct attention to it is another matter. I should say you could serve it better by adding something to it.[1]

But I'm not a good person to assist you, I fear, for I know the titles of very few Californian books. My reading has not lain much in that direction. You will infer, and correctly, that I have not a very high opinion of the body of writings which it is your intention to collect. A few books by a few authors (you and I, of course, among them) would comprise *my* collection in your place. Californian writers are accustomed to send me their books, God knows why. Shall I forward them to you henceforth?

As you have given away the copy of my book which you bought perhaps you will give me permission to replace it.

As to the photograph I have none. None has been taken these last fifteen years or so. One about that old was recently found by a friend somewhere and she had it enlarged at some gallery, but I don't remember whose, and have given away all the copies sent me. Mr. Chas. H. Kaufman, 307 Montgomery St.,[2] will tell you the name of the photographer, as it was he who had the copies made for my friend. I don't think the picture can be much like me now, but it is the latest—and last.

So you have stopped your sketches of writers in the *Wasp*. I have seen none excepting those that you kindly sent me. They seemed to me to run rather too much to eulogium, the almost invariable fault of that kind of work. But I dare say you think nothing but good of all mankind. Well, I think nothing but good of you, for your reward.

Sincerely yours,
Ambrose Bierce.

1. Ella Sterling Cummins (1853–1934; later Ella Sterling Mighels) compiled *The Story of the Files: A Review of Californian Writers and Literature* ([San Francisco: Cooperative Printing Co.,] 1893; rpt. San Leandro, Calif.: Yosemite Collections, 1982), an account of literature in California, for the 1893 World's Fair. AB is discussed, and his journalism liberally quoted, on pp. 177–84. Mighels's later compilation, *Literary California* (1918), includes AB's poems "Invocation" and "Science."

2. Kaufman was AB's adviser in San Francisco during his Black Hills days. He accompanied AB when AB went to Chico to investigate the death of his son Day.

[22] To Blanche Partington[1] [ALS, BL]

Angwin,
July 31, 1892.

My dear Blanche,

You will not, I hope, mind my saying that the first part of your letter was so pleasing that it almost solved the disappointment created by the other part. For *that* is a bit discouraging. Let me explain.

You receive my suggestion about trying your hand (I remember just how your hand looks, by the way) at writing, with assent and apparently pleasure. But, alas, not for love of the art, but for the purpose of helping God repair his botchwork world. You want to "reform" things, poor girl—to rise and lay about you, slaying monsters and liberating captive maids. You would "help to alter for the better the position of working-women." You would be a missionary—and the rest of it. Perhaps I shall not make myself understood when I say that this discourages me; that in such aims (worthy as they are) I would do nothing to assist you; that such ambitions are not only impracticable but incompatible with the spirit that gives success in art; that such ends are a prostitution of art; that "helpful" writing is dull reading. If you had had more experience of life I should regard what you say as entirely conclusive against your possession of any talent of a literary kind. But you are so young and untaught in that way—and I have the testimony of little felicitous and purely literary touches (apparently unconscious) in your letters—perhaps your unschooled heart and hope should not be held as having spoken the conclusive word. But surely, my child—as surely as anything in mathematics—Art will laurel no brow having a divided allegiance. Love the world as much as you will, but serve it otherwise. The best service you can perform by writing is to write well with no care for anything but that. Plant and water and let God give the increase if he will, and to whom it shall please him.

Suppose your father were to "help working-women" by painting no pictures but such (of their ugly surroundings, say) as would incite them to help themselves, or others to help them. Suppose you should play no music but such as—but I need go no further. Literature (I don't mean journalism) is an *art*;—it is not a form of benevolence. It has nothing to do with "reform," and when used as a means of reform suffers accordingly and justly. Unless you can *feel* that way I cannot advise you to meddle with it.

It would be dishonest in me to accept your praise for what I wrote of the Homestead Works quarrel[2]—unless you should praise it for being well written and true. I have no sympathies with that savage fight between the two kinds of rascals, and no desire to assist either—except to better hearts and manners. The love of truth is good enough motive for me when I wrote of my fellow men. I like many things in this world and a few persons—I like you, for example; but after they are served I have no love to waste upon the irreclaimable mass of brutality that we know as "mankind." Compassion, yes—I am sincerely sorry that they are brutes.

Yes, I wrote the article "The Human Liver".[3] Your criticism is erroneous. My opportunities of knowing women's feelings toward Mrs. Grundy are better than yours. They hate her with a horrible antipathy; but they cower all the same. The fact that they are a part of her mitigates neither their hatred nor their fear.

[. . .]

I'm sure your father will do interesting work of the kind that he has undertaken, and hope it will bring him something. I should advise him to send it to Mr. Chamberlain,[4] of the *Examiner*, by Richard, or take it himself. Chamberlain is a nice and sensible fellow, but Noble,[5] the editor of the Sunday Supplement, is a fool.

[. . .]

    Sincerely your friend,
        Ambrose Bierce.

1. Blanche Partington (d. 1951) was part of a family several of whose members were acquainted with AB. Her father, John H. E. Partington (1843–1899), was a painter and an illustrator for several San Francisco newspapers who painted AB's portrait, which was exhibited at the 1893 World's Fair. One sister, Gertrude, was an actress and painter; another sister, Phyllis, was a singer; another sister, Katie, was married to Frederick Peterson; and her brother, Richard (1869–1929), was a journalist and painter. AB corresponded sporadically with all of them, but chiefly with Blanche.

2. A reference to a bitter miners' strike at Homestead, Pennsylvania, lasting from July to November 1892. AB, generally hostile to labor strikes, wrote harshly of the miners in "Prattle," *SF* (24 July 1892): 6.

3. "The Human Liver," an unsigned editorial in *SF* (24 July 1892): 6, concerning the "tyranny of fashion."

4. Samuel S. Chamberlain, an editor for the Hearst newspapers and, later, briefly editor of *Cosmopolitan*.

5. Frank L. H. "Cosy" Noble, a member of Hearst's "Harvard Brigade" from their days on the *Harvard Lampoon*.

[23] To Blanche Partington [ALS, BL]

                St. Helena,
                Aug. 15, 1892.

I know, dear Blanche, of the disagreement among men as to the nature and aims of literature; and the subject is too "long" to discuss. I will only say that it seems to me that men holding Tolstoi's view are not properly literary men (that is to say, artists) at all.[1] They are "missionaries", who, in their zeal to lay about them, do not scruple to seize any weapon that they can lay their hands on; they would grab a crucifix to beat a dog. The dog is well beaten, no doubt (which makes him a worse dog than he was before) but note the condition of the crucifix! The work of these men is better, of course, than the work of men of truer art and inferior brains; but always you see the possibilities—possibilities to *them*—which they have missed or consciously sacrificed to their fad. And after all they do no good. The world does not wish to be helped. The poor wish only to be rich, which is impossible, not to be better. They would like to be rich in order to be worse, generally speaking. And your working woman (also generally speaking) does not wish to be virtuous; despite her insincere deprecation she would not let the existing system be altered if she could help it. Individual men and women can be assisted; and happily some are worthy of assistance. No *class* of mankind, no tribe, no nation is worth the sacrifice of one good man or woman; for not only is their average worth low, but they like it that way; and in trying to help them you fail to help the good individuals. Your family, your immediate friends, will give you scope enough for all your benevolence. I must include your*self*.

In timely illustration of some of this is an article by Ingersoll in the current *North American Review*[2]—I shall send it you. It will be nothing new to you; the fate of the philanthropist who gives out of his brain and heart instead of his pocket—having nothing in that—is already known to you. It serves him richly right, too, for his low taste in loving. He who dilutes, spreads, subdivides, the love which naturally *all* belongs to his family and friends (if they are good) should not complain of non-appreciation. Love those, help those, whom from personal knowledge you know to be worthy. To love and help others is treason to *them*. But, bless my soul! I did not mean to say all this.

But while you seem clear as to your own art, you seem undecided as to the one you wish to take up. I know the strength and sweetness of the illusions (that is, *de*lusions) that you are required to forego. I know the abysmal ignorance of the world and human character which, as a girl, you necessarily have. I know the charm that inheres in the beckoning of the Britomarts,[3] as they lean out of their dream to persuade you to be as like them as is compatible with the fact that you exist. But I believe, too, that if you are set thinking—not reading—you will find the light.

You ask me of journalism. It is so low a thing that it *may* be legitimately used as a means of reform or as a means of anything deemed worth accomplishing. It is not an art; art, except in the greatest moderation, is damaging to it. The man who can write well must not write as well as he can; the others may, of course. Journalism has many purposes, and the people's welfare *may* be one of them; though that is not the purpose-in-chief, by much.

I don't mind your irony about my looking upon the unfortunate as merely "literary material." It is true in so far as I consider them *with reference to literature*. Possibly I might be willing to help them otherwise—as your father might be willing to help a beggar with money, who is not picturesque enough to go into a picture. As you might be willing to give a tramp a dinner, yet unwilling to play "The Sweet Bye-and-Bye," or "Ta-ra-ra-boom-de-ay,"[4] to tickle his ear.

You call me "master". Well, it is pleasant to think of you as a pupil, but—you know the young squire had to watch his arms all night before the day of his accolade and investiture with knighthood. I think I'll ask you to contemplate yours a little longer before donning them—not by way of penance but instruction and consecration. When you are quite sure of the nature of your *call* to write—quite sure that it is *not* the voice of "duty"—then let me do you such slight, poor service as my limitations and the injunctions of circumstance permit. In a few ways I can help you.

You say you destroy my letters. You need not do that if you do not wish—at least not until I ask you. I suppose you are not likely to let them go out of your control.

Since coming here I have been ill all the time, but it seems my duty to remain as long as there is a hope that I *can* remain. If I get free from my disorder and the fear of it I shall go down to San Francisco some day and then try to see your people and mine. Perhaps you would help me to find my brother's new house—if he is living in it.

With sincere regards to all your family, I am most truly your friend,

Ambrose Bierce.

Your letters are very pleasing to me. I think it nice of you to write them.

1. In *What Is Art?* (1898), Russian novelist Leo Tolstoi (1818–1910) maintained that art should be accessible to the masses rather than merely to the educated elite, that it should be a guide to life, and that it should clearly show the distinction between good and evil. His views were no doubt propagated in the press long before the publication of this treatise.
2. Robert G. Ingersoll (1833–1899), "Thomas Paine," *North American Review* 155 (August 1892): 181–95. Ingersoll was a renowned agnostic lecturer and writer, whom AB defended in his columns; see "A Dead Lion" (*CW* 10). The article is a general overview of Paine's literary and journalistic work.
3. In Spenser's *The Faerie Queene*, Britomart is a maiden knight who represents chastity.
4. "The Sweet By and By" (1867; words by Sanford Fillmore Bennett; music by Joseph Philbrick Webster) was a popular gospel song of the nineteenth century. "Ta-ra-ra-boom-de-ay" (1891; words and music by Henry J. Sayers).

[24] To Blanche Partington [ALS, BL]

St. Helena,
Aug. 17, 1892.

Dear Blanche,

It was not that I forgot to mail you the magazine that I mentioned; I could not find it; but now I send it.

My health is bad again, and I fear that I shall have to abandon my experiment of living here, and go back to the mountain—or some mountain. But not directly.

You asked me what books would be useful to you—I'm assuming that you've repented your sacrilegious attitude toward literature, and will endeavor to thrust your pretty head into the crown of martyrdom otherwise. I may mention a few from time to time as they occur to me. There is a little book entitled (I think) simply "English Composition." It is by Prof. John Nichol[1]—elementary, in a few places erroneous, but on the whole rather better than the ruck of books on the same subject.

Read those of Landor's "Imaginary Conversations"[2] which relate to literature.

Read Longinus, Herbert Spencer on Style, Pope's "Essay on Criticism" (don't groan—the detractors of Pope are not always to have things their own way) Lucian on the writing of history—though you need not write history. Read poor old obsolete Kames' notions; some of them are not half bad. Read Burke "On the Sublime and Beautiful."[3]

Read—but that will do at present. And as you read don't forget that the rules of the literary art are deduced from the work of the masters who wrote in ignorance of them or in unconsciousness of them. That fixes their value; it is secondary to that of *natural* qualifications. None the less, it is considerable. Doubtless you have read many—perhaps most—of these things, but to read them with a view to profit *as a writer* may be different. If I could get to San Francisco I could dig out of those artificial memories, the catalogues of the libraries, a lot of titles additional—and get you the books, too. But I've a bad memory, and am out of the Book Belt.

I wish you would write some little thing and send it me for examination. I shall not judge it harshly, for this I *know:* the good writer (supposing him to be born to the trade) is not made by reading, but by observing and experiencing. You have lived so little, seen so little, that your range will necessarily be narrow; but within its lines I know no reason why you should not do good work. But it is all conjectural—you may fail. Would it hurt if I should tell you that I thought you had failed? Your absolute and complete failure would not affect in the slightest my admiration of your intellect. I have always half suspected that it is only second rate minds, and minds below the second rate, that hold their cleverness by so precarious a tenure that they can detach it for display in words.

God bless you,
A. B.

1. John Nichol (1833–1894), *English Composition* (1878).

2. Walter Savage Landor (1775–1864), Britsh poet and critic. His *Imaginary Conversations* (1824–53) are prose dialogues between historical personages and are regarded as his great work. AB himself wrote numerous such "imaginary conversations" between his contemporaries, chiefly of a political nature (e.g., the section "Two Administrations" in *CW* 12).

3. Longinus was the reputed author of a Greek work, *Peri hypsous* (*On the Sublime*), dating to the first century C.E. Herbert Spencer (1820–1903) was a leading English sociologist and philosopher of the nineteenth century. His *Philosophy of Style* (1873) was much reprinted in its time. Alexander Pope was the greatest British poet and satirist of the first half of the eighteenth century. His poem *An Essay on Criticism* (1711) addresses the art of writing. Lucian of Samosata was a Greek satirist of the second

century C.E. His *Pōs dei historian syngraphein* (*How to Write History*) is a satire on contemporary historians. Henry Home, Lord Kames (1696–1782) was a lawyer, agriculturalist, and philosopher. His *Elements of Criticism* (1762) was an influential discussion of the notions of beauty and ugliness. Edmund Burke (1729–1797) was a prominent British statesman, parliamentary orator, and political thinker during the later eighteenth century. His *A Philosophical Enquiry into the Origin of Our Ideas of the Sublime and Beautiful* (1757) attempted to distinguish between the two aesthetic concepts.

[25] To Blanche Partington [ALS, BL]

St. Helena,

Sept. 28, 1892.

My dear Blanche,

[...]

I'm sending you and your father copies of my book.[1] Not that I think you (either of you) will care for that sort of thing, but merely because your father is my co-sinner in making the book, and you in sitting by and diverting my mind from the proofsheets of a part of it. Your part, therefore, in the work is the typographical errors. So you are in literature in spite of yourself.

I appreciate what you write of my girl. She is the best of girls to me, but God knoweth I'm not a proper person to direct her way of life. However, it will not be for long. A dear friend of mine—the widow of another dear friend—in London wants her, and means to come out here next Spring and try to persuade me to let her have her—for a time at least. It is likely that I shall. My friend is wealthy, childless and devoted to both my children. I wish that in the meantime she (the girl) could have the advantage of association with *you*.

[...]

My (and Danziger's) book, "The Monk and the Hangman's Daughter,"[2] is to be out next month. The Publisher—I like to write it with a reverent capital letter—is unprofessional enough to tell me that he regards it as the very best piece of English composition that he ever saw, and he means to make the world know it. Now let the great English classics hide their diminished heads and pale their ineffectual fires!

So you begin to suspect that books do not give you the truth of life and character. Well, that suspicion is the beginning of wisdom, and, so far as it goes, a preliminary qualification for writing—books. Men and women are certainly not what books represent them to be, nor what *they* represent—sometimes believe—themselves to be. They are better, they are worse, and far more interesting.

With best regards to all your people, and in the hope that we may frequently hear from you, I am very sincerely your friend,

Ambrose Bierce.

Both the children send their *love* to you. And they mean just that.

1. *Black Beetles in Amber* (San Francisco & New York: Western Authors Publishing Co., 1892), a collection of AB's satirical verse, culled from his newspaper columns.

2. *The Monk and the Hangman's Daughter* (Chicago: F. J. Schulte & Co., 1892). The work is a translation by AB and Gustav Adolphe Danziger (1859–1959) of a short novel by Richard Voss, *Die Mönch des Berchtesgaden,* first published in *Vom Fels zum Meer* 1 (1890–91) and later in book form. Danziger brought his own translation to AB probably sometime in 1891; AB extensively revised it, and it was serialized in *SF* (13, 20, and 27 September 1891). Danziger later contended that AB had little to do with the work; see his *Portrait of Ambrose Bierce* (New York: Century Co., 1929), 125–38; 275–80.

[26] To Blanche Partington [ALS, BL]

Angwin,

Dec. 25, 1892.

My dear Blanche,

[...]

It was uncommonly nice of Hume[1] to entertain so good an opinion of me; if you had seen him a few days later you would have found a different state of affairs, probably; for I had been exhausting relays of vials of wrath upon him for delinquent diligence in securing copyright for my little story[2]—whereby it is uncopyrighted. I ought to add that he has tried to make reparation, and is apparently contrite to the limit of his penitential capacity.

No, there was no other foundation for the little story than its obvious naturalness and consistency with the sentiments "appropriate to the season." When Christendom is guzzling and gorging and clowning it has not time to cease being cruel; all it can do is to augment its hypocrisy a trifle.

Please don't lash yourself and do various penances any more for your part in the plaguing of poor Russell;[3] he is quite forgotten in the superior affliction sent upon James Whitcomb Riley.[4] *That* seems a matter of genuine public concern, if I may judge by what I heard in town (and I heard little else) and by my letters and "esteemed" (though testy) "contemporaries." Dear, dear, how sensitive people are becoming!

[...]

Seeing Harry Bigelow's article in the *Wave* on women who wrote[5] (and it's unpleasantly near to the truth of the matter) I feel almost reconciled to the failure of my gorgeous dream of making a writer of *you*. I wonder if *you* would have eschewed the harmless, necessary tub and danced upon the broken bones of the innocuous toothbrush. Fancy you with sable nails and a soiled cheek, uttering to the day what God taught in the night! Let us be thankful that the peril is past.

The next time I go to "the Bay" I shall go to 1019 *first.*

God bless you for a good girl.

Ambrose Bierce.

1. Hugh Hume, editor of the *Wave*. AB had numerous stories published in the *Wave* in 1892.
2. "The Applicant," *Wave*, Christmas 1892 (17 December 1892): 16–17; rpt. *CW* 2.
3. AB had written disparagingly about Edmund Russell, a San Francisco critic and lecturer, in "Prattle," *SF* (11 December 1892): 6. AB also wrote a fable about him; see "Fables and Anecdotes," *SF* (11 February 1893): 6; rpt. *The Collected Fables of Ambrose Bierce*, ed. S. T. Joshi (Columbus: Ohio State University Press, 2000), 241 (Fable 699).
4. James Whitcomb Riley (1849–1916), Indiana poet remembered for nostalgic dialect verse and called "the poet of the common people." AB repeatedly needled him in his newspaper and magazine work.
5. Henry Derby "Harry" Bigelow, "Literary Wives," *Wave* 9, no. 26 (24 December 1892): 9

[27] To Blanche Partington [ALS, BL]

Angwin,

Jan. 9, 1893.

Dear Blanche

[...]

So you are good enough to be amused by my Riley criticism.[1] Well, I am going to slip into this letter some of the criticisms on *me* elicited by mine on him; and I do hope that when you learn from them what an unworthy person you are honoring with your friendship you will reform—me. I will not ask you to read more of them than enough to amuse you, and you may send them back if you will; my collection is not yet complete.

Yes, I know Blackburn Harte[2] has a weakness for the proletariat of letters—though the Foss person is unknown to me[3]—and doubtless thinks Riley good *because* he is "of the people," peoply. But he will have to endure me as well as he can. You ask my opinion of Burns. He has not, I think, been translated into English, and I do not (that is, I can but *will* not) read that gibberish.[4] I read Burns once—that was once too many times; but happily it was before I knew any better, and so my time, being worthless, was not wasted.

I wish you could be up here this beautiful weather. But I dare say it would rain if you came. In truth, it is "thickening" a trifle just because of my wish. And I wish I *had* given you, for your father, all the facts of my biography from the cradle—downward. When you come again I shall, if you still want them. For I'm worried half to death with requests for them, and when I refuse am no doubt considered surly or worse. And my refusal no longer serves, for the biography-men are beginning to write my history from imagination.[5] So the next time I see you I shall give you (orally) that "history of a crime", my life. Then, if your father is still in the notion, he can write it from your notes, and I can answer all future inquiries by enclosing his article.

Do you know?—you will, I think, be glad to know—that I have many more offers for stories at good prices, than I have the health to accept. (For I am less nearly well than I have told you.) Even the *Examiner* has "waked up" (I woke it up) to the situation, and now pays me $20 a thousand words; and my latest offer from New York is $50.

[...]

        Sincerely yours,
                Ambrose Bierce.

1. See "Prattle," *SF* (18 December 1892): 6: "It is to be hoped that Mr. James Whitcomb Riley may be arrested and returned forthwith to his reservation in Hoop-pole county, Indiana; he appears to be calculated for that meridian. If he would have the goodness to confine his ambition to the reading of his dreary literature to his audiences (whom it serves royally right) he could be suffered in silence, and might even exact a temperate approval as a minister of doom charged with punishment of sin. Unfortunately, he wreaks himself upon the just and the unjust alike, by utterance of his mind in the newspapers concerning the things whereof Heaven has not seen fit to let him be informed. With a frankness which is three parts effrontery and one part inability to master the struggle of his tongue, he first explains that he knows nothing, and then proves it by expounding the nature of poetry. He did not need: his ignorance is as a tower looking toward Damascus, and his notions of poetry are shouted out in every raucous line that he writes. True, men of sense do not, and men of sensibility cannot, read what he writes; but if I rightly understand his mission he was not sent upon men of sense and sensibility, but upon those who forget God."
2. Walter Blackburn Harte (1867–1899), editor of the *New England Magazine* and a friend of AB. An article by him on AB appeared in the *New England Magazine* (22 February 1896).
3. Sam Walter Foss (1858–1911), poet and author of *Back Country Poems* (1892) and other books. Of Foss, AB later wrote: "Sam Walter Foss—a dialect man; a son o' the people; a feeble imitator of all that is most abominable in James Whitcomb Riley!" "Prattle," *SF* (13 January 1895): 6
4. Robert Burns (1759–1796), Scottish poet, most of whose work is in Scottish dialect.
5. See AB's criticism ("Prattle," *SF* [26 August 1888]: 4; rpt. *A Sole Survivor* 240–41) of the biographical sketch of him that appeared in *Mark Twain's Library of Humor* (1888).

[28] To Gustav Adolphe Danziger[1] [ALS, VA]

                        Angwin, Cal'a,
                        Feb'y 1, 1893.

My dear Danziger,
        If you had not written in "hot haste" you would probably not have written as you did—unless you have gone "clean daft". You say: "The money that you owe me is simply my share from the publication in the *Examiner*". That simply "lays over" anything that I have yet seen from your pen; your last published story "isn't in it" with that remarkable statement!

You had not only "your share" "from the publication in the *Examiner*", but my share too.[2] The story brought $199.^{00}. You took it all and I hold your receipts for every cent of it. What can you mean by writing such things as that?

I shall owe you $67.33/100 as soon as I get that much profit from further publication of the story. At present *you* owe *me* for every copy of "Black Beetles in Amber" that has been sold since you made a statement to me—November 16, I think.³ Forty dollars additional are acknowledged in that statement. The fact that I don't press you for the money that *you* owe *me* might be entitled to consideration when you press me for money that *I do not* owe *you*. But apparently it counts for nothing; it does not even secure me another statement from you. Yet you complain that (in another matter) Schulte does not make a statement to you. The other matters between us (the Schulte matter) I shall not discuss. You already know my position in that. I have no knowledge of what Schulte means to do, but if you are going to "fight" him it would hardly improve your chance of success to fight me too; I would be rather more useful, one would think, as an ally. I have a one-third interest in the copyright of that book, and the fact that the copyright stands in your name does not enable you to do as you please with it; you are bound by the contract. If Schulte does not pay we will see what we can do to make him pay, but you must not attempt to do anything without my concurrence. You should remember (if you know) that at least one reason why, as you say, you are "luckless in dealing with others" is your headlong way of doing things. Another reason is your occasional inability to distinguish your friend from your enemy.

I will again ask you to make me a statement in the matter of "Black Beetles in Amber". That you will withdraw anything in your last letter is, I fear, too much to expect.

        Sincerely yours,
        Ambrose Bierce.

1. Danziger was a German-born fiction writer, poet, and scholar (*Jewish Forerunners of Christianity* [1903]), whose relationship with AB was, to say the least, tortured. According to GS (see GS's introduction to AB's *In the Midst of Life* [New York: Modern Library, 1926], x), "Danziger was the person over whose head Bierce broke his cane to fragments. . . ." He later changed his name to Adolphe de Castro, adopting his mother's maiden name. In the early 1920s he went to Mexico to investigate AB's disappearance, later writing the somewhat unreliable memoir, *Portrait of Ambrose Bierce* (1929).

2. AB and Danziger squabbled over payment for the appearance of "The Monk and the Hangman's Daughter" in *SF*, and later argued over whose role in its publication was greater, forgetting that they had merely translated the work of another writer. See AB, "Prattle," *SF* (13 August 1893): 6: "I wrote every word of 'The Monk and the Hangman's Daughter' as published. Until Dr. Danziger saw that it was a creditable book he never, so far as I know, professed to have done more than translate the German story by Dr. Voss upon which it was founded. I have never seen that story and do not read German; what changes he may have made I do not know, nor care. If there was as little of Dr. Voss in his version as there is of him in mine, I am unable to conjecture what the original yarn was like. It was for lying about that and other matters that I punished him; and apparently he is not yet reformed."

3. *Black Beetles in Amber* was published in 1892 by the Western Authors Publishing Company, a firm established by AB, Danziger, and others.

[29] To Blanche Partington [ALS, BL]

Angwin,
Feb'y 5, 1893.

My dear Blanche,

What an admirable reporter you would be! Your account of the meeting with Miller in the restaurant and of the "entertainment" are amusing no end. I think you must have written the account of the latter event in the *Wave*. So *that's* what the Lezinsky[1] looks like! By the way, I observe a trooly offle "attack" on me in the Oakland *Times* of the 3rd (I think) which I suspect him of writing, or inspiring.[2] (I know of course it means me—I always know that when they pull out of their glowing minds that old roasted chestnut about "tearing down" but not "building up"—that is to say, effacing one imposture without giving them another in place of it.) The amusing part of the business is that he points a contrast between me and Realf[3] (God knows there's unlikeness enough) quite unconscious of the fact that it is I and no other who have "built up" Realf's reputation as a poet—published his work, and paid him for it, when nobody else would have it; repeatedly pointed out its greatness, and when he left that magnificent crown of sonnets behind him protested that posterity would know California better by the incident of his death than otherwise—not a soul, until now, concurring in my view of the verses. Believe me, my trade is not without its humorous side.

[...]

My health is very good now, and Leigh and I take long walks. And after the rains we look for Indian arrow-heads in the plowed fields and on the gravel bars of the creek. My collection is now great; but I fear I shall tire of the fad before completing it. One in the country must have a fad or die of dejection and oxidation of the faculties. How happy is he who can make a fad of his work!

By the way, my New York publishers (The United States Book Company)[4] have failed, owing me a pot of money, of which I shall probably get nothing. I'm beginning to cherish an impertinent curiosity to know what Heaven means to do to me next. If your position as one of the angels gives you a knowledge of such matters please betray your trust and tell me where I'm to be hit, and how hard.

But this is an intolerable deal of letter.

With best regards to all good Partingtons—and I think there are no others—I remain your affectionate uncle by adoption,

Ambrose Bierce.

Leigh has brought in some manzanita blooms which I shall try to enclose. But they'll be badly smashed.

1. David Lesser Lezinsky (1864–1894), a young poet and critic in San Francisco, author of *Daniel, Daddy, Ruth and Company* (1894). AB repeatedly made fun of Lezinsky's work in his columns of the early 1890s. AB's enemies maintained that Lezinsky took his own life because of AB's unfavorable notices of his work, a charge AB denied.

2. S. Woetley, *Oakland Times* (3 February 1893): 1: "Nothing is more pleasant to the venomous mind than to eject poisonous darts at their enemies in the face of the world, and then to gloat over said enemies' imaginary annihiliation, which however, never comes. But such debasing efforts rarely do more than to excite pity in the reader that the evident genius of the writer was not used to uplift instead of making high-sounding but ineffectual efforts to destroy.

"Of course, as every schoolboy knows, there is nothing original about this tattle. It is but a moderately successful attempt to imitate Voltaire. It savors in many instances of the mud stirred in a bowl of water by a medium sized frog. In the ocean the frog's existence would be ignored."

3. Richard Realf (1834–1878), British-born poet and author of *Guesses at the Beautiful* (1852) and other volumes published posthumously, including *Poems* (1898). He had been raised by Lord Byron's widow. He committed suicide after writing some sonnets on his deathbed. AB wrote a memoir of him: "Richard Realf," *SF* (3 March 1895): 11; rpt. in William McDevitt, *Ambrose Bierce on Richard Realf* (San Francisco: Recorder-Sunset Press, 1948). See further letter 41, notes 3 and 4.

4. The United States Book Company had reprinted *Tales of Soldiers and Civilians* in 1892.

[30] To Gustav Adolphe Danziger [ALS, VA]

Angwin,

Feb'y 11, 1893.

My dear Danziger,

"What I want," and all that I have *ever* wanted, is the $500⁰⁰ that I put in. Your proposal to pay me the $200⁰⁰ balance and keep the books is accepted, of course: it is precisely, in effect, the proposal that I made to you months ago in St. Helena—to let me have back what money I had put in, and you take the whole edition. If you had accepted then what a lot of vexation and "strained relations" we would have been spared.[1]

But it seems as if you cannot help reaffirming old and abandoned claims.

You have *not* "a half-interest" in those books, nor *any* interest until my outlay is paid back.

You did *not* put your money in to "satisfy my desire". I hold your written acknowledgment that I urged you to keep your money and yourself out of it.

You talk to me about performing my promises to help you get back your losses by Langton.[2] Those promises were always conditional on your good behavior in carrying out the contract. I hold *your* written promise that you will *not* attach those books. Shall I perform conditional promises while you break absolute ones?

You can attach the books, but you will not. You could better afford to lose as many thousand dollars as there are books.

But all this is needless if you are sincere in your proposal. I too am anxious to be on good terms with you; we may need each other in the Schulte matter, and I am desirous of peace and good will for other reasons.

Send me the remaining $200 and take the books. It is very simple.

I don't wish to go down to San Francisco; if you compel me I will never forgive you. I doubt if I should live to forgive you, but I won't forgive you even when I'm an angel.

Sincerely yours,
Ambrose Bierce.

1. The dispute is over money AB invested in the Western Authors Publishing Company for the publication of *Black Beetles in Amber*.
2. William Langton, a business associate of Danziger's.

[31] To James Tufts[1] [ALS, CC]

Angwin
Apr. 16, '93.

Dear Tufts,

I do not see how I could write the article that you suggest without making it so plain that I wrote out of my own experience that I might as well frankly confess it as a personal defense. That, indeed, is what you seem to want. Well, I'm not on the defensive. I'm in no hurry to be "understood of the people"—time enough when I'm dead. So long as they find me interesting in one way and another (and that they do I have superabundant evidence) it is not important what they think of me. The article—if I'm to be the subject of it, and that's what you intimate your preference for—would come with better grace if less light from another hand.

No—with reference to your other suggestion—I certainly will not take a hand in the game of story-writing that you propose setting afoot; and if anybody else does who *can* write I shall be, not, perhaps, surprised, but disgusted. I have, I hope, too high a regard for my art to practice it as a play or a puzzle. You, of course, in your present place, look at the matter from another viewpoint, and are not concerned about the dignity of literature; I *am*. Morrow's recent performance with that "unfinished" story surprised me, for Morrow can write.[2] It struck me as disagreeable that he would be willing to make literature ridiculous with such a mountebank trick. I only wish you would let me express in print my notions of such things; but I fear my expression of them would set the paper on fire.

I should be pleased, too, to air my opinion of prize-story contests and of those who compete in them. Your notion of "bringing out talent" in that way must amuse even you now in the light of the disgusting but inevitable result. The stories all disgraced California in the eyes of those thoughtless mortals who believe in that method of "bringing out talent," yet have sense enough to perceive the nice distinction between a good story and a bucket of swill. By the way, I've observed that the "first prize" goes always to a woman. But *that* woman—yah!

Doubtless conservation of the dignity of literature and the good name of the State do not come within the scope of your duties as editor of the Sunday Sup.—and you will smile a free, long smile at all this. Smile and be doodled, old man, but all the same you can't draw me into that sort of thing with a team of oxen.

[...]

    Yours sincerely,
        Ambrose Bierce.

1. James Tufts, managing editor of *SF*.
2. W[illiam] C[hambers] Morrow (1854–1923), short story writer, novelist, and friend of AB. AB highly praised his volume of weird tales, *The Ape, the Idiot and Other People* (1897). In 1892 Morrow had written for *SF* the beginning of a tale, "The Unfinished Story," and the paper then offered prizes for the best conclusion sent in by readers.

[32] To Percival Pollard[1] [BL (transcript)]

        Angwin, Cala.
        April 22, 1893.

Dear Mr. Pollard,

    I am glad if my opinion of your stories[2] pleased you; it is an entirely honest one—the stories are good and if you are (as I think) a young man they promise great work to come. Your fault is—you will not mind my saying so—a rather loose and careless use of words, whereby you sacrifice precision. The devil of it is with us all that our newspaper work corrupts us.

I get Figaro regularly, for which I thank you.

Yes I'm sorry to miss Harte from the *New England,* and am writing him to know if it is forever. I can't imagine the mental state that would persuade one to read anything but his stuff, in that magazine.

Here's fun. Gladstone bought a book of mine the other day—of which I was promptly advised by postal card from Robert Barr, of the *Idler*.[3] The incident has started some of the London newspapers—notably the *Chronicle*—gabbling about me and my London "career" of twenty years ago. The gabble has increased in volume as it rolled westward into California, and is echoed in the newspapers here with variations. The fun of it (apart from the toadyism) is that the book is d—— rot, long out of print and righteously forgotten. I do not doubt that Gladstone chucked it into the fire forthwith. He was probably attracted by the title: *The Fiend's Delight.* If his confounded curiosity result in another edition I hope that God will not fail to debit him with the offense.

        Sincerely yours,
                Ambrose Bierce.

    1. Percival Pollard (1869–1911), fiction writer, critic, and good friend of AB. In 1893, Pollard's Chicago-based magazine *Figaro* reprinted several of AB's fables, a short story, and other journalism.
    2. *Figaro Fiction* (1893), an anthology of stories (most of them by Pollard) gathered from *Figaro*. AB praised the book in "Prattle," *SF* (2 April 1893): 6.
    3. As reported in the London *Daily Chronicle* (17 March 1893), Gladstone purchased a copy of *The Fiend's Delight* from a second-hand catalogue. See "Prattle," *SF* (3 July 1893): 4: "Rt. Hon. W. E. Gladstone—Sir: I am surprised to receive a note conveying your thanks for a book said to have been sent to you by me. No book has been sent to you by me, nor with my consent or knowledge. And if the one in question has my name on the title page I beg leave to say that it seems to me a serious impertinence in any one to ask your attention to my work."

[33] To Blanche Partington [ALS, BL]

                              Angwin, Cal'a,
                              April 26, 1893.

My dear Blanche,
        What you tell me of Hume & Cosgrave[1]—their treatment of your father—is not surprising only because Leigh had already told me; it was surprising then. I do not think, though, that the paragraph in *The Wave* was meant to reflect upon the artists, but upon the "process" men.[2] I am writing Hume about it; I'm sure there is something that we don't know—about his assurance and his subsequent ignoring of it. He spoke to me in the warmest terms of your father, and has repeatedly written me to the same effect. With Cosgrave I have never been in correspondence and have not seen him for a year and a half.

    Hearst[3] passed Sunday evening and yesterday with me, and I showed him some of your father's work. He did not know until I told him that *The Wave* had stopped the pictures. If the place that he wanted your father to take is not filled he will probably renew his offer.

    I did not intend to write all this to you, but to your father. But it can't make much difference, I suppose. For that matter, I don't quite know why I write it at all.

    I accept your sympathy for my misfortunes in publishing. It serves me right (I don't mean the sympathy does) for publishing. I should have known that if a publisher cannot beat an author otherwise, or is too honest to do so, he will do it by failing. Once in London a publisher gave me a check dated two days ahead, and then (the only thing he could do to make the check worthless)—ate a pork pie and died.⁴ That was the late John Camden Hotten, to whose business and virtues my present London publishers, Chatto and Windus, have succeeded. They have not failed, and they refuse pork pie, but they deliberately altered the title of my book.⁵

All this for your encouragement in "learning to write." Writing books is a noble profession; it has not a shade of selfishness in it—nothing worse than conceit.

[...]

I trust your mother is well of her cold—that you are all well and happy, and that Phyllis will not forget me. And may the good Lord bless you regularly every hour of every day for your merit, and every minute of every hour as a special and particular favor to

Your Uncle.

The coyote sings and plays the piano, but "howls" only at Madge Morris.⁶

1. John O'Hara Cosgrave (1864–1947), was a reporter for the *San Francisco Call* before becoming co-editor (with Hugh Hume) and publisher of the *Wave*. He joined *Everybody's Magazine* as managing editor in 1900, and was its editor from 1903 to 1911.

2. John H. E. Partington's art had appeared in several issues of the *Wave* for 1893. In "Splashes" (*Wave*, 22 April 1893), the magazine announced it was going to discontinue using illustrations because of the great expense of reproducing them.

3. William Randolph Hearst (1863–1951) began his newspaper and magazine empire in 1887, when his father gave him *SF*. He was AB's employer from 1887 to 1909. AB wrote briefly of his relationship with Hearst in "A Thumb-Nail Sketch" (*CW* 12; rpt. *A Sole Survivor*).

4. AB recounts this anecdote at length in "A Sole Survivor" (*A Sole Survivor* 301–2).

5. Chatto & Windus changed the title of *Tales of Soldiers and Civilians* to *In the Midst of Life*, by which the collection subsequently became known.

6. AB alludes to Madge Morris's poem, "To the Colorado Desert" (*Lippincott's Magazine*, September 1892): "The shadowy, gray coyote, born afraid, / Steals to some brackish spring and laps, and prowls / Away, and howls and howls and howls and howls" (ll. 9–11). Aside from repeatedly disparaging the poem, AB maintained that a coyote does not howl, but barks and yelps. AB's comments sparked the article, "Does the Coyote Howl? A Pot-Pourri of Opinions by Poets, Politicians and Litterateurs" (*SF*, 23 April 1893).

[34] To Percival Pollard [MEG (transcript)]

Berkeley, Cal.,
July 20, 1893.

Dear Mr. Pollard,

Your question about the Cassell Company I am unable to answer definitively. Mrs. Atherton¹ sends me a note from her latest publisher (Tait) in which he says he "thinks" the affairs of the Company are now conducted by a receiver. I am myself too much disgusted to inquire, or very greatly care. The failure of four publishers out of five in one year rather takes away my interest in the tribe. Schulte, the U.S. Book Company, a private person named Langton (who "undertook" my *Black Beetles in Amber*) and now the Cassells—that is a fairly good array of notches in my rifle-stock, is it not? I had read about 3/4 of the proofs of my new book of yarns when the trouble occurred—the proofs stopped coming and that's all I know.[2]

You mistake about my mentioning you to Charles Edwin Markham;[3] I do not know him personally. I suppose he read what I wrote of you.

I think you will succeed in your *Figaro* venture—newspapering is, after all, our only permanent hold upon our bone, even if the meat upon the bone is not altogether to our liking.

Yes, I get *Belford's* and *Figaro* regularly, and thank you very much for them. Would you mind taking the trouble to alter the address to the *Examiner* office San Francisco, until I am "settled"? Ill health has compelled me to be rather a nomad lately. I did not know that *Belford's* was in trouble and am sorry to learn it.

Enclosed is a slip from the Oakland *Saturday Press* (Cal.) of the 17th July.

Success attend you.

       Ambrose Bierce.

1. Gertrude Atherton (1857–1948), prominent Californian novelist and friend of AB. She wrote of her encounters with AB in *Adventures of a Novelist* (1932).
2. Cassell's did not fail, and it issued AB's *Can Such Things Be?* in December 1893.
3. Edwin Markham (1852–1940), California poet who later achieved spectacular success with "The Man with the Hoe" (1899), a poem AB deprecated as political propaganda.

[35] To Messrs. Stone & Kimball [ALS, HL]

       Berkeley, Cal.,
       Nov. 7, 1893.

Messrs. Stone & Kimball,
  Gentlemen,

Your proposal, dated Nov. 1, to publish a selection from the book "Black Beetles in Amber," has been attentively considered. But I am unable to make a selection of pieces which seem to me free from your objection to the book as a whole. If you can do so, and will send me the book with such pieces marked as you would wish to bring out I will put them in shape and return them, with corrections—for the book is full of errors. Any of the verses which suit you are good enough for me, and I think my suggestion would give the result most satisfactory to you.

I will then submit to Mr. Steele your proposal to have the two books sold together, and have no doubt that he will assent.[1]

Please let me know if you accept my suggestion.

I am very truly yours,

Ambrose Bierce.

P.S.—I shall probably get a little advertising during the next few months, as I expect to publish another book, in New York. I suppose it will help.

A. B.

1. This venture came to nothing. In January 1896, AB submitted the ms. of a book he called *The Fall of the Republic and Other Satires* to Stone & Kimball, but it was rejected.

[36] To Messrs. Stone & Kimball [ALS, HU]

Berkeley, Cal.,
Dec. 4, 1893.

Messrs. Stone & Kimball,

Gentlemen,

Replying to yours of Nov. 24, I wish to say that you seem to have misunderstood my proposal regarding a selection from my book "Black Beetles in Amber". I did not propose that you "edit" it, but merely that you indicate which of the pieces *I* should edit—which of them would be acceptable. On undertaking to make the selection myself, though, I find that if the obscurity (in the East) of the persons satirized is a fatal objection no considerable selection can be made. It does not appear to be an objection in such works as the "English Bards and Scotch Reviewers", the "Dunciad", and most of the satires which have lived; but of course I am not a Byron nor a Pope.[1] Nevertheless, I cannot see how the quality or interest of a piece is affected by application to a real, though unknown, person instead of presenting it as a general satire, with perhaps a fictitious name. If the verse is good it *makes* the victims known; if not good it is not worth publishing anyhow.

But if your objection is valid a selection is impossible—not enough of the book is about men of national eminence to make another, of nearly the size that you suggest.

Very truly yours,

Ambrose Bierce.

1. George Gordon, Lord Byron, *English Bards and Scotch Reviewers* (1809); Alexander Pope, *The Dunciad* (1728; rev. 1742), two of the best-known satirical poems in English.

[37] To Mrs. E. L. G. Steele [ALS, VA]

[3 July 1894?]

Dear Mrs. Steele

I know I can write nothing that you will care to read, but it can at least do no harm to say—what you must already know—that I feel very deeply for you and the children. And I think you will hardly need to be told that I am not wholly untouched by the blow that has fallen you. The world seems not altogether the same without my friend. It was hard on me, too, not to be able to look upon his face after he was gone. I was very ill through it all, as I believe Miss Partington was kind enough to inform you—she happened to be with me when Ed's note came.[1]

Sometime when you are willing to see me I hope you will let me come in and talk with you a few minutes. In the mean time if I can in any way serve you please do not hesitate to command me.

I am, dear Mrs. Steele, most sincerely yours,

Ambrose Bierce.

101½ Washington St.,
Tuesday.

1. Edward Steele, son of E. L. G. Steele, with whom AB briefly corresponded in the later 1890s.

[38] To Warring Wilkinson[1] [ALS, BL]

Los Gatos,
June 18, 1895.

Dear Dr. Wilkinson,

Unless you direct me otherwise I shall bring the young deaf mute girl (Lily Walsh)[2] to you on Saturday next, sometime before the noon hour. I have been in Santa Cruz to learn about her, and I am more than before convinced that she is an uncommonly clever girl, considering her disability and disadvantages; and I am anxious to have your judgment of her.

Sincerely yours,

Ambrose Bierce.

1. Warring Wilkinson (1834–1918), a physician and board member of the California Institution for the Deaf and Blind.
2. Elizabeth (Lily) Walsh (1872–1895), a deaf-mute girl whose poetry AB admired. Myles Walsh was her brother. She was cared for by Dr. C. W. Doyle and Harriet Hershberg. AB sent her to Wilkinson's school for the deaf in Berkeley, where she died in October.

[39] To Carroll Carrington[1] [ALS, VA]

Los Gatos,
June 26, 1895.

My dear Carrington,

While you were writing me I was in your town. But I was very ill, or I should have seen you. If I had known of the change in your fortunes I should have seen you anyhow.

I hardly know what to advise. Certainly there can be no doubt of your great ability—none of the expediency of your ambition. You are an unusually good writer; you know that as well as I. But for reasons other than those concerning your ultimate advantage, I should rejoice at your "taking off". That paper is no place for you; and now that you are out of it, I hope it will no longer print my praise of it. If it do—I shall "kick". But all this is not to the point and purpose of your letter.

I fear Mr. Millard[2] is in love with his *Examiner* work. If so, there is probably no chance for you there—in that department. Why should you be on *The Wave* or *The Argonaut?* My "influence" counts for nothing, I suppose with Cosgrave; I know it counts for nothing with Hart.[3] But I'll enclose a note introducing you to Cosgrave and maybe you can "do the rest". You'd make a good literary department if C. would let you.

[...]

I'm too ill to write much.

Sincerely yours,
A. B.

1. Carroll Carrington (1872?–1901), a California journalist who wrote occasionally for *SF* and for the *Oakland Saturday Press*.
2. Frank Bailey Millard (1859–1941), prolific California journalist who wrote for *SF* and other San Francisco newspapers and was briefly (1905–6) editor of *Cosmopolitan*. He also wrote novels and short stories.
3. Jerome A. Hart (1854–1937) took over editorship of *Argonaut* in 1895 upon the death of Frank Pixley. He wrote about AB in *In Our Second Century: From an Editor's Note-book* (San Francisco: Pioneer Press, 1931).

[40] To Ray Frank[1] [ALS, AJHS/MEG]

Los Gatos,
July 13, 1895.

Dear Miss Frank,

I am so accustomed to having my letters considered "ill-natured," "sarcastic," and so forth, that I can't say it gives me any particular sensation, other than a mild disgust. I did not, however, expect this kind of thing from *you*. The letter in question was written in illness, but it happens that illness does not make me "cross", that I had no reason to be surly with you, and that the letter was, in point of fact, absolutely good natured. Its adversity lay in the mind of the reader. As I say, this commonly occurs; and what else commonly occurs is that I *do* then write a not very friendly letter, and that it is the last to *that* correspondent. I shall depart from my rule in this instance, and tell you what I think of your manuscript, as I undertook to do. But as yet I've had no time to read it all.

The Colonel[2] was in to see me yesterday. She is as pretty and lively and long-suffering as ever, but declares herself lonely at the Springs.

Thank you for your good wishes anent my health—which is better.

Sincerely yours,

A. B.

1. Rachel (Ray) Frank (1861–1948), American Jewish advocate born in San Francisco. Beginning in the late 1880s, Frank lectured, taught, and wrote extensively on Judaism throughout the American West. She married Simon Litman in 1901 and they eventually settled at the University of Illinois in Urbana, where she counseled the Jewish students on the campus. See Simon Litman, *Ray Frank Litman: A Memoir* (Studies in American Jewish History, Number 3) (New York: American Jewish Historical Society, 1957). AB's letters to her apparently are at the American Jewish Historical Society (Worcester, Mass.), although librarians there maintain that they are not. However, photocopies of the ALSs, identified as coming from the historical society, exist among the M. E. Grenander Papers at the State University of New York at Albany.

2. AB's affectionate name for Belle Hershberg, sister of Harriet (see letter 55), one of the several women he befriended during this period.

[41] To Herman Scheffauer[1] [BL (transcript)]

Los Gatos,
Sunday.
[August 12, 1895]

My dear Scheffauer,

I have your letter of Friday. Your other was received in due time, so your solicitude about it is, as usual, of mine own making. My correspondence is so large that I do not answer (nor in most cases read) letters when received; they must wait—there is no other way. Even now I cannot hope to "answer" much of your letter. The poem is, as I said, too good to throw aside. It is not all good—no poem of that length is; in any long one the major part is mere *recitative*—necessary to connect and correlate the other parts. But it is impossible in a letter to criticise adequately your work; *that* I cannot undertake. In conversation I could do something toward it while the poem is fresh in memory. So I'm sorry we are not to meet and talk it over, but must accept your reasons for not coming to Los Gatos—which, however, is not so far away as you seem to think.

I must strongly advise you against the attempt to put it into hexameters. If there is a more difficult thing than blank verse it is hexameters. I know of *no* satisfactory English hexameter work; the poverty of our tongue in spondees would, alone, prevent success.

My counsel, then, is let the work lie unless, or until, you care to take the trouble to rewrite it. In the meantime study and practise blank verse; that will not harm you, even if you don't apply your results to this poem. I'm not sure but (assuming that you do not care to take the trouble, or are unable, to become proficient in blank) it would be worth while to try to recast it into the English heroic—the iambic rhymed pentameter. There is something in that meter—a greater difference than mere addition of the rhyme to blank verse—which gives freedom and facility where blank verse cramps and restrains. Try a page or two as an experiment. I shall return the manuscript.

You are full of ideas—your letters swarm with them. Your feeling is not, apparently, deficient or erroneous. I hardly know what ails you—whether it is a defective ear or imperfect study. Most likely the latter, for young poets have usually "lisped in numbers for the numbers came".[2] It has been thought that the young poet ("born unto singing",[3] as Realf hath it) is recognizable by the fact that his thoughts *sing* themselves. Yet I believe you a born poet and cannot but think you were, in this case, overcome by the weight of your theme: "the meaning outmastered the meter",[4] to quote Realf again. Perhaps you hit it off in your other letter when you asked: "What have I, in the spring of life, to do with the deaths of worlds?"

I may go back to Oakland soon, for awhile.

Meantime I'm very sincerely yours,

Ambrose Bierce.

Is it Room 58 or 82? Some of your envelopes have the one, some the other number.

---

1. Herman George Scheffauer (1878–1927), California poet, playwright, and translator, was AB's leading disciple until the emergence of GS. Scheffauer later moved to Germany, where he wrote numerous tracts condemning America's involvement in World War I; he also achieved celebrity as one of the earliest English translators of Thomas Mann.

2. Alexander Pope, *An Epistle to Dr. Arbuthnot* (1734), l. 128 (referring to himself).

3. Richard Realf, "Written on the Night of His Suicide," l. 20; in Realf's *Poems* (New York: Funk & Wagnalls, 1898), 34.

4. Realf, "Indirection," l. 4; in *Poems*, 152.

[42] To Ray Frank [ALS, AJHS/MEG]

St. Helena,
Sept. 5, 1895.

Dear Miss Frank,

It was "nice" of you to go out and see my little daughter of silence, who, poor thing, needs a deal of encouragement. She seems more solicitous about me than herself, but I fear she is seriously ill.

As to me. It is impossible yet to know the nature and extent of my injuries.[1] They are serious enough at the best. Whether my kneecap is broken or not the swollen condition of the leg prevents us from determining. If so it is likely that I shall have a stiff leg as a bequest (I scorn to say leg-acy) of the incident. One arm is useless at present, and the other can do nothing of greater utility than write to you. Doubtless I shall remain in bed a long time, but I have an excellent physician (who abstains, mostly, from advice) and the best of care. So you need not worry about doing anything for me.

I must exculpate the bicycle—the accident was, as usual, the fault of the rider. (This to encourage Miss Esther.)[2]

Yes, it was indiscreet of you to tell Miss Walsh that you had read her letter—you would not like that yourself. But I always expect something to go wrong when I bring my women friends together—it is a law of nature, to be deprecated but accepted. Happily no great interests are involved.

[...]

A. B.

1. AB suffered a serious accident on his bicycle a few days prior to writing this letter. AB later wrote humorous verses concerning a bicycle accident in "Prattle," *SF* (12 July 1896): 6. He published nothing between 18 August and 13 October because of his injuries.
2. Esther Frank was Ray's sister. One letter by AB to her (29 August 1895) survives.

[43] To Warring Wilkinson [ALS, BL]

St. Helena,
Sept. 24 1895.

Dear Dr. Wilkinson,

I hardly know what to say in reply to your letter about Lily Walsh. Her illness has been a deep disappointment to me, but I did not know it was so serious. In one of her letters she seemed very despondent, and even expressed a fear that she would not recover; but in one written yesterday she is cheerful again, and says she is much better and growing stronger daily. Perhaps I should make some allowance for her natural desire to spare me anxiety in my own rather bad condition. It is surprise to me to learn that "her illness is of long standing" and that she has "passed much [or any] of her life in hospitals". True, I had never questioned her about her health. It did not occur to me to do so, although it was obvious that she was not very sturdy and robust.

What should be done with her is a question that my present helplessness forbids me to consider in any practical way. I have myself been three weeks in bed, under medical treatment. I have a daughter ill in Redlands, a son out of employment here, and am, in short, sailing through the Financial Straits, generally. So it is little that I can do for the poor girl at present. As I cannot back my views, I don't feel at liberty to entertain any. You, in any case, will know best, as I am absolutely ignorant of hospitals, who is put into them, and how the unfortunates are maintained. I wish I could see you and consult you in the matter, but it is impossible for me to go to Berkeley this week. I hope to be taken down to Oakland (to the Washington House, Washington St.) on Friday if I get no worse, but the journey will doubtless lay me up for a while.

I shall write to my friend Dr. Doyle,[1] of Santa Cruz, who has been kind to Lily, asking him to see her uncle and ascertain his wishes and will in the matter, if he has any. Lily sends me a letter from her brother in New York, promising her a remittance and asking how much he shall send. I doubt if he is able to do much. It is far from my intention to abandon the poor child; as soon as I can get at work I shall help her again. At present my resources are not equal to her maintenance at a private hospital. Is there a public one to which she is entitled to admittance, where she could have good care, and where our influence would secure it for her?

You see I am not only ignorant but nearly powerless; so I shall have to ask you to do what is best for the time being, until I can get down there and stir up some of my well-to-do friends to an interest in the girl. If they are half as good as you have been I shall be glad and—surprised.

Sincerely yours,
Ambrose Bierce.

P.S.—My injuries are painful but not dangerous. And it was not the fault of the "bike".

1. C. W. Doyle (1852–1903), author of *The Taming of the Jungle* (1899) and *The Shadow of Quong Lung* (1900).

[44] To Lily Walsh [ALS, UC]

1101½ Washington St.,
Oakland, Oct 13, '95.

Dear Lily,

It is pleasant to learn that you are feeling so much better. I should like to go to you, but last evening my own illness took a sudden bad turn, and to-day I'm unable (after a night of suffering) to rise from my chair. I shall have to go back to Los Gatos the moment I can be moved. I've been here now for more than two weeks, and growing worse all the time. No day have I felt well enough even to cross the bay to San Francisco, where I have urgent business.

Before I go your brother will be with you—I have not felt like leaving you entirely alone among strangers, for although I could do nothing for you, it seemed as if it must be pleasant for you to know that I was near by in case anything should happen to you—I mean if you should get worse. But now you will be all right. Of course I should like to see your brother if he will call. Maybe I shall not be able to talk much to him, but if he does not mind that please ask him to call. I shall try to see you again before going away.

You must not hesitate to let me know, dear child, when I can serve you in any way, no matter where I am. And please let me hear from you—how you are and all about you. Address me as usual—"Box 73".

Be brave—"with a heart for any fate".[1] And if the need of all your courage should come, remember that I confidently count upon your having it. Whatever may *seem*, remember that God, Nature—whatever it is that orders things, if things are ordered at all—is not going to be hard upon poor little harmless *you*.

A. B.

1. Henry Wadsworth Longfellow (1807–1882), "A Psalm of Life" (1839), l. 34.

[45] To C. W. Doyle [BL (transcript)]

Los Gatos,
Oct. 21, 1895.

Dear Dr. Doyle,

I have been at Oakland to-day, but did not dare to remain overnight; nor do I dare to go up again to-morrow, to Lily's funeral, for I returned this evening distinctly asthmatic. I'm going to send my boy. There was little that I could do, but I saw Lily's body at the undertakers, looking very sweet and peaceful. I'm not a believer in a future life, nor can I think of anything better to wish her than what I believe she has—rest.

I thank you for your sympathy—I had really become very much attached to her—as much as if she had been my daughter; probably because of her misfortunes, her helplessness, and that odd habit of the heart which makes us love those whom we befriend, rather than those who befriend *us*. And I shall always think that the poor child's natural "gift" amounted to no less than genius.

No, don't send me her letters—I need no proofs of her affection; but if you had any evidences that I was ever worthy of it they would be welcome.

Some day when you can think of nothing better to do come over the mountain and learn that there's a tribe on this side. Why don't you live here and be well?

Sincerely yours,
A. B.

[46] To C. W. Doyle [BL (transcript)]

Los Gatos,
Nov. 22, 95.

Dear Dr. Doyle,

[...]

Myles Walsh has written me. He is back in his old place, his successor having had the thoughtfulness to be unsatisfactory. By the way, I shall probably be going go New York soon. Mr. Hearst wants me there on his new paper,[1] but I'm trying to put him off until spring, being hardly fit to travel—with my knee in an elastic band and my wrist in a splint. Your "medical advice" not to travel in that condition is gratefully assumed.

I share your opinion of Howells. I once gave him a tremendous dressing down in several columns. Soon afterward he reviewed one of my books, with all sorts of pleasant praise, and has written the sweetest things of me since.[2] What will you do if he acts in that shockingly irregular (not to say unfair) manner with you.

Sincerely,
Ambrose Bierce.

1. Hearst had recently purchased *NYJ*.
2. AB excoriated novelist and critic William Dean Howells (1837–1920) in "Prattle" (*SF*, 22 May 1892; rpt. in *A Sole Survivor* 242–47). Although AB's remarks on Howells were reprinted in part in the essay "The Short Story" (*CW* 10), it is unlikely that Howells ever read them. Neither William M. Gibson and George Arms, *A Bibliography of William Dean Howells* (New York: New York Public Library, 1948), nor Vito J. Brenni, *William Dean Howells: A Bibliography* (Metuchen, N.J.: Scarecrow Press, 1973), list any review by Howells of a book by AB; nor does such a review seem to be among AB's numerous clippings of reviews of his books. Howells included "An Occurrence at Owl Creek Bridge" in *The Great Modern American Stories* (New York: Boni & Liveright, 1920), where he wrote: "I think Mr. Ambrose

Bierce has done nothing more imaginative than *An Occurrence at Owl Creek Bridge*, where he carries further the sort of post-mortem consciousness which Tolstoy and Turgenev were the first to imagine. It is very excellent work, and is all the more interesting in the expression of Confederate feeling, which is less known to fiction than Union feeling in the war dear alike to North and South" (xii).

[47] To C. W. Doyle [BL (transcript)]

Los Gatos,
Dec. 22, 1895.

Dear Dr. Doyle,

    Your assurance that Fresno has appreciated your worth, and your attributing it to *my* commendation are amusing. The "Republican" is the "organ" of Poet Waterhouse[1]—in which all his abuse of me appears. Really, he must feel somewhat as President Lincoln when, having failed to secure a man an appointment in one of the Departments, he said: "I fear I have no influence with this administration."

Thank you for Mark Tapley's latest—he is funny.[2]

You are funny too. The notion of my publishing a book "in which A. B. as he is known to his friends will shine forth" tickles exceedin'. What shall it be?—"The Autobiography of a Much Misunderstood Man"? or "An Angel Defledged"? or "The Open Tiger—Displaying the Bowels of Compassion"? "The Rattlesnake *sans* Fangs, Just as God Made Him"? or "The Worthy Man Unmasked by His Own Hand"? or "The Lovable Fiend in Human Shape—a Character Sketch by the Fiend"? or "A Jordanful of the Milk of Human Kindness"? or "Life and Times of an Amiable Assassin"? or "Saint Satan"? or "A. B., Criminal Philanthopist?" or "One of God's Devils"? or "The Cherub That Would a Raw-head-and-bloody-boning go"?

Now answer me this. What does it matter how one is known to (say) isosceles triangles, abracadabras, strangers, vacua, and such small hypothetical deer?

I have found my remarks on Miller's poem on Tennyson's death, but cannot find the poem;[3] and the remarks would be unintelligible without it. It was in the Sunday Examiner next after the event. If you'll get it it will seem to you worth the trouble, and then I'll send you my remarks to let you know how it seems to me. There's enough of the good and great in Miller's work (sometimes) to make your scant praise-and-blame of him seem inadequate. He subtends a larger angle than he looks to you, I'm sure.

    Sincerely yours,
        Ambrose Bierce.

    1. Alfred James Waterhouse (1855–1928), California journalist and author of *Some Homely Little Songs* (1899) and *Lays for Little Chaps* (1902). At the time, AB was gibing Waterhouse regularly in

SF, the following sentiment being representative: "I never doubted the intrepidity of Mr. A. J. Waterhouse; his poetry is what I take the liberty to be an agnostic about. Its publication appears to be the only miracle authenticating it" ("Prattle," *SF* [2 June 1895]: 6).

2. A local columnist, using as a pseudonym the name of a character in Dickens's *Martin Chuzzlewit*.

3. Joaquin Miller, "The Passing of Tennyson." AB commented favorably on the poem in "Prattle," *SF* (16 October 1892): 6.

[48] To Myles Walsh [ALS, UC]

(Box 567)
Washington, D.C.,
Feb'y 16, 1896.

My dear Mr. Walsh,
    I have been trying ever since my arrival here[1] to find time to reply even briefly to your letter of a month ago. I am living in a whirl of "moil and turmoil," and hardly get time to eat and sleep. So all my correspondents are neglected. I came here (with my boy) three weeks ago, and since then have been in New York three times: so you can see that I'm "on the jump" a little. Even when there I saw none of my friends, and had no time to look you up—though I don't know if you are to be found there.

[...]

Since coming here I have written Mrs. Hirshberg instructions about beautifying Lily's grave; she kindly undertook to do so. Before I left not enough rain had fallen to settle the little mound and make it possible to get the grass going. It will be all green now, and when I go back I shall give it a border and a stone; or if I do not go back soon Mrs. Hirshberg will attend to it for me. My movements are uncertain; I am on a special mission here for "The Examiner," but it may expire any day, and then it is likely I shall go to New York for "The Journal," for awhile. I was summoned up there by telegraph a week ago to-day to write one editorial.[2]

Your village experiences with the sages of the parish must amuse you. As yet I have been unable to find Mahwah on any map.[3] Has it been discovered by any body but you?

My boy Leigh is in N.Y. working in the art department of "The Journal." I suppose he would care to see you.

    Sincerely yours, Ambrose Bierce.

1. Hearst had sent AB to Washington to report on the attempt of railroad magnate Collis P. Huntington (1821–1900), one of the "Big Four" railroad tycoons, to persuade Congress to pass a funding bill that would give an almost indefinite extension for his repayment of debts to the government for construction of the Southern Pacific Railroad. See "Bierce on His Way to Washington," *SF* (21 January 1896): 1, containing AB's "Telegram to William Randolph Hearst" (18 January 1896). AB pub-

lished more than sixty articles on the matter in *SF* (and a few more in *NYJ*) from February to May 1896. AB attacked Huntington mercilessly, and the bill was defeated, largely because of AB's reporting.
2. "An Unwilling Convert," *New York Journal* (10 February 1896): 4 (unsigned).
3. Walsh lived in Mahwah, a town in northeastern New Jersey.

[49] To C. W. Doyle [BL (transcript)]

Washington, D.C.
M'ch 22, 1896.

Dear Dr. Doyle,
      I know that it is a month and a day since the day of your latest letter, and I know that it is no "palliation" to say that I have been more uncivil to others than to you. But it is true that I have had to stop writing personal letters, for mere lack of time. The life of a newspaper correspondent here has only one advantage—brevity. It is a little longer than that of a car-horse, but not much. Here is an outline of what I have been trying to do. Be at the Capitol by 10 a.m. Attend committee meeting and keep an eye on both Houses at the same time. Talk with dozens of men of my speciality. When both Houses have adjourned go home to dinner—no time for luncheon. Between 7 and 10 telegraph to N.Y. "Journal" an editorial on Cuba,[1] and the substance of my later dispatch to "Examiner." Then rewrite and amplify (and fortify) for "Examiner"—enabled to do so by the three hours difference in time. Home to bed at, say, 2 a.m., to be routed out probably once or oftener by telegrams. No Sundays.

O wouldn't you like to be in this business? 'Fore God, I don't know how I have taken time to relate it.

I've had to give up the N.Y. part of it now, but other duties have come in, somehow, to take its place. It is what we call "a dog's life", in compliment, I suppose, to the diligent assiduity of that animal in lying all day on a door-mat with a southern exposure.

You say I "ought to be happy". Well, I'm in a bit of a shindy; that's all that makes it endurable; and I'm having rather the better of it. And I'm (as yet) well.
[. . .]
    Sincerely yours, as ever,
        Ambrose Bierce.

1. Not located. AB may not be referring to a specific article.

[50] To C. W. Doyle [BL (transcript)]

Washington, D.C.,
May 25, 1896.

Dear Dr. Doyle,
    I'm sending you the photograph of a human wreck. May it remind you of our pleasant hours at Santa Cruz.

My work here is virtually finished, and I know you'll be pleased to learn that it is finished my way. But it has been a trifle hard on me, and in a day or two I shall mount my wheel and try again to escape on it from the demon Insomnia—as you remember I did once before.

After a few weeks of rest I shall probably go to New York—that is the arrangement now. I should be sorry to think I should not eventually return to California, but all is uncertain. Of *this,* I do not want any more. I know I've done good work for California, and that consciousness is something, though subject to deduction from the consciousness that California will never give me or my work a thought, unless in disparagement.

I hope you are well and happy and prosperous. Please let me know about you.
    Sincerely yours,
        Ambrose Bierce.

[51] To Ray Frank [ALS, AJHS/MEG]

Englewood, N.J.,
July 13 1896.

My dear Ray,
    During my long illness my correspondence and memory have fallen into such confusion that I hardly know, and in many instances cannot ascertain, whom I have written to, or when. But I think I must have sent you a line before leaving Washington a month ago. My health is only just now restored, for I had a bad relapse after coming here. But enough of myself—*you* are a more interesting topic—do you remember how interesting I used to find you those evenings at your house? And you are recovering too. Who would not, living the natural life that you have done up there in God's country? Do you go bare-footed as well as bare-headed and bare-hearted?
    [. . .]

This is a very beautiful place, with a different beauty from that of your surroundings—a highly cultivated garden studded with superb country dwellings of rich persons—a suburb of New York, only a half-hour distant by train, and only two miles from the Hudson river at "the Palisades." And the Hudson at that point is the noblest river I know anywhere. Perhaps you know about it—I forget if you have been "in these parts."

My future is still in the shadow, but doubtless I shall be hereabout the rest of the season. This will be my address for awhile, anyhow.

Please give my love to Esther, the sweet girl—and may the God of your fathers always bless you.

        A. B.

[52] To Ray Frank [ALS, AJHS/MEG]

              Hunter, Greene Co., N.Y.,
              Oct. 30, 1896.

My dear Ray,

  I don't remember if you were among the many whom I recently notified by card that I was about to leave New York and had no address. And if you were perhaps the notification was not clear, for I was very ill, and full of chloroform. Well, I'm *here,* though I was nearly three weeks coming, having to stop at several towns en route, from inability to travel. "Here" is a little village in the Catskills, away up in the air. The mountains are always good to me, as to you, and my health is already improved. Is it not odd—we two taking the mountain cure with all those needless leagues between? How little one is captain of his fate is shown in the fact that I am not with you—or you with me. The mountain cure is not like that dreimannerwein which requires three men to drink a glass of it—one to take it down while the others keep his courage up—but surely it would be more agreeable if "the both of us" took it together.

[. . .]

When am I coming home? Dear child, I don't know. I've been too ill to do any of the many things (for myself) which I remained in this country to do. If well all winter I can do them and go back to California and stay there—if you are very good. You are now—or will be then—so well and beautiful and happy that, with all those gifts, much will be expected of you. Is that not reasonable?

I sincerely hope you will get back all your voice—and not lose it again in the service of a sentiment and in the vain pursuit of an appreciable result.

But I must say good night and God bless you.

Mentioning God reminds me that I have been re-reading the Hebrew "Scriptures"—such as we have in translation—reading them *critically.* I think I've some new light on their quality as literature. But you know them so much better than I that it would be presumption in me to utter judgment.

Again good night—and again (and again) God bless you.

        Ambrose Bierce.

Thank you for the pretty pebbles—what are they?

[53] To C. W. Doyle [BL (transcript)]

Los Gatos,
Feb'y 8, 1897.

My dear Doctor,

I hope you will not mind my having quoted from your letter in the "Examiner" of yesterday.[1] Really the temptation was irresistible. I should think your statement of the grounds for your diagnosis of the cause of Fat Jack's taking off (stated with due professional gravity) would be good reading. If I fingered the "Examiner's" purse I should be after it (the statement) with the price of a prince's ransom.

I was not insensible to Miss Dawson's's[2] striking treatment of music, but felt a little insecure of my footing on that ground. I'm proud of Miss Dawson—she is a "pupil" of mine, and was once kind enough to write, too generously, that she owes all her success (in writing well—she has achieved little of the other kind) to me. Still, I think that has had nothing to do with my good opinion of her book.

I live in the hope that you and Carrington will carry out the amiable intention of coming to Los Gatos. From Mrs. Martin I have heard no more.[4]

Sincerely yours,
Ambrose Bierce.

I know you'll be glad to hear that "little sister" Lily's grave is now permanently preserved from effacement, and suitably marked.
B.

1. In "A Voice from Palo Alto," *SF* (7 February 1897): 32, a review of several books including Emma Frances Dawson's *An Itinerant House and Other Stories* (San Francisco: William Doxey, 1897), AB quotes a letter by C. W. Doyle in which he states that a knowledge of music is necessary to understand Dawson's stories, "just as one must be a physician to appreciate Shakspeare's wonderful description of the death of Falstaff."
2. Emma Frances Dawson (1851–1926), short-story writer and poet whose earliest work had appeared alongside AB's in *Argonaut* in the late 1870s. See also "Prattle," *SF* (10 January 1897): 6; rpt. as "Emma Frances Dawson" (*CW* 10).
3. Presumably Mrs. Mabel Martin (*née* Wood), the wife of Lieutenant C. F. Martin, of West Point, a "pupil" of AB.

[54] To Edwin Markham [ALS, WC]

Los Gatos
May 19, '97.

Dear Mr. Markham,

I am sending back the poems. I found little to suggest but the remarks I did make are to be taken *merely* as suggestions. The finish that you have given the verses is quite surprising. If the book's critics find as little fault as I it will be well with you—if the critics count for anything in the estimate of a book.

It did not seem to me wise to indicate a preference as to the relative merits of the poems: that is a matter which the author should—and best can—determine for himself. I will only say that your own judgment as indicated by your marks (X)—which Miss Hazen[1] says mean a less confident approval—seems to me, in the main, good. I think, though, that your best work is in the larger themes—not the birds and the flowers, etc. As an example of what I mean take the poem on Semiramis.[2] Thus, I fear I go counter to your own judgment, for you seem fond of the smaller subjects.

In conclusion, I must congratulate you on the work, which is something of a revelation to me. I did not think you had yet so "discovered" yourself.

Sincerely yours,
Ambrose Bierce.

The delay was caused by lack of time to consider the matter as it should be—and eventually was—considered.

1. Jean Hazen, Markham's secretary.
2. "A Look into the Gulf," in *The Man with the Hoe and Other Poems* (New York: Doubleday & McClure Co., 1899). Semiramis was the legendary queen of Assyria.

[55] To Harriet Hershberg [ALS, VA]

Los Gatos,
July 11, 1897.

Dear Hattie,

I owe you a kiss for every cake; when you want to be paid present your bill—like the dear little bird that wants a worm. It was very nice of you to remember that I like ginger—and for the Colonel to remember it at about the same time. It is not likely that you would both have thought of it if God had not put it into your hearts. I'm convinced that he really does put things in such places. The cakes are delicious; I've been trying to share them with my horned-toads, but the little hoodlums are not educated up to them and prefer grasshoppers.

I think Belle a wicked girl to pass through here and not let me see her. You may tell her so.

No, child, a trip to Oakland would not "do me good". The last one cost me a month of illness. But don't you think that you need the air of Los Gatos, and the fruit, and the sitting on the hotel porch of an evening, in a shirt-waist and under a big straw hat, with nothing to do but talk to me and look prettier than the other girls? (That is my notion of "an iridescent dream"[1]—what do *you* think of it?) If so, just run away and come along, and if your folks come after you I'll set the hotel dog on them. Of course you may bring that impossible paragon, the Pittsburg sister—whom, however, I verily believe to be a myth, like "Marjorie Daw", in Aldrich's story of that name.[2] Or if she really exists outside the exuberant imaginations of you and the Colonel I've no doubt she is homely and dull. But I suppose I shall never know until I go and see—which maybe I shall do, after all.

Meantime, a thousand angels guard and love you.

Ambrose Bierce.

1. "The purification of politics is an iridescent dream. Government is force." John James Ingalls (1833–1900), from an article in the New York *World* (1890). Ingalls was U.S. senator from Kansas (1873–91) and incurred AB's lasting hostility for being a vigorous advocate of pensions for the Grand Army of the Republic.

2. Thomas Bailey Aldrich (1836–1907), American poet, short story writer, and editor whose use of the surprise ending influenced the development of the short story. His best-known prose work is *Marjorie Daw and Other People* (1873), a collection of short stories. AB called him "a nerveless, colorless jelly-fish of literature" ("Prattle," *Wasp* [17 February 1883]: 5). "Marjorie Daw" concerns a man who falls in love with a mythical woman described in letters by the man's friend.

[56] To Ray Frank [ALS, AJHS/MEG]

Wright's Station,
Oct. 3, 1897.

My dear Ray,

I'm sorry that you feel (or rather felt, for I cannot think so strange a mood could last) just *that* way about so trivial an occurrence as my attending that party and meeting those persons. That it was in "the camp of the enemy" may or may not be true; I can only say that in that camp I have never heard you spoken of otherwise than in terms of respect and friendship. And if you correctly understood what was said in answer to your question about me (on Wednesday evening) I think it was intended rather to avoid giving you pain than, for any other reason, to deceive. For the person giving the answer knew that I had not called on you—though, of course, not why. So far as I know, she is an admiring friend of yours.

As to the two gentlemen whom you mention (whom I did not know that I was to meet, and one of whom, at least, came especially to meet *me*) I am very certain that neither of them mentioned or in any way alluded to you. Whatever grievance you may conceive yourself to have, or may really have, against them, you could hardly expect it to influence my social relations with fellow guests at the house of a friend, even if it had been known to me.

I should not in any case have called on you that day or evening, for the reason that I don't always know the secret springs of your—shall I say temper? nor just what your mood may be. I was, in fact, at the railway station, and had bought my ticket to Los Gatos when persuaded to remain. All things considered, I cannot think there was anything related in my letter that ought to have caused you the slightest annoyance—certainly nothing to cause you feelings which you describe in so bitter and, it seems to me, extravagant words.

Dear Ray, you really should habituate yourself to more just and cheerful views of things. The hand of everybody is not against you. The things that rouse your anger are not always significant of unfriendliness, as in my own case I know. I suppose you have had much to embitter you, but adversity, injustice, even wrong, should *not* embitter; they should sweeten and soften. In their tendency to embitter lies all their evil. Deny them the power to do that and you are invulnerable. All else that disaster and malevolence can do to us is a trifle compared with the wreck that they *may* make of our dispositions—our characters.

I called you once a daughter of light and fire. Don't let the light blind you, nor the fire consume. If you have not my philosophy of indifference—if you must *care* what your enemies do and say—then you should cultivate the habit of considering whether you have so many as you seem (to yourself) to have, and whether it is likely that they do and say all that you suspect. I'm rather an expert in enmities and antagonisms, and I find they have not so large and important a place in one's life and affairs as one has a tendency to think.

Pardon all this, dear friend; I am older and worldly-wiser than you, and have worn war-paint all my life. It is not worth while to hate anybody, nor to assume that anybody is taking much trouble to be malignant and vengeful. Men and women have as slack a diligence in doing evil that profits them nothing as in nearly all else. They're a lazy lot and a forgetful. I think it unlikely that you have any enemies. *Some* that you think such I *know* are not.

Let me hear from you sometimes, and believe me (despite my preaching at you),
   Sincerely your friend,
      A. B.

[57] To Percival Pollard [BL (transcript)]

Los Gatos, Cal.,
Oct. 12, 1897

My dear Pollard,

I am greatly obliged to you for "speaking" to the Town Topicist.[1] I hardly expected he would pay me what he did when I was having a bit of a boom (which by writing no more stories I suffered to expire) but as he has not said what he *will* pay I shall not proceed in the matter—at least not until I know. Perhaps I shall ask him.

Why, of course I shall be grateful for your interest, in *any* quarter. I am so far away, and so little acquainted with the lay of the literary land. You see, with nothing saved, I have voluntarily surrendered a salary of $75.00 a week in order, partly, to preserve my self-respect, partly to do more congenial and in the end profitable work.[2] That I shall eventually "win out" I don't doubt; in the meantime if I find my belly and my back too closely associated it will be nothing more than natural.

The Examiner is unwilling to let me go, and I have consented to give it some work during the absence of the present editor in New York—have just sent it a story in fact.[3] But Prattle is dead, and nothing but the direst straits would induce me to revive it. The salary is *all* there was in it.

[...]

Sincerely yours,
Ambrose Bierce.

1. *Town Topics* was a society magazine published in New York. AB's "The Damned Thing" appeared there in the issue of 7 December 1893. He published no more work in the magazine except for a few brief pieces in 1909 and 1910.
2. The reference is to AB's resignation from *SF*, the first of several occasions when he attempted to resign from working on the Hearst newspapers.
3. "The Eyes of the Panther," *SF* (17 October 1897): 3.

[58] To Myles Walsh [ALS, UC]

Los Gatos, Cal.,
Nov. 14, 1897.

My dear Walsh,

Yours of Oct. 29 received. I have not "cut Hearst", but have dropped "Prattle", and my connection with his papers is less close and more precarious, for I fear he won't "be good".

I'm still on salary but working only when I feel like it, and at whatever I please.[1]

Tell your sister that Benedicta's bad bread-making was doubtless prophetic, for her "cake is all dough"[2] at the last. I was but the humble instrument of Providence in revealing darkly her future.[3]

I have not forgotten your desire to come to California, but, alas, have been unable to do anything toward its gratification. I go to San Francisco only once in several months.

You will, I hope, be pleased that Putnams are to bring out a new edition of "Soldiers and Civilians," which has never had a chance. Also, "Can Such Things Be" is to be published in London, and Way & Williams of Chicago are to publish two books of mine next spring if they don't "assign" before that time.[4]

Sincerely, but somewhat egotistically, yours,
           Ambrose Bierce.

1. AB published only five items in *SF* from 7 November 1897 to 6 February 1898, when he resumed writing more frequently.
2. Thomas Becon, *The Flower of Godly Prayers* (1559): "Your cake is dough, and all your fat in the fire."
3. AB refers to chapter 26 of *The Monk and the Hangman's Daughter*, where Benedicta, the hangman's daughter, amused by the monk Ambrosius's inability to make bread properly, prepares a cake for him. Later Ambrosius, jealous that she loves another man, kills her.
4. G. P. Putnam's Sons brought out an augmented edition of *Tales of Soldiers and Civilians* (now titled *In the Midst of Life*) in 1898. There was no London reprint of *Can Such Things Be?* at this time (see further letter 62). Way & Williams had apparently accepted a collection of AB's political satires (*The Fall of the Republic*) as well as a volume of fables, but by May 1898 the manuscripts were "coolly returned" (AB to Myles Walsh, 19 May 1898; ALS, UC). Putnam's brought out *Fantastic Fables* in 1899, but the book of political satires was not issued; its contents, however, were included in *CW* 1.

[59] To C. W. Doyle [BL (transcript)]

                                  Los Gatos,
                                  Dec. 26, 1897.

Dear Dr. Doyle,
    [. . .]

How I hate Christmas! I'm one of the curmudgeons that the truly good Mr. Dickens found it profitable to hold up to the scorn of those who take such satisfaction in being decent and generous one day in 365. Bah! how hollow it all is! Always on Christmas, though, I feel my own heart soften—toward the late Judas Iscariot. Why, even Mrs. Martin has wished me a "merry Christmas". Great Scott! who could want to be "merry"? Is one to grin through a horse-collar, or walk on one's hands, because a babe was born in Bethlehem?

Yours ever,
           Ambrose Bierce.

[60] To Jean Hazen [ALS, WC]

Los Gatos
March 16, 1898.

Dear Miss Hazen,

Thank you for the one "quotation," and may Heaven deal with you ungently for withholding the other. Please perform an act of base treachery, like a good girl, and let me know what she wrote.

Of course I shall be always glad to hear from her, and should have written her if I had known how to address her.

Am I well? You shall judge—tomorrow morning I go to Livermore to put myself under the treatment of my good friend Dr. Robertson of the "Sanitarium."[1] I've been in the care of a physician here for a week, and he's evidently not willing that I should die on his hands—so he consents to my going away.

God be good to you,
Ambrose Bierce.

Don't imagine that this disciple of Epictetus worries, nor for a moment forgets his brief philosophy—his before Zeno stole it from him—that "nothing matters."[2]

Did I tell you that I got my ailment at Bohemia?[3]

1. Dr. John W. Robertson, founder of the Livermore Sanitarium in Livermore, California.
2. Zeno of Citium (333?–262 B.C.E.), founder of the Stoic school of philosophy. Epictetus (50?–120?), Stoic philosopher. It is a considerable exaggeration to state that "Nothing matters" is representative of Stoic thought.
3. Bohemia was the name of the home of Lella Cotton, a friend of AB's in Wright's. In the 1890s AB frequently took meals there with Cotton and her family.

[61] To C. W. Doyle [BL (transcript)]

Los Gatos,
May 8, 1898.

My dear Doyle,

Let us bless God for the typewriter—if He *will* afflict us with scrivener's paralysis; for which, to be just and logical, let us "unbless" him.

[...]

So you are "in disgrace" with Mrs. Martin. It seems to be a rather easy performance, this falling into disgrace with her. One may do it without knowing how to do it, or how it was done. In my case it seems to have been done this way: After a long silence (succeeding her failure to keep the engagement that you wot of and my declining to make another) she wrote me a very friendly letter complaining of the length of her "punishment", asking me to pass a few days at her house in town, and promising to make it pleasant for me. I replied that my health did not permit, and she was then good enough—at my suggestion, I suppose,—to promise to come here some day; ending the letter with an assurance of eternal friendship, proof against all things adverse and "firm as a rock". These are not her words—I'll send you the letters if you think it would be right, under the circumstances, and am more than willing that you should see mine. I write, and hope to receive, no letters that the whole world may not read.

In reply I pointed out how short a time she would have here if she came and returned the same day—that she could not have the ramble or picnic that she had had long in mind, nor the "midnight supper" which is my pride and joy. (Perhaps *that* alarmed her). Well, *you* know whether the m. s. is alarming; it is rather famous and in good favor among my friends of her sex, not all of whom, I hope, are bad; even my landlady approves. Knowing that she, the mother of young girls, could not visit Los Gatos and remain overnight alone, I suggested that she bring a companion. All this in good faith, cordially and playfully, but with no thought of the possibility of offence or misconstruction. The letter ended with an assurance, though, that whatever was her wish in the matter would be mine; I did not wish her to think me greedy in asking so much of her time and society.

To this letter there was no reply. After a long wait I wrote, briefly but not unfriendly, *suggesting* a reply. None came. On the Christmas day soon following she sent me a little present (which unfortunately fell into the fire) but no note.

And then she told you that I thought her "a bad woman". Even then it did occur to me that she might mean more by "bad" than we commonly do mean by it. It occurs to me now, and that in reading my letter and having in her mind what was not in mine she may have put a base construction on it; or somebody may have done so for her. I think I've told you something of the annoyance to which I am subject to persons who read into my letters what I do not write into them—assuming that I am this or that kind of scoundrel, in addition to the kind that I am. I had cautioned her against this folly, and it was, as I recollect, in reply to my caution that she affirmed her unalterable favor, as mentioned before.

Now, my dear Doyle, I did not mean to say so much, but I fancy it is as well. It was through you that I knew her and I suppose (and hope) that despite your jocular reference to your "disgrace" you are still friends. It is disagreeable to me to think that you could have even the faintest doubt of my honor in such an affair, and if you care to see the entire correspondence I am, as intimated, desirous that you should, though on second thoughts, and on rereading her letters, I fancy I cannot submit them to you without her assent, even if they are necessary to an understanding of mine—which you have my permission to see.

I do not think and have not thought Mrs. Martin "bad" in the sense that she may have had in mind, nor has she ever given me the faintest justification for such an opinion of her; but I do think that unless something has occurred beyond my conjecture her treatment of me has been incredibly base. I'm accustomed to base treatment, and it doesn't hurt as much as it once did, but—well, I don't want you to think that I would or could be unworthy of your friendship—which I should if I deserved the treatment that I have received from your friend.

Sincerely yours,
Ambrose Bierce.

[62] To Percival Pollard [ALS, NYPL]

Wright's Cal.,
Jan. 8, 1899.

Dear Mr. Pollard,

I've no better excuse for not writing to you than my "upsetting sin", procrastination, which is no excuse at all. So—please forgive me.

I am sorry to infer from the tone of your last letters that things are not going your way. (Does it ever go right with anybody?) No, I shall not "call you a fool" for your notion that you are not booked for longevity; it is a natural notion, and thirty years ago I too cherished the conviction that my life was to be brief—and was rather satisfied with it. Well, I'm 56 all right; and so, no doubt, you will be. As to having accomplished nothing, why, there's nothing worth accomplishing.

I infer from your former letter that you are connected with "The Criterion",[1] and sometimes I fancy I detect your hand in "Town Topics". Is that so?

Yes, I resumed "Prattle"—Hearst talked me into it, when I would have sworn, and *had* strongly affirmed, that nothing would move me to do so.[2]

It is interesting, what you tell me of Cowley-Brown.[3] He promised to bring out a London edition of my "Can Such Things Be?" I sent him the copy, &c., and never could get a word from him about it. I did not particularly care for his delinquency, but he might have replied to my civil inquiries. He seems to be an odd kind of chap.

I have not read Mrs. Atherton for years, nor heard from her since I was in New York. I hear that she occasionally writes a good word of me, which is very nice of her. I know not of "The Californians,"[4] but mean to look through it some day.

By the way, I hear distressing reports of Blackburn Harte—that is, I hear *one* such report, which I'd rather not repeat. Do you know anything of him? He never writes to me.

As to me—I'm living all alone on the top of a mountain, wasting my life with newspapers, a rifle and frivolity generally. The Putnams have published a book of

"Fantastic Fables" for me, but not a copy of it have I seen. I did not even read the proofs; my boy attended to that, indeed, to the whole business. If encouraged I shall publish some more soon—not fables but other things.

I hope your troubles whatever their nature have vanished or will vanish soon, and that you'll not continue despondent. When *I'm* in trouble and distress I read Epictetus, and can warmly commend that plan to you. It does not cure, but it helps one's endurance of the ill. I go to Epictetus with my mental malady as one consults one's family physician for one's physical—and misfortunes themselves are nothing except in so far as they affect us mentally. For we of our class do not suffer hunger and cold, and the like, from our failures and mischances—only dejection. And dejection is unreasonable.

If you meet my boy (he lives at 14 W. 28th St.) I wish you'd report upon him. I should like to have your judgment of him—I have only his own.

Please let me hear from you; and do be able to tell me that you don't mind the buffetings of Fate very much.
        Sincerely yours,
        Ambrose Bierce.

1. The *Criterion* (1897–1905) was a New York–based literary magazine for which Pollard served as drama critic. For *Town Topics* see letter 57, n. 1.
2. After 26 September 1897, AB wrote no more "Prattle" columns until 30 October 1898, although he wrote a large number of pieces (both in a regular column entitled "War Topics" and in separate articles) on the Spanish-American War. These have now been collected as *Skepticism and Dissent: Selected Journalism from 1898–1901*, ed. Lawrence I. Berkove (Ann Arbor, Mich.: Delmas, 1980; rev. Ann Arbor, Mich.: UMI Research Press, 1986).
3. British editor John Stapledon Cowley-Brown's short-lived magazine, *The Anti-Philistine* (1897), reprinted several of AB's stories and fables. See further letter 93, n.4. Cowley-Brown's article about AB, "The American Kipling," had appeared in *Black and White* 17 (7 January 1899): 14–15.
4. Gertrude Atherton, *The Californians* (1898), a novel dealing with the conflict between American and Hispanic families in San Francisco in the 1880s.

[63] To Eleanor Vore[1] [ALS, BL]

        Wright's, Cal.,
        Jan. 27, 1899.

My dear Nellie,
        Your mother reminds me that I have neither acknowledged your picture nor answered your letter. My delay in thanking you for the pretty picture (which I do now) is inexcusable; but I cannot undertake always to answer letters "promptly"—sometimes they wait for months unless something in them *requires* a reply immediately. You see, my child, I get dozens of letters every week, and cannot afford

to employ a secretary to assist me in attending to them. With your letter, in my "unanswered" box, are at least fifty others. If you and I replied to each other's letters "promptly" we'd have little time to do anything else.

I like the picture very much, and you will please thank your mama and the Apaches for their contribution to my "Christmas".

I hope you have been at Altadena and enriched your herbarium and your collection of spiders' nests. When you visit me you shall see my pets. I have a chipmunk, a pigeon and a pair of quails. My quails are not shut up, but go where they please in my parlor, and they commonly please to go on my lap or shoulder. Besides these I have a lot of bird visitors every day, some of which come into the house if I open the window; and there's a whole flock of my neighbor's pigeons that fight for places on my knees. I can call them down out of the sky whenever I see them flying over, for I always carry a pocketful of wheat for all the birds that I meet. I had a lovely little owl about as big as a base-ball, and as round, but it died a few days ago.

Tell your mother to bear with me as well as she can. When I get rich, I shall do nothing but write letters; but I'll write to her, I dare say, before that happy day.

And some day I'll write to you again, whether you "answer" this or not, though I hope you'll not altogether forget that an old chap up this way likes to hear from you sometimes.

Sincerely your friend,
Ambrose Bierce.

1. AB had been corresponding with Elizabeth Vore (author of "The Men Who Make Our Books," *Overland Monthly* 14, no. 4 [April 1903]: 252–59, which discusses AB in part), when her daughter, Eleanor (age fifteen), answered one of AB's letters to her in 1898. The ensuing correspondence continued until AB's disappearance in 1913.

[64] To Edwin Markham [ALS, WC]

Wrights
March 14, '99.

My dear Markham,

I have not enough knowledge of the two publishing houses—Macmillan's and McClure's—to advise you. My general notion is that it can't make much difference to a fellow which cannibal devours him. For I suppose these firms are, like their fellows in the business, gifted with a sweet-tooth for authors. I cannot help remembering, in connection with this matter, that it was one of the Macmillans who recently advised authors (with absolute gravity) to have some other vocation than writing! I think he has no other than publishing, however.[1]

McClure would doubtless spread your light more widely than the other fellows.

Yes, I've done what I could to help on your "boom," but the credit of starting it is due to Millard.² Discussion (as Stedman points out) is *life*. It does not so greatly matter *what* is said about you, so that *something* is said. If I had known that you cared to be "put in the papers" before publication of your book I would have cheerfully have done so at any time. You ought to have signified your wish—it simply did not occur to me that you would care for it. Nor do I think any "boom" would have come of what I should have selected for publication and commendation. You see I am sceptical of the legitimacy of it all, and think your *poetic* merit (the only thing that I value in your work) has nothing to do with it. I don't believe you are preaching the gospel that *you* think you are, but a doctrine of hate which has successfully appealed to the worst side of human nature. I don't think you quite knew that you were doing so; but you know how, and I hope you will no longer dwell in the tents of the demagogue, nor preach vague dreams to the cranks of that association—what's its name?

Sincerely yours,
Ambrose Bierce.

On second thoughts, I guess the "dreams" do no great harm—except in encouraging those impracticables and futilitarians to think that they think.

By the way, I sent the "Man With a Hoe" (you observe I will *not* say "The" hoe) to the N.Y. "Journal," with Millard's comments and my own and the picture and all, as a special article, the week that they appeared, telling the editor that they were bound to make a sensation. I think he did not "see it"—anyhow, I did not see the article.³

B.

1. AB repeats this anecdote in "The Passing Show" under the heading "On Putting One's Brain into One's Belly," *Cosmopolitan* 40, no. 5 (March 1906): 596.
2. AB refers to the sensation created by the publication of Markham's "The Man with the Hoe" in *SF* (15 January 1899).
3. "The Man with the Hoe" never appeared in *New York Journal*.

[65] To Edmund Clarence Stedman¹ [ALS, CU]

Wright's, Cal.,
March 19, 1899.

My dear Mr. Stedman,

The verses that Markham was kind enough to ask me for, for submission to you, hardly "represent" my humble muse. I am not, properly speaking, a poet—the writing of a few desultory poems gives one but little title to that distinction. The greater part, by far, of my verse is satirical and intended to be, not poetical, but witty. The taste for that kind of thing is like that for dry wines—it comes of cultivation. It is not understood in this country, nor will it be, probably, for generations. It is thought malicious and ascribed to personal rancor. Humor our people understand (if it is coarse enough) but not wit. Nevertheless, following the line of least resistance, I have commonly gone that way.

In compliance with your request—at least with the spirit of it—I am sending you my book—long out of print—"Black Beetles in Amber", which is, of course, hardly known outside California. As intimated, it has for "the general reader" no *intrinsic* value, out of its relation to the nobodies named in it, whom I might, perhaps, more profitably have designated by the impersonal names affected by those who believe in censuring sin and letting sinners enjoy the performance with immunity. I "go for" the sinner.

Much of my verse cannot obtain a publisher in the East for the reason that its themes are "Californian", naturally. It has been rejected *for that reason* by the same houses that grabbed at Bret Harte's stories! My boy in New York has, or soon will have, a typescript volume of my verse (all sorts) which I shall instruct him to loan to you.[2]

If you care to use anything in that, or in the book I'm sending, please do so. I must apologize for the slovenly proofreading, and some of the paging, in "Black Beetles in Amber;" the book was put together while I was absent from San Francisco and ill.

Your confirmation of my technical criticisms of Markham's poem (we all regard you as the leading authority in such matters) gave me great satisfaction—the more as it seemed to show that literary criticism is not *all* personal taste.[3]

Sincerely yours,
Ambrose Bierce.

1. Edmund Clarence Stedman (1833–1908), a leading American critic and editor of the period. At this time he was in the process of compiling an important poetry anthology, *An American Anthology* (1900). See also letter 67.

2. Leigh Bierce was circulating the manuscript of *SC* (1903).

3. Stedman had written to Markham about his "The Man with the Hoe," criticizing its absence of caesuras, with the result that "Your poem . . . is written in a novel, and I may say staccato sort of unrhymed pentameter." AB's independent comments were similar; see "Prattle," *SF* (22 January 1899): 12.

[66] To S. O. Howes[1] [ALS, HL]

Wright's,
May 4, 1899.

Dear Mr. Howes,

Be assured that your kind words of appreciation are most welcome and encouraging.

I am not writing much just now. I "threw up my job" of "Prattle" because Mr. Hearst let his fools, fakers and freaks do what they would with it in the N.Y. Journal—the which I could nowise abide. They yellowed it every way they knew how, and mangled it at will.

Thanking you for your kindly interest, I am very sincerely yours,
Ambrose Bierce.

1. Silas Orrin Howes (1867–?) of Galveston, Texas, assembled a collection of AB's political and social criticism, *The Shadow on the Dial* (San Francisco: A. M. Robertson, 1909), culled from his newspaper columns; it was later reprinted with additions in *CW* 11.

[67] To Edmund Clarence Stedman [ALS, CU]

Wright's, Cal.,
May 4, '99.

My dear Mr. Stedman,

I am greatly obliged to you for the assurance that I am to have a place in the anthology. Use your own judgment, of course, as to the pieces that go in; though I confess to a slight disappointment that "The Passing Show" did not commend itself to you as suited to your purpose.[1] The only poem of mine that has ever "caught on" and been much discussed (usually in connection, lately, with Kipling's "Recessional") is "Invocation".[2] If you get the "Outlook" (London) you may have observed that in the issue of Apr. 1st Mr. John Cowley writes of it, and in those of the 8th and 15th Robert Barr has a lot of talk about it and me.[3] I never thought so much of it myself, and think it "struck" by its patriotism rather than its poetry—as our friend Markham's "boom" is due more to his "industrial discontent" than to his art in being discontented. One could wish that these things were otherwise.

Very sincerely yours,
Ambrose Bierce.

1. Stedman selected "The Death of Grant," "The Bride," "Another Way," "Montefiore," "Presentiment," "Creation," and "T. A. H." from the ms. of *SC*. Stedman may have felt that "The Passing Show," the very first poem in *SC*, at 76 lines was too long for inclusion in his anthology.

2. "Invocation," *SF* (5 July 1888): 2, a poem of 112 lines recited by AB during a commemoration of the fourth of July at the San Francisco Opera House. See Edward F. Cahill, "Bierce's 'Invocation' and Kipling's 'Recessional,'" *SF* (23 October 1898): magazine section, p. 8.

3. John Cowley[-Brown] wrote a letter to the editor—published as "California Poets," *Outlook* (London) no. 61 (1 April 1899): 292—in which he discussed AB and quoted eleven stanzas of "Invocation." Robert Barr then wrote a two-part article, "Bierce, Kipling, Popularity, and Criticism," *Outlook* no. 62 (8 April 1899): 326; no. 63 (15 April 1899): 357–58.

[68] To S. G. Blythe[1] [ALS, VA]

Wright's, Cal.,
Nov. 27, 1899.

S. G. Blythe, Esqr.,
    Editor of The Cosmopolitan Magazine,
        Dear Sir,

In reply to your favor of the 6th I would say that I have lately done nothing in fiction. I have, moreover, uniformly declined to write for the magazines, being dissatisfied with the indefinite character of their proposals and the uncertainty as to when the work if accepted will be published. Perhaps your system is different from that of the others,—your magazine certainly is different, and better than most of them.[1]

Very truly yours,
    Ambrose Bierce.

1. Samuel George Blythe (1868–1947), author of *The Making of a Newspaper Man* (1912).

2. AB ultimately did write for *Cosmopolitan* from 1905 until 1909, after it had been purchased by Hearst, although his tenure there was marked by considerable frustration.

[69] To S. O. Howes [ALS, HL]

Wright's, Cal.,
Nov. 29, 1899.

Dear Mr. Howes,

I am greatly obliged to you for your letter of the 16th. The "News" certainly has no right to say that my stuff from the "Journal" and "Examiner" is "special" to itself.[1] What right it has to use it at all I do not know, but shall ascertain.

It was kind of you to apprise me.

In a few weeks I expect to go to Washington, D.C., where I shall probably remain. It is simply a change of residence without a change of duties, excepting that I shall probably do more work for "The Journal" and less for "The Examiner".[2]

If you should ever go to Washington I should be pleased to meet and greet you.
Sincerely yours,
Ambrose Bierce.

1. Evidently some of AB's work for *NYJ* and *SF* was being reprinted without authorization in other newspapers.
2. AB's work was published in both papers, usually first in *NYJ/New York American* and lagging by several days (or weeks) in *SF*. Much of his work for *NYJ/New York American* did not appear in *SF*. On rare occasions, pieces published in *SF* did not appear in *NYJ/New York American*.

[70] To Herman Scheffauer [BL (transcript)]

Washington, D.C.,
June 8, 1900.

Dear Scheff,
I've reached your last letter on my pile. It is always a pleasure to get down to yours. It is like penetrating the nethermost stratum of barren rock and striking ore. By the way, I did not say that I was going to "discontinue writing letters", I think, but that I had given up "answering" letters. A true "answer", I take it, follows close upon receipt of the letter "answered".

Now that Congress has adjourned I shall know soon whether I can remain here. Be sure I shall do my best to remain a while at least. Nothing short of the loss of my "job" for insubordination would move me, and I'm not sure that that would.

I'm living a few miles out of town now, at a roadside club-house on the bank of the Potomac and am comfortable. I ride my bike, loaf under the trees, entertain my friends, dream a good deal (that river always sends me into that dreamland that we call the Past) and work a little. When you come—ah, when you come—shall I ever be able to bring it about? Well, I shall try.

[...]
Sincerely yours,
Ambrose Bierce.

You are the only one to whom I confess my wish to remain away from California. Please do not let any of the others know. Some would be hurt by it. Time will "break it gently" to them. And some day I'll come back.

[71] To Gustav Adolphe Danziger[1]

Washington,
Aug. 21, 1900.

[Dear Dr. Danziger,]
One or two points in your last letter demand attention. If any of your friends told you that I said anything very bad about you (anything half so bad as you say of yourself) they lied. I have made it a rule not to speak of you at all unless I had to—to treat the subject as if you were dead; and I do not speak ill of the dead—have, indeed, refused to write of the late C. P. Huntington.

Some of my friends came to me with tales of *what you* said of *me*—that you were always talking of "The Monk" as entirely your work, I having simply lent my name to it, and so forth. I always said that was not true—when I said anything, which was not commonly the case; but the matter troubled me not at all nor angered me. My peace of mind is not at the mercy of tale-bearers, even if I believe the tales. If it were my life would be miserable indeed, for "that of an hour's age doth hiss the speaker."[2]

I have read twice and carefully, your proposed original addition to "The Monk," and you must permit me to speak plainly, if not altogether agreeably, of it. It will not do—for these reasons and others:

1. The book is almost perfect as you did it; the part of the work that pleases me least is *my* part.[3]

2. The proposed change would make another book; the last part utterly incongruous and unlike the first. By my rewriting that part congruity of style could be obtained, but congruity of character nothing could give it—not even the necessary recasting of the whole book. I am surprised that you should yield to the school girl desire for that shallowest of all literary devices, a "happy ending," by which all the pathos of the book is effaced to "make a woman holiday." It looks as if you had accepted a hint from the magnate of a circulating library.

3. With the additional chapters the last of the other part, all about the stabbing of Benedicta, becomes a mere unworthy trick upon the reader—not only needless, but dishonest and resentable.

4. The change would sacrifice the noble and natural simplicity of the book, these chapters making a complicated and unnatural and impossible plot. Complicated and impossible plots are the stock-in-trade of second- and third-rate writers: they are unworthy of *you*. So much did I feel their unworthiness that I hesitated a long time before even deciding to have so much "odious ingenuity" and "mystery" as making Benedicta the daughter of the Saltmaster and inventing her secret love for Ambrosius instead of Rochus.

5. In your new chapters Benedicta, the very life and soul of the book's interest, ever holding the center of the stage, is almost effaced. She disappears, actually "soaks in"—

to reappear for one moment as a shadow, a lay figure, a "dummy," among the cheap tale-worn properties of the melodramatic stage. Then you really kill her (with old age presumably) leaving the reader to *infer* their happiness meantime.

6. "Dramatic action," which is no less necessary in a story than in a play, requires that so far as is possible what takes place shall be *seen* to take place, not related as having previously taken place. There is hardly a touch of it in these chapters: they are taken up with explanation—explanation of needless mysteries and impossible foregone events. Compare Shakspeare's Cymbelline with his better plays. See how he spoiled it the same way. You need not feel ashamed to err as Shakspeare erred. Indeed, you did better than he, for his explanations were of things already known to the reader, or spectator, of the play. *Your* explanations are needful to an understanding of the things explained; it is *they* that are needless. But all "explanation" is unspeakably tedious, and is to be cut as short as possible. Far better to have nothing to explain—to *show* everything that occurs, in the very act of occurring. We cannot always do that, but we should come as near to doing it as we can. Anyhow, the "harking back" should not be done at the end of the book, when the dénouement is already known and the reader's interest in the *action* exhausted. Theatre audiences who begin to leave the house before the curtain comes down are not so much to blame as some think.

7. Ambrosius and Benedicta are unique in letters—you and I are not entitled to all the credit of their creation. Their nobility, their simplicity, their sufferings—everything that is theirs stamps them as "beings apart." They live in the memory sanctified and glorified by theese qualities and sorrows. They are, in the best and most gracious sense, children of nature. All this you would efface at the last, leaving another taste in the mouth. You transform them into commonplace persons. Ambrosius a "prince"—Benedicta a "princess"! How *could* you? It is unthinkable—insupportable! Are princes and princesses more grateful in the memory than saints in Heaven? Is it sweeter to think of their tawdry new magnificence than of their old innocence in the wilderness? Does it give a tenderer and more solemn satisfaction to lay them in a gorgeous "mausoleum" at the end of a life of vulgar splendor than to leave them lying there in the lovely valley of the gallows, where Ambrosius shuddered as his foot fell on the spot where he was destined to sleep? Ah, my friend, your restless mind has robbed me of a fascinating memory; it must not rob others.

Look here: the power of your work is not to be disregarded, nor denied its fruits. Why not make a new book, all your own? Why not alter names and some incidents in your ingenious chapters and make another story to fit them? You could begin at the beginning and write up to them. With some of the hints which I have tried to give you—some modifications—you could make a better story than you have yet written—a far better story than *this* book would be, or could be made, by *anybody's* alterations. Think it over.

I must dissent, too, from your proposed new title, in which I see no good but alliteration—if that is good. "The Monk and the Maiden" is deadly commonplace and does not stimulate curiosity. In what world have you been existing since we breathed the same atmosphere? Have the Philistines had you in keeping and training? Have you listened to the voice of Miss Nancy and sat at the feet of Sweet Sixteen? I don't understand.

Let "The Monk and the Hangman's Daughter" alone. It is great work and *you* should live to see the world confess it. But for Schulte's failure and our estrangement the acknowledgment would have come already. It is not too late, but I could never consent to its alteration by so much as a single line.

This is a long letter, but I have felt that in asking you to renounce a project evidently dear to you I "owed you much reasons."

Let me know if my faith in your faith in me is an error. You once believed in my judgment; I think it is not yet impaired by age.

    Sincerely yours,
        Ambrose Bierce

1. This letter apparently does not survive in manuscript; the text is taken from Adolphe (Danziger) de Castro, *Portrait of Ambrose Bierce* (New York: Century Co., 1929), 275–78.
2. Shakespeare, *Macbeth* 4.3.175.
3. Danziger would later use this sentence to augment the impression that *The Monk and the Hangman's Daughter* was largely his own work. See his preface to the revised (1926) Boni & Liveright edition of *The Monk and the Hangman's Daughter* (with *Fantastic Fables*).

[72] To Herman Scheffauer [BL (transcript)]

                18 Iowa Circle,
                    Washington,
                        Dec. 1, 1900.

Dear Scheff,

    I've just returned from New York where I remained for two weeks, neither receiving letters nor writing any. That is why I have not acknowledged the "working pans" of Queen Lella's seal.[1] I shall now look for a competent man to cut it, but doubt if he can be found here. I may have to send to Tiffany's or some other place in New York. Please do not bother with the tortoise suggestions. I had no idea that it would entail so much work for you. It was only a passing fancy, anyhow. I rather wish I had asked you to have Stott, of San Francisco, do the work on Lella's seal. He is, I think, competent, and as he likes me he would have done his best. Do you know him?—A. W. Stott, 131 Post St. If not go and see him—he and his work may amuse you for an hour. Here's a card which will introduce you.

I'm awaiting the arrival of my painting and candlestick, which Lella is to send—probably has already sent. It will be like a breath of pinewood fragrance from the Santa Cruz hills to get them again.

It is very sweet and lovely (as a woman might say) of Sam Davis[2] to write all that about me, in a letter to you. O, yes, I like Sam, but I have sometimes feared that you and he might not take to each other if you met. He's a hospitable soul. Moreover, he has done some good stories which he was unable to find a publisher for—which is disgusting.

I note all you say of Swinburne, but whether you like his alliteration or not you have something to learn, as all of us have, from his mastery of metre. As to alliteration, it is as legitimate as rhyme, which is indeed itself alliteration of a kind. And once alliteration proper was counted in our poetry an ornament superior to rhyme. We've the other fashion now; and some day rhyme may go out of fashion, too, and be carefully avoided by the fastidious poets.

I'm pleased with your quotations from Goethe. (I have been unable to obtain here his "Conversations with Eckermann".)[3] As the Nicaragua Canal matter will soon be "on" again in Congress, I shall use some of his words on that subject—the transisthmian waterway. It is very "timely".[4]

[. . .]

I wish you were here and am still not without hope, now that members of Congress are returning. I mean to tackle some of them to help in the matter of finding a Government official willing to appoint you to something that can be had without the "competitive examination" and "list of eligibles" nonsense. But it is weary work to do *any*thing for *any*body, here.

The poem is good and grim. If it had been briefer I had been tempted to print it (without your consent) in my department of the "Journal-American"–"Examiner".[5] But my editor does not approve of giving up much of my limited space to the work of others, even if it is better than my own, which this certainly is. If I've a criticism to make it is that the speech of the Markham should make an even stanza or two stanzas.

I've a screed from Doyle-sahib recounting his successes in the struggle of letters . . . whereof I am joyant. I wish you were similarly fortunate. Perhaps you would be if you wrote tales in prose. Why not try it? It is a lottery; nobody knows, or can find out, what makes a story "popular". Maybe you have it.

Sincerely yours,
Ambrose Bierce.

---

1. Lella Cotton was designing for AB a seal, possibly for a signet ring.
2. Samuel Post Davis (1850–1918), editor of the Carson [Nev.] *Appeal* and author of *Short Stories*

(1886), *The History of Nevada* (1913), and other volumes. In 1894 AB attempted to find a publisher to reissue Davis's *Short Stories*, to no avail.

3. Johann Wolfgang von Goethe (1749–1832) and Johann Peter Eckermann (1792–1854), *Conversations with Eckermann* (1832). See AB, "Goethe Was a Prophet as Well as a Poet," *NYJ* (23 May 1901): 16; *SF* (12 June 1901): 16.

4. The United States had long pondered the feasibility of a canal connecting the Atlantic and Pacific Oceans. AB at this time supported the building of the canal in Nicaragua rather than in Panama (see "The Nicaragua Canal Is Not Yet Assured," *NYJ*, 17 January 1900). See also "Ambrose Bierce Says: We Must Control the Nicaragua Canal," *NYJ* (23 November 1900; *SF*, 10 December 1900).

5 AB had reprinted Scheffauer's "The Republic" in "The Passing Show" (*NYJ* and *SF*, 25 February 1900).

[73] To Gustav Adolphe Danziger[1]

[late December 1900?]

[Dear. Dr. Danziger,]

        I have your distressing letter. I had no idea that your illness was so serious, and cannot now think it so bad as you deem it. No, I shall not believe your diagnosis of your own case—the patient is not in a condition to appraise his own disease.

    I wish I could go to you, but that is not possible now. Leigh will call on you, and I have ventured to send him a little money with which to help you a bit if needful. You know I cannot have you suffer for anything that I am able to procure for you.

    If you had been a little more candid with me regarding your *needs* it would have been better. I was very inconsiderate not to suspect the depth of your adversity. But I had expected to have a whole evening with you before leaving, and had thought of questioning you then about it. For I *did* fear that you had not perhaps told me all.

    Well, I came away at the last very suddenly; and then your cheerful letters made me think you were all right. That you "did not eat regularly" never for a moment occurred to me.

    I have seen Kahn twice about the consulship—the second time only an hour ago.[2] You say you need a change of climate. Now, it happens that the Consulships that give an American the most complete change of climate are those for which there are the fewest applicants—places in the tropics. So it may be possible to procure you an appointment to one of them. Of course the best paying ones are not to be had for the asking, but Kahn is now looking over the list of the smaller places in the hope of finding something that will serve and can be got soonest. We are not going to believe that it is too late.

    Of course, my dear friend, if you should die I will do all that you ask, and more. Don't give yourself any uneasiness about that. The interests and rights of your heirs will be to me a sacred trust.

But you'll not die. You'll get well and we will find a place for you in this big brutal world.

Don't worry to write to me. Leigh will keep me informed about you.

Sincerely yours,
Ambrose Bierce

P.S.—My hasty action on reading your letter was based on the belief that you were now in the hospital. That is why I sent the money to Leigh, instead of to you directly. It is now too late to correct the error, but you'll not mind, will you?

A. B.

1. Text from de Castro, *Portrait of Ambrose Bierce*, 290–91.
2. Julius Kahn (1861–1924), U.S. representative from California (1898–1903, 1905–24). Danziger in fact became U.S. vice-consul to Spain around this time.

[74] To C. W. Doyle [ALS, NYPL (H. L. Mencken Papers)]

Washington, D.C.
Jan. 23, 1901.

My dear Doyle:

Your letter of the 16th has just come and as I am waiting at my office (where I seldom go) I shall amuse myself by replying "to onct." See here, I don't purpose that your attack on poor Morrow's book[1] shall become a "continuous performance", nor even an "annual ceremony". It is not "rot". It is not "filthy". It does not "suggest bed-pans;"—at least it did not to me, and I'll wager something that Morrow never thought of them. Observe and consider: If his hero and heroine had been man and wife, the bed-pan would have been there, just the same; yet you would not have thought of it. Every reader would have been touched by the husband's devotion. A physician has to do with many unpleasant things; whom do his ministrations disgust? A trained nurse lives in an atmosphere of bed-pans—to whom is her presence or work suggestive of them? I'm thinking of the heroic Father Damien[2] and his lepers; do you dwell upon the rotting limbs and foul distortions of his unhappy charges? Is not his voluntary martyrdom one of the sanest, cleanest, most elevating memories in all history? Then it is *not* the bed-pan necessity that disgusts you; it is something else. It is the fact that the hero of the story, being neither physician, articled nurse, nor certificated husband, nevertheless performed their *work*. He ministered to the helpless in a natural way without authority from church or college, quite irregular and improper and all that. My noble critic, there speaks in your blood the Untamed Philistine. You were not caught young enough. You came into letters and art with all your beastly conventionalities in full mastery of you. Take a purge. Forget that there are Philistines. Forget that they have put their abominable pantalettes upon the legs of Nature. Forget that their code of morality and manners (it stinks worse than a bed-pan) does *not* exist in the serene altitude of great art, toward which you have set your toes and into which I want you to climb. I know about this thing. I, too, tried to rise with all that dead weight dragging at my feet. Well, I could not—now I could if I cared to. In my mind I do. It is not freedom of act—not freedom of living for which I contend, but freedom of thought, of mind, of spirit; the freedom to see in the horrible laws, prejudices, customs, conventionalities of the multitude, something good for them, but of no value to you *in your art*. In your life and conduct defer to as much of it as you will (you'll find it convenient to defer to a whole lot), but in your mind and art let not the Philistine enter, nor even speak a word through the keyhole. My own chief objection to Morrow's story is (as I apprised him) its unnaturalness. He did not dare to follow the logical course of his narrative. He was too cowardly, (or had too keen an eye upon his market of prudes) to make hero and heroine join in the holy bonds of *bed*lock, as they naturally, inevitably and rightly would have done long before she was able to be about. I daresay that, too, would have seemed to you "filthy", without the parson and his fee. When you analyse your objection to the story (as I have tried to do for you) you will find that it all crystalizes into that—the absence of the parson. I don't envy you your view of the matter, and I really don't think you greatly enjoy it yourself. I forgot to say: Suppose they had been two men, two partners in hunting, mining, or exploring, as frequently occurs. Would the bed-pan suggestion have come to you? Did it come to you when you read of the slow, but not uniform starvation of Greeley's party in the arctic?[3] Of course not. Then it is a matter, not of bed-pans, but of sex-exposure (unauthorized by the church), of prudery—of that artificial thing, the "sense of shame", of which the great Greeks knew nothing; of which the great Japanese know nothing; of which art knows nothing. Dear Doctor, do you really put trousers on your piano-legs? Does your indecent intimacy with your mirror make you blush?

    There, there's the person whom I've been waiting for (I'm to take her to dinner, and I'm not married to even so much of her as her little toe) has come; and until you offend again, you are immune from the switch. May all your brother Philistines have to "Kiss the place to make it well."[4]

    Pan is dead! long live Bed-Pan!
        Yours ever,
            Ambrose Bierce.

1. W. C. Morrow, *A Man: His Mark* (Philadelphia: J. B. Lippincott Co., 1900), a historical romance.
2. Father Damien (Joseph de Veuster, 1841–1889) was a Belgian priest who devoted his life to mis-

sionary work among the Hawaiian lepers at Molokai. He contracted leprosy in 1884, but refused treatment as it would have meant leaving his work. His story was popularized by Robert Louis Stevenson in *Father Damien: An Open Letter to the Reverend Dr. Hyde of Honolulu* (1890).

3. Adolphus Washington Greely (1844–1935) was a U.S. Army officer whose scientific expedition to the Arctic resulted in the exploration of Ellesmere Island, Canada, and coastal Greenland. The mission, however, ended in tragedy. Greely commanded the U.S. station at Fort Conger on Ellesmere Island, beginning in August 1881. When a relief ship failed to arrive in early August 1883 his party abandoned Fort Conger and moved southward in small boats. Covering 500 miles in 51 days, the men landed at Bedford Pym Island, north of Cape Sabine, in Smith Sound, on 15 October, where they faced a winter of 250 days with rations for 40 days. Before the ordeal was over, they were reduced to eating their own leather clothing. Only Greely and six others survived. AB mentions the ill-fated expedition in several columns in *Wasp* for 1884, hinting at cannibalism.

4. Ann Taylor (1782–1866), "My Mother" (1804), l. 23.

[75] To Herman Scheffauer [BL (transcript)]

234 W. 52d St., N.Y.,
March 29, 1901.

Dear Scheff,

Your letter of the 22d has just reached me, forwarded from Washington. I can't "answer" it, nor answer your other. For two weeks I have been at the bedside of a dying son.[1] That cannot last much longer, but even when it is past I shall be hardly in the mind of writing letters. I got the photograph of yourself, and thank you. The one I promised you I cannot at present supply. I haven't the negative, which is, I suppose, locked up in my boy's desk at his office.

About Hubbard.[2] Why not write him yourself, telling him what you can do? Refer to me for corroboration. I *can't* write him, nor anybody, of anything. Hubbard was here the other day (in New York) and some friends gave him a great dinner. Of course I did not see him—see nobody. Thank you for your good letter from Bohemia. O yes, I should like to kiss Lady Betty[3]—I've not got beyond *that*, nor could any trouble ever put me beyond it.

Address me at Washington as usual—if you will not expect an answer. God bless you.

A. B.

1. Leigh Bierce died of pneumonia on 31 March. AB's other son, Day, had died in 1889 at the age of sixteen in a quarrel over a girl. His death is not mentioned in the few surviving letters of that period.

2. Elbert Hubbard (1856–1915), American author, publisher (whose Roycroft Press promoted hand craftsmanship and fine books), and proponent of rugged inividualism; author of the inspirational essay "A Message to Garcia" (1899). AB owned Hubbard's *So Here Cometh White Hyacinths* (1907).

3. May Elizabeth McAlister, a friend and correspondent of AB since the 1890s.

[76] To Herman Scheffauer [BL (transcript)]

New York,
April 2, 1901.

Dear Scheff,

My boy died on Sunday morning. I'm a bit broken in body and mind—you'll not expect a "letter". Shall go back to Washington next week, I hope.

Sincerely yours,
Ambrose Bierce.

[77] To George Sterling[1] [ALS, NYPL]

Washington,
May 22, 1901.

My dear Sterling,

I enclose a proof of the poem—all marked up. The poem was offered to the Journal, but to the wrong editor. I would not offer it to him in whose department it could be used, for he once turned down some admirable verses of my friend Scheffauer which I sent him. I'm glad the Journal is *not* to have it, for it now goes into the Washington Post—and the Post into the best houses here and elsewhere—a good, clean unyellow paper. I'll send you some copies with the poem.[2]

I think my marks are intelligible—I mean my remarks. Perhaps you'll not approve all, or anything, that I did to the poem; I'll only ask you to endure. When you publish in covers you can restore to the original draft if you like. I had not time (after my return from New York) to get your approval and did the best and the least I could.

Thank you for your kind offer of a domicile to my boy's widow, but a reconciliation has come about and she is again with her mother. My daughter is with me, but will return to Los Angeles. As to me, I neither question the future nor care to affect it.

My love to your pretty wife and sister.[3] Let me know how hard you hate me for monkeying with your sacred lines.

Sincerely yours,
Ambrose Bierce.

(over)

Yes, your poem recalled my "Invocation" as I read it; but it is better, and not too much like—hardly like at all except in the "political" part. Both, in that, are characterized, I think, by decent restraint. How Markham would, at those places, have ranted and chewed soap!—a superior quality of soap, I confess.

A. B.

1. George Sterling (1869–1926), California poet best known for such volumes as *The Testimony of the Suns and Other Poems* (1903), *A Wine of Wizardry and Other Poems* (1909), *The House of Orchids* (1911),

and *Selected Poems* (1923). AB's most notable poetic pupil, he became the unofficial "Poet Laureate of San Francisco" and a leading Californian man of letters in the first three decades of the twentieth century.

2. "Memorial Day, 1901," *Washington Post* no. 9115 (26 May 1901): 26; rpt. in *The Testimony of the Suns and Other Poems*. It is his first published poem.

3. GS's wife was Carolyn ("Carrie" Rand) Sterling (d. 1918); they divorced in 1913. He had six sisters, but AB seemed particularly attracted to a younger sister, Marian.

[78] To Myles Walsh [ALS, UC]

Washington, D.C.
Sept. 7, 1901.

My dear Walsh,

I know you wrote me, but do not know when nor what; nor do I know where the letter is.

I have been very ill—five weeks of it—and am still engaged in recovering. That is not the worst, not by much. My daughter, who has been with me since we saw you, is down with typhoid fever, and I expect to lose her as I did her brother. She is in a hospital under the care of the Sisters, and all is done for her that is possible in the way of nursing and medical attention, but I think she will die.

So don't expect me to write letters now.

Sincerely yours (with affectionate regards for the pretty sister)

Ambrose Bierce.

Address:
N.Y. Journal Bureau,
Washington, D.C.

[79] To Herman Scheffauer [BL (transcript)]

The Olympia,
Washington, D.C.

My dear Scheff,

I have your letter all right, though unable at this moment to lay hand to it. You've had a devil of a tussle with the enemy, old man, and I judge from the tone of your report that it was your maiden engagement with him. Well, I congratulate you on your victory, and that's about the end of the incident, or ought to be. There is no use in dwelling on, or brooding over, the familiar fact that illness and adversity are disagreeable and even painful. Take the word of one who is of ripe experience in suffering: it doesn't all amount to much as an episode in the scheme of things, and is of little importance to ourselves even, so long as we pull through with unscarred *minds*. I think you will be the better writer for it. I *know* you will; so am unable to commiserate as I might in the case of a poor devil to whom the experience would be valueless.

You must look at it that way yourself, and be thankful that you have learned in suffering what you are to teach in song.[1]

I have myself just gone through ten weeks of hell physical, with a continuous performance of hell mental; but an the gods please I can stand some more of the same and be damned to them!

[. . .]

  Sincerely yours,
    Ambrose Bierce.
Oct. 17, 1901.

P.S.—Perhaps I told you of my daughter's illness, coincident in point of time with my own. If so you will be glad to know that I have just taken her from the hospital, where she lay eight weeks with a dreadful case of typhoid fever, and hope she will be soon able to go home to Los Angeles. Having typhoid fever is a favorite form of popular diversion here in Washington.

      A. B.

1. Percy Bysshe Shelley, *Julian and Maddalo: A Conversation* (1818), l. 546: "They learn in suffering what they teach in song."

---

[80] To George Sterling [ALS, NYPL]

    The Olympia,
     Washington, D.C.

My dear Sterling,

  I enclose the poems, with a few suggestions. They require little criticism of the sort that would be "helpful". As to their merit, I think them good, but not great. I suppose you do not expect to write great things every time. Yet in the body of your letter (of Oct. 22) you do write greatly—and say that the work is "egoistic" and "unprintable". If it were addressed to another person than myself I should say that it is "printable" exceedingly. Call it what you will, but let me tell you it will probably be long before you write anything better than some—many—of these stanzas.

You ask if you have correctly answered your own questions. Yes; in four lines of your running comment:

"I suppose that I'd do the greater good in the long run by making my work as good poetry as possible."

It is the "questions" that are great, *because* they are "good poetry". The succeeding questions whereby you rather obscurely and unconfidently "answer" them are less good.

Of course I deplore your tendency to dalliance with the demagogic muse.¹ I hope you will not set your feet in the dirty paths—leading nowhither—of social and political "reform". I hope you will not follow Markham in making a sale of your poet's birthright for a mess of "popularity."² If you do I shall have to part company with you, as I have done with him and at least *one* of his betters, for I draw the line at demagogues and anarchists, however gifted and however beloved.

Let the "poor" alone—they are oppressed by nobody but God. Nobody hates them, nobody despises. "The rich" love them a deal better than they love one another. But I'll not go into these matters; your own good sense must be your salvation if you are saved. I recognise the temptations of environment: you are of San Francisco, the paradise of ignorance, anarchy and general yellowness. Still, a poet is not altogether the creature of his place and time—at least not of his to-day and his parish.

By the way, you say that Blanche is your only associate that knows anything of literature. She is a dear girl, but look out for her; she will make you an anarchist if she can, and persuade you to kill a President or two every fine morning. I warrant you she can pronounce the name of McKinley's assassin to the ultimate zed,³ and has a little graven image of him next her heart.

Yes, you can republish the Memorial Day poem without the *Post's* consent—could do so in "book form" even if the *Post* had copyrighted it, which it did not do. I think the courts have held that in purchasing work for publication in his newspaper or magazine the editor acquires no right in it, *except for that purpose.* Even if he copyright it that is only to protect him from other newspapers or magazines. The right to publish in a book remains with the author. Better ask a lawyer though—preferably without letting him know whether you are an editor or an author.

I ought to have answered (as well as able) these questions before, but I have been ill and worried, and have written few letters, and even done little work, and that only of the pot-boiling sort. Am better now.

My daughter has recovered and returned to Los Angeles.

Please thank Miss Marian for the beautiful photographs—I mean for being so beautiful as to "take" them, for doubtless I owe their possession to you.

I wrote Doyle about you and he cordially praised your work as incomparably superior to his own and asked that you visit him. He's a lovable fellow and you'd not regret going to Santa Cruz and boozing with him.

Thank you too for the picture of Grizzly and the cub of him.⁴

Sincerely yours, with best regards to the pretty ever-so-much-better half of you,

Ambrose Bierce.

P.S.

I enclose a letter from Percival Pollard, to whom I gave a copy of your Memorial

Day poem. Think you may care for his opinion of it. You need not return the letter.

A. B.

Dec. 16, 1901.

    1. GS, under the influence of his friend Jack London, was attracted to a kind of sentimental socialism at this time.
    2. Genesis 25:33–34: "And he [Esau] sold his birthright unto Jacob. Then Jacob gave Esau bread and pottage of lentils."
    3. President William McKinley was shot at Buffalo on 6 September 1901 by the anarchist Leon Czolgosz.
    4. "Grizzly" was AB's nickname for his brother Albert. Late in life he also refered to him as "Sloots."

[81] To George Sterling [ALS, NYPL]

The Olympia,
Washington, D.C.

My dear Sterling,

    Where are you going to stop?—I mean at what stage of development?[1] I presume you have not a "whole lot" of poems really writ, and have not been feeding them to me, the least good first, and not in the order of their production. So it must be that you are advancing at a stupendous rate. This last beats any and all that went before—or I am bewitched and befuddled. I dare not trust myself to say what I think of it. In manner it is great, but the greatness of the theme!—that is beyond anything.

    It is a new field, the broadest yet discovered. To paraphrase Coleridge,

> You are the first that ever burst
> Into that ~~silent~~ unknown sea—[2]

a silent sea because no one else has burst into it in full song. True, there have been short incursions across the "border", but only by way of episode. The tremendous phenomena of Astronomy have never had adequate poetic treatment, their meaning adequate expression. You must make it your own domain. You shall be the poet of the skies, the prophet of the suns. Don't fiddle-faddle with such infinitesimal and tiresome trivialities as (for example) the immemorial squabbles of "rich" and "poor" on this "mote in the sun-beam".[3] (Both "classes", when you come to that, are about equally disgusting and unworthy—there's not a pin's moral difference between them.) Let them cheat and pick pockets and cut throats to the satisfaction of their base instincts, but do thou regard them not. Moreover, by that great law of Change which you so clearly discern, there can be no permanent composition of their nasty strife. "Settle" it how they will—another beat of the pendulum and all is as before; and ere another, Man will again be savage, sitting on his naked haunches and gnawing raw bones.

Yes, circumstances make the rich "what they are." And circumstances make the poor what *they* are. I have known both, long and well. The rich—*while* rich—are a trifle the better. There's nothing like poverty to nurture badness. But in this country there are no such "classes" as "rich" and "poor": as a rule, the wealthy man of today was a poor devil yesterday; the poor devils of today have an equal chance to be rich tomorrow—or would have if they had equal brains and providence. The system that gives them the chance is not an oppressive one. Under a really oppressive system a salesman in a village grocery could not have risen to a salary of one million dollars a year because he was worth it to his employers, as Schwab[4] has done. True, some men get rich by dishonesty, but the poor commonly cheat as hard as they can and remain poor—thereby escaping observation and censure. The moral difference between cheating to the limit of a small opportunity and cheating to the limit of a great one is to me indiscernible. The workman who "skimps his work" is just as much a rascal as the "director" who corners a crop.

As to "Socialism". I am something of a Socialist myself; that is, I think that the principle, which has always coexisted with competition, each safeguarding the other, may be advantageously extended. But those who rail against "the competitive system", and think they suffer from it, really suffer from their own unthrift and incapacity. For the competent and provident it is an ideally perfect system. As the other fellows are not of those who effect permanent reforms, or reforms of any kind, pure Socialism is the dream of a dream.

But why do I write all this. One's opinions on such matters are unaffected by reason and instance; they are born of feeling and temperament. There is a Socialist diathesis, as there is an Anarchist diathesis. Could you teach a bulldog to retrieve, or a sheep to fetch and carry? Could you make a "born artist" comprehend a syllogism? As easily as persuade a poet that black is not whatever color he loves. Somebody has defined poetry as "glorious nonsense".[5] It is not an altogether false definition, albeit I consider poetry the flower and fruit of speech and would rather write gloriously than sensibly. But if poets saw things as they are they would write no more poetry.

Nevertheless, I venture to ask you: *Can't* you see in the prosperity of the strong and the adversity of the weak a part of that great beneficent law, "the survival of the fittest"? Don't you see that such evils as inhere in "the competitive system" are evils only to individuals, but blessings to the race by gradually weeding out the incompetent and their progeny?

I've done, i' faith. Be any kind of 'ist or 'er that you will, but don't let it get into your ink. Nobody is calling you to deliver your land from Error's chain. What we want of you is poetry, not politics. And if you care for fame just have the goodness to consider if any "champion of the poor" has ever obtained it. From the earliest days down to Massaniello, Jack Cade and Eugene Debs[6] the leaders and prophets of "the masses" have been held unworthy. And with reason too, however much injustice is mixed in with the right of it. Eventually the most conscientious, popular and successful "demagogue" comes into a heritage of infamy. The most brilliant gifts cannot save him. That will be the fate of Edwin Markham if he does not come out o' that, and it will be the fate of George Sterling if he will not be warned.

You think that "the main product of that system" (the "competitive") "is the love of money." What a case of the cart before the horse! The love of money is not the product, but the root, of the system—not the effect, but the cause. When one man desires to be better off than another he competes with him. You can abolish the system when you can abolish the desire—when you can make Man, as Nature did *not* make him, content to be as poor as the poorest. Do away with the desire to excel and you may set up your Socialism at once. But what kind of a race of slugs and sloths will you have?

But, bless me, I shall *never* have done if I say all that comes to me.

Why, of course my remarks about Blanche were facetious—playful. She really is an anarchist, and her sympathies are with criminals, whom she considers the "product" of the laws, but—well, she inherited the diathesis and can no more help it than she can the color of her pretty eyes. But she is a child—a good child—and except in so far as her convictions make her impossible they do not count. She would not hurt a fly—not even if, like the toad, it had a precious jewel in its head that it did not work for. But I am speaking of the Blanche that *I* knew. If I did not know that the anarchist leopard's spots "will wash", your words would make me think that she might have changed. It does not matter what women think, if thinking it may be called, and Blanche will never be other than lovable.

Lest you have *not* a copy of the verses addressed to me I enclose one that I made myself.[7] Of course their publication could not be otherwise than pleasing to me if you care to do it. You need not fear the "splendid weight" expression,[8] and so forth—there is nothing "conceited" in the poem. As it was addressed to me, I have not criticised it—I *can't*. And I guess it needs no criticism.

I fear for the other two-thirds of this latest poem. If you descend from Arcturus to Earth, from your nebulae to your neighbors, from Life to lives, from the measureless immensities of space to the petty passions of us poor insects, won't you incur the peril of anti-climax? I doubt if you can touch the "human interest" after those high themes without an awful tumble. I should be sorry to see the poem "peter out," or "soak in". It would be as if Goethe had let his "Prologue in Heaven"[9] expire in a coon song. You have reached the "heights of dream" all right, but how are you to stay there to the end? By the way, you must perfect yourself in Astronomy, or rather get a general knowledge of it, which I fear you lack. Be sure about the pronunciation of Astronomical names.

I have read some of Jack London's work and think it clever.[10] Of Whitaker I never before heard, I fear.[11] If London wants to criticise your "star poem" what's the objection? I should not think, though, from his eulogism of Markham, that he is very critical. Still, I trust he knows more of poetry than Clough[12] and Millard do.

Where are you to place Browning? Among thinkers. In his younger days, when he wrote in English, he stood among the poets. I remember writing once—of the thinker: "There's nothing more obscure than Browning except blacking."[13] I'll stand to that.

No, don't take the trouble to send me a copy of these verses: I expect to see them in a book pretty soon.

My love to Mrs. Sterling and Miss Marian, whose pictures still make beautiful my wall. If Mrs. Sterling comes East, as you seem to think she may, I hope she will "take in" Washington and let me see her.

Sincerely yours,

Ambrose Bierce.

March 15, 1902.

1. AB is expressing his reaction to the first part of GS's "star poem," *The Testimony of the Suns*, which conveys GS's sense of wonder and awe at the vastness of the cosmos.

2. Samuel Taylor Coleridge, *The Rime of the Ancient Mariner* (1798), ll. 105–6 ("We were" for "You are" in Coleridge). AB had initially written "silent" (matching Coleridge's text), but then struck it out and wrote "unknown."

3. Geoffrey Chaucer, "The Wife of Bath's Tale" (from *The Canterbury Tales*), l. 868.

4. Charles M. Schwab (1862–1939), American industrialist and president of the Carnegie Steel Company (later U.S. Steel) from 1897 to 1903. He then founded the Bethlehem Steel Company, which became U.S. Steel's chief rival.

5. AB may be referring to Isaac Barrow's definition of poetry as "ingenious nonsense" (*Sermons*, 1678).

6. Massanielo is the byname of Tommaso Aniello (1620–1647), leader of a popular insurrection in Naples against Spanish rule and oppression by the nobles. Jack Cade is the arrogant leader of the rebellious peasants in Shakespeare's *Henry VI, Part 2*. Eugene Victor Debs (1855–1926) was a labor organizer and Socialist Party candidate for U.S. president five times between 1900 and 1920.

7. AB refers to GS's "To Ambrose Bierce" (written August 1901), later used as the dedicatory poem in *The Testimony of the Suns and Other Poems*.

8. GS, "Dedication: To Ambrose Bierce": "I tremble with the splendid weight" (l. 5) of the laurels AB has figuratively placed on GS's brow.

9. Included in Goethe's *Faust: Part One* (1808).

10. AB had mixed feelings about Jack London (1876–1916), largely because of the latter's entrenched Socialism. But cf. letters 93 and 96.

11. Herman Whitaker was a friend of GS's and a prominent member of the Ruskin Club, an informal Socialist group in Oakland.

12. Edward H. Clough, a California journalist and friend of AB since the 1890s. He had written a favorable review of *Tales of Soldiers and Civilians* for the *Oakland Times*.

13. From AB's poem "With a Book" (*CW* 5.170).

[82] To Robert H. Davis[1] [ALS, NYPL]

The Olympia,
Washington, D.C.
[Summer 1902?]

My dear Davis,

I hope there's nothing wrong with the *other* "Little Johnny" stuff; I sent you three batches of it last week.

By the way, do you know any fool publisher up there to whom you would care to suggest making a book of "Little Johnny" stuff? It is the only stuff I ever wrote which I think would sell *well* in covers. I've been writing it in London, San Francisco and New York for more than thirty years, and all editors grab at it; but I've not had any annoyance from the eager importunities of publishers.[2] Block wrote me a long time ago that I would probably get an offer from Stokes, "after the holidays."[3] Stokes has since rejected two books of mine, but the offer for *that* one has not come.

Don't take any trouble in the matter, but if you happen to know personally any publisher that you'd like to do an ill turn to you might mention the matter to him. Do you?

Sincerely yours,
Ambrose Bierce.

1. Robert H. Davis (1869–1942), longtime editor of *Munsey's* and other magazines in Frank A. Munsey's publishing empire.
2. AB had begun writing the Little Johnny sketches—about an enthusiastic young writer with a serious problem in spelling—for *Fun* in 1874, and continued to publish them in nearly every subsequent magazine and newspaper for which he worked. They typically appeared under the byline of "Little Johnny," and under AB's name only in error (sometimes AB is referred to as Little Johnny's advocate or benefactor). The last of them appeared in *Cosmopolitan* in May 1909.
3. Rudolph Block (1870–1940), journalist and short-story writer who also wrote under the pseudonym Bruno Lessing.

[83] To Herman Scheffauer [BL (transcript)]

July 2, 1902.

The Olympia,
Washington, D.C.

Dear Scheff,

I'm sending you the book-that-is-never-to-be, by express, having just got it back from Stokes.[1] Your men will not have it—nobody will have it—of that I'm convinced. It is something new in literature, and in the eyes of publishers whatever is new is "no good". At least it is doubtful; and quite naturally they prefer to be on the safe side of a doubtful situation.

You'll find—if you care to read it—that it is a book of all-sorts, unclassified and not to be classified. You'll object to much that is in it, as trivial and worse. True, but the objections have all been duly considered and overruled.

I authorize you to make such terms with the publishers as you can, short of my surrender of the copyright. You will naturally be consulted as to the appearance of the book—the binding, etc. I know your taste can be relied on. Don't persist upon more than ten per cent. of the retail price; that is the customary "royalty"; and I don't care if I don't get a cent.

If the publishers are afraid of libel suits and the like, why, these are all outlawed by lapse of time. Moreover I will be liable (and am financially responsible) for all that.
  Yours in some haste,
  Ambrose Bierce.

1. *SC*, a collection of poetry that was issued in 1903 by an obscure San Francisco publisher, W. E. Wood, by arrangement with Scheffauer and GS.

[84] To George Sterling [ALS, NYPL]
         The Olympia,
          Washington, D.C.
My dear Sterling,
  About sending that poem to the Atlantic. You say that rejections might pain you—"wound" you is what you say. That is almost funny in one so indifferent to fame as you seem to be, and to the opinions of those unable to appreciate great work. If rejection wounded, all writers would bleed at every pore. Its length would be a valid reason for rejection, with most magazines, but if you think the first part could stand alone why not send that? Nevertheless, not my will but thine be done.[1] Of course I shall be glad to go over your entire body of work again and make suggestions if any occur to me. It will be no trouble—I could not be more profitably employed than in critically reading you, nor more agreeably.

As to the relative excellence of your star poem—for which I have not been able to find a title. I had not thought to make a comparison between it and the poems you mention, and the attempt now seems to give me no light. As to *your* superiority to the *authors* of those poems—your superiority as a poet—there is no question of that. You can beat them in a canter.[2]

Of course your star poem has one defect—if it is a defect—that limits the circle of understanding and admiring readers—its lack of "*human* interest." We human insects, as a rule, care for nothing but ourselves, and think that is best which most closely touches such emotions and sentiments as grow out of our relations, the one with another. I don't share the preference, and a few others do not, believing that there are things more interesting than men and women. The Heavens, for example. But who knows, or cares anything about them—even knows the name of a single constellation? Hardly any one but the professional astronomers—and there are not enough of them to buy your books and give you fame. I should be sorry not to have that poem published—sorry if you did not write more of the kind. But while it may impress and dazzle "the many" it will not win them. They want you to finger their heart-strings and pull the cord that works their arms and legs. So you must finger and pull—too.

[. . .]

Send me the typewritten book when you have it complete.

Sincerely yours,

Ambrose Bierce.

July 10, 1902.

1. Luke 22:42: "Father, if thou be willing, remove this cup from me: nevertheless not my will, but thine, be done."
2. GS (letter to AB, 28 June 1902; ALS, NYPL) had asked AB to tell him "if my poems can compare with [W. E.] Henley's 'Song of the Sword', Kipling's 'Recessional' or 'Last Chanty', and [William Vaughn] Moody's 'Ode in Time of Hesitation'. These men are my contemporaries, and I'd like to know if I nick shoulders with them."

[85] To Herman Scheffauer [BL (transcript)]

Aug. 2, 1902.   The Olympia,
                                                                                                    Washington, D.C.

My dear Scheff,

I am glad to learn that Robertson[1] encourages you to think that he will bring out your poems, for there is a chance in a thousand that he will. By the way, why did you not send them for consideration of the Neale Publishing Company, of this city?[2] I'm sure I suggested it. It is not a large and famous concern, but any house here is better than any there. But to whomsoever you submit them you will probably find all manner of objections urged against them. I should not be surprised if Robertson discovered an insuperable objection to the fact that they will not make a big, fat book.

Thank you for your Gettysburg poem,[3] and for the other fellow's. Fancy putting Gen. Sickles[4] on the committee of award simply because he *fought* at Gettysburg and would know the *facts!* And fancy the "successful competitor" deliberately stealing [from] a popular song his repetend: "as the sun went down"! If you *couldn't* write a better poem than that I should cut your acquaintance. (I enclose some strolling comments on the incident.) It serves you right, though, to lose; you should not play the game of literature for prizes; it is unworthy of you to do so, as it is of Doyle.

[...]
Now I wish I might have been with you on your Yosemite trip and your bicycle whirl down-coast. I still wheel, getting up commonly at 4:30 a.m. to do so, for the rest of the day is too warm here. And the world in the early morning is another and better world, as I hope you know. And one has it all to oneself, which is much. Sometimes I take a girl with me, sometimes go alone; get great physical, mental and moral profit out of it. (I'm not so sure about the "moral", but it always goes with the other words, you know.)

By all means write up your Yosemite tour—I want to read it. Your photographs alone would make a magazine editor grab at it.

I read Aunty Jo's account of the forest fire with pleasure and amusement—they are not always the same feeling.[5] I shall never forget the poor, wild half-clad creature who came to my cottage that morning and refused to stay because she must "warn the neighbors", although the flames, tree-high, were visible and audible to all. Jo. is a peach, all the same.

[...]

May I ask you not to talk of my private business? I mean the book which you are so kindly, and vainly, attempting to place. It is very distasteful to me to have foolish women and gossiping girls apprised of my affairs and asking me about them. I supposed that book matter was confidential. Of course it is mere thoughtlessness on your part to discuss it with others, but please don't—I'd rather the book were never submitted to anybody. And, anyhow, nothing will come of it.

By the way, I wonder why it never occurs to a publisher to employ an experienced newspaper editor to tell him what the public wants. One would think that would be the very man he'd look for.

    Sincerely yours,
    A. B.

1. A[lexander] M[itchell] Robertson (1855–1934), San Francisco bookseller; publisher of most of GS's poetry volumes and of Scheffauer's *Of Both Worlds* (1903).
2. The Neale Publishing Co. (Washington, D.C.) was founded by Walter Neale (1873–1933), who published *CW* and other books by AB. We first hear of Neale in 1902, when he wished to reprint *The Monk and the Hangman's Daughter* (the reprint did not occur until 1907). In 1903 Neale reprinted *Can Such Things Be?*
3. "Pickett's Charge," *Of Both Worlds*, 40–43.
4. General Daniel Edgar Sickles (1819–1914) executed a controversial maneuver during the Battle of Gettysburg on 2 July 1863, resulting in the effective end of his military career. He was subsequently U.S. minister to Spain (1869–73) and U.S. representative from New York (1893–95).
5. Josephine Clifford McCrackin (1838–1920) traveled from Kansas to New Mexico in a covered wagon with her husband, and later came to California, where she assisted Bret Harte in founding the *Overland Monthly*. See her story collections, *Overland Tales* (1877), *Another Juanita and Other Stories*

(1893), and *The Woman Who Lost Him* (1913), for which AB wrote an introduction. In 1899 her ranch burned to the ground, despite efforts by AB and Scheffauer to save it.

[86] To Herman Scheffauer [BL (transcript)]

The Olympia,
Washington, D.C.
[September 1902?]

My dear Scheff,

First about "Shapes of Clay". I should have no difficulty in getting all my books published if I would let the publishers edit them. They all propose, and insist upon, alterations and omissions. Yet the books seem right enough when published as I want them.

Of course I had duly considered all the matters mentioned in your letter—knowing what objections would be made. They were made by all my friends in the case of "Black Beetles in Amber", which all said would fail, for this reason and for that. It didn't fail, but made money, despite the fact that its only possible market was the Pacific Coast, for its matter was strictly limited to Pacific Coast topics and persons.

It is hopeless to discuss these things with publishers, but I will with you, for your friendly service entitles you to consideration.

As to the "*personal* satires". In satirizing real persons I follow the example of *all* satirists who succeed. It does not at all matter how obscure, or how anything-else, the persons satirised may be; the merit is *in the satire*. Do you suppose that the merit of Heine's, of Pope's, or Byron's attacks on *persons*—has any relation to the personality or des. . . .[1] of the objects of it. The merit is *intrinsic*. Nobody cares who was hit—nobody reads, for example, the explanatory notes to "The Dunciad" or the "English Bards and Scotch Reviewers", which fool publishers think it necessary to insert. These things of mine would have the same literary value (and I'm bound to assume that they have *some*) if they bore any other names than the ones they do bear. Would it add anything to the interest of a personal satire to entitle it "Atticus" instead of "Arthur McEwen"?[2] I'm not running a guessing game: I prefer human names as Byron did. But the publisher will say I am not a Byron. Good; he thereby discloses the *real* nature of his objection, which is not the *personal* character of the work, but its *inferiority*. Why not say so? I am a little surprised that you, with knowledge and literary taste, should call the publisher's objections on *this* score "quite right".

The interest of none of these pieces has "passed away with the occasion that brought them forth"—if they ever had any they have it now, for I have omitted a thousand whose only interest *was* of that sort. You seem not to have duly considered the difference between the *intrinsic* (permanent and literary) interest and the *extrinsic*—

arising from circumstances and occasions. If one is a good, or great writer it does not matter of whom or what he writes. Again to compare my methods with those of my masters (whom I study as to method while preserving my own style) do you not see that if publishers subjected Byron's, Pope's or Heine's satirical verses to the same criticism that you would commend we should have no new editions of these works?

I cannot consent to publication of my *poetry* apart from my wit. I am not a poet; the poetry is incidental. I am a satirist and, if anything, a wit. It is not that my poetical work is debased by personal satire, but that my satire is sometimes enriched with poetry. As to Mr. Robertson's notion that "the American public has never properly understood satire, nor would yours (mine), however brilliant," how do you explain the success of "Black Beetles in Amber", which has *nothing* but satire? How do you explain—or how would he explain, that I have all my life made a very decent living in America (*and* England) as a professed satirist—known as nothing else? What besides wit and satire was in my "Prattle" or my "Passing Show" all those long years? The only reason that I am not writing that same stuff, now at the desire of Mr. Hearst and his editors, is that I don't submit to the censorship of *one* editor, whom, nevertheless, he finds too valuable in other directions to dispense with. Hundreds of letters are still received, asking for the rehabilitation of the "Department", and I alone am obdurate.

As to classification of my stuff under several heads—that, too, has long been considered and the notion rejected. A thing does not need to be labeled "Wit", "Humor", "Satire" or "Poetry" in order to be known for what it is. Moreover, it may be a little of two, or three, or all, these things—in my work it is quite likely to be.

As to publishing only the "poetry", there is less understanding of that in the American public than of "satire"—why does a publisher wish to address a book to only *one class of readers* (and that the smallest class) instead of to the whole public that reads *any* kind of verse? I, at least, want a larger public than "American lovers of poetry". To publish a book of "poetry" is like publishing a newspaper with only one kind of news—church news for example. Do such succeed? Mr. Hearst very cleverly explained once that he was compelled to make a large newspaper because he had so small a public: he had to address *all* tastes.

Mr. Robertson may think that the trade demands a "thin" volume of poetry. I know something, naturally, about what the public wants: I have been supplying it longer than he has. The reason that volumes of poetry (commonly published at the expense of the authors) are "thin" is because the brains that produce them are "thin", or in such a hurry for publication that they cannot wait until they have produced enough. I should be ashamed (as an old writer) to put out a "thin" volume of poetry.

But it will amuse you to know that "Shapes of Clay" is thick because three publishing houses objected to its thinness—among them Harpers. It was then two thirds the length that it is now.

There is not enough "poetry" in this book for a separate volume, and what there is is not good enough; and I would not publish it separate from the humorous and satirical verse if there were enough and it were good enough.

But we now come to common ground on which we can stand: If the book's size is the only insuperable objection I will cut it down to the desired magnitude. But I shall not alter its character, for the reasons given. I shall not throw out any *kind* of stuff, but only any desired—or rather undesired—quantity. I shall leave out some of the poetry, some of the satire, some of the humor, for another book just like it. If that doesn't suit please send it back.

You are in error as to the character of the book that I showed you. All of that is in this was in that and the character of its contents has not been altered by additions. I never intended publishing a book of pure poetry, and never shall. To the name of the poet I do not aspire; to that of a satirist I do. I have that, but if not permitted to strengthen and confirm it by publication of my best stuff in covers *in my own way* the stuff will lie unpublished while I live. Meantime, I shall be making a pretty good living by selling to the "American public" what the American public is thought (by publishers, not by editors) "not to understand".

This is an insufferably long letter *all* about my own affairs; I shall have to postpone the discussion of yours. Thank you, however, for the verses.

  Sincerely yours,
    Ambrose Bierce.

Of course the book will require an index.[3]

1. The transcriber of this letter evidently could not read AB's handwriting here.
2. Arthur McEwen (1851–1907), a well-known San Francisco journalist with whom AB had tangled frequently in the 1890s. See the squib, "Arthur McEwen" (1895; *CW* 4.87).
3. A table of contents.

[87] To Herman Scheffauer [BL (transcript)]

            1321 Yale St., N.W.,
             Washington, D.C.

Dear Scheff,

  Whatever Robertson may be pleased to do about *my* book, I'm glad that he will publish yours—more glad than his publishing mine could make me. But why "early next year"? That is a long time to wait.

I'm sending back some verses of yours with a few marks on them. The verses are good; you are getting too strong for me to spank you.

By the way, about Robertson. He seems to be your only reliance. Is he the only publisher in that neck of woods? I had it in mind in sending my stuff that it was going to Elder and Shepard.[1] Did I get that notion from my inner consciousness, or did you intend at first to deal with them? And have you tried them? Perhaps *they* would be willing to take the stuff as it is.

Do not fail to send me the story that has been taken by the unnamed magazine. [...]

I do not see any way to help you in the matter of the Bohemian Club. It is more than 20 years that I resigned, and I did not visit it it once in two years afterward. Indeed, I don't think much of the club as it is, and cannot advise you to join it. It has ruined more young men than I can count. You are, I know, of sterner stuff than most of them, but even to you membership in that "boozing ken"[2] would mean a sinful waste of time. True, *I* belong to a club here (and have just been unanimously elected a Director).[3] But I am old and my habits are fixed, and I have no life work before me,—no aim, for I have fired. Really, I shall hear of your joining that club with serious misgivings. But that is not the reason that I do not help you in the matter. I don't know how I could. I'm without influence there, and the Greer Harrisons (they are mostly Greer Harrisons there) would whack any man that I should back.[4]

Doyle Sahib has tired of writing to me, I guess, but it is good to know that he has a foothold in England. He ought to be famous there and here. I fear he feels his obscurity as an author.

So, you spoke of my affairs "only" to two women. Well, you are an innocent, truly, not to know that to speak of a thing to even one woman is to tell it to the world. I must say, though, in justice to the ladies mentioned, that my allusion to "brainless girls" had no reference to them, nor either of them. It's all right, anyhow, and no harm done.

I have finished the "Conversations" and was pleased to find in the latter part of the book that Goethe had approved them. So they may be held to be a fair expression of his views, I suppose, if Eckermann did not alter them afterward, which there is no reason to believe. But isn't it awful to think of Goethe's view of Hugo and his "Notre Dame de Paris"? It is hard to believe that such a criticism by the greatest of Germans on the greatest of men is genuine.[5]

          Sincerely yours,
              Ambrose Bierce.

Oct. 5, 1902.

1. Paul Elder (1872–1948) was a renowned specialty publisher in San Francisco. Morgan Shepard (1865–1947) was his partner until 1903. Although Elder did not publish SC, in 1907 he did issue a slim volume of two AB stories, *A Son of the Gods and A Horseman in the Sky*, with an introduction by W. C. Morrow.

2. From "A Piratical Ballad" (1891; l. 9), a song by Henry Waller (music) and Young E. Allison

(words), based on the quatrain "Fifteen men on a dead man's chest . . ." from Robert Louis Stevenson's *Treasure Island* (1883).

3. The Army and Navy Club.

4. William Greer Harrison (1835–1916) was another San Francisco journalist, author of *The Outdoor Life of California* (1905?) and *Making a Man: A Manual of Athletics* (1915?), with whom AB quarreled in the 1890s. See "Prattle," *SF* (13 October 1895): 6, to which Harrison responded with an article, "The Degeneracy of Ambrose Bierce," *San Francisco Call* (20 October 1895).

5. In a conversation with Eckermann late in life (27 June 1831), Goethe had excoriated Victor Hugo's *Notre-Dame de Paris*, calling it "the most horrible book ever written." AB had praised Hugo lavishly in "Prattle," *Wasp* no. 461 (30 May 1885): 5.

[88] To Herman Scheffauer [BL (transcript)]

1321 Yale St.,
Washington, D.C.

My dear Scheff,

As to the book matter, I think it hardly worth while to go on. There is, apparently no hope of an agreement, and the only advantage of continuing the negotio is that it will add an amusing chapter to my memoirs.

I confess that the scheme of making two books of the stuff in covers designed by you is captivating; I could wish for nothing better, and the same free hand that I would give you in that I must be allowed in the text. If not allowed it I will not play. I will tell you why, though I thought I had made myself pretty clear already.

First, as to titles. "Shapes of Clay" will have to stand for the title of one. You err in thinking it a "limited" title, applicable to only a part of the persons mentioned in the books. It is the "broadest" title that could be got, for it means all the human race. Is not every one familiar with the notion that we are all made of earth? Is the Book of Genesis not pretty well known? Turn to stanzas LXXXII et seq. of the Rubiat (or Rubaiyat if you prefer) and learn that that is what Omar meant by the phrase.[1]

As to such titles, or sub-titles as "Poesy and Humor" and "Wit and Satire", they will hardly do. I cannot consent publicly to declare myself a poet, a wit, a humorist, or a satirist. When I am dead publishers may call me what they will if they think it necessary to call me anything. A descriptive title handicaps any book—I mean any *literary* book. The ideal title is one that arouses curiosity, but sends the reader to the book for its gratification.

If Mr. Robertson wants to observe the meaningless traditions of his craft and have everything classified I'll concede the point and do it, though it will entail a long delay; but those words are barred. I'll find others, *not* descriptive. But I fancy the necessity will not arise, for I cannot accept his proposed elisions of the text.

I agreed, as a matter of courtesy, to omit names of his *personal friends;* farther than that I cannot go. Fancy, for example, omitting that of Stanley, the explorer,[2] because he is an honorary member of the Bohemian club! Fancy, that is to say, me squaring my literary judgment with the tastes of that aggregation of shop clerks, insurance steerers and literary pretenders—with a handful of good fellows to save it from the fate of Sodom and the other place! If a more grotesque proposal was ever made it is not on record.

Your notion that it is customary to indicate persons by initials *in satire* is erroneous. It was once customary to conceal the identity of the victim who happened to be powerful enough to inspire fear in the satirist. I don't know of any one so powerful as to inspire fear in me; if I did I would not let him alone. Certainly I would not advertise my cowardice. My judgment of public men may be right or wrong; it goes.

A little while ago one objection urged was the *obscurity* of my "victims"; it seems now that it is partly because of their eminence. Maybe in some instances it is because they are dead. As to that I refer to the preface of the book. These things were written of men who were alive and were published years before their death. They did not "kick"—they did not dare to, for they are all rascals. The stuff is all safe now under the statute of limitations.

I will mention a few in the list of proposed exempts:

Arthur McEwen, an anarchist who is to-day one of the most mischievous men in the country, and very famous here in the east. As I don't recollect the verses on him and haven't a copy I'll deny myself the benefit of doubt. He may be omitted to suffer later.[3]

Allan Forman,[4] a blackmailing writer who in one column told 26 lies about [me] in defence of a friend of his own kidney. That's why I have ever since called him "Allan Forman, 26"—a name which has "stuck." He afterwards threw over his friend and wrote to a friend of mine offering to apologise *if assured of pardon*. As that is not the way to apologise, and as there was no promise to become a truthful man, he did not get the assurance.

Greer Harrison.[5] You say he is a friend of Mr. Robertson. Sorry for Mr. Robertson, but will omit him.

Morehouse,[6] a boodling State Senator, legitimate object of ridicule.

Stoneman,[7] an incompetent Governor,   "   "   "   "

Stanley, vide supra.

Anderson,[8] an idiot Theosophist. If a friend of Mr. Robertson he can have a fictitious name.

Newman,[9] a Methodist parson and professional rich man's parasite. Leland Stanford gave him ten thousand dollars to come out to California and preach a sermon on Stanford's deceased adopted son. He earned his money by comparing the boy, all through the sermon, with Jesus Christ, greatly to the disadvantage of the latter.

Mike de Young[10] I need not describe. His name may be omitted if Mr. Robertson admires or fears it. I've taken all the "rise" out of him that I care to.

Stephen Dorsey,[11] a notorious politician indicted for complicity in the famous "Star route" frauds and saved from the penitentiary which swallowed his pals by the personal friendship of President Grant. Politically dead, but still stinks.

Stephen J. Field,[12] the most corrupt man that ever disgraced the U.S. Supreme Court. All conceded his ability, nor doubted his rascality.

Jay Gould.[13] Concerning the skit on him you say: "Can see no point in this." Dear old Scheff, you know that the sense of humor is not your strongest equipment. That's why you are a poet: if you saw the humorous sides of things it would be bad for poetry, for even poetry has its humorous sides. If it is not witty to represent the mourners at a funeral weeping, not because they think the man dead, but because they think him alive, I have lived in vain. But I find that I used the same notion in "Black Beetles", in an epitaph on General Barnes.[14] Glad you mentioned it—let Jay Gould aside.

Ingalls,[15] a shining mark in his day and something of a satirist himself. I only gave him a dose of his own medicine, he liked it. Don't recollect what I wrote of him, but it will have to stand.

Fairchild,[16] noted politician famous for his intemperate and blackguardly protest against President Cleveland's proposal to restore to the South its captured flags. There have been other Fairchilds, equally undeserving—Lee of that ilk, for horrible example.

"Puck".[17] That may stand if you like. I cut it out because it applied only to the "Puck" of the time when it was written. The "Puck" of to-day ought not, I suppose, to bear the sins of its predecessor. By affixing a date to the skit it would, I suppose, be all right.

Now, it ought to occur to Mr. Robertson that if these things are witty they will not hurt the book, and they *must* be just or some of the persons aggrieved would have haled me into court and kept me in jail a great part of the nearly thirty years that I was engaged in writing and publishing them. Only once was that attempted, and that attempt failed.[18] The fellows hated me badly enough, and gave me reasons a-plenty to know it; but they did not dare to prosecute me, for they knew that I did not libel wantonly nor to gratify a personal grudge.

I thought I had sufficiently expounded my satirical "method" in a former letter—to lash, not the sin, but the sinner. How can I do that without naming him? If he is an illustrious sinner, why, that is the sort of game that satire flies at. If he is an obscure one, I flatter myself that he will be obscure no longer when I have done with him. Anyhow publication in my lifetime is not so sweet a dream that I am willing to throw over every one of my lifelong principles, nor *any* of them, in order to make it come true. I expect soon to publish all my books myself. (There will be a few that you do not know about.) So I must beg you to close the incident Robertson if there is further insistence on impossible conditions. You are working for a result that the situation does not promise. It is awfully good of you, and my sense of that is all that has induced me to discuss the matter of alterations in my original design at all. Neither you nor Mr. Robertson, not the two of you together are likely to make a suggestion regarding the matter in that book that I have not considered many times. I was not born yesterday, as the slang hath it, and I have not pursued my art without some knowledge of what I am about. In the words of Heine, I know who I am.

As to "terms" of publication, I am less particular. Those that you mention are good enough.

I think I have covered all the points in your letter. Please convey my decision on them to Mr. Robertson as nicely as possible, for I do not doubt that he is the good fellow that you say he is. But the craft of authorship has not fallen to quite so low an estate as to make the author a mere registrar of the views of the publisher in matters not really affecting him, or affecting him only remotely.

I'll have to write you another letter, soon, on pleasanter themes; this has grown to an unconscionable length.

  Ever and most sincerely yours,
   Ambrose Bierce.
October 23, 1902.

1. The phrase "shapes of clay" appears in stanza 82 of *The Rubáiyát of Omar Khayyam*, in reference to the human race.
2. Sir Henry Morton Stanley (original name John Rowlands; 1841–1904), British-American explorer of central Africa, famous for his rescue of the Scottish missionary and explorer David Livingstone and for his discoveries in and development of the Congo region. He was knighted in 1899. See "Stanley" (*SC* 184–85; *CW* 4.204–5).
3. *SC* contains the poem "Arthur McEwen" (1895).
4. Allan Forman, editor of the *Maquereau*, the New York organ of the Pacific Coast Women's Press Association. See "Diagnosis" (*SC* 362; *CW* 4.319).
5. See letter 87, n.4. *CW* 5 contains two poems about Harrison; "A Playwright" (1895) did not appear in the first edition of *Black Beetles in Amber* (1892), and was probably the poem omitted from *SC*.
6. There is no poem about H. V. Morehouse, a California state senator, in *SC*, but he is the subject of "Genesis" (*Black Beetles in Amber* 135; *CW* 5.49).
7. General George Stoneman (1822–1894) served as governor of California (1883–87). AB had criticized him for what he believed to be undue leniency toward criminals. See "A Merciful Governor" (1885; *CW* 5). SC contains no poems about Stoneman. Those in *CW* 5 had appeared previously in *Black Beetles in Amber*.
8. There is no poem about Anderson in *SC*, although AB's "Laus Lucis" (*CW* 4) is about Theosophists. The poem "Theosophistry" (1897; *CW* 5; as "A Fool" in *Black Beetles in Amber*) mentions Anderson by name.
9. John Philip Newman (1826–1899), Methodist bishop, chaplain of the U.S. Senate (1872–73), and resident bishop of California (1896–99). See "To a Professional Eulogist" (*SC* 271; *CW* 4.268–69).
10. Meichel Henry De Young (1849–1925), founder and editor of the *San Francisco Chronicle*. AB repeatedly attacked him in both his columns and his verse. There is no poem about De Young in *SC*.

11. Stephen Dorsey (1842–1916) was a Civil War veteran who, while serving as U.S. senator from Arkansas (1873–76), defrauded the state of more than a million dollars on behalf of railroad interests. In 1881 he stood trial for a similar defrauding of the federal government in the Star Route Scandal and eventually pleaded guilty. See AB's "Stephen Dorsey" under "Some Ante-Mortem Epitaphs" (*SC* 344; *CW* 4.348–49).

12. Stephen J. Field (1816–1899) came to California during the gold rush of 1849 and subsequently became a member of the California Supreme Court (1858–63). He was then appointed an associate justice of the U.S. Supreme Court (1863–97). Field championed individual and corporate liberty, but a ruling in 1879 favorable to the Union Pacific Railroad probably ensured AB's hostility to him. See "Stephen J. Field" (later "Mr. Justice Field") under "Some Ante-Mortem Epitaphs" (*SC* 344; *CW* 4.349).

13. Jay Gould (1836–1892), American financier whose shady tactics involving the Erie Railroad led to the stock market crash of 1869. He later obtained control of most of the railroads in the Southwest. There is no poem about him in *SC*, but AB wrote a fable about him; see "Fables and Anecdotes," *SF* (24 October 1891); rpt. *The Collected Fables of Ambrose Bierce*, 241 (Fable 648).

14. General W. H. L. Barnes was a prominent attorney and Republican politician in San Francisco. See the untitled poem "This grave holds Barnes in all his glory—" (*Black Beetles in Amber* 277; *CW* 5.378).

15. John James Ingalls (1833–1900), U.S. senator from Kansas (1873–91) who earned AB's wrath by relentlessly advocating greater and greater pensions for the former Union soldiers who made up the Grand Army of the Republic. See AB's "Ingalls on Pensions," *SF* (11 March 1888): 4. See also "A Kit" (*CW* 4.351).

16. Lucius Fairchild (1831–1896), Union soldier and governor of Wisconsin (1866–72) who, as National Commander of the Grand Army of the Republic (1886–87), delivered a speech in Harlem, N.Y., in June 1887 denouncing President Grover Cleveland's order for the return of the Confederate battle flags. AB attacked Fairchild on this point in "The Confederate Flags" (*SC* 385–87; *CW* 4.335–37). Lee Fairchild was a poet and journalist in Seattle whom AB repeatedly ridiculed in his columns of the early 1890s.

17. AB refers to H[enry] C[uyler] Bunner (1855–1896), a poet, fiction writer, and playwright, who was a prolific contributor to the New York humor magazine *Puck*. The verses in question appear to be those published in "Prattle," *SF* (6 September 1896): 6 ("Giant with pencil, but with pen, / Pigmy..."); they did not appear in *SC*.

18. AB refers to the failed attempt of a theater owner, George T. Russell, to sue AB and the *San Francisco News Letter* for libel in 1871–72. See *A Sole Survivor* 101–04.

[89] To Herman Scheffauer [BL (transcript)]

Washington, Feb. 5, 1903.

Dear Scheff,

[...]

About *my* book. Of course we should prefer that it be published by Elder & Shepard, but if they will not have it, or if they insist on editing it, or otherwise cause you trouble, I would not bother with them. You had had a lot of trouble in the matter already and I'm getting weary of it myself. As to your Mr. Woods, I don't know what to say.[1] He, no doubt, is all right, but if he is to use the money of any friend of mine it will be necessary for me to know who the friend is. I could not consent to put myself under an obligation of that kind blindly. I don't think you have many friends from whom you would care to accept assistance of a pecuniary sort in the dark. I should have to know.

[. . .]

So my remaining here is a riddle to you. It is very simple. I like Washington and Washington life. I am doing more work than you see, for more papers than you know about, though I really am not overworked. As to being in a "whirl", I live rather quietly—the life of an elderly and tolerably respectable clubman; loaf about the Capitol a little (a certain chair in the House restaurant is known as "Bierce's seat in Congress") have a little circle of friends of both sexes, to which I hope to add you some day, and busy myself with the small affairs that I care about. So I await the end, with absolute indifference as to when it shall come.

Now is't not a sensible program for the latter end of a life of—well, a life of any kind? Sure.

You know I was ever given to trifling, even in my work. Why not? Nothing (at sixty) is worth serious consideration, as may you live long enough to learn.

Expect the poems in a few days.

Sincerely yours,
Ambrose Bierce.

1. W. E. Wood, a San Francisco businessman who published *SC* (1903).

[90] To George Sterling [TLS, NYPL]

1321 Yale St.,
Washington, D.C.

My dear Sterling,

You are a brick. You shall do as you will. My chief reluctance is that if it become known, or *when* it becomes known, there may ensue a suspicion of my honesty in praising you and *your* book; for critics and readers are not likely to look into the matter of dates. For your sake I should be sorry to have it thought that my commendation was only a log-rolling incident; for myself, I should care nothing about it. This eel is accustomed to skinning.

It is not the least pleasing of my reflections that my friends have always liked my work—or me—well enough to want to publish my books at their own expense. Everything that I have written could go to the public that way if I would consent. In the two instances in which I did consent they got their money back all right,[1] and I do not doubt that it will be so in this; for if I did not think there was at least a little profit in a book of mine I should not offer it to a publisher. "Shapes of Clay" *ought* to be published in California, and it would have been long ago if I had not been so lazy and so indisposed to dicker with publishers. Properly advertised—which no book of mine ever has been—it should sell there if nowhere else. Why, then, do *I* not put up the money? Well, for one reason, I've none to put up. Do you care for the other reasons?

But I must make this a condition. If there is a loss *I* am to bear it. To that end I shall expect an exact accounting from your Mr. Wood, and the percentage that Scheff purposes having him pay to me is to go to you. The copyright is to be mine, but nothing else until you are entirely recouped. But all this I will arrange with Scheff, who, I take it, is to attend to the business end of the matter, with, of course, your assent to the arrangements that he makes.

I shall write Scheff to-day to go ahead and make his contract with Mr. Wood on these lines. Scheff appears not to know who the "angel" in the case is, and he need not, unless, or until, you want him to.

[...]

Pardon the typewriter; I wanted a copy of this letter.
      Sincerely yours,
      Ambrose Bierce.
March 1, 1903.

1. AB apparently refers to the hoax *The Dance of Death* (1877), published by William Herman Rulofson, and *Tales of Soldiers and Civilians* (1891), published by E. L. G. Steele.

[91] To Herman Scheffauer [BL (transcript)]
      1321 Yale St.,
      Washington, D.C.,
      March 27, 1903.

Dear Scheff,

The books came to-day and I'm greatly obliged to you. I had vainly tried to get them through dealers. I enclose money order in payment.

I note what you say about Wood's intentions regarding "Shapes of Clay". By the way, Professor Syle, whom I think you know, has kindly offered to write an introduction, which I think will be of value to the book.[1] He is here now, but is going to Los Angeles, where I suppose Wood can send him advance sheets to assist. He has read most of it in an imperfect copy which I have, but will need the entire work before him.

I should have written you before, but have been in New York, returning only Wednesday. In that city of the giants one cannot write letters. I hate the place—that is, I should hate to live there—but I admire and wonder. Really it is amazing; everything on so colossal a scale. You must not fail to pass a week or two in New York on your way— here. The architecture may not please you; it doesn't please me. It only stuns me. In calling it a city of giants I unintentionally expressed the feeling it gives me. But where are the giants? Alas! it is infested by pigmies, or at least the giants remaining are seen only away up in the sky rearing new structures for their masters, the pigmies. They look like ants, these titans up there, but of course one knows they are a hundred feet in stature. Even so I think the gods must come down from Olympus to take a hand in the work, especially in that of bridge-building. O yes, you must see New York, preferably under my guidance.[2]

Thank you for your criticism of the Guiteau skit, it doesn't explain itself. "Poor Guiteau" means that he was judicially murdered, for he was as crazy as a wet cat, which everybody knew, and none more clearly than those who thirsted for his blood—that is to say, the entire country, virtually. The "dust" is that of his flesh; his skeleton is actually a museum. *This* "Fairchild" was a statesman of the period, famous for his rancour, but now forgotten.[3]

As to irregularity in versification, which you mention in a former letter. It is true that Milton is so in many of his minor poems, though not in his epics, but I think you err in saying that Shakspeare is. In the plays, of course, for those that are not in blank verse proper, but what is known as *dramatic* blank, in which almost anything goes. In all his other works he is "regular" as Doyle-Sahib could wish.

I think you err, too, when you exclude quantity from our English prosody. Mainly it is based on accent, as you say, but he has much to learn of the power and sweetness of our language who ignores the effect of long and short voweling. Take, for example, Tennyson's song in "The Princess", beginning,

"The splendour falls on castle walls."[4]

Observe the difference between the first stanza and the second: the first with its long open vowels producing a wonderfully sonorous effect; the second having mostly short ones compelling you to read it a whole octave higher, as befits the sense. I could multiply examples. Here's another—I don't remember where I got the lines; and probably they are incorrectly quoted:

"The lonely tarn that sleeps upon the mountain."[5]

"The busy rivulet that threads the valley."[6]

They have the same metrical construction, the same length, the same accents (stresses) in the same places. But how different they are in all else! The one has a lordly dignity;

the other none at all—just liveliness. So you see that in English verse quantity is not "a negligible quantity". You cannot do better than study it with an attentive ear and an open mind.

As to "Heaven", "fire", and so forth, being monosyllables.[7] If you cannot so pronounce them do not bother about them, but when you "defy" me to, why, I can and do. And in certain circumstances *you* can.

The fire is out and Heaven is far.[8]

Is not that an eight syllable line all right enough? Would you make it a ten? Of course it can be done.

But even when followed by consonants, or not followed at all, such words are easily, with a little practice, pronounced as monosyllables, though perhaps it is not worth while.

It would be pleasing to me, surely, to have our books (and Sterling's too) come out together. I mean (unless there is objection, as presiding officers say) to dedicate mine to you and Sterling, thereby bringing into conjunction two names dear to me, whose owners I hope will learn to be friends.[9]

But this is grown into a pretty long letter. God be with you.
Ambrose Bierce.

1. Louis DuPont Syle (1857–?), a professor at the University of California and author of *Essays in Dramatic Criticism* (1898). SC had no introduction by Syle, but a preface by AB.

2. Shortly after writing this letter, AB embodied his impressions of New York in much the same terms in "A Letter from a Btrugumian" (*New York American*, 30 April 1903), later incorporated into "The Land Beyond the Blow" (*CW* 1).

3. Charles J. Guiteau assassinated President James A. Garfield in 1881. See "Prattle," *SF* (14 August 1887): 4: "I have myself an assured faith in the expediency of hanging criminal lunatics, but if Guiteau's victim had been anybody but a President and I had advocated the assassin's execution, every man but the public prosecutor would have treated my views with contumelious disdain. If ever a penitent country commissions me to write Guiteau's epitaph it will be something like this:

>   Within this gorgeous mausoleum
>   Poor Guiteau's flesh you'll find;
>   His bones are kept in a museum,
>   And Fairchild has his mind.
>   Three creatures profit by his fall:
>   Worm, showman, fool—God bless them all!"

The verses appeared (somewhat shorter) untitled in *SC* and as "Disjunctus" in *CW* 5, and referred to a "Tillman" instead of to Fairchild. For "Fairchild" (probably Lucius Fairchild), see letter 88, n. 16.

4. Tennyson, *The Princess*, 3.348.

5. Possibly a misremembrance of Tennyson's "Slumbers not like a mountain tarn" ("Supposed Confessions of a Second-Rate Sensitive Mind," l. 129).

6. Unidentified.

7. Cf. *The Devil's Dictionary*: "Dissyllable, *n*. A word of two syllables. The following words are dissyllables, according to the ancient and honorable usage of all the San Francisco poets: Fire, hire, tire, flour, hour, sour, scour, chasm, spasm, realm, helm, and slippery elm."

8. Apparently AB's own invention, designed for purposes of metrical illustration.

9. The dedication to *SC* reads as follows: "With pride in their work, faith in their future and affection for themselves, an old writer dedicates this book to his young friends and pupils, George Sterling and Herman Scheffauer."

[92] To Herman Scheffauer [BL (transcript)]

1321 Yale St.,
Washington, D.C.
[May 6, 1903?]

Dear Scheff,

Your telegram about poor Doyle-Sahib hit me hard—how hard I cannot explain.¹ Of course I knew that I was foolishly fond of him—with something of the affection that one has for a woman—but *how* fond I did not know. Poor fellow! I fear his disappointment by the world's indifference to his really great work in letters had something to do with it. His recent letters to me have been full of a pathetic despondency. He was not made of so stern stuff as you and I.

I am almost sorry I ever set him to writing by acquainting him with his talent for the trade.

You will, of course, tell me all there is to tell about his death—all that you know. And you will, perhaps, write some kindly verses of him.² That is a thing I could never do—write anything for the public on the death of a friend. At least I have never done it in a way to satisfy me that I ought to do it again. I thank Heaven, though, that I said a few things of Doyle when he was with us that pleased him. And I hope he got my last letter, which must have got to Santa Cruz at about the time he was leaving.

His last letter to me ended thus:

"Won't you come back? . . . . . Good God! what a difference your leaving California has made to me! How I might have blossomed into a ———! God bless you, dear Bierce,—you have helped me so much—more, more than you know."

Dear Scheff, I shall never be able to read that with dry eyes; and I don't want to.

I could not write of this sooner—I cannot write of it as I feel it, even now. If I did I should set you weeping, old man; and tears for the dead—why, they are the invention of a humorist. It is for the living that we should weep.

Sincerely yours,
Ambrose Bierce.

1. Doyle had committed suicide. In a previous letter (18 April 1903; BL [transcript]), AB wrote to Scheffauer: "I'm sorry for what you tell me of Doyle—his addiction to drink, his unsuccess, his despondency."
2. Scheffauer's poem "In Memory of Dr. C. W. Doyle" appears in *Of Both Worlds* (p. 93).

[93] To George Sterling [ALS, NYPL]

The N.Y. "American" Bureau,
Washington, D.C.

Dear Sterling,

It is good to hear from you again and to know that the book is so nearly complete as to be in the hands of publishers. I dare say they will not have it, and you'll have to get it out at your own expense. When it comes to that I shall hope to be of service to you, as you have been to me.

So you like Scheff. Yes, he is a good boy and a good friend. I wish you had met our friend Dr. Doyle, who has now gone the long, lone journey. It has made a difference to me, but that matters little, for the time is short in which to grieve. I shall soon be going his way.

No, I shall not put anything about the Robertson person into "Shapes of Clay."[1] His offense demands another kind of punishment and until I meet him he goes unpunished. I once went to San Francisco to punish him (but that was in hot blood) but Jack Cosgrave of "The Wave" told me the man was a hopeless invalid, suffering from locomotor ataxia. I have always believed *that* until I got your letter and one from Scheff. Is it not so?—or *was* it not? If not he has good reason to think me a coward, for his offense was what men are killed for; but of course one does not kill a helpless person, no matter what the offense is. If Jack lied to me I am most anxious to know it; he has always professed himself a devoted friend.

The passage that you quote from Jack London strikes me as good.[2] I don't dislike the word "penetrate"—rather like it. It is in frequent use regarding exploration and discovery. But I think you are right about "rippling"; it is too lively a word to be outfitted with such an adjective as "melancholy". I see London has an excellent article in "The Critic" on "The Terrible and Tragic in Fiction".[3] He knows how to think a bit.

What do I think of Cowley-Brown and his "Goosequill"? I did not know that he had revived it; it died several years ago. I never met him, but in both Chicago and London (where he had "The Philistine", or "The Anti-Philistine", I do not at the moment remember which) he was most kind to me and my work. In one number of his magazine—the London one—he had four of my stories and a long article about me which called the blushes to my maiden cheek like the reflection of a red rose in the petal of a violet.[4] Naturally I think well of Cowley-Brown.

You make me sad to think of the long leagues and monstrous convexity of the earth separating me from your camp in the redwoods. There are few things that I would rather do than join that party; and I'd be the last to strike my tent and sling my swag. Alas, it cannot be—not this year. My outings are limited to short runs along this coast. I was about to set out on one this morning; and wrote a hasty note to Scheff in consequence of my preparations. In five hours I was suffering from asthma, and am now confined to my room. But for eight months of the year here I am immune—as I never was out there.

[. . .]

I tried in vain to dissuade Scheff. from joining the Bohemian Club, which I have known to ruin many a promising youngster. Let us hope for better things in his case.

You will have to prepare yourself to endure a good deal of praise when that book is out. One does not mind when one gets accustomed to it. It neither pleases nor bores; you will have just no feeling about it at all. But if you really care for *my* praise I hope you have quoted a bit of it at the head of those dedicatory verses, as I suggested. That will give them a raison d'être.

With best regards to Mrs. Sterling and Katie I am sincerely yours,
                                                    Ambrose Bierce.
June 13, 1903.

P.S.—If not too much trouble you may remind Dick Partington and wife that I continue to exist and to remember them pleasantly.

1. Louis Alexander Robertson (1856–1910), a San Francisco poet and journalist, and also an invalid. Author of *The Dead Calypso and Other Verses* (1901), *Beyond the Requiems and Other Verses* (1902), *Cloistral Strains* (1902), *From Crystal Choirs* (1904), and *Through Painted Panes and Other Poems* (1907), all published by A. M. Robertson. The specific offense committed by Robertson is unknown, but Walter Neale suggests that Robertson (not named by Neale) had claimed in print that AB was "guilty of an unnatural sex act" (*Life of Ambrose Bierce* [New York: Walter Neale, 1929], 140).
2. GS had written (30 May 1903; ALS, NYPL): "By the way, here's an extract from London's last book, 'The Call of the Wild,' that 'goes nearer to be' literature. Would it trouble you too much to criticize it: we had arguments over one or two words, as I didn't like 'penetrated', and though 'rippling' out of color with the rest of the sentence. Here it is:

'In the fall of the year they penetrated a weird lake country, sad and silent, where wild-fowl had been, but where then there was no life nor sign of life—only the blowing of chill winds, the forming of ice in sheltered places, and the melancholy rippling of waves on lonely beaches.'"

3. Jack London, "The Terrible and Tragic in Fiction," *Critic* 42, no. 6 (June 1903): 539–43. The article discusses Poe, Stevenson, and other writers of horror fiction; AB is cited in one paragraph.
4. AB had seven stories reprinted in *The Anti-Philistine* in three issues in 1897. "Chickamauga,"

"The Damned Thing," and "A Son of the Gods" appeared in the issue of 15 August 1897. The issue of 15 September 1897 contained "My Favorite Murder," "The Realm of the Unreal," and "A Watcher by the Dead." Appended to the appearance of "A Son of the Gods" was a lengthy unsigned note by Cowley-Brown (168–72) lavishly praising AB's stories. Cowley-Brown's *Goose-Quill* reprinted "My Favorite Murder" in two separate issues: March 1900 and April 1902.

[94] To Herman Scheffauer [BL (transcript)]

N.Y. "American" Bureau,
Washington, D.C.
[July 1903]

Dear Scheff:

I got the proofs yesterday, and am returning them by this mail. The "report of progress" is every way satisfactory, and I don't doubt that a neat job is being done.

The correction that you made is approved. I should have wanted and expected you to make many corrections and suggestions, but that I have had a *purpose* in making this book—namely, that it should represent my work at its average. In pursuance of this notion I was not hospitable even to suggestions, and have retained much work that I did not myself particularly approve; some of it trivial. You know I have always been addicted to trifling, and no book from which trivialities were excluded would fairly represent me.

I could not commend this notion in another. In your work and Sterling's I have striven hard to help you to come as near to perfection as we could because perfection is what you and he want, and as young writers ought to want, the *character* of your work being higher than mine. I reached my literary level long ago, and seeing that it is not a high one, there would seem to be a certain affectation, even a certain dishonesty, in making it seem higher than it is by republication of my best only. Of course I have not carried out this plan so consistently as to make the book *dull;* I had to "draw the line" at that.

I say all this because I don't want you and Sterling to think that I disdain assistance: I simply decided beforehand not to avail myself of its obvious advantages. You would have done as much for the book in one way as you have done in another.

I'll have to ask you to suggest that Mr. Wood have a man go over all the matter in the book, and see that none of the pieces are duplicated—as I fear they are. Reading the titles will not be enough: I might have given the same piece two titles. It will be necessary to compare first lines, I think. That will be drudgery which I'll not ask you to undertake: some of Wood's men, or some of the printer's men, will do it as well; it is in the line of their work.

The "Dies Irae"[1] is the most earnest and sincere of religious poems; my travesty of it is mere solemn fooling, which fact is "given away" in the prose introduction, where

I speak of my version being of possible service in the church! The travesty is not altogether unfair—it was inevitably suggested by the author's obvious inaccessibility to humor and logic—a peculiarity that is, however, observable in *all* religious literature, for it is a fundamental necessity to the religious mind. Without logic and a sense of the ludicrous a man is religious as certainly as without webbed feet a bird has the land habit.

It is funny, but I am a "whole lot" more interested in seeing your cover of the book than my contents of it.[2] I don't at all doubt—since you dared undertake it—that your great conception will find a fit interpreter in your hand; so my feeling is not anxiety. It is just interest in what is above my powers, but in which *you* can work. By the way, Keller, of the old "Wasp" was *not* the best of its cartoonists. The best—the best of *all* cartoonists if he had not died at eighteen—was another German, named Barkhaus. I have all his work and have long cherished a wish to republish it with the needed explanatory text—much of it being "local" and "transient". Some day, perhaps—most likely not. But Barkhaus was a giant.[3]

How I envy you! There are few things that would please me so well as to "drop in" on you folks in Sterling's camp. Honestly, I think all that prevents is the (to me) killing journey by rail. And two months would be required, going and returning by sea. But the rail trip across the continent always gives me a horrible case of asthma, which lasts me for weeks. I shall never take *that* journey again if I can avoid it. What times you and they will have about the campfire and the table! I feel like an exile, though I fear I don't look and act the part.

I did not make the little excursion I was about to take when I wrote you recently. Almost as I posted the letter I was taken ill and have not been well since.

Poor Doyle! how thoughtful of him to provide for the destruction of my letters! But I fear Mrs. Doyle found some of them queer reading—if she read them. I am thankful that they are gone—one never knows into what hands one's letters may fall, nor (if one has a little notoriety) whether they will not be *published*. The law (to our discredit be it said) permits that. Great Scott! if ever they begin to publish mine there will be a circus! For of course the women will be the chief sinners, and—well, they have material a-plenty; they can make many volumes, and your poor dead friend will have so bad a reputation that you'll swear you never knew him. I dare say, though, you have sometimes been indiscreet, too. *My* besetting sin has been in writing to my girl friends as if they were sweet-hearts—the which they'll doubtless not be slow to affirm. The fact that they write to me in the same way will be no defense; for when I'm worm's meat I can't present proof—and wouldn't if I could. Maybe it won't matter—if I don't turn in my grave and so bother the worms.

As Doyle's "literary executor" I fear your duties will be light: he probably did not leave much manuscript. I judge from his letters that he was despondent about his work and the narrow acceptance that it had. So I assume that he did not leave much more than the book of poems which no publisher would (or will) take.

You are about to encounter the same stupid indifference of the public—so is Sterling. I'm sure of Sterling, but don't quite know how it will affect *you*. You're a pretty sturdy fellow, physically and mentally, but this *may* hurt horribly. I pray that it do not, and could give you—perhaps have given you—a thousand reasons why it *should* not. You are still young and your fame may come while you live; but you must not expect it now, and doubtless do not. To me, and I hope to you, the approval of one person who knows is sweeter than the acclaim of ten thousand who do not—whose acclaim, indeed, I would rather not have. If you do not *feel* this in every fibre of your brain and heart, try to learn to feel it—practice feeling it, as one practices some athletic feat necessary to health and strength.

Thank you very much for the photograph. You are growing too infernally handsome to be permitted to go about unchained. If I had your "advantages" of youth and comeliness I'd go to the sheriff and ask him to lock me up. That would be the honorable thing to do, if you don't mind.

God be with you—but inattentive.

    Ambrose Bierce.

---

1. "Dies Iræ" is a mediaeval hymn describing Judgment Day, sung in some masses for the dead. AB claimed to have undertaken his own "translation" of "Dies Iræ" (printed in its entirety in *SC*) because of his disappointment with the translation by General John A. Dix. Actually, AB once wrote that Dix "was the author of one of the noblest translations of the *Dies Iræ*" ("Prattle," [San Francisco] *Argonaut* [10 May 1879]: 4).

2. The background of Scheffauer's cover design of *SC* shows a group of people silhouetted against an immense moon. The foreground shows a throng of upturned faces, overcome by fumes from a flaming brazier or censer, before a sculpture of a seated figure that appears to be Anubis.

3. AB refers to G. Frederick Keller (d. 1883) and Henry Barkhaus. Cf. AB to S. O. Howes (19 January 1906; ALS, HL): "Your commendation of the 'Wasp's' cartoonist, Keller, is all right, but he was a lisping babe compared with the later Barkhaus. Barkhaus was a boy—only seventeen—with no art education. But what a great chap he was! To reproduce his cartoons in portfolio form and write the needful explanatory note to each has always been one of my heart's desires, but of course I shall never have the time to do it, and could not afford the expense. He left us and went to Germany to study, as was right; but he died there, as was wrong, at about the age of eighteen. No caricaturist that I know of was born to the trade as he." Some of Keller's and Barkhaus's cartoons are included in Kenneth M. Johnson, comp., *The Sting of the Wasp* (San Francisco: Book Club of California, 1967).

[95] To Herman Scheffauer [BL (transcript)]

Aurora,
Preston Co.,
W. Va.

Dear Scheff,

I have been compelled to "flee to the mountains;" so here I am, on the summit of the Alleghenies, where already I am recovering. I came up a week ago.[1]

It is to be an interesting country, for at Oakland, Maryland, twelve miles from here, my age and my youth met—the latter a trifle wan, ghostly and absent-minded, inhospitable to questioning. What I mean is that I was in Oakland (Md.) forty-odd years ago, as a young soldier, when there were new things under a new sun. And I was the newest of all. This country has been Dreamland to me ever since. I know I should not have sought it again, to dispel the illusions, but I just *had* to; and I mean to go over all my old campaigning routes and battle grounds, even if I die of disappointment. It all makes me feel a bit lonely and de trop, like a man from Mars.

I so like the spirit of your letter of July 7! It gives me assurance of your future. You are to do *great* work, believe me. I shall not see it all, but that does not greatly matter, having the assurance of it.

What I feared—though not greatly, indeed—was not that ignorant criticism might pain and discourage you, but that the stolid, stupefied indifference of the public *might*. To a man of sensibility—and you are that or you'd not be a poet—nothing, surely, can be so hard to endure. You see I'm playing the part of "prophet of evil". It is hardly possible that either your work or Sterling's will find the immediate acceptance that it merits. It is too good for your contemporaries—they will not understand. In this country the "public" that knows and loves poetry is a few thousands in number, badly scattered, mostly inaccessible because incredulous through frequent disappointment. The publishers and "critics" have so often and so loudly cried: "Poet! Poet!" when there was no poet that when one comes he is unheeded.

Since you ask me, I hardly agree with your criticism of Sterling's dedicatory verse,

"Ah, glad to thy decree," etc.,[2]

but I'd rather not discuss it, it being so personal a matter—to me. It seems to me very nearly perfect in both sentiment and construction.

Your general appreciation of Sterling's work is as pleasing to me as your friendly feeling for his personality. May you and he always be friends—always in your lives confirming our twinship in my mind and heart.

I have not read Nietzsche, but shall when I get back to Washington, since you and Sterling think so well of him.

[...]
When am I to see you on your way to Europe? I shall probably remain in this wilderness, or hereabout, until October. It is always difficult for me to part with the mountains, even when (unlike the Santa Cruz range) they hold nothing dear in memory or life. I've two nice girls with me and expect two more; so I'm not lonely.[3]
[...]
    Sincerely yours,
    Ambrose Bierce.
Aug. 4, 1903.

    1. Presumably to find relief from his asthma. Cf. Luke 21:21: "Then let them which are in Judea flee to the mountains...."
    2. AB treats the poem as untitled, the line given being the first of the poem.
    3. AB refers to Carrie Christiansen (d. 1920), a schoolteacher who was AB's longtime secretary, and Priscilla Shipman. Both were his fellow lodgers at the Olympia in Washington, D. C.

[96] To George Sterling [ALS, NYPL]

    Aurora, W. Va.,
    Sept. 12, 1903.
Dear Sterling,
[...]
I'm glad you like London; I've heard he is a fine fellow and have read one of his books—"The Son of the Wolf", I think is the title—and it seemed clever work mostly.[1] The general impression that remains with me is that it is always winter and always night in Alaska.
[...]
Do I think extracts from "Prattle" would sell? I don't think anything of mine will sell. I could make a dozen books of the stuff that I have "saved up"—have a few ready for publication now—but all is vanity[2] so far as profitable publication is concerned. Publishers want nothing from me but novels—and I'll die first!

Who is "Tully"—and why? It is good of London to defend me against him.[3] I fancy all you fellows have a-plenty of defending me to do, though truly it is hardly worth while. All my life I have been hated and slandered by all manner of persons except good and intelligent ones; and I don't greatly mind. I knew in the beginning what I had to expect, and I know now that, like spanking, it hurts (sometimes) but does not harm. And the same malevolence that has surrounded my life will surround my memory if I am remembered. Just run over in your mind the names of men who have told the truth about their unworthy fellows and about human nature "as it was given them to see it". They are the bogie-men of history. None of them has escaped vilification. Can poor little I hope for anything better? When you strike you are struck. The world is a skunk, but it has rights; among them that of retaliation.

Yes, you deceive yourself if you think the little fellows of letters "like" you, or rather if you think they will like you when they know how big you are. They will lie awake nights to invent new lies about you and new means of spreading them without detection. But you have your revenge: in a few years they'll all be dead—just the same as if you had killed them. Better yet, you'll be dead yourself. So—you have my entire philosophy in two words: "Nothing matters."

[...]

My girls have returned to Washington, and I'm having great times climbing peaks (they are knobs) and exploring gulches and cañons—for which these people have no names, poor things. My dreamland is still unrevisited. They found a Confederate soldier over there the other day, with his rifle alongside. I'm going over to beg his pardon.

Ever yours,
Ambrose Bierce.

1. Jack London, *The Son of the Wolf* (1900), a collection of short stories based on London's Alaskan experiences.
2. Ecclesiastes 1:21: "Vanity of vanities, ... all is vanity."
3. GS had written to AB: "I'm getting very fond of Jack London. When I first made his acquaintance, about two years ago, he was, through ignorance, a lukewarm admirer of yourself. Under my tutelage he has changed, and last week actually took up the cudgels in your behalf when Tully and his wife began a verbal assault on you at a literary (?) gathering. I was not present, as I had refused to meet Tully, on the grounds that he was no friend of yours" (5 September 1903; ALS, NYPL). In identifying Richard Walton Tully (1877–1945) for AB, GS wrote: "This fellow Tully is the chap who 'butted in' at the time of your flaying of Gayley. He was then on the staff of one of the U.C. papers. Since then he married one May Eleanor Gates [1875–1951], author of 'The Biography of a Prairie Girl', who is a pushing little creature who's doing a heap of posing on account of its 'success'. Tully is now writing melodramas in New York. Both are protégés of Mrs. Hearst, who has wasted a lot of money on them" (10 October 1903; ALS, NYPL).

[97] To Herman Scheffauer [BL (transcript)]

Aurora, W. Va.,
Sept. 27, 1903.

Dear Scheff,

[...]

About George's sister. I have no fear that you will tamper with her pretty body; her heart is the thing to which you are a peril; and a woman's heart is a mighty precious thing—to her. In order to spare it one must walk with circumspection thereabout—

must sometimes be even rude and unmannerly. But bless you, I am not at all concerned in the matter and would not have you think I presume to lay down the law to you in this or any other affair.

I did not know about your Nemesis, and suppose myself unacquainted with her. You'll find Nemesis anew afore you're as old as I, and most of them will be vindictive because you treated them honorably, refusing to be seduced by them. An angry or slighted woman has always one trump card to play, and so far as I know always plays it to the great applause from the onlookers at the game. She gratifies at once her malice and her vanity by affirming one's ineffectual attempts to seduce *her*. This you have to expect many, many times unless you escape by dying young—which you'll wish you had done.

As to the advice I once gave you at Los Gatos I recollect it right well, and it was good advice with the small glimmer of light that I thought I had. "Seduction" has an ugly sound; "murder" has an ugly sound; so have all the names of sins and crimes. Yet there may be circumstances in which any one of them would be right; that is, promotive of the sum of human happiness, including that of the "victim". The virtues are good; they are the things that promote happiness. But sometimes don't. Sometimes they decrease it; and then, performing the office of the vices, they are equally reprehensible. A truth, for illustration, that produces the effect commonly produced by a lie is no better than a lie and in that instance not as good. There is no sanctity inhering in the virtues; they are practical means to a desirable end. Considered without reference to its effect, an act is neither moral nor immoral—just unmoral. Moral principles are for those who have not the brains, the right instincts, or the time to judge each case as it comes up. The moral principle simply pledges one to a certain course of action in advance of the time for it. It is a rough, easy and generally expedient guide to conduct. Some of us, automatically honorable or with the insight to be honorable by taking thought, do not need it—one of us in a thousand perhaps. To the others it is better to affirm the divine origin and universal authorities of the virtues. But what the devil am I preaching for? Really, I must be getting deep into my dotage.

[. . .]

I knew it is thought in some quarters that I had a "patron" in the late Ed. Steele, in re my first book of tales. On the contrary, it was a commercial transaction. What he contributed was his faith; all the money that he put in he got back—and more too—from the sales of the book; and for a long time I continued to pay his widow, although I have his written refusal of any sum in excess of his expenditure. And finally I *bought* her rights rather than claim mine. She is a good friend of mine and to-day she does not know.

And to this day one-third of the profits of that book go to the estate (the mother) of my dead friend, Charlie Kaufman, who did not put a cent into it, whom I did not owe a cent and who had nothing to do with the publication. Why do I do this? Because he *was* to have a third interest if he got a publisher. He failed to do so, but worked like a Trojan trying to, until Steele—without his knowledge—made me *his* proposal. Kaufman gladly gave it up.

And not long ago when I proposed to buy out his mother's no rights she insisted on the legality of her claims and asked me a price greatly in excess of all that I ever got from all my books—or even expect to. Why do I tell you all this? I'm damned if I know—unless to disillusionize you a bit if you have any illusions to which this is apropos. And then—I'm garrulous to-night. It is my night to be this way. My landlord lies dead near by and I feel as if I were sitting up with a corpse. It is the rule to be loquacious.

"The Devil's Dictionary"—no; I'll bet a pretty penny that not a publisher on this side of the continent will look at the stuff unless I will give it another title.[2] It is ready for compilation, but not compiled. It will consist of definitions (somewhat original) of such words that struck my fancy, regularly arranged as in a real dictionary. Some of the definitions stand alone, some are followed by a few lines of illustration or comment, some run to the length of small essays. Many are in verse or partly in verse—a bit cynical.

I shall compile it next winter and that, doubtless, will be the end o' it. My intention, by the way, is a secret known (now) to you only. Keep it, please.

I shall leave here the day after to-morrow, Deo volente, and shall then have no address for a week or two. Then I shall go back to Washington, where, doubtless, I shall find my book and a letter or two from you. And I guess the letters will get themselves opened first.

Yes, you must come to Washington on your way to Europe. I feel what Blanche Partington once called "a you famine".

    Ever yours,
        Ambrose Bierce.

1. An allusion to the statue of Memnon in Egypt occurs in stanza 18 of "Invocation" (1888; *CW* 4).
2. When the book first appeared in 1906, it was titled *The Cynic's Word Book*.

[98] To Herman Scheffauer [BL (transcript)]

                                  Washington, D.C.

Dear Scheff,

        Returning here I find the box of books, for which many thanks. They are great!—I mean artistically and mechanically. I cannot quite adequately express my sense of the way in which all the work has been done. Your cover-designs are all that I could have expected and I find barely a trace of the imperfections in the printing which your letter pointed out. I only wish the contents were more worthy of their setting. I shall write to to Mr. Wood my satisfaction with his admirable work.

My rambles in the Alleghanies were charming. I traveled all over my old lines of march; visited my old battle-fields; inspected the forts which I assisted to build and those which I assisted to take and try to take; found the graves of my comrades in the national cemetery at Grafton and those lonely ones in the valleys and on the hills, from which they had been removed.[1] What most impressed me were the neglected and now barely distinguishable graves of the Confederates, near their old camps where the poor fellows still lie among the trees that have grown up above them and under the fallen leaves that fill the depressions that once were mounds. If I had your gift, old man, what a poem I should make of that!

I'm sending you a little book of sonnets—not for the sonnets—not even for the instructive introduction; but as a souvenir of the mountains. It will at least amuse you.

Ah, how I wish your visit hereabout could have been so timed that you'd have been with me there!

My health is again "restored"—it requires such a lot of restoring.

I'll write you soon—I'm struggling to discharge a thousand duties and obligations.
   Sincerely yours,
      Ambrose Bierce.
Oct. 12, 1903.

1. AB published some of his reflections on this trip in "The Passing Show" (*New York American*, 22 November 1903), reprinted as "A Bivouac of the Dead" (*CW* 11; rpt. *A Sole Survivor*). He also wrote of the cemetery in a lengthy letter published in the *Ninth Indiana Veteran Volunteer Infantry Association: Proceedings of the Eighteenth Annual Reunion* (1904), later reprinted as *Battlefields and Ghosts* (1931); rpt. *A Sole Survivor*.

[99] To Herman Scheffauer [BL (transcript)]
      Washington, D.C.,
      Nov. 11, 1903.
Dear Scheff,
 [...]

As to your estimate of the proportion of German blood in the American vein why did you suppose me ignorant that a great many Germans do not care to live in Germany? But why consider all those other tribes German, to the exclusion of still others. By going back far enough you could make an even better showing, for even the Norman strain in the English and American is German. The Franks themselves were of the Germanic race, and the French are their descendants.

Your grotesque notion of the "degeneracy" of the French invites a smile too—it is worthy of an untraveled Missourian.

Dear Scheff, if it were not for the German ichor in the lenses of your eyes you'd see *so* much better. The tribal instinct is as strong in you as if you wore skins and ate raw meat, asquat upon your haunches. Fancy all that intemperate tirade provoked by my simple comparison between the German soldier and the French one! *Don't* be German. Don't be American. Leave those ugliest of all possible things, tribal pride and tribal animosity, to the frankly unveneered barbarian. They are not worthy of *you*. Your funny picture of the British Empire squirming impotently under German feet amuses, but it also grieves. All over the world the educated German has the bad repute of brutal and offensive conceit. He is even worse than the American, for the conceit of the latter is tinctured with a dash of humorous braggadocio like that of the Gascon, as if he took himself only half seriously. An you love me Scheff you'll try to physic all the little that you have of that out of you. If you don't I honestly advise you to write your poetry in the German tongue, for as sure as sin the cloven feet will appear in the spirit of all you write.

Take this in good part, my friend, and smile as you finish reading it. But I fear you should not trust yourself to "reply" to it, for the very word "German" is a red rag to the bull in you. (You see, I'm trying to spare myself a castigation.)

You think your German blood helps you to be a good American. You think it gives you lofty ideals, knowledge, and much else. The same claim could be (and is, doubtless) made for every other nationality. Each tribesman thinks his tribe is best and greatest—even the Hottentot. None is best; none (pardon the paradox) is worst. In all that distinguishes civilization from barbarism the French lead, but *their* conceit, too, is something dreadful; it offsets all the good in them. But enough of this—the subject is disgusting.

I await your advent with impatience.

    Sincerely yours,
        Ambrose Bierce.

[100]   To George Sterling [ALS, NYPL]

                                          Washington, D.C.

My dear George,

        Thank you so much for the books and the inscription—which (as do all other words of praise) affects me with a sad sense of my shortcomings as writer and man. Things of that kind from too partial friends point out to me with a disquieting significance what I ought to be; and the contrast with what I am hurts. Maybe you feel enough that way sometimes to understand. You are still young enough to profit by the pain; *my* character is made—*my* opportunities are gone. But it does not greatly matter—nothing does. I have some little testimony from you and Scheff and others that I have not lived altogether in vain, and I know that I have greater satisfaction in my slight connection with your and their work than in my own. Also a better claim to the attention and consideration of my fellow-men.

Never mind about the "slow sale" of my book; I did not expect it to be otherwise, and my only regret grows out of the fear that some one may lose money by the venture. *It is not to be you.* You know I am still a little "in the dark" as to what *you* have really done in the matter. I wish you would tell me if any of your own money went into it. The contract with Wood is all right; it was drawn according to my instructions and I shall not even accept the small royalty allowed me if anybody is to be "out". If *you* are to be out I shall not only not accept the royalty, but shall reimburse you to the last cent. Do you mind telling me about all that? In any case don't "buy out Wood" and don't pay out anything for advertising nor for anything else.

The silence of the reviews does not trouble me, any more than it would you. Their praise of my other books never, apparently, did me any good. No book published in this country ever received higher praise from higher sources than my first collection of yarns.[1] But the book was never a "seller", and doubtless never will be. That *I* like it fairly well is enough. You and I do not write books to sell; we write—or rather publish—just because we like to. We've no right to expect a profit from fun.

[. . .]

You whet my appetite for that new poem. The lines

"The blue-eyed vampire, sated at her feast,
Smiles bloodily against the leprous moon"[2]

give me the shivers. Gee! they're awful!

Sincerely yours,
Ambrose Bierce.

Jan. 8, 1904.

1. AB kept scrapbooks (now at VA) of reviews of some of his books; the scrapbook for *Tales of Soldiers and Civilians* contains dozens of reviews from newspapers and magazines.
2. "A Wine of Wizardry," ll. 196–97.

[101]   To George Sterling [ALS, NYPL]

Washington, D.C.,
Jan. 31, 1904.

Dear George,

Your letter of Jan. 24 has surprised me more than I care to say. And what surprises me most is that I have occasion for surprise—that I was misled by you. Of course I supposed that you had put up something for my book, but not that you had done all, or any more than I could easily repay.

So my contract with Wood is a "dummy" contract! And he is not a publisher taking a chance of loss in hope of a possible gain, but merely a "dummy" publisher, with no clientele, no trade connections, no advertising machinery—nothing whereby he can get back any considerable part of your outlay.

It is gratifying to know that I have in you a friend willing to whack up all that money for me, but it is a trifle too much. I can't let you do for me what I had repeatedly refused to do for myself—not even if my refusal to let *you* compels *me* to do it.

My small service to you has no such value as you put upon it, and would in my eyes have none at all if you paid me for it in this way, or in any way.

If Mr. Wood or any other man in the publishing business (as I supposed him to be) had chosen (as I supposed he had) to take the risk, or most of the risk, of publishing the book, and had lost—that would have been his affair—a legitimate business loss, which I should not have felt bound to make good. But *you*—no; that "does not go".

Not having a cent, I don't see my way clearly just now to "making good"; but I shall make good. Perhaps I can learn the trick of saving. I don't suppose that under the circumstances one hundred dollars of your outlay will return to you from sales of the book. Only a publisher in the regular currents of trade *can* sell a book—I beg you will not attempt it and so "throw good money after bad."

I should think it might be well, perhaps, to arrange with The American News Company to take over the whole edition (you do not say how many volumes were printed) for whatever they will give, if they will give anything. If they will not perhaps you can arrange with them to sell on commission—any commission. Let's get out on the best terms we can, but get out. Of course I don't know how you may be tangled up with Wood and unable to act on these suggestions, or any suggestions. I only know that *he* cannot sell that book to the trade, nor to the public.

I know what you will say—that you don't want your money back, and so forth. Don't take the trouble to say it; it will count for nothing. I shall have my way, but unfortunately cannot have it at once, as I'm carrying some pretty heavy burdens.

I dare say your outlay in this matter was far greater than you expected it to be. It certainly is greater than it ought to have been—a cheaper book would have done as well. The splendid work put into this one is no longer gratifying to me. In short, I wish the manuscript had been flung into the fire.

Dear George, if there is anything else that I do not know about this unfortunate affair I beg you to let me know it at once. I am profoundly grateful to you for the goodwill that your act has shown and keenly admire the generosity of it. I don't think I've another friend who would have done that. But you hardly stopped to reflect—to ask yourself would I permit. Well, I can't and won't.

I shall reply to the rest of your letter later—this revelation has upset me a bit.

Sincerely yours,
Ambrose Bierce.

[102]   To Herman Scheffauer [BL (transcript)]

Washington, D.C.
Feb'y 12, 1904.

Dear Scheff,

I'll have to ask you to pardon me for using the machine: I've a poverty of ink and no time to go out and replenish. How could you think that I wanted that careless letter back because I mistrusted you? Surely I explained that it was because nobody can control his letters—I mean those that he has "on hand". You might die, for example, and all literary history shows that in such matters the wishes of the dead count little with the living. There are many ways for letters to get into print against the wish of both writer and writee.

[. . .]

I think you are right about Wood; he is not enterprising; but then he is, as I understand the matter, hardly a publisher at all; and only a publisher *can* market a book. For illustration, a publisher will have a list of booksellers who will take a certain number of *any* book that he puts out—any book in their line. That is enough, in some cases, to recoup him for his whole outlay. There are many ways to market a book that are impossible to one not regularly in the trade. Wood sent on here, to Brentano's, our principal bookseller, forty or fifty copies of My book. (That capital M slipped in quite unconsciously to me.) They have never been even so much as put on the counter. The newspapers have not had them for review, nor have they been advertised, so far as I can learn. Who can know about them? Of the many persons here who know me probably not six know that I have recently published a book. (I'm rather glad of that, for every one of them would expect me to give him a copy. I dare say you have been taught *that*.) I suppose Wood does the best he can, but—he is not a publisher. And I fear he hasn't a cent's interest in the sale of the book. Well, I hope *your* man is in the current of the trade and will make your book go a little. I'm not concerned about my "fame", but just a trifle about my pocket.

[...]
Of course you did not like to see my newspaper stuff "illustrated".¹ But fancy how "mad" it made *me!* I put a stop to it at once. The stuff is bad enough without the pictures. These little Eastern editors, and Hearst's Presidential ambition, have pretty nearly done me up. By the way, here is a story. A little girl asked her father, "Papa, what is a gelding?" "A horse", he replied, "that has been edited."

I am glad that you are to start so soon upon your travels; not that I shall see you, but that if you take the right spirit with you, and leave a little something behind, it will make you different and better. As you say, you will learn what you cannot get out of books. I like your enthusiasm and your high purposes—that is how a young poet ought to feel. O that it were possible to have always oil for that flame! Alas, for the disillusion that we call wisdom! Pray God it be many years before the altar grows cold. I can bless your new guide for at least one service to you—for overturning one of your idols: the horrible God of the Hebrew mythology, horrible even in his softened character, as we now have him. But be careful that you set not up a mortal in his place. I have not yet listened to Nietzsche, but all men are stammerers—all the philosophers from Aristotle down speak brokenly of what they know not. At your age I devoured them all; at mine you will turn from them, smiling sadly, and go "back, back to Nature".² I would rather see you lying on your back on a hillside, studying the blue sky, than "dipping your nose in the Gascon wine"³ of the bookmen.

I fear you go too far in condemnation of our modern poetry and its reverent loyalty to the great Past. The ancients, as Dr. Johnson pointed out, "had the first rifling of the beauties of nature". That accounts for much. They had, too, the advantage of ignorance. Don't sneer: consider if the Odyssey could have been written by one who knew what lay beyond his Mediterranean horizon and the Pillars of Hercules—who knew there was no land of the Shades and no shades. Our trumpery knowledge has killed imagination and has given us no wisdom. Great poetry is still possible where George has found it—in the unknown fields of Space, where imagination can still fly with a free wing.

I am a little alarmed by your new passion for revolution, innovation. The best innovation is superior excellence. The great men are those who excel in their art as they find it; the revolutionaries are commonly second and third rate men—and they do not revolutionize anything. Of course there are exceptions. But the game of poetry is good enough as it is to him who knows how to play it. He does not need a game with new rules. Think how many have tried to revolutionize even the *forms* of English verse—have invented metres and forsworn *all* metre; have substituted irregularity for regularity, discarded rhyme and written blank verse in lines of varying length and so forth. What has become of their work and of their fame? None of them lives fifty years. I pray you go slowly in the matter of innovation. It does not innovate. What we need is not a new poetry, but a better; as much better as is possible in a world that has substituted knowledge for wisdom and science for imagination.

[...]

I'm expecting to have to go to the mountains sometime in May—depends on the movements of my friend the asthma. My health is robust now.

       Yours in all sincerity,
            Ambrose Bierce.

  1. AB's "Passages from the 'Best-Selling' Books" (*SF*, 14 October 1903) and "The Passing Show" (*SF*, 3 January 1904) contained cartoonlike illustrations (the latter even with captions abstracted from the text).

  2. AB alludes to Scheffauer's poem, "Back, Back to Nature" (*Of Both Worlds*, 5).

  3. William Makepeace Thackeray (1811–1863), "The Age of Wisdom," l. 30 ("my" for "your" in Thackeray).

[103] To George Sterling [ALS, NYPL]

                      "N.Y. American" Office,
                      Washington, D.C.

Dear George,

        I wrote you yesterday. Since then I have been rereading your letter. I wish you would not say so much about what I have done for you, and how much it was worth to you, and all that. I should be sorry to think that I did not do a little for you—I tried to. But, my boy, you should know that I don't keep that kind of service *on sale*. Moreover, I'm amply repaid for what *you* have done for *me*—I mean with your pen. Do you suppose *I* do not value such things? Does it seem reasonable to think me unpleasured by those magnificent dedicatory verses in your book? Is it nothing to me to be called "Master" by such as you? Is my nature so cold that I have no pride in such a pupil? There is no obligation in the matter—certainly none that can be suffered to satisfy itself out of your pocket.

You greatly overestimate the sums I spend in "charity." I sometimes help some poor devil of an unfortunate over the rough places, but not to the extent that you seem to suppose. I couldn't—I've too many regular, constant, *legitimate* demands on me. Those, mostly, are what keep me poor.

Mr. Mackay and wife passed the evening with me a little while ago—Mackay of "Success."[1] He has been reading your book and has a tremendous admiration of you. He said he was going to review your book and Scheff's in his magazine.

By the way, I wish if you print "The Wine of Wizardry" you would send me a few proof-slips of it. Maybe I can place it—anyhow I want to give a few to friends and have one for myself.

Maybe you think it odd that I've not said a word in print about any of your work except the "Testimony." It is not that I don't appreciate the minor poems—I do. But I don't like to scatter; I prefer to hammer on a single nail—to push one button until someone hears the bell. When the "Wine" is published I'll have another poem that is not only great, but striking—notable—to work on. However good, or even great, a short poem with such a title as "Poesy", "Music", "To a Lily", "A White Rose",[2] and so forth, cannot be got into public attention. Some longer and more notable work, of the grander manner, may *carry* it, but of itself it will not go. Even a bookful of its kind will not. Not till you're famous.

Your letter regarding your brother (who has not turned up) was needless. I could be of no assistance in procuring him employment. I've tried so often to procure it for others, and so vainly, that nobody could persuade me to try any more. I'm not fond of the character of suppliant, nor of being "turned down" by the little men who run this Government. Of course I'm not in favor with this Administration, not only because of my connection with Democratic newspapers, but because, also, I sometimes venture to dissent openly from the doctrine of the divinity of those in high station—particularly Teddy.

I'm sorry you find your place in the office intolerable. That is "the common lot of all" who work for others. I have chafed under the yoke for many years—a heavier yoke, I think, than yours. It does not fit my neck anywhere. Some day perhaps you and I will live on adjoining ranches in the mountains—or in adjoining caves—"the world forgetting, by the world forgot".[3] I have really been on the point of hermitizing lately, but I guess I'll have to continue to live like a reasonable human being a little longer until I can release myself with a conscience void of offense to my creditors and dependents. But "the call of the wild" sounds, even in my dreams.

You ask me if you should write in "A Wine of Wizardry" vein, or in that of "The Testimony of the Suns." Both. I don't know in which you have succeeded the better. And I don't know anyone who has succeeded better in either. To succeed in both is a marvelous performance. You may say that the one is fancy, the other imagination, which is true, but not the whole truth. The "Wine" has as true imagination as the other, and fancy into the bargain. I like your grandiose manner, and I like the other as well. In terms of another art I may say—rear great towers and domes. Carve, also, friezes. But I'd not bother to cut single finials and small decorations. However exquisite the workmanship, they are not worth your present attention. If you were a painter (as, considering your wonderful sense of color, you doubtless could have been) your large canvases would be your best.

[. . .]

I passed yesterday with Percival Pollard, viewing the burnt district of Baltimore.[4] He's a queer duck whom I like, and he likes your work. I'm sending you a copy of "The

Papyrus", with his "rehabilitation" of the odious Oscar Wilde. Wilde's work is all right, but what can one do with the work of one whose name one cannot speak before women?[5]

I'm so glad Maid Marian's armament is lighter than I feared it was. I shall not run away if I ever meet her.

Sincerely yours,
Ambrose Bierce.

Feb. 29, 1904. (over)

I enclose some of the clippings you kindly sent but retain the one from the San Jose paper for myself for you can easily replace it.

A. B.

1. Robert Mackay (1871–?) was editor of the popular magazine *Success* and a late associate of AB.
2. All the poems cited are in GS's *The Testimony of the Suns*.
3. Alexander Pope, "Eloisa to Abelard" (1717), l. 208.
4. An enormous fire on 7–8 February 1904 destroyed 2600 buildings in an 80-block area of the business district of Baltimore, resulting in property loss of $80,000,000.
5. Percival Pollard, "Oscar Wilde: A Rehabilitation," *The Papyrus: A Magazine of Individuality* 2, no. 2 (February 1904): 12–19. AB excoriated Wilde in his poem "To Oscar Wilde," *Wasp* no. 296 (31 March 1882): 197, and "Prattle," 198, at a time when Wilde was making a much-publicized tour of the United States. The last sentence refers to the cloud surrounding Wilde's name as a result of his trial and conviction for homosexuality in 1895.

[104]   To Herman Scheffauer [BL (transcript)]

Washington,
March 20, 1904.

Dear Scheff,

[...]

I'm a little amused by your earnestness in repudiating the head god of the Hebrew mythology and your determination to keep him out of your poetry. Don't do that. He is a far more impressive poetical figure than the Zeus of the Greeks or the Romans. You would not think of excluding *them* on the ground that you don't believe in them. A poet's gods—his "machinery"—are not supposed to represent outside his imagination. They are a part of his poetry, just as his other fables are. Is the reader to suppose that you *believe* in "Shagalon", in "Thelma", in "Lilith" and the rest? Faith is poetical, religion is picturesque; as such they belong in poetry. If the poet writes only his *convictions*—but he would not be a poet. Don't be a proponent, an exponent, an opponent of *anything*—in poetry. Be true to nothing but your imagination and your art.

Lay the whole world under contribution to *them*. "Beauty and Truth only are my gods", you say. One of these is enough—Beauty. We know nothing of the other in poetry.
[...]
I hope I shall be here when you arrive. I shall not leave until my health compels, and then perhaps I shall be nearer to you than I am here and you can stop off on your way. It would be better to see you in the mountains than here.

Au reste, I shall not discuss George's faults as a poet with you; nor your own and Josephare's abilities to equal his great lines (happily, happily you both [have] unlimited opportunity to prove that); nor whether they are really great; nor whether great poetry is not made up of great lines; nor my own competence as a critic. There is much that you and I can more pleasantly and profitably do than argue. But this I will say, though I'll not discuss it: You'll have to get the eyes of your mind open a lot wider in order to take in the full stature of George Sterling. I can wish you nothing better than that you may do so.
Sincerely yours,
Ambrose Bierce.

[105]   To George Sterling [ALS, NYPL]
Washington, D.C.,
May 11, 1904.
Dear George,
[...]
Yes, I've dropped "The Passing Show" again, for the same old reason—wouldn't stand the censorship of my editor.[1] I'm writing for the daily issues of The American, mainly, and, as a rule, anonymously.[2] It's "dead easy" work.
[...]
My favorite translation of Homer is that of Pope, of whom it is the present fashion to speak disparagingly, as it is of Byron. I know all that can be said against them, and say *some* of it myself, but I wish their detractors had a little of their brains. I know too that Pope's translations of The Iliad and The Odyssey are rather paraphrases than translations. But I love them just the same, while wondering (with you, doubtless) what so profoundly affected Keats when he "heard Chapman speak out loud and bold."[3] Whatever it was, it gave us what Coleridge pronounced the best sonnet in our language; and Lang's admiration of Homer has given us at least the next best.[4] Of course there must be something in poems that produce poems—in a poet whom most poets confess their king. I hold (with Poe) that there is no such thing as a *long* poem— a poem of the length of an Epic.[5] It must consist of poetic passages connected by

recitativo, to use an opera word; but it is perhaps better for that. If the writer cannot write "sustained" poetry the reader probably could not read it. Anyhow, I vote for Homer.

I am passing well, but shall soon seek the mountains, though I hope to be here when Scheff points his prow this way. Would that you were sailing with him!

I've been hearing all about all of you, for Eva Crawford[6] has been among you "takin' notes," and Eva's piquant comments on what and whom she sees are delicious reading. I should suppose that *you* would appreciate Eva—most persons don't. She is the best letter writer of her sex—who are all good letter-writers—and she is much beside. I may venture to whisper that you'd find her estimate of your work and personality "not altogether displeasing."
[...]

Sincerely yours,
Ambrose Bierce.

1. "The Passing Show" (*New York American*, 20 March 1904; *SF*, 3 April 1904) was AB's last, although he continued to publish numerous other articles.

2. AB's scrapbook (Stanford University Library) contains numerous clippings of unsigned squibs from the *New York American* from this time.

3. John Keats, "On First Looking into Chapman's Homer" (1816), l. 8, referring to George Chapman's translation (1598–1616) of the *Iliad* and the *Odyssey*.

4. Andrew Lang (1844–1912) wrote several sonnets on Homer and the Homeric poems, but AB probably refers to the most celebrated and widely reprinted of them, "The Odyssey," in *Ballades and Verses Vain* (1884).

5. Edgar Allan Poe had condemned the long poem in "The Philosophy of Composition" (1846) and "The Poetic Principle" (1849).

6. Eva Crawford was a pupil of Lella Cotton whom AB first met in the late 1890s.

[106]   To Herman Scheffauer [BL (transcript)]

Haines' Falls,
Greene Co.,
N.Y.

Dear Scheff,

A dearth of ink must excuse the machine writing. I have your letter of the 15th. It is pleasant to know that you are enjoying yourself. Permit me to remark that nothing is more enjoyable.

I too am having a lovely time in a different way, loafing in the woods and along the ways, overlooking the lowlands and underlooking the bluest of skies with their mountain-born clouds aping the forms and matching the magnitude of their parents. Nevertheless I envy you your wheel trip in England and Scotland. If you do wheel through England I hope you will take in Stratford-on-Avon (a poet can do no less) and see Coventry, Warwick and Kenilworth—a region in which I idled away many a month.[1]

It was indeed unfortunate that, through my fault, we did not meet that last evening of the Navarre, since you prove that you would have gone up river with me. I hope you hunted up Mrs. Martin, anyhow, using my letter to introduce yourself.

The enclosed postal-card was doubtless intended for my reading as well as yours—anyhow I naturally read it. It suggests a pleasant dinner and thereat some hearts that "fondly turn to thee".[2] You will think of them a bit while abroad, and sometimes, I trust, one who in love of you yields to none of the younger breed.

Of course you understand that I have no personal acquaintance with Barr—at least I think I told you so; he and I have not met. But he has a kindly feeling for me, I think, and will recognize my right to introduce you. Please convey to him my best wishes and my sense of his great kindness to me and to my work in letters. I don't know his address but you will easily learn it.

The girls send love. Farewell, and peace attend you.

    Sincerely yours,
        Ambrose Bierce.
July 17, 1904.

1. AB wrote about all these British locales in his letters to the *Alta California* in 1872, reprinted in part as "Notes Written with Invisible Ink by a Phantom American" in *Nuggets and Dust* (1873) and more exhaustively in *A Sole Survivor* 106–24.
2. Byron, *Hints from Horace* (1811), l. 618 ("turn'd" in Byron).

[107]   To George Sterling [ALS, NYPL]

                              Haines' Falls,
                                  Greene Co.,
                                      N.Y.

Dear George,

        I haven't written a letter, except on business, since leaving Washington, June 30—no, not since Scheff's arrival there. I now return to earth, and my first call is on you.

You'll be glad to know that I'm having a good time here in the Catskills. I shall not go back so long as I can find an open hotel.

I suppose Scheff has written you about his visit to me—he is a better letter writer than I. We visited New York and Saybrook, Connecticut, together and the boy seemed to think he was having a pretty good time. I greatly enjoyed him. He was, to me, the modest, unassuming boy that I knew, though unknown to him I pricked one or two of his bubbles. In our correspondence he had given me the impression, for example, that he was something of a linguist—that he was especially at home in French. He knows almost nothing of French, and his pronunciation of the little that he does know—just what everybody knows—is one of the seven wonders of the world.

Well, all that is for your own eye, and is most ungracious, for, as I said, he showed none of the presumption and egotism whereof he has been accused by more than one of his friends, and mine. Nor was the Lothario element in evidence.

I should like to hear from you about our—or rather your—set in California, and especially about *you*. Do you still dally with the Muse? Enclosed you will find two damning evidences of editorial incapacity. Harper's now have "A Wine of Wizardry", and they too will indubitably turn it down.

I shall then try The Atlantic where it should have gone in the first place; and I almost expect its acceptance.[1]

I'm not working much—just loafing on my cottage porch; mixing an occasional cocktail; infesting the forests, knife in hand, in pursuit of the yellow-birch sapling that furnishes forth the walking stick like yours; and so forth. I knocked off work altogether for a month when Scheff came, and should like to do so for *you*. Are you never going to visit the scenes of your youth?

The newspaper clipping is from Sam Davis's paper. He sends it to me and swears he will stand to it. Let's let him.

It is awfully sad—that latest visit of Death to the heart and home of poor Katie Peterson. Will you kindly assure her of my sympathy?

Love to all the Piedmontese.

Sincerely yours,

Ambrose Bierce.

Aug 4, 1904.

1. Despite numerous submittals to leading magazines, the poem went unpublished until it appeared in *Cosmopolitan* (September 1907).

[108]   To George Sterling [TLS, NYPL]

Washington,
October 5, 1904.

Dear George,

[...]

Please don't persuade me to come to California—I mean don't *try* to, for I can't, and it hurts a little to say nay. There's a big bit of my heart there, but—O never mind the reasons; some of them would not look well on paper. One of them I don't mind telling; I would not live in a State under union labor rule. There is still one place where the honest American laboring man is not permitted to cut throats and strip bodies of women at his own sweet will. That is the District of Columbia.

I am anxious to read Lilith; please complete it.[1]

[...]

Yes, in The Cynic's Dictionary I did "jump" from A to M. I had previously done the stuff in various papers as far as M, then lost the beginning. So in resuming I redid that part (quite differently, of course) in order to have the thing complete if I should want to make a book of it.[2] I guess the Examiner isn't running much of it, nor much of anything of mine.

I had forgotten your man Ridgely Torrence (never before heard of him) but will get the August Critic and see what he has to say about you.[3] I can easily get it.

So Joaquin is still in the ring as a dandy seducer. He was pretty good at the game ere Decay's effacing fingers toyed with him. When impotent he will doubtless brag about his virtue and denounce lechery even more shrilly than he does now.

I like your love of Keats and the early Coleridge.

Sincerely yours,
Ambrose Bierce.

1. AB refers to GS's verse drama, *Lilith: A Dramatic Poem* (San Francisco: A. M. Robertson, 1919; San Francisco: Book Club of California, 1920). GS called it an allegorical tragedy, which he at the time planned to call "Lilith, or Temptation." He did not complete it until 1918.

2. In June and July 1904, AB published two installments of "The Cynic's Dictionary" after a sixteen-year hiatus. His "Devil's Dictionary" had run fairly steadily during his tenure with *Wasp* (1881–86), and was followed by two sporadic columns (retitled "The Cynic's Dictionary") in *SF* in 1887 and 1888. When it ceased, AB ended with the word "Lyre." GS probably had neither seen nor was aware of these earlier columns. The two new installments in 1904 contained definitions of words starting with the letter A, and were presumably AB's attempt to reconstruct or fill in for definitions that he had published in 1875 as "The Demon's Dictionary," of which he no longer had a copy. Within two weeks, AB had given up on his plan of going all the way back to the letter A as preparatory work to his planned book, and he resumed with the letter M, thus causing the "jump" that GS had spotted. See *The Unabridged Devil's Dictionary*, xvi–xxi.

3. Ridgely Torrance (1875–1950), "Verse—Recent and Old," *Critic* 45, no. 2 (August 1904): 151–56 (esp. 155). A review of *The Testimony of the Suns*.

[109]   To Robert H. Davis [TLS, NYPL]

The N. Y. American Office,
Washington, D. C.,
Oct. 12, 1904.

My dear Davis,

The "bad eminence" of turning down Sterling's great poem is one that you will have to share with some of your esteemed fellow magazinists—for examples, the editors of The Atlantic, Harper's, Scribner's, The Century, and now The Metropolitan, all of the elite. All these gentlemen, I believe, profess, as you do not, to know literature when they see it, and to deal in it.

Well, *I* profess to deal in it in a small way, and if Sterling will let me I propose some day to ask judgment between them and me.

Even *you* ask for literature—if my stories are literature, as you are good enough to imply. (By the way, all the leading publishers of the country turned down that book until they saw it published without them by a merchant in San Francisco and another sort of publishers in London, Leipzig and Paris.) Well, you wouldn't do a thing to one of my stories!

No, thank you; if I have to write rot I prefer to do it for the newspapers, which make no false pretences and are frankly rotten, and in which the badness of a bad thing escapes detection or is forgotten as soon as it is cold.

I know how to write a story (of the "happy ending" sort) for magazine readers for whom literature is too good, but I will not do so so long as stealing is more honorable and interesting.

I've offered you the best stuff to be had—Sterling's poem—and the best that I am able to make; and now you must excuse me. I do not doubt that you really think that you would take "the kind of fiction that made 'Soldiers and Civilians' the most readable book of its kind in this country," and it is nice of you to put it that way; but neither do I doubt that you would find the story sent a different kind of fiction and, like the satire which you return to me, "out of the question." An editor who has a preformed opinion of the stuff that he is going to get will always be disappointed with the stuff that he does get. I know this from my early experience as an editor—before I learned that what I needed was, not a particular kind of stuff, but just the stuff of a particular kind of writer.

All this without any feeling and only by way of explaining why I must ask you to excuse me.

Sincerely yours,
Ambrose Bierce.

[110]   To Herman Scheffauer [BL (transcript)]

Washington, Nov. 4, 1904.

Dear Scheff,

At last I have a letter from you—dated in London, Sept. 15, but finished in Augsburg, Oct. 18. You mention another letter, but I got none. The postals, the map, and so forth, came, but I awaited a letter. Maybe it was not "nice" o' me, but I have thought you ought to write me, even a little one, from somewhere, you having so much to tell and I so little. By the way, did you ever observe that the difficulty of writing a letter, or rather the reluctance to write, increases in the ratio of the square of the distance that it has to go? That is odd, but it is so, at least with me.

Of myself there is little to say. I stayed in the Catskills three months outstaying the girls by a month—outstaying nearly everybody and leaving only when compelled by the closing of the hotels for the season. It was a great time that I had—my health excellent and my indolence indulged to the limit of decency. On my way home I stayed three or four days with my pretty friend at West Point and came down to New York on the sky-deck of a steamer under the harvest moon. I'm sorry you didn't carry out your intention of going to West Point. It is the most beautiful place in America and one of the most interesting, though it would be less so, doubtless, to you than to me. Au reste, I am content with Washington and an entirely charming autumn.

I find your letter most interesting, especially your account of your trips in Scotland, Wales and England. It stirs some memories in me, for of course I am familiar with the history and literature of the places that you visited, even those of them that I never cared to visit myself. To say the thing that is, I don't greatly care for places—I mean their outward and visible aspect—and would as lief see them through the eyes of others as through my own. Their people *do* interest me, and I would rather live long enough among a few of them to know them than to *see* all that they have to show in castle, town and country. To me a citizen is more interesting than a city, a peasant than a field. I'd stop over three months to study a custom, but not go a Sabbath day's journey to see a famous cathedral. That, I suppose, is because I am not a poet and an artist. God forbid that I press my individual tastes upon you, yet I could wish that your itinerary contemplated some longish stops here and there. The back of a bicycle or a seat in an express train is not the best view-point from which to learn what is best worth knowing about alien peoples. One must *live* with them. In this way I know—really and truly *know*— only one people besides my own: the English. You'll not mind, I hope, if I smile a little at your judgment of them. You will smile yourself when you are as old as I am.

Nov. 5.

I'm glad I was unable to complete this screed yesterday, for the interruption enables me to convey to you the cordial greetings of the Pollards. They came in to-day, from St. Louis, en route to Saybrook, and are to dine with me this evening. Pollard was up in the mountains with me three or four happy days. By the way, Miss Christiansen desires to be kindly remembered by you.

[...]

By the way, this is a good place to say that [the] reason why—*one* reason why—I made no reply to a certain long controversial letter of yours, nor made any allusions to it, was not the wish to be uncivil, but a dislike of the tone of it, despite the professions of respect. (As to the matter and methods of it, they seemed to me unworthy of you and of my attention). I once wrote you that I had to do a little defending of you, as well as you of me. It was against some of our best friends; and although in my personal intercourse with you I found nothing in their criticism of you (and have so assured them) that little controversy, as far as I permitted it to go, deprived me at the time of the pleasure of confuting them.

It was said of Goethe that he placed his finger on humanity, saying: "Thou ailest here and here."[1] God knoweth I don't want to do that to you, yet you have some tribal traits which I ardently hope that in the wider horizon that comes of travel will be less marked. That, not mere sight-seeing, is the best purpose of travel. You mention the polish that travel gives, and that is much; but far better is the cosmopolitan mind. We all ail here and here, but the healthiest intellect and disposition are his who has learned (most difficult of all lessons) to think of himself not as a German, an American, a Frenchman, or a Hottentot, but a human being, a man—, who takes no greater pride in the character or achievements of his countrymen than in those of any other nationality and hears them criticised, justly or unjustly, with no more feeling. Constantly to strive for this high ideal makes travel, thought, reading as nothing else can. But if, consciously or otherwise, we make these things subserve and harden and confirm our tribal instincts and patriotic prejudices, we travel, think, and read in vain. The tribesman is pretty strong in you, as in all young men, but if I had not "the faith to believe" that travel will sensibly diminish his power in you I should be sadder than I am.

You call me Magister, and I am proud of my pupil. It is the business of a master to teach—you'll say this is not teaching, but preaching. All right, but these things have a distinct and most important relation to your literary work; hence my concern about them. The broader outlook will make you the greater poet. The wider sympathies will humanize all your work.

So—I commend you to "whatever gods may be"[2] and remain your devoted friend,
Ambrose Bierce.

1. From Matthew Arnold's "Memorial Verses" (1850) on Goethe, l. 22.
2. From William Ernest Henley (1849–1903), "Invictus," l. 3.

[111]   To George Sterling [ALS, NYPL]

My permanent address   The Army and Navy Club,
                                               Washington, D.C.
Dear George,
    It's a long time since the date of your latest letter, but I've been doing two men's work for many weeks and have actually not found the leisure to write to my friends.[1] As it is the first time that I've worked really hard for several years I ought not to complain, and don't. But I hope it will end with this session in Congress.
    I think I did not thank you for the additional copies of your book—the new edition. I wish it contained the new poem, "A Wine of Wizardry".[2] I've given up trying to get it into anything. I related my failure to Mackay, of "Success", and he asked to be permitted to see it. "No", I replied, "you too would probably turn it down, and I will take no chances of losing the respect that I have for you". And I'd not show it to him. He declared his intention of getting it, though—which was just what I wanted him to do. But I dare say he didn't.
    Yes, you sent me "The Sea Wolf."[3] My opinion of it? Certainly—or a part of it. It is a most disagreeable book, as a whole. London has a pretty bad style and no sense of proportion. The story is a perfect welter of disagreeable incidents. Two or three (of the kind) would have sufficed to *show* the character of the man Larsen; and his own self-revealings by word of mouth would have "done the rest". Many of these incidents, too, are impossible—such as that of a man mounting a ladder with a dozen other men—more or less—hanging to his leg and the hero's work of rerigging a wreck and getting it off a beach where it had stuck for weeks, and so forth. The "love" element, with its absurd suppressions and impossible proprieties, is awful. I confess to an overwhelming contempt for both the sexless lovers.
    Now as to the merits. It is a rattling good story in one way; something is "going on" all the time—not always what one would wish, but *something*. One does not go to sleep over the book. But the great thing—and it is among the greatest of things—is that tremendous creation, Wolf Larsen. If that is not a permanent addition to literature it is at least a permanent figure in the memory of the reader. You "can't lose" Wolf Larsen. He will be with you to the end. So it does not really matter how London has hammered him into you. You may quarrel with the methods, but the result is almost incomparable. The hewing out and setting up of such a figure is enough for a man to do in one life-time. I have hardly words to impart my good judgment of *that* work.
    I never received the book of the "amateur astronomer"—Irving?—"How to Know the Starry Heavens."[4] Think he wrote me about it, but do not distinctly remember. If he sent the book to New York he might as well have thrown it into the sea; I'd have been as likely to get it.

I remember meeting Mary Shaw—twice, I think—and having luncheon with her. The cab indicent I do not recall. Nor do I think we had any argument, "warm" or otherwise. If I really did *not* "try to seduce her" in a cab it may have been because the conditions were unfavorable. It can't be done in a cab—crede expertum.[5] I rather liked the lady and am sorry if my austere virtue pained her.

That is a pretty picture of Phyllis as Cleopatra—whom I think you used to call "the angel child"—as the Furies were called Eumenides.

[...]

I'm enclosing a review of your book in the St. Louis "Mirror" a paper always kindly disposed toward our little group of gifted obscurians. I thought you might not have seen it; and it is worth seeing. Percival Pollard sends it me; and to him we owe our recognition by the "Mirror."

I hope you prosper apace. I mean mentally and spiritually; all other prosperity is trash.

Sincerely yours,
Ambrose Bierce.

Feb'y 18, 1905.

1. AB was at this time contributing heavily to the *New York American*, both with a recurring column of commentary, "The Views of One," and with other pieces.
2. A. M. Robertson published a second edition of *The Testimony of the Suns and Other Poems* in 1904. "A Wine of Wizardry" appeared in *A Wine of Wizardry and Other Poems* (San Francisco: A. M. Robertson, 1909).
3. Jack London, *The Sea Wolf* (1904), a novel about Wolf Larsen, a brutal ship captain heading to the Bering Sea to hunt seals. The novel is told from the point of view of Humphrey Van Weyden, a sailor on Larsen's ship, the *Ghost*, who falls in love with Maud Brewster, a young woman picked up by the *Ghost*. In the end, all of Larsen's crewmen desert the ship, and he deventually dies, while Van Weyden and Brewster are rescued by a revenue cutter.
4. Edward Irving (1856–?), *How to Know the Starry Heavens: An Invitation to the Study of Suns and Worlds* (New York: Frederick A. Stokes Co., 1904). The book contains numerous references to and quotations from GS's *The Testimony of the Suns*.
5. *Crede expertum* (properly *crede experto*) means "Believe one who has experienced it." GS has added a marginal comment: "O yes it can—crede expertum!"

[112]   To Herman Scheffauer [BL (transcript)]

The Olympia,
Washington, D.C.

Dear Scheff,

Your letter of March 27 from Augsburg has just come. I have many postal cards from you, and right glad I have always been to get them. In fact, I have liked them better than your letters. As you seem to take my silence seriously, and as I should be most unwilling either to pain or offend you—though I fear that I shall now do both—I break it to explain, with such consideration as is consistent with absolute candor, why I have not written to you. It was for this reason. I found the correspondence unsatisfactory. My habit in such cases is to stop it—at my end—and say nothing. For what can one say that will not be disagreeable? In a personal interview it would be easier, but in correspondence a statement entails a reply; an explanation may look like a complaint; a protest is magnified to an accusation. Everything looks unfriendly—everything seems exaggerated, and of controversy there is no end. The best preserver of goodwill and peace is silence. Believe me, it has been no easy matter for me *not* to write to you; it has not troubled you half as much as it has me.

Lest you should think that I refer to matters that have been in controversy between us, I will say that I have them not at all in mind. Some of the things that have affected me unpleasantly I will here set down. That may profit you in your correspondence and intercourse with others; and for the effect upon *our* relations—that is as God pleases. You have questioned me—I answer.

I do not like your Byronic (and Heineic) accounts of your love adventures. No kind of narration can make such matters acceptable; they are things of which one should not write, nor speak—not even to one's best friend.

I do not like your oracular way of *informing* me of many things which I knew as a schoolboy before you were born, and which I have always supposed *every* schoolboy knew. Such things, as that Hamburg belonged to the Hanseatic League; that Bremen is a great sea-port; etc., etc., etc. Really, either you must have been very ignorant if most of what you take the pains to tell me seems new to you, or you must think me so. There have been travelers and historians before you.

I do not like, for similar reasons, your care to translate for me the commonest foreign words and locutions—those that may almost be said to be a part of the English language as it is known to men who read. You need not translate French at all; I can manage that for myself. By the way, I am glad to know that you propose to learn it. I don't say that I *know* it myself, but I observed at Saybrook that your pronunciation of it was the eighth wonder of the world—at which, remembering certain things in our correspondence, I was naturally surprised.

I once wrote you that I had to do some defending of you, as well as you of me. It was not your work that I had to defend, but something else. You may now know what I have never told you: that I am, and all along have been, in correspondence with more of your friends and acquaintances in California than you would guess. My dear boy, the consensus of opinion is that you have changed a bit, particularly since the publication of your admirable book—that modesty is no longer your most charming virtue, as I had always found it to be, and that in the new character of Don Juan you were not pleasing. I was told by most of them—*George* has never had any but admiring and affectionate words for you; it all came from the other sex—that I would find you different from my notion of you. I did not find you different, except in two instances: you spoke disparagingly of George's sister and of Shatsie—which greatly pained me, for I think I knew them fairly well. (One of them complained to me of your manner toward her, and I had begged her to overlook it.) So—I took great pleasure in giving the earnest assurance, all round, that I had found you the same modest, gentlemanly fellow whom I knew as boy and man.

I know that all this will hurt, and suppose that some of it will anger, but you have asked me. And I know that if you read this letter twenty years hence, when I am dead, it will be with a softer feeling for the writer than I hope that you will have now. For if you *have* changed it is impossible for a man of your brains not to change back. I would advise—if I have the right—that you pay no attention to all this, even to the extent of replying; for poets (and men of the pen generally) are prone to epistolary violence, "as the sparks fly upward",[1] and pleasant relations of years are frequently destroyed by an unconscious dash of ink. I accept the danger with open eyes and a clear conscience, and if the result is a dead friendship—well, peace to its ashes; it was pleasant while it lived, and we shall both survive it.

Au reste, I am glad that you enjoy your breathless racing through many lands. I would not do it for ten thousand a year (I could get five thousand and expenses) but it will, I hope, do you no harm if little good; and you certainly have gratified your eyes. If you return you will be just [as] welcome in Washington as you were before—just as welcome as if nothing disagreeable had even been said or written between us.

I expect to pass a part of the summer at Saybrook—that is about all that I have in the way of news that you are not likely to [know] already from others.

I am, as ever, sincerely yours,
      Ambrose Bierce.
April 10, 1905.

My *permanent* address is The Army and Navy Club, Washington, D.C.

1. Job 5:7.

[113]   To George Sterling [ALS, NYPL]
Army and Navy Club,
Washington,
D.C.
Dear George,
　　Bailey Millard is editor of "The Cosmopolitan" Magazine, which Mr. Hearst has bought. I met him in New-York two weeks ago. He had just arrived and learning from Hearst that I was in town looked me up. I had just recommended him to Hearst as editor. He had intended him for associate editor. I think that will give you a chance, such as it is. Millard dined with me and I told him the adventures of "A Wine of Wizardry." I shall send it to him as soon as he has warmed his seat, unless you would prefer to send it yourself. He already knows my whole good opinion of it, and he shares my good opinion of you.
[...]
　　If you hear of my drowning know that it is the natural (and desirable) result of the canoe habit. I've a dandy canoe and am tempting fate and alarming my friends by frequenting, not the margin of the upper river, but the broad reaches below town, where the wind has miles and miles of sweep and kicks up a most exhilarating combobbery. If I escape I'm going to send my boat up to Saybrook, Connecticut, and navigate Long Island Sound.
　　Are you near enough to the sea to do a bit of boating now and then? When I visit you I shall want to bring my canoe.
　　I've nearly given up my newspaper work, but shall do something each month for the Magazine.[1] Have not done much yet—have not been in the mind. Death has been striking pretty close to me again, and you know how that upsets a fellow.
Sincerely yours,
Ambrose Bierce.
May 16 1905.

1. AB was beginning to contribute to *Cosmopolitan*, but he continued to write numerous pieces—primarily very small installments (almost daily) of "The Views of One" and "Little Johnny" sketches—for *SF* and *New York American* until July 1906.

[114]   To Myles Walsh [ALS, UC]

The Army & Navy Club,
Washington,
June 6, 1905.

Dear Myles,

I think Lydia a good name, for the same reasons that make you like it. But you err in thinking that I would be surprised to know about that wee Walshette. I hear from Claire sometimes, and naturally heard all about it. If I didn't believe with Schopenhauer that it is a crime to bring a child into

"This place of wrath and tears"[1]

I'd felicitate you. Now that she's here I vote to let her remain; it would be hardly fair to put her to death.

No, my lad, you never read anything of mine before I "joined the crowd of phonetic-spelling humorists," if you refer to the "Little Johnny" things; they were begun in London before your birth.[2] And [they] are not "phonetic spelling" humor at all; the spelling is done for *vraisemblance* and is intended to represent the actual spelling of such a kid. As to the "crowd", they are mostly my imitators, as far as they are able to be. I've seen the rise and fall of more than a hundred "Little Willies", "Little Sammies", and so forth. The American (in Mr. Hearst's absence in Europe) has laid on a "Little Bobbie".[3] The editor, who doesn't love me, knew that that would make me quit, and it did. But there is a day of reckoning for him. Now I've no doubt that your taste is infallible, but perhaps if you were doing something commended in thousands of enthusiastic letters annually—many of them from more distinguished *littérateurs* than Myles Walsh, you'd look at the matter a little differently—particularly if the man from whom you got a hundred dollars a week were "stuck on" the stuff himself.

Would you mind knowing something of what you are talking about before talking about it? There is really something in the newspaper trade that you would be more competent to discuss if you knew a little about the conditions under which newspaper work is done. Anyhow, I'm not hungering and thirsting for your views of my work, nor for anybody's.

I'm expecting to be in New York soon and if you've been good meanwhile I'll look you up and let you buy me a drink. Nothing could be fairer than that—except Mrs. Walsh, to whom my best regards.

Sincerely yours,
Ambrose Bierce.

1. Possibly a misremembrance of Tennyson's "All flooded with the helpless wrath of tears" (*Enoch Arden*, 1.32). AB's reference to Schopenhauer is to the essay "On the Sufferings of the World" in the posthumous volume of essays, *Studies in Pessimism* (1893).
2. As noted, AB began publishing his "Little Johnny" sketches in London in September 1874. He wrote more than four hundred such items through 1909, containing more wordage than his complete fiction.
3. Sketches about "Little Bobbie," written by William F. Kirk (1877–1927), began appearing around this time in *New York American*. Kirk was the author of *The Norsk-Nightingale: Being the Lyrics of a Lumberyack* (1905).

[115]   To George Sterling [ALS, NYPL]

Washington,
June 16, 1905.

Dear George,
I'm your debtor for two good long letters. You err in thinking your letters, of whatever length and frequency, can be otherwise than delightful to me.

No, you had not before sent me Upton Sinclair's article explaining why American literature is "bourgeois".[1] It is amusingly grotesque. The political and economical situation has about as much to do with it as have the direction of our rivers and the prevailing color of our hair. But it is of the nature of the faddist (and of all faddists the ultra socialist is the most untamed by sense) to see in everything his hobby, with its name writ large. He is the humorist of observers. When Sinclair transiently forgets his gospel of the impossible he can see well enough.

I note what you say of Millard and know that he did not use to like me, though I doubt if he ever had any antipathy to you. Six or eight years ago I tackled him on a particularly mean fling that he had made at me while I was absent from California. (I think I had not met him before.) I told him, rather coarsely, what I thought of the matter. He candidly confessed himself in the wrong, expressed regret and has ever since, so far as I know, been just and even generous toward me. I think him sincere now, and enclose a letter which seems to show it. You may return it if you will—I send it mainly because it concerns your poem. The trouble—our trouble—with Millard is that he has voluntarily entered into slavery to the traditions and theories of the magazine trade, which, like those of all trades, are the product of small men. The big man makes his success by ignoring them. Your estimate of M. I'm not disposed to quarrel with, but do think him pretty square.

I have written Scheff a nice, friendly letter, with no reference to my other, nor to anything disagreeable. I sent him the "Wine of W." in the hope that he might "place" it. He'll need to place a lot of his own things if he is going to live by literature. It is unlikely that he can do it, but he is young and footloose, and there'll be no harm in his having his try at the game.

No, I don't care any more about your indiscretion *in re* "Town Talk",[2] and have no further curiosity to know what I said that you thought it worth while to "pass to print."

Bless you, don't take the trouble to go through the Iliad and Odyssey to pick out the poetical parts. I grant you they are brief and infrequent—I mean in the translation. I hold, with Poe, that there are no long poems—only bursts of poetry in long spinnings of metrical prose. But even the "recitativo" of the translated Grecian poets has a charm to one that it may not have to another. I doubt if any one who has always loved "the glory that was Greece"[3]—who has been always in love with its jocund deities, and so forth, can say accurately just how much of his joy in Homer (for example) is due to love of poetry, and how much to a renewal of mental youth and young illusions. Some part of the delight that we get from verse defies analysis and classification. Only a man without a memory (and memories) could say just what pleased him in poetry and be sure that it was the poetry only. For example, I never read the opening lines of the Pope Iliad—and I don't need the book for much of the first few hundred, I guess—without seeming to be on a sunny green hill on a cold windy day, with the bluest of skies above me and billows of pasture below, running to a clean-cut horizon. There's nothing in the text warranting that illusion, which is nevertheless to me a *part* of the Iliad; a most charming part, too. It all comes of my having first read the thing under such conditions—at the age of about ten. I *remember* that; but how many times I must be powerfully affected by the poets *without* remembering why. If a fellow could cut out all that extrinsic interest he would be a fool to do so. But he would be a better critic.

You ought to be happy in the contemplation of a natural, wholesome life at Carmel Bay—the "prospect pleases," surely. But I fear, I fear. Maybe you can get a newspaper connection that will bring you in a small income without compelling you to do violence to your literary conscience. I doubt if you can get your living out of the ground. But I shall watch the experiment with sympathetic interest, for it "appeals" to me. I'm a trifle jaded with age and the urban life, and maybe if you can succeed in that other sort of thing I could.

I never understood why you did not care to let me know your brother.[4] I know that he was worth knowing. By the way, I'm expecting every day a call from a bright young woman whom he interested in me by reading my work to her, and who, naturally, knows much about *you*. Your brother was her pastor and her friend.

As to Marian the Superb. Isn't Sag Harbor somewhere near Saybrook, Connecticut, at the mouth of the river of that name? I'm going there for a month with Percival Pollard. Shall leave here about the first of July. If Sag Harbor is easily accessible from there, and Marian would care to see me, I'll go and call on her. She has been so long the chief adornment of my "sitting room" that I feel like thanking her for the service. But maybe I'd fall in love with her and, being now (alas) eligible,[5] just marry her alive!—or be turned down by her, to the unspeakable wrecking of my peace! I'm only a youth—63 on the 24th of this month—and it would be too bad if I got started wrong in life. But really I don't know about the good taste of being jocular about Marian. I'm sure she must be a serious enough maiden, being your sister, with the sun of a declining race yellow on her hair. Eva Crawford thinks her most lovable—and Eva has a clear, considering eye upon you all.

I'm glad to know that Wood is square and will do the right thing by you. Please let me know, as soon as convenient, just how much money you are *out* on the "Shapes of Clay"—that's all I care to know about the bad business. (And let me ask you not to be "out" any more, under any circumstances—I don't care what becomes of the book.) That sum and the price of the books I have had is what I "hold myself holden" for. And I want to begin right away to discharge the obligation, which I shall do with pleasure. And with gratitude too. Do, please name the sum in your next.

This is assuming that Robertson will *not* "take over the whole edition for whatever you have put into it"—I'm sure he will be no such idiot. Commercial idiot, I mean. Why should he do so, when he would not touch it in the first place?

I'm going to send up my canoe to Saybrook and challenge the rollers of the Sound. Don't you fear—I'm an expert canoist from boyhood.

My felicitations (if they are not premature) to Katie. And my cordial regards to Carrie.

Sincerely,
Ambrose Bierce.
(over)

I don't recall Hopper, nor my letter to him, but shall look out for something of his in the magazines.[6]

Of course I shall be glad to read Mary Austin's book[7] if given time—I don't read many books—and will freely tell you what I think of it.

Yes, "Charly" Stoddard and I were friends (almost chums) ages ago, but for years have not cared for each other. Something came between. A part of it was my feeling that he was something of a toady and a bit affected. Maybe he has reformed. Hope so.

This is the sure-enough end of this letter.

A. B.

1. Upton Sinclair (1878–1968), *Our Bourgeois Literature* (Chicago: Charles H. Kerr Co., 1905), a reprint of "Our Bourgeois Literature: The Reason and the Remedy," *Collier's* 34 (18 October 1904): 22–25.

2. GS had sent AB's comment on London's *The Sea Wolf* (from letter 111) to Theodore Bonnet, the editor of *Town Talk*, where it appeared in Bonnet's unsigned column, "The Saunterer," in *Town Talk* no. 653 (4 March 1905): 13, under the heading "Bierce on London."
3. Edgar Allan Poe, "To Helen" (1831), l. 9.
4. GS writes in a marginal note: "(Jim)," referring to his younger brother James Davenport Sterling.
5. AB, although separated from his wife Mollie since 1889, had never divorced her. Mollie began divorce proceedings in December 1904 but died on 27 April 1905 before they could be finalized.
6. James Hopper (1876–1956), prolific novelist and short story writer, and friend of GS.
7. Mary Hunter Austin (1868–1934), novelist, short story writer, and suffragist. The book referred to is *The Land of Little Rain* (1903), a series of poignant sketches about the Southwest. Following GS's death, Austin wrote "George Sterling in Carmel," *American Mercury* 11, no. 1 (May 1927): 65–72.

[116]   To S. O. Howes [ALS, HL]

Army & Navy Club,
Washington,
D.C.

Dear Mr. Howes,

Your letter is nearly a month old. I was ill nearly all the time at Lyme—too ill to write letters, or anything, and am only just now able. Have been home five days.

No, I shall not be able to visit you at Galveston, though I should dearly like to do so if I had the leisure. I've tried going away from home to work. The plan is a bad one, resulting in no work; and now I *must* work.

As to the book.[1] It is nice of you to offer to do so much of the work, just for love of it. But the only reason that I have never done it myself (aside from my conviction that it would not pay) is that I have no time to give to it—for my newspaper grind is not all that I do, by much, though not all is for immediate publication, nor even for publication in the near future.

No, I don't think the book you have in mind would "go," but if you think otherwise, and care to do the work, you are welcome to all the profit. It was in that sense that I expressed to Pollard my approval of the notion.

Of course I could assist by sending you material—enough for the book (with what you have) even with the severest censorship and most fastidious selection. I should claim only the right of last revision.

Let me know how that strikes you—I hardly think you'd care to undertake it, and can't conscientiously advise you to do so. I should want your name on the title-page, as editor or compiler, and you might care to write an introduction.

I've not heard from Pollard since leaving Lyme, on the fifth. He was about to go to Iowa, and Mrs. Pollard with him. I was a week in New York, recovering breath for the rest of my journey.

You'll be pleased to know that the canoe with which I tried to assassinate you proved a gallant deep-sea boat, and in her I had many a tussle with the big waves of the Sound. This in my brief flashes of good health.

Miss Christiansen desires that you remember her and I that you come again to Washington some day.

        Sincerely yours,
                Ambrose Bierce.

Sept. 17, 1905.

1. *The Shadow on the Dial* (1909).

[117]   To S. O. Howes [ALS, HL]

                              Washington,
                                  D.C.

Dear Mr. Howes,
        [. . .]

I'm compiling "The Devil's Dictionary" at the suggestion of Doubleday, Page & Co., who doubtless think it a lot of clowneries like the books to which it gave the cue.[1] When they find that it is only sense, wit and good English they will probably turn it down in a hurry. I'm not sure but I shall make another book of anecdotes, fables and epigrams for publishers to flash their swords upon.

I've not heard from Pollard for a little time. He was "moving" at last advices. I'd buy that shack of his if I could be well there, but I proved that I could not.

I'm going to have my canoe decked and rigged for sailing as well as paddling. Come up and "serve before the mast".

Miss Christiansen sends love—that's her word.

        Sincerely yours,
                Ambrose Bierce.

Nov. 4, 1905.

I'm greatly obliged for the pleasure of reading about myself in the articles enclosed.

1. The book was published as *The Cynic's Word Book* (New York: Doubleday, Page & Co., [October] 1906). AB refers to Harry Thompson's *The Cynic's Dictionary* (Philadelphia: Henry Altemus, 1905) and other imitators.

[118] To John O'Hara Cosgrave[1] [ALS, VA]

> The Army and Navy Club,
> Washington,
> D.C.

My dear Cosgrave,

I really had no feeling in the matter of the reported conversation between you and Cowley-Brown. I merely wanted to know, you know.

Your letter surprises me—your recollection is so different from mine. I don't recollect that you ever asked me for a *story*. I don't recollect that I ever sent you a poem—I remember only some fables in verse,[2] sent in response to a published free-to-all invitation in the magazine. I do remember that I cared nothing for their rejection, but resented an editorial note in the next number, insulting to all those who had responded. I do not recollect that you, personally, ever asked me to write *anything* for the magazine. Maybe you did, but I do not recall the circumstances.

As to my sending you a poem, and then not letting you have it, when you wanted it—*that* is incredible. For what purpose under the sun could I have sent it?

You're right in thinking that I must have been frequently solicited to write for the magazines. I think there is not one of a year's standing that has not asked me—some of them repeatedly. But you are wrong in inferring that my "impracticality" accounts for my not doing so. In the first place, I do not admire American (and English) magazines. Secondly, I have always had a sufficient income from the newspapers—in which I prefer to write such stuff as the magazines want, if write it I must, for there it is forgotten the day after publication. There are other reasons which you are at liberty to give "when asked why you (I) are not in 'Everybody's'" or any other magazine except Mr. Hearst's. Their suggestions that I write for them never come from the man who passes last judgment on the stuff. A writer who thinks himself dealing with the chief finds himself dealing with a powerless subordinate. That is not business-like.

The suggestion always is that I "submit" my stuff, but no price for accepted stuff is ever "submitted" to me. That is not business-like.

The editor (for soliciting purposes) commonly wants a particular kind of stuff—if a story, a particular kind of story. That is a little *too* business-like, or rather small-tradesman-like; for that is a matter which no good writer can control. A story—a good story—writes itself; that is, it developes spontaneously under the pen. One incident *entails* another, as in life, and the dénouement, as in life, is beyond control. Remember, I am speaking of *good* stories; bad ones can be written on preconceived lines, but I don't care to write bad stories; at least I don't care to publish them—with a waste-basket within easy reach.

So far as I can see, what the very small men who mostly edit magazines want is stories in which nothing occurs, with a "happy ending". (The only good story that I ever saw in "Everybody's" was prefaced with an editorial apology for printing it and a promise never to print another like it.) Seeing a good story in a book—say one of those which you are kind enough to say that you admire in my books—the editor may *think* he would like to have one like it; but getting the same kind of story in manuscript, he would be scared to death and could not send it back quickly enough to suit him. I fancy I know whereof I speak.

Our good friend Mackay recently wrote me a letter of extravagant praise regarding a published "story" of mine called "Ashes of the Beacon".[3] A few months before, it had been submitted to him, exactly as afterward published, and he had turned it down with his own lily-white hand and given abundant reasons.

You were once pleased to say that I am a man of genius. Carlyle points out that the first impression of a work of genius is disagreeable. Editors have to go by first impressions—which is a trifle hard on men of genius. I sometimes send the work of my friends and pupils (they are such *because* I think I detect their great talent, for I am not fool enough to waste gratuitous instruction on incompetents.) to the magazines. I *know* beforehand which of their things will be turned down—those that are incomparably the best. I recently sent George Sterling's "A Wine of Wizardry", the greatest poem in English since Keats and Coleridge, to the eleven leading magazines. They all rejected it, and not one of their notes showed the slightest consciousness that it was in any way "out of the common". Amongst these rejecting editors were three—I think four—Californians familiar with my work in literature, all of whom had expressed the highest opinion of my critical judgment,—two had pronounced it, in poetry, "infallible". Now what do you think of that? Nothing, probably.

When I write for a magazine I write only literature. Honestly, how many editors of American magazines do you think have been appointed for their knowledge of literature by proprietors having a knowledge of literature and of good judges of literature? How many have enough commercial sense to want it?—are "practical" enough to want it?

So it may be, my dear Johara, that the "fault" of my virtual exclusion from the magazines is not entirely mine. It may be that having looked at both sides of the matter you will think me less impractical than you *had* thought me. Possibly if you know, and would ask, some of my editors (say C. P. Mooney and W. P. Anderson, of "The American", and Bailey Millard of "The Cosmopolitan") you would strike a different judgment of me and learn that I'm not so terribly difficult to deal with, after all. And then, when asked why I am not in "Everybody's" you would know what to say without asking me to prompt you.[4]

No, I don't want a controversy, or I care nothing about our difference of opinion regarding so trivial a matter as my personal and professional character. You are afflicted with this interminable screed because I have had the leisure to write it, and have no other "medium" for it than personal correspondence. Unless I had Lawson's money I could never get my notions of American magazines and their editors into print to save my soul and theirs.

I have the friendliest regard for you, old man, and shall never forget your kindness to me when I needed kindness pretty badly. Perhaps that is why I care to have you think me less a fool than you seem to do.

I am yours, as ever,
Ambrose Bierce.
Nov. 19, 1905.

1. Cosgrave (see letter 33, n. 1) was at this time managing editor of *Everybody's Magazine*.
2. Some of AB's fables in verse appeared in *NYJ* (3 September and 17 September 1901; 15 September 1902), later reprinted in the section "Fables in Rhyme" in the revised edition of *Fantastic Fables* (*CW* 6), but not in Cosgrave's magazine.
3. "The Ashes of the Beacon: Written in 3940: An Historical Monograph," *New York American* (19 February 1905: 22), *SF* (26 February 1905: 44), an exhaustive revision of "The Fall of the Republic: An Article from a 'Court Journal' of the Thirty-first Century," *SF* (25 March 1888): 12; revised again as "Ashes of the Beacon" (*CW* 1); both versions rpt. in *The Fall of the Republic and Other Political Satires*, ed. S. T. Joshi and David E. Schultz (Knoxville: University of Tennessee Press, 2000).
4. Ultimately AB had only one piece published in *Everybody's Magazine*, the article "Have We a Navy?" (October 1909).

[119]   To George Harvey[1] [ALS, BL (Mark Twain Papers)]
Washington, D.C.
George Harvey Esqr.,
    Dear Sir,
        I regret that I am unable to accept your kind invitation to the Mark Twain dinner.[2] New York is such a long way off and the walking so bad. I rejoice, however, in everything—even in overeating—that tends to the greater glory of the only man in America who, always talking, writing and doing, has never to my knowledge said or done a foolish thing.
    I am sincerely yours,
        Ambrose Bierce.
Nov. 19, 1905.

1. George Harvey (1864–1928), a leading journalist of the period and editor of the *North American Review* (1899–1926) and *Harper's Weekly* (1901–13).
2. Twain's seventieth birthday party was held on 5 December 1905 in New York.

[120]   To George Sterling [ALS, NYPL]

Washington, D.C.

Dear George,
          I have at last the letter that I was waiting for—didn't answer the other, for one of mine was on the way to you.
    About "business". I'm not expecting Robertson to sell many of those books, and you shall not only *not* send me back any money for those he does sell, but you shall have back from me all that you have paid out that you don't get back from him. It's going to be a long transaction, apparently, but that's the way it's to be closed. And by way of beginning to close it I shall send you $236^{00} in a few days—the binders' bill.
    You need not worry yourself about your part of the business. You have acted "mighty white," as was to have been expected of you, and, caring little for any other feature of the matter, I'm grateful to you for giving my pessimism and growing disbelief in human disinterestedness a sound wholesome thwack on the mazzard.
    Scheff has not the chance, if he had the inclination, to "make amends", for I have returned one of his letters unopened, and should another. Please don't reprove him for what he cannot help; his offense goes to character. I'm infinitely sorry, and hope that he will some day be a better man; but as for our friendship—his and mine—that chapter is closed. It is not the first time that I've given of my heart without inquiry (I never knew a single one of his friends out there, whereas he knew many of mine) and have paid the penalty of disillusion.
    Yes, I was sorry to whack London,[1] for whom, in his character as author, I have a high admiration, and in that of publicist and reformer a deep contempt. Even if he had been a personal friend I should have whacked him, and doubtless much harder. I'm not one of those who give their friends carte blanche to sin. If my friend dishonors himself he dishonors me; if he makes a fool of himself he makes a fool of me—which another cannot do. However, I don't fancy London did more than smile when smitten on the brazen cheek of him.
    [...]
    Your description of your new environment, in your other letter, makes me "homesick" to see it. I cordially congratulate you and Mrs. Sterling on having the sense to do what I have always been too indolent to do—namely as you please. Guess I've been always too busy "warming both hands before the fire of life." And now, when

> "It sinks and I am ready to depart,"[2]

I find that the damned fire was in *me* and ought to have been quenched with a dash of cold sense. I'm having my canoe decked and yawl-rigged for deep water and live in the hope of being drowned according to the dictates of my conscience.

By way of proving my power of self-restraint I'm going to stop this screed with a whole page unused.
Sincerely yours, as ever,
Ambrose Bierce.
Dec. 3, 1905.

1. It is not entirely clear what AB is referring to here. His only published comment on London at this time occurs in the column "The Views of One" (*New York American*, 26 October 1905: 18; *SF*, 1 November 1905: 20), which contains the following lines:

Who would not laugh if such a man there be?
Who would not weep if London Jack were he?

AB became increasingly vexed by London, chiefly for his socialist politics.
2. Both quoted lines are from Walter Savage Landor, "Dying Speech of an Old Philosopher" (1859), ll. 3–4 ("warmed" in Landor).

[121]   To George Sterling [ALS, NYPL]

Washington,
D.C.

Dear George,
    [...]
I have read Mary Austin's book with unexpected interest. It is pleasing exceedingly. You may not know that I'm familiar with the *kind* of country she writes of, and reading the book was like traversing it again. But the best of her is her style. That is delicious. It is a slight "tang" of archaism—just enough to suggest "lucent sirups tinct with cinnamon",[1] or the "spice and balm" of Miller's sea-winds. And what a knack at observation she has! Nothing escapes her eye. Tell me about her. What else has she written? What is she going to write? If she is still young she will do great work; if not—well, she *has* done it in that book. But she'll have to hammer and hammer again and again before the world will hear and heed.
    As to me I'm pot-boiling. My stuff in the N.Y. American (I presume that the part of it that you see is in the Examiner) is mere piffle, written without effort, purpose or care. My department in the Cosmopolitan is a failure, as I told Millard it would be. It is impossible to write topical stuff for a magazine. How can one discuss with heart or inspiration a thing that happens two months or so before one's comments on it will be read? The venture and the title were Hearst's notion, but the title so handicaps me that I can do nothing right. I shall drop it.[2]
    I've done three little stories for the March number (they may be postponed) that are ghastly enough to make a pig squeal.[3]

Your friend Wells is a long time "getting down to business" in his story of the comet—unless his business is now socialism, not literature.[4] Apropos of socialism, I enclose a skit on Jack London which has just caught my attention. It is harsh, but seems to me not altogether undeserved and not wholly unfair. Also one on Markham, which is amusing, though I don't know how fair it may be. I never see Markham and he has lost his interest to me since he has made a whore of his Muse for the wage of the demagogue. As a poet he was great; as a "labor leader" and "walking delegate" he disgusts.
My love to "Carrie".
Sincerely yours,
Ambrose Bierce.
Feb'y 3, 1906.

1. John Keats, *The Eve of St. Agnes* (1820), l. 267.
2. AB had resumed "The Passing Show" in *Cosmopolitan*, but the delay between the time he wrote it and the time it appeared in print made it difficult for him to address topical issues as he had been able to do in a daily or weekly column in the newspaper (see letter 124). The column continued until June, and AB did not replace it until February 1907, when he began "Small Contributions."
3. "Some Uncanny Tales" ("One Summer Night," "John Mortonson's Funeral" [with Leigh Bierce], and "Staley Fleming's Hallucination"), *Cosmopolitan* (March 1906); all rpt. *CW* 3.
4. H. G. Wells (1866–1946), *In the Days of the Comet* (1906), one of his utopian novels. It was serialized in the U.S. in *Cosmopolitan* (December 1905–October 1906), where presumably AB read it. AB's comment "Your friend Wells" refers to GS's brief correspondence with Wells in 1904, after GS sent him *The Testimony of the Suns and Other Poems*.

[122]   To George Sterling [ALS, NYPL]

Washington.
My dear George,
First, about the "Wine". I dislike the "privately printed" racket. Can you let the matter wait a little longer? Neale has the poem, and Neale is just now inaccessible to letters, somewhere in the South in the interest of his magazine-that-is-to-be.[1] I called when in New York, but he had flown and I've been unable to reach him; but he is due here on the 23^d. Then if his mag is going to hold fire, or if he doesn't want the poem for it, let Robertson or Josephare have a hack at it.[2]
[...]
I was greatly interested in your account of Mrs. Austin. She's a clever woman and should write a good novel—if there is such a thing as a good novel. I won't read novels.
Yes, the "Cosmopolitan" cat-story is Leigh's and is to be credited to him if ever published in covers.[3] I fathered it as the only way to get it published at all. Of course I

had to rewrite it; it was very crude and too horrible. A story may be terrible, but must not be horrible—there is a difference. I found the manuscript among his papers.

[...]

I had seen that group of you and Joaquin and Stoddard and laughed at your lifelike impersonation of the Drowsy Demon.

I passed the first half of last month in New York. Went there for a dinner and stayed to twelve. At the last—a low bohemian affair, very enjoyable—I met Isabel Frayser, sat by her, let her pet me all she wanted to, and bit her fingers when she fed me with nuts. She seems a goodish sort—is she? Sam Davis and Homer Davenport were of the party.[4]

Sam was here for a few days—but maybe you don't know Sam. He's a brother to Bob, who swears you got your Dante-like solemnity of countenance by coming into his office when he was editing a newspaper.

You are not to think I have thrown Scheff over. There are only two or three matters of seriousness between us and they cannot profitably be discussed in letters, so they must wait until he and I meet if we ever do. I shall mention them to no one else and I don't suppose he will to any one but me. Apart from these—well, our correspondence was disagreeable, so the obvious thing to do was to put an end to it. To unlike a friend is not an easy thing to do, and I've not attempted to do it.

[...]

When are you coming to Washington to sail in my canoe?

Sincerely yours,

Ambrose Bierce.

March 12, 1906.

1. Neale was planning a magazine devoted to Southern literature and culture, but it never materialized.

2. GS was considering the possibility of a limited edition of "A Wine of Wizardry" to be issued by A. M. Robertson or Lionel Josephare (1876–?), a California poet who was then working in a printing office.

3. AB and Leigh Bierce, "John Mortonson's Funeral" (see letter 121, n. 3). The story was included in the revised version of *Can Such Things Be?* (*CW* 3). It concerns a cat who was inadvertently locked in a casket, eats a part of the corpse, and then nonchalantly walks away when the casket is opened for the final viewing of the deceased.

4. For Sam Davis see letter 72, n. 2. Homer Davenport (1867–1912) was a cartoonist for the Hearst papers, especially *NYJ*.

[123]   To George Sterling [ALS, NYPL]
[The Army and Navy Club.
Washington.]
Dear George,
I write in the hope that you are alive and the fear that you are wrecked.[1] Please let me know if I can help—I need not say how glad I shall be to do so. "Help" would go with this were I sure about you and the post-office.

It's a mighty bad business and one does not need to own property out there to be "hit hard" by it. One needs only to have friends there.

We are helpless here, so far as the telegraph is concerned—shall not be able to get anything on the wires for many days, all private dispatches being refused.

Pray God you and yours may be all right. Of course anything that you may be able to tell me of my friends will be gratefully received.

Sincerely yours,
Ambrose Bierce.
April 20, 1906.

1. AB writes after hearing of the catastrophic earthquake in San Francisco on 17 April 1906.

[124]   To George H. Casamajor[1] [TLS, BL]
Washington, April 22, 1906.
My dear Mr. Casamajor,
I regret that I shall be unable to send you the "Passing Show" this month. I have it all written, but it is so bad that I will not stand for it, and I've been so hard hit by the San Francisco disaster that I'm unable to do anything creditable in place of it.

The trouble is deeper than that. I have all along found that the department [is] most difficult and unsatisfactory work that I have ever done, as I have repeatedly pointed out to Mr. Millard, who, I think, understands. The reason is this: The title, "The Passing Show," compels the stuff to be topical, to deal with passing events, things going on. But to write of passing events that which cannot be published until the events are a month-and-a-half dead is a thing that it is impossible to do intelligently. This I foresaw from the first, and ventured to give my stuff another (though not a good) title, although the title now used was suggested by Mr. Hearst. He requested that I use the title that he had chosen, and I have done so, but it mastered me—handicapped me. The work has been bad except where I have departed from the topical character that it implies.

Mr. Hearst, doubtless, has so many other and larger affairs engaging his attention that he has not thought much about this small one. I hope, at least, that he has not thought as much about it as I have; to me it has been a veritable nightmare. It is like the consciousness of being a dealer in stale champagne.

Of course I like to work for the magazine, and I have no objection to a "department." My notion is that some such work as that in the August number (with a better head) is what I can do best and is best for the mag, but I'm hospitable to suggestion.[2] Will you kindly let me know if my proposal meets with your approval? Perhaps, if the matter seems to you of sufficient importance, you will submit it to Mr. Hearst.

Regretting that I have "fallen down" and that I have a congenital inability to do uncongenial work,

I am sincerely yours,
                    Ambrose Bierce.

1. Casamajor was presumably a sub-editor at *Cosmopolitan*, working under Bailey Millard.
2. In the August 1905 *Cosmopolitan*, AB had the column "Diversions of an Idler" and the satirical sketch "The Jury in Ancient America" (later incorporated into "Ashes of the Beacon"). It is the latter item that AB refers to as his "best."

[125]   To George Sterling [ALS, NYPL]
                                                Washington,
                                                D.C.
Dear George,
            Your letter relieves me greatly. I had begun to fear that you had "gone before."[1] Thank you very much for your news of our friends. I had already heard from Eva Croffie. Also from Grizzly.

I don't think there will be a second edition of Shapes of Clay;[2] so I think you'd better close up the deal and let me know how much you are out of pocket. I've never paid for the copies that I've had—don't know how many. Wood probably knows. *Please* let me get the matter out of mind.

Thank you for Mr. Eddy's review of "Shapes". But he is misinformed about poor Flora Shearer. Of course I helped her—who would not help a good friend in adversity? But she went to Scotland to a brother long ago, and at this time I do not know if she is living or dead.

But here I am forgetting (momentarily) that awful wiping out of San Francisco. It "hit" me pretty hard in many ways—mostly indirectly, through my friends. I had rather hoped to have to "put up" for you and your gang, and am a trifle disappointed to know that you are all right—except the chimneys. I'm glad that tidal wave did not come, but don't you think you'd better have a canoe ready? You could keep it on your veranda stacked with provisions and whiskey.

My letter from Ursus (written during the conflagration) expresses a keen solicitude for the Farallones, as the fire was working westward.

If this letter is a little disconnected and incoherent know, O King, that I have just returned from a dinner in Atlantic City, N.J. I saw Markham there, also Bob Davis, Sam Moffett,³ Homer Davenport, Bob Mackay and other San Franciscans. (Can there be a San Franciscan when there is no San Francisco? I don't want to go back. Doubtless the new San Francisco—while it lasts will be a finer town than the old, but it will not be *my* San Francisco and I don't want to see it. It has for many years been, to me, full of ghosts. Now it is itself a ghost.)

I return the sonnets. Destruction of "Town Talk" has doubtless saved you from having the one on me turned down.⁴ Dear old fellow, don't take the trouble to defend my memory when—or at least until—

"I am fled
From this vile world, with vilest worms to dwell."⁵

I'm not letting my enemies' attitude trouble me at all. On the contrary, I'm rather sorry for them and their insomnia—lying awake o' nights to think out new and needful lies about me, while I sleep sweetly. O, it is all right, truly.

No, I never had any row (nor much acquaintance) with Mark Twain—met him but two or three times. Once with Stoddard in London. I think pretty well of him, but doubt if he cared for me and can't, at the moment, think of any reason why he *should* have cared for me.

"The Cynic's Dictionary" is a-printing. I shall have to call it something else, for the publishers tell me there is a "Cynic's Dictionary" already out. I dare say the author took more than my title—the stuff has been a rich mine for a plagiarist for many a year. They (the publishers) won't have "The Devil's Dictionary." Here in the East the Devil is a sacred personage (the Fourth Person of the Trinity, as an Irishman might say) and his name must not be taken in vain.

No, "The Testimony of the Suns" has not "palled" on me. I still read it and still think it one of the world's greatest poems.

You ask me if Markham mutilated Poe in the editing.⁶ I don't know—haven't seen the work. He is capable of that crime if he could thereby help along the cause of Liberty, Fraternity and Insanity. He is now rubbing shoulders with that bomb-throwing peasant, Maxime Gorky.⁷ I'll enclose (if I don't forget to) an account of their meeting—as ridiculous a bit of posing as you are likely to see. Fancy Marky striking an attitude and delivering himself of his studied Thriller: "We stand for humanity!" And Max doesn't understand a word of English!

Well, God be wi' ye and spare the shack at Carmel.
                        Sincerely yours,
                        Ambrose Bierce.
May 6, 1906.

On second thoughts I'll keep the sonnet about me for of course you have a copy, and of course, too, I can't criticise it.

1. Charles Lamb, "Hester" (1803): "Gone before / To that unknown and silent shore" (ll. 25–26).
2. Many unsold copies of *SC* were destroyed in the San Francisco earthquake and fire.
3. Samuel Erasmus Moffett (1860–1908) was a writer for various newspapers, including *SF* and *NYJ*. AB discusses his treatise, *The Tariff: What It Is and What It Does* (1892), in "A Backslider" (*SF*, 4 March 1892); rpt. in *The Fall of the Republic and Other Political Satires*.
4. AB refers to GS's sonnet, "To Ambrose Bierce," in *A Wine of Wizardry*. It did in fact appear later in *Town Talk* (4 December 1915).
5. Shakespeare, Sonnet 71.3–4.
6. *The Works of Edgar Allan Poe*, with an introduction by Edwin Markham. Cameo ed. New York: Funk & Wagnalls, 1904.
7. AB took a dim view of Russian writer Maxim Gorky (1868–1936), especially after Gorky published an article, "The City of Mammon: My Impressions of America," *Appleton's Magazine* 8, no. 2 (August 1906): 176–82, condemning American thirst for money. Gorky and his companion, Maria Andreyeva, had arrived in the United States in April 1906 and remained until September, staying mostly in New York. They created a scandal because they were not married.

[126]   To S. O. Howes [ALS, HL]

Washington,
D.C.

Dear Howes,

Do as you will in the matter of Joel Chandler Harris.[1] I don't care to "swat" him. I've cut up these things a good deal. The revelation of how carelessly I used to write, and doubtless do yet, is appalling! I'm sure you don't respect me any more. But then you must have observed it before. Doubtless carelessness is the upsetting sin of the newspaper trade—in which one kind of writing "goes" as well as another, and the temptation to "get it off and have done it" is irresistible. But I wouldn't have believed myself such a sloven if this reviewing my stuff had not drawn my attention to the matter.

I have finished the proofs of "The Cynic's Word Book"—not the page-proofs, but the others. I think D. P. & Co. mean to have to out in October.

We are sweltering here. I should like a lungful of your gulf air, blown across a mint julep. But it's not for me.

Sincerely yours,
Ambrose Bierce.

June 9, 1906.

1. Joel Chandler Harris (1848–1908), journalist and short-story writer who achieved celebrity and critical renown for his tales of Uncle Remus, with their faithful recreations of African American dialect

and folk myth. AB briefly acknowledged Harris in "Small Contributions," *Cosmopolitan* 45, no. 5 (October 1908): 566: "[Harris's] 'Uncle Remus' stories are his best work, and [...] have a particular value as negro folk-lore; ... [they] are good reading; they have no other value, and need none. Their author was not a student and investigator. He was just a writer, and wrote these things out of his head, as 'folk-lore' is commonly, and preferably, written. Harris's chief service to literature in these tales was in recording the negro dialect of his time and place; nobody else has had so true an ear for it, nor so great skill in putting it upon paper with the clumsy and disobedient means that our alphabet supplies."

[127]   To George Sterling [ALS, NYPL]

Washington, D.C.

Dear George,

Your poem, "A Dream of Fear," was so good before that it needed no improvement, though I'm glad to observe that you have "the passion for perfection." Sure—you shall have your word "colossal", applied to a thing of two dimensions, an you will.[1]

I have no objection to the publication of that sonnet on me. It may give my enemies a transient feeling that is disagreeable, and if I can do that without taking any trouble in the matter myself it is worth doing. I think they must have renewed their activity, to have provoked you so—got up a new and fascinating lie, probably. Thank you for putting your good right leg into action themward.

What a "settlement" you have collected about you at Carmel![2] All manner of cranks and curios, to whom I feel myself drawn by affinity. Still I suppose I shall not go. I should have to see the new San Francisco—when it has foolishly been built—and I'd rather not. One does not care to look upon either the mutilated face of one's mashed friend or an upstart impostor bearing his name. No, *my* San Francisco is gone and I'll have no other.

[...]

You are wrong about Gorky—he has none of the "artist" in him. He is not only a peasant, but an anarchist and an advocate of assassination—by others; like most of his tribe, he doesn't care to take the risk himself. His "career" in this country has been that of a yellow dog. Hearst's newspapers and Markham are the only friends that remain to him of all those that acclaimed him when he landed. And all the sturdy lying of the former cannot rehabilitate him. It isn't merely the woman matter. You'd understand if you were on this side of the country. I was myself a dupe in the matter. He had expressed high admiration of my books (in an interview in Russia) and when his Government released him from prison I cabled him congratulations. O, my!

Yes, I've observed the obviously lying estimates of the San Francisco dead; also that there was no earthquake—just a fire; also the determination to "beat" the insurance companies. Insurance is a hog game, and if they (the companies) can be beaten out of their dishonest gains by superior dishonesty I have no objection; but in my judgment they are neither legally nor morally liable for the half that is claimed of them. Those of them that took no earthquake risks don't owe a cent.

Please don't send Mary Austin's verses to me if you can decently decline. I should be sorry to find them bad, and my loathing of the Whitmaniacal "form" is as deep as yours. Perhaps I should find them good otherwise, but the probability is so small that I don't want to take the chance.

How *could* you think that the poet who I said could not write without solecisms was *you?*[3] Of course I meant Joaquin. And the two others unkindly criticised are Markham and Riley. That leaves *you* in sole possession of the crown. You never commit errors in taste and sense. You are not ignorant. You don't have lapses into anarchy and plow-tail philosophy. You don't write "dialect".

[...]

I've just finished reading the first proofs of "The Cynic's Word Book," which Doubleday, Page & Co. are to bring out in October. My dealings with them have been most pleasant and one of them whom I met the other day at Atlantic City seems a fine fellow.

I think I told you that S. O. Howes, of Galveston, Texas, is compiling a book of essays and sich from some of my stuff that I sent him. I've left the selection entirely to him and presented him with the profits if there be any. He'll probably not even find a publisher. He has the work about half done. By the way, he is an enthusiastic admirer of you. For that I like him, and for much else.

I mean to stay here all summer if I die for it, as I probably shall.

Luck and love to you.

      Sincerely yours,
      Ambrose Bierce.

June 11, 1906.

 1. GS, "A Dream of Fear," in *A Wine of Wizardry and Other Poems* (1909). AB refers to GS's use of "colossal" to describe "cerements" (l. 56).

 2. GS had persuaded many of his literary colleagues to reside in Carmel, making it a Bohemian literary colony of significance. It included such individuals as Mary Austin, Upton Sinclair, Grace MacGowan Cooke, the photographer Arnold Genthe, and, later, Sinclair Lewis.

 3. See "The Passing Show," *Cosmopolitan* 40, no. 4 (February 1906): 473–74: "Of the four living Americans most splendidly gifted by nature for the poet's art, one, through poverty in youth and indolence afterward, is so devoid of 'that fine sense of expression which belongs to him by the right of genius,' as to be unable to write ten consecutive lines without setting one's teeth on edge by some insupportable solecism; and two others are so frankly peasant in sentiment and sympathies that most of their work fades before it is dry."

[128]   To William Randolph Hearst [TLS, BL]
Army and Navy Club,
Washington,
D. C.

Dear Mr. Hearst,

If you have had the time to observe the absence of my work from the Cosmopolitan you may have inferred that the work was not done. That would be an erroneous inference: both the Cosmopolitan and the magazine that died a-bornin' have at all times had heaps of my stuff on hand, and it is still there, most of it in type. I do not know why more of it has not been used; it was accepted all right.

The American hasn't any, and I guess it will not have, for in my little differences with that paper which were referred to you I had the misfortune to win the decisions. That made me impossible. From a recent note of yours I infer, though, that you don't particularly care to have me work for your newspapers if there is room for me in the Cosmopolitan, and that suits *me*. A seven years' policy of repression by your editors has left me powerless to do any work for them that I care to do, and I'm "out of it" (with your assent, I hope) forever.

Mr. Maxwell and I have concluded an arrangement which I think will meet your approval and will last. It will last if he sticks to his agreement.

When the magazine was new you wanted me to do a department of current topics, under the head of "The Passing Show." That seemed easy enough, but when I came to do the work I learned what we did not know—that you can't (or rather, that *I* can't) discuss passing events intelligently in a monthly magazine. You can point out the show as it passes, but it has gone by a month-and-a-half before the spectator looks out of the window. You being inaccessible in Europe, I took the liberty of altering the head and the character of the stuff. I explained the reasons to Millard. On your return he informed me that you insisted on the original head, and I of course yielded.[1] But a few trials confirmed my notion that one can't make a daily newspaper out of a magazine: all the attempts of the other magazines [to] do so I find to be lamentable failures. The heading so handicapped me that I could do no fit work under it. So I gave it up and wrote stories and other things instead. Unless Millard explained my reasons to you, as I asked him to do, you may have thought my action capricious and unfair, not to say insubordinate. I want to make sure that you know my reasons; hence this letter. In order to feel sure that you get it I shall send it to your house. I had the bad taste once to tell your secretary to go to the devil. I observe with pain that he has not gone, and I think him capable of suppressing my letters if he has to eat them.

Sincerely yours,
Ambrose Bierce.

October 12, 1906.

1. "The Passing Show" was not resumed after June 1906.

[129]   To Perriton Maxwell[1] [TLS, BL]

The Army and Navy Club,
Washington,
D. C.

Dear Mr. Maxwell,

[...]

You say that "two contributions by one author in the same number is, I think, something that no good editor will endure." The traditions of every business are the creation of the small men in it—they being in an overwhelming majority. They sometimes make small successes. The great successes are made by men great enough to disregard them and their traditions. I have succeeded in some things myself (editing, among others) but never did so in any other way. That is the "secret" of Mr. Hearst's success—in business. It is the secret of every man's success. That is a matter for you to decide, however; it is none of my affair. But I understood Mr. Hearst to want more of my work in the magazine, and you told me that he did. How can he get it under that rule? We agreed on a department. That, of course, will go in every month, and it will bear my name. You have told me that you want stories too, and I know that Mr. Hearst wants them, for *he* told me so. You rule excludes them. (I have one already written and was about to make another, but of course I shall not send any now.) Pardon me, but you seem a little inconsistent.

The title "Matters of Fact" will hardly do for my department, for much of the work will have nothing to do with fact. Some of that which you have is not related to fact at all; much of it being imaginary and much being opinion. "Matters of Fact" was a subhead for the first paragraphs only. My preference for a title is "Small Contributions."

I shall expect it to go as written, the verses, the epigrams, the dialogue and all. You assured me that I should have "absolute liberty"; the work would have no charm for me if I had not.

I sincerely hope that we shall not have irreconcilable views about my place in the scheme of the magazine. It is not to my interest to have any place in it, but if I have one it must suit me. It suits me to do as little as you think Mr. Hearst will stand, but none will be anonymous (I wish the law permitted *nobody* to write anonymously) and you must not take the cream and throw away the milk, or what you consider the milk. That *I* would not stand.

Sincerely yours,
Ambrose Bierce.

Nov. 23, 1906

1. Perriton Maxwell (1868–1947) was an editor at *Cosmopolitan* (1906–10) and, later, *Nash's*.

[130]   To S. O. Howes [ALS, HL]
[The Army and Navy Club
Washington, D.C.]
My dear Howes,
   Your letter is nearly a month old, and unanswered! Fact is, I thought I *had* answered it till I found it to-day in my "unanswered" pigeon-hole.
   You are a little hard on Doubleday, Page & Co., don't you think?[1] We can hardly expect a publisher (who is a mere tradesman) to act against the advice of his salaried readers, and can hardly expect *them* to take any chances of a commercial loss on books that are different from what they are accustomed to. D. P. & Co. would doubtless willingly pay $50,000 a year to an infallible reader; and for the bad guessing of the fallible ones that they have they pay more heavily than any rejected author. Of course their "sugared words" are hard ("for the likes o' we") to hear, but most persons offering manuscripts would swear if they did not get a little sugar in their gall-and-wormwood of rejection. I never feel any resentment when my stuff is turned down; the publisher has to walk a dimly defined line between the devil and deep sea, and my sympathies are with him, generally speaking. I fancy you'll have opportunity for a lot of practice in charity before you get that book taken.
   [...]
   I'm doing very little—just the "Cosmopolitan" stuff. When I pointed out to Hearst, the other day, that I had quit his newspapers and found little to do in his magazine I ventured to suggest a readjustment of my salary. His reply was: "You haven't heard me shrieking about that, have you?" I was compelled to admit that I had not.
   I, too, hear no more from Pollard, but have a trembling hope that we shall soon see his play.
   We had eight inches of snow two weeks ago, and much of it is still with us. Can you imagine that—in Galveston?
      Sincerely yours,
         Ambrose Bierce.
February 19, 1907.

1. Howes had apparently offered *The Shadow on the Dial* to Doubleday, Page, and had been turned down.

[131] To George Sterling [ALS, NYPL]

Washington.

My dear George,

If you desert Carmel I shall destroy my Jorgensen picture,[1] build a bungalow in the Catskills and cut out California forever. (Those are the footprints of my damned canary, who will neither write himself nor let me write. Just now he is aperch on my shoulder, awaiting the command to sing—then he will deafen me with a song without sense. O he's a poet all right.)

I entirely approve your allegiance to Mammon. If I'd had brains enough to make a decision like that I could now, at 65, have the leisure to make a good book or two before I go to the waste-dump. Stick to your nunky[2] and get yourself a fat bank account—there's no such friend as a bank account, and the greatest book is a checkbook; "You may lay to that!" as one of Stevenson's pirates puts it.

That's good news you tell me of Mrs. Partington's recovery through "Christian Science". Not that I believe a word of it—that is, I don't believe she had cancer, or, having cancer, was cured. I've been reading the Christian Scientists lately, and have not found one of them who knows how to think. And of such is the kingdom of untruth.

[...]

If I could stop you from reading that volume of old "Argonauts" I'd do so, but I suppose an injunction would not "lie". Yes, I was a slovenly writer in those days, though enough better than my neighbors to have attracted my own attention. My knowledge of English was imperfect "a whole lot". Indeed, my intellectual status (whatever it may be, and God knows it's enough to make me blush) was of slow growth—as was my moral. I mean, I had not literary sincerity.[3]

Yes, I wrote of Swinburne the distasteful words that you quote.[4] But they were not altogether untrue. He used to set my teeth on edge—could *not* stand still a minute, and kept you looking for the string that worked his legs and arms. And he had a weak face that gave you the memory of chinlessness. But I have long renounced the views that I once held about his poetry—held, or thought I held. I don't remember, though, if it was as lately as '78 that I held them.

You write of Miss Dawson. Did she survive the 'quake? And do you know about her? Not a word of her has reached me.

Notwithstanding your imported nightingale (upon which I think you should be made to pay a stiff duty) your Ina Coolbrith poem is so good that I want to keep it if you have another copy. I find no amendable faults in it. I'm not enamored of its subject. She made me heaps of needless trouble.[5]

The feller that told you that I was an editor of "The Cosmopolitan" has an impediment in his veracity. I simply write for it, for a hundred a week, and the less of my stuff the editor uses the better I'm pleased.

Neale was down the other day and we boozed on champagne till it ran out at our ears—*his* notion of a good time. He swears his mag *will* come out in the spring. So I let matters rest as they were. I guess it will come out—sometime; and certes your poem will be in the first number.

[...]

By the way, Neale says he gets almost enough inquiries for my books (from San Francisco) to justify him in republishing them.

[...]

Ambrose Bierce.

February 21, 1907.

1. AB recently had paid $50 for a watercolor of "a bit of Carmel Beach" by Christian A. Jorgensen (1860–1935), who had had an exhibition of his Californian work in Washington, D.C.
2. GS's wealthy uncle, Frank C. Havens, for whom he was working.
3. This sentence added later by AB.
4. GS had quoted the sentence "We happen to know Mr. Swinburne. Physically, he is a choreatic weakling, faced like a fool" ("Literature," *Argonaut* 2, no. 4 [2 February 1878]: 7 [unsigned]).
5. "To Ina Coolbrith," in *A Wine of Wizardry*. Coolbrith (1841–1928), the poet laureate of California, was a longtime librarian in Oakland.

[132]   To George Sterling [ALS, NYPL]

[The Army and Navy Club
Washington, D.C.]

Dear George,

I'm enclosing a note from Sam Chamberlain, the new editor of the Cosmopolitan. I've given him your address (at Carmel—you wrote that you'd go there this month) and told him I knew nothing as to the matter of payment. Maybe you'd better write him your "terms" if you have any. I'm inclined to think he'll want to be fair.

I have told him also that it would hardly be agreeable to you to be made the subject of any controversy with Ambassador Bryce—I had already mentioned you in a paragraph in disproof of Bryce's assertion that we have no poets.[1]

Neale tells me that he wrote you about making a book of your work. He says publication in the magazine will not interfere with that project.

Sincerely yours,
Ambrose Bierce.

June 11, 1907.

160 Selected Letters

On second thought I'll enclose my fool article that is to go with the poem.[2] I knew the public would not see anything in the poem unless it were pointed out to them in the manner of a pedagogue at a blackboard.

A. B.

There is nothing in my article that will be new to *you*.

1. See AB, "Small Contributions," *Cosmopolitan* 43, no. 4 (August 1907): 461: "Mr. [James] Bryce, the venerable British ambassador, is pleased to lament the fact that America has no great poets. Mr. Bryce has the distinction to be ignorant, or he is inaccessible to poetry. In Mr. George Sterling and Mr. William Vaughn Moody we have two young poets of a high order of genius who have 'arrived,' and others are on the way."
2. "A Poet and His Poem," *Cosmopolitan* (September 1907); rpt. *CW* 10.

[133]   To William Randolph Hearst [ALS, BL]
Army and Navy Club,
Washington,
D. C.

Dear Mr. Hearst,

Ihmsen[1] has told me of your wishes in the matter of the Pulitzer person.[2] As my first impulse is naturally to please you, I undertook to punish the fellow, provided I could do so in the magazine, but that, I find, is impracticable, owing to the exigencies of magazine work. He would have sixty whacks to our one and we should be always two months behind.

And on reflection I see other reasons. I know nothing about the quarrel—did not know there was one—and know nothing about *him*. I should have to rely on your fellows in New York for my material facts, and there are not many of them whom I would believe under oath.

But here is my chief reason for asking you to excuse me—and please don't read any "sarcasm" into this friendly note. Since coming East I have not been allowed a free hand in your papers. You have yourself (as was your right) limited my liberty of attacking the men whom *I* think the worst enemies of the country. Your editors have gone much further in a policy of repression. I could not even write book-reviews unless I conformed to *their* views. (For examples, I wrote one on the work of Upton Sinclair and another on that of Maxim Gorky, considered *merely as literature*. Both were turned down because these gentlemen were "going to" do something for the paper—which they didn't do. In a few weeks the paper was abusing Gorky as if he had been a thief!) So I retired to the Cosmopolitan. It was my last ditch. I tried to earn my salary on it, but Mr. Maxwell would not let me. I was willing to write the whole magazine, covers and all, but more than half my stuff was thrown out, and they have now on hand three "ghost stories" of mine[3] and a review of a poem. (Maybe Chamberlain will run them; he says he will, but it was on account of him that I quit your newspapers.) All this time the magazine has found plenty of room to run a story by Mr. Block *every month.*

In brief, I have wasted eight years trying in your papers to make the same reputation here that you permitted me to make in California, and I have given it up. But if I cannot fight the men whom I think public enemies I will not fight anybody. I don't like the job of chained bulldog, to be let loose only to tear the panties off the boys who throw rocks at *you.* You wouldn't like it yourself in my place. Henceforth I won't *bite anybody;* a nice quiet life for mine. I'm going to be a literary gent, thank you—it is nicer, and there is nobody that can say me nay.

From what I have said it follows you have a right to my resignation from your service. It is hereby tendered, and on its acceptance I will be "heard to cease."[4] Please notify me by wire and say that you don't mind.

I am very sincerely yours,

Ambrose Bierce.

July 8, 1907.

1. Max F. Ihmsen, Hearst's political manager.
2. Presumably a reference to Hearst's wish that AB attack Joseph Pulitzer (1847–1911), owner of the *New York World* and other newspapers, and Hearst's chief journalistic rival. Pulitzer had strongly opposed Hearst's unsuccessful campaign for governor of New York in 1906.
3. The only ghost stories by AB that appeared in *Cosmopolitan* in the latter half of 1907 were "The Other Lodgers" (July) and "Beyond the Wall" (December). No other such work appeared until "The Man" (later titled "A Resumed Identity") was published in September 1908.
4. The phrase (which AB quoted repeatedly, presumably because he found it quaintly paradoxical) is from Joaquin Miller's "The Passing of Tennyson" (1892), ll. 23–24.

[134]   To William Randolph Hearst [ALS, BL]

Army and Navy Club,
Washington,
D. C.

Dear Mr. Hearst,

From the tenor of your telegrams to Ihmsen I judge that you have been dissatisfied with the amount of my work—not with its quality, I hope. You could not be any more dissatisfied than I was, as I explained in my other letter. You will recall, I think, that in my last conversation with you I told you that I could no longer work for your paper, and as I was allowed only a little space in the magazine I suggested a change in my salary. Your reply was that you were not shrieking. Of course, then, it was not up to me to shriek. Still I felt that you ought to have more work for your money. Your editor seemed to think differently, limited my department to three pages and, on the foolish ground that he did not want my name *twice* in the table of contents, would run nothing else of mine. I enclose carbon copies of two of my letters about this matter, in order that you may see that I did all that I could to earn my salary from the magazine.

Chamberlain is now showing a disposition to give me a square deal—or rather give you one—by running the stuff that Maxwell would not.

I never knew anything about the ownership of the magazine, or which of your publications paid my salary. I supposed that was merely a matter of bookkeeping.

No, I cannot again work for your newspapers under the kind of men that run them. They know that I detest them—most of them—and in gratification of their revenge they do not hesitate to sacrifice your interests along with mine when the two are mixed. Even your express wishes, communicated to me and to them, count for nothing with them. It was not so in California, and there I did great work for you; but it has always been so here and always would be so.

The purpose of this note is simply to clear me of any suspicion that you may possibly have entertained that I took your money without *trying* to earn it. The delinquency, I think you will admit, was not mine.

  Sincerely yours,
    Ambrose Bierce.
July 13, 1907.

[135] To George Sterling [ALS, NYPL]

    [The Army and Navy Club
    Washington, D.C.]
    Aug. 17, 1907

Dear George,

  I guess several of your good letters are unanswered, as are many others of other correspondents. I've been gadding a good deal lately—to New York principally. When I want a royal good time I go to New York; and I get it.

[...]

Thank you for taking the trouble to send Conan Doyle's opinion of me. No, it doesn't turn my head; I can show you dozens of "appreciations" from greater and more famous men. I return it to you corrected—as he really wrote it. Here it is:

"Praise from Sir Hugo is praise indeed." In "Through the Magic Door," an exceedingly able article on short stories that have interested him, Conan Doyle pays the following well-deserved tribute to Ambrose Bierce, whose wonderful short stories have so often been praised in these columns: "Talking of weird American stories, have you ever read any of the works of Ambrose Bierce? I have one of his books before me, "In the Midst of Life." This man ~~has~~ had a flavor quite his own, and ~~is~~ was a great artist. It is not cheerful reading, but it leaves its mark upon you, and that is the proof of good work."[1]

[...]
I'm being awfully pressed to return to California. No San Francisco for me, but Carmel sounds good. For about how much could I get ground and build a bungalow—for one? That's a pretty indefinite question; but then the will to go is a little hazy at present. It consists, as yet, only of the element of desire. And that is new-born of this morning's reflection that there is, virtually, nobody here for whom I care a tinsmith's imprecation. The folk here are so damned different—and difference is a deadly sin.

The "Cosmopolitan", with your poem, has not come to hand but is nearly due—I'm a little impatient—eager to see the particular kind of outrage Chamberlain's artist has wrought upon it. He (C.) asked for your address the other day; so he will doubtless send you a check. If I were to guess I should say a hundred dollars. God knows that's little enough, considering the stuff for which they pay *me* that much.

[...]
"The other half of the Devil's Dictionary" is in the fluid state—not even liquid. And so, doubtless, it will remain.[2]

Sincerely yours,
Ambrose Bierce.

1. From an unidentified newspaper article. In the penultimate sentence, AB has crossed out "has" and "is" and written "had" and "was," respectively, thereby bringing the text in line with the original. See Sir Arthur Conan Doyle (1855–1930), *Through the Magic Door* (London: Smith, Elder & Co., 1907), 125–26. Evidently Conan Doyle thought AB deceased.

2. The Doubleday, Page edition of *The Cynic's Word Book* proceeded only through the letter L. If it had sold well, Doubleday would have issued a second volume containing the balance of the alphabet, but evidently it did not sell well. The remaining text did not appear until it was included in *CW* 7.

[136]   To George Sterling [ALS, UP]
[The Army and Navy Club
Washington, D.C.]
My dear George,
I'm awfully glad that you don't mind Chamberlain's yellow nonsense in coupling Ella's name with yours.[1] But when you read her natural opinion of your work you'll acquit her of complicity in the indignity. I'm sending a few things from Hearst's newspapers—written by the slangers, dialecters and platitudinarians of the staff, and by some of the swine among the readers. (The papers have no other kind of readers.)[2]

Note the deliberate and repeated lying of Brisbane in quoting me as saying the "Wine" is "the greatest poem ever written in America".[3] Note his dishonesty in confessing that he has commendatory letters, yet not publishing a single one of them. But the end is not yet—my inning is to come, in the magazine. Chamberlain (who professes an enthusiastic admiration of the poem) promises me a free hand in replying to these ignorant asses. If he does not give it me I quit. I've writ a paragraph or two for the November number (too late now for the October) by way of warning them what they'll get when December comes.[4] So you see you must patiently endure the befouling till then.

[...]

I am serious in wishing a place in Carmel as a port of refuge from the storms of age. I don't know that I shall ever live there, but should like to feel that I can if I want to. Next summer I hope to go out there and spy out the land, and if I then "have the price" (without sacrificing any of my favorite stocks) I shall buy. I don't care for the grub question—should like to try the simple life, for I have already two gouty finger points as a result of the other kind of life. (Of course if they all get that way I shan't mind, for I love uniformity.) Probably if I attempted to live in Carmel I should have asthma again, from which I have long been free.

I came here (to New York) two days ago. Yesterday I sought Phyllis, but she's gone to California—of which I am glad, for her family must wish to see her, and it is a better place for her. Try to dissuade her from the stage.

[...]

I expect to go to Galveston to visit Howes next month. Wish you and Scheff could meet me there. Howes, too, would be delighted.
           Sincerely yours,
                     Ambrose Bierce.
New York,
   Sept. 7, 1907.

1. An editorial note prefacing "A Wine of Wizardry" in *Cosmopolitan* (September 1907), combating James Bryce's belief that there were no poets in the United States, reads: "Obviously Mr. Bryce had not read Ella Wheeler Wilcox's splendid poem, 'Abelard and Heloise.'" Wilcox (1850–1919) was a prolific poet and essayist whose work appeared frequently in *SF*. AB had a low regard for her poetry.
2. *SF* for 4 and 7 September 1907 featured an editorial (written by Arthur Brisbane, according to AB) and readers' comments on "A Wine of Wizardry." For several weeks thereafter, *SF* was filled with comments from readers, journalists, and prominent writers about the poem.
3. In "A Poet and His Poem" AB had written: "I steadfastly believe and hardily affirm that George Sterling is a very great poet—incomparably the greatest that we have on this side of the Atlantic. And of this particular poem ["A Wine of Wizardry"] I hold that not in a lifetime has our literature had any new thing of equal length containing so much poetry and so little else" (*CW* 10.181). AB never stated that "A Wine of Wizardry" was the greatest poem written in America; in fact, he declared frequently that he believed GS's own *The Testimony of the Suns* a superior poem.
4. In "Small Contributions" (*Cosmopolitan*, November 1907) AB wrote briefly of the controversy over "A Wine of Wizardry." His more exhaustive comment, "An Insurrection of the Peasantry," appeared in *Cosmopolitan* for December 1907.

[137] To Herman Scheffauer [BL (transcript)]

Washington,
D.C.

Dear Scheff,

[...]

Murphy wrote me of your kind offer to write to the London publishers in behalf of my book of satires.[1] I have told him to do what he will with the book. I'd rather that it would come out there than here, but don't think it will find favor in either country. May I send Chamberlain a copy of your criticism of the work of that fool artist that made the borders for George's poem? I told him much of the same when I saw the proofs of the thing, but knowing that I was not an artist he gave me little attention—perhaps it was too late to alter the thing by making another border.

I'm having "heaps" of fun with the pigs that have snouted that poem and squealed their lack of appetite for its pearls.

You ask my opinion of Shaw. I've read little of him, but enough to observe that he has ideas. I should say that he sometimes falls short of sincerity. O, yes, I've noticed his indebtedness to me in some of his utterances (have not read nor seen any of his plays) but he's not alone in that. I have been a fairly rich mine for the "high-graders"—as I think the miners are called who steal the high-grade ore and sell it. I don't greatly mind, though it will make many passages in the Howes book look like plagiarism. But probably the Howes book will never find a publisher and I shall be spared.

No, George has not acquainted me with the nature of his trouble, and of course I have not asked him. Something about Jack London, wasn't it? I detest Jack London. He has a lot of brains, but neither honesty nor shame. According to his own conf—no, boasting, he is a tramp, a thief, a liar and a general all-around criminal. I'll put it another way when convinced that leopards change their spots. I know nothing of his character except what he has himself related in his disgusting Cosmopolitan articles.[2] He stinks.

[...]

I'm expecting to go to Galveston to visit Howes in November. Should have gone in October, but shall wait for Pollard, who wants to go too. George says he may run down there while I'm there. Of course he will not, but you—it is not far out of your way as you go to New York. Washington, though, is more directly in line.

I never hear from Millard now.
    Sincerely yours,
        Ambrose Bierce.
September 30, 1907.

1. AB refers to Scheffauer's offer to market *The Fall of the Republic and Other Satires* to British publishers. AB also refers to Daniel Murphy, a literary agent.
2. London published a series of autobiographical articles in *Cosmopolitan* (May 1907–March 1908) on his adventures as a hobo and in the underworld. They were collected in *The Road* (1907).

[138] To W. C. Morrow [ALS, SC]
            The Army and Navy Club,
              Washington,
                D.C.
My dear Morrow,
     Whether you "prosper" or not I'm glad you write instead of teaching.[1] I have done a bit of teaching myself, but as the tuition was gratuitous I could pick my pupils, so it was a labor of love. I'm pretty well satisfied with the results.

No, I'm not "toiling" much now. I've written all I care to, and having a pretty easy berth (writing for The Cosmopolitan only, and having no connection with Mr. Hearst's newspapers) am contented.

I have observed your story in Success,[2] but as I never never read serials shall await its publication in covers before making a meal of it.

You seem to be living at the old place in Vallejo street, so I judge that it was spared by the fire.[3] I had some pretty good times in that house, not only with you and Mrs. Morrow (to whom my love, please) but with the dear Hogan girls. Poor Elodie! she is nearly a sole survivor now. I wonder if she ever thinks of us.

I hear from California frequently through a little group of interesting folk who foregather at Carmel—whither I shall perhaps stray some day and there leave my bones. Meantime, I am fairly happy here.

I wish you would add yourself to the Carmel crowd. You would be a congenial member of the gang and would find them worth while. You must know George Sterling: he is the high panjandrum and a gorgeously good fellow. Go get thee a bungalow at Carmel, which is indubitably the charmingest place in the State. As to San Francisco, with its labor-union government, its thieves and other impossibilities, I could not be drawn into it by a team of behemoths. But California—ah, I dare not permit myself to remember it. Yet this Eastern country is not without charm. And my health is good here, as it never was there. Nothing ails me but age, which brings its own cure.

God keep thee!—go and live at Carmel.
    Sincerely yours,
        Ambrose Bierce.
Oct. 9, 1907.

1. Around 1899 Morrow had opened a writing school. See AB, "The Passing Show," *SF* (29 August 1899): 13.
2. Morrow's novel *Lentala of the South Seas* was serialized in *Success* and published in book form in 1908.
3. AB refers to his assumption that Morrow's residence on Vallejo Street (a major thoroughfare in northern San Francisco) was not damaged during the earthquake and fire of 1906.

[139]   To Robert H. Davis [TLS, NYPL]

                              The Army and Navy Club,
                                    Washington, D.C.

My dear Davis,
        Maybe you did *not* ask me for a ghost story. Certainly you did not ask me for a soldier story, nor for a story about a family disagreement, nor for a story of the vicinity of a certain village in Tennessee. Any one of these features would have been a fatal objection—if you did not want to take the story. That it began with the words "In the year 1861" would have served your need of a reason, for you did not ask me for a story beginning with those words.[1]

Let us see what you did ask me for.

            From your letter of October 11, 1904:

"There is, however, a type sticker caressing his machine against the day you send us some of the kind of fiction that made 'Soldiers and Civilians' the most readable book of its kind in this country."

            From your letter of October 15, 1904:

"'Just the stuff of a particular kind of writer,' to use your own phrase, is just what I want. That particular writer is the author of 'SOLDIERS AND CIVILIANS' which are the particular kind of stories desired."

And that is the particular kind of story that you got.
Now let us see how badly you caused me to think that you wanted it.

From your letter of October 21, 1904.

"No, I do not repent my proposal, and the misty hope you hold out to some day 'try a story' makes me feel like a blushing girl, sitting in the moonlight, voiceless and trembling for fear that a single word will cause her foolish lover to withdraw his hand. Therefore, I wait with patience and in hope."

Now for my view (at that time) of how much all this meant.

From my letter of October 17, 1904:

"As explained in my last, I have no feeling in the matter of your turning down my stuff (though I must remind you that God sees you when you turn down George Sterling's) and my objection to writing you a story is the conviction that it would disappoint you. My recollection is that every one of my stories has disappointed even the editor who has reluctantly accepted it, because it was not like the story that he had in mind."

Yet you seem to like these stories fairly well when you see them in a book.

From my letter of October 12, 1904:

"Even you ask for literature—if my stories are literature, as you are good enough to imply..... Well, you wouldn't do a thing to one of my stories."

And you didn't.

From the same letter:

"I do not doubt that you really think that you would take 'the kind of fiction that made "Soldiers and Civilians" the most readable book of its kind in this country,' and it is nice of you to put it that way; but neither do I doubt that you would find the story sent a different kind of fiction."

How is that for prophecy? I don't say that I knew you better than you knew yourself, but I knew, I knew. It is natural that you are averse to a "dispute;" a man who does recollect what he said that he didn't mean is at some small disadvantage in that sort of thing, no?

I have three times tested your sincerity in repeatedly asking me for work. You seem to like my copyright stories well enough when I give them to you (others have to pay for them) but work that would cost you something runs up against some insuperable objection forthwith. That is all right, but if I may claim some of the consideration due to a vertebrate mammal I will ask you not again to entice me off my comfortable reservation for the mere pleasure of shooting me. That is painful to my self-respect.
    Sincerely yours,
        Ambrose Bierce.
October 13, 1907.

1. AB refers to "Three and One Are One," *Cosmopolitan* (October 1908); rpt. *CW* 3.

[140]   To James D. Blake[1] [ALS, SFPL]

The Army & Navy Club,
Washington,
D.C.
[29 October 1907?]

James D. Blake, Esqr.,
    Dear Sir,
        It is a matter of no great importance to me, but the republication of the foolish books that you mention would not be agreeable to me. They have no kind of merit or interest. One of them, "The Fiend's Delight," was published against my protest; the utmost concession that the compiler and publisher (the late John Camden Hotten, London) would make was to let me edit his collection of my stuff and write a preface.[2] You would pretty surely lose money on any of them.

If you care to republish anything of mine you would, I think, do better with "Black Beetles in Amber," or "Shapes of Clay." The former sold well, and the latter would, I think, have done equally well if the earthquake-and-fire had not destroyed it, including the plates. Nearly all of both books were sold in San Francisco, and the sold, as well as the unsold copies—I mean the unsold copies of the latter—perished in the fire. There is much inquiry for them (mainly from those who lost them) and I am told that they bring fancy prices. You probably know about that better than I.

I should be glad to entertain proposals from you for their republication—in San Francisco—and should not be exacting as to royalties, and so forth.

But the other books are "youthful indiscretions" and are "better dead."
Sincerely yours,
Ambrose Bierce.

1. James D. Blake was a wealthy bookseller who apparently offered to subsidize the publication of some of AB's works.
2. *The Fiend's Delight* (1873). The other "youthful indiscretions" are *Nuggets and Dust Panned Out in California* (1873) and *Cobwebs from an Empty Skull* (1874). All were published as by "Dod Grile."

[141]   To Helen (Bierce) Cowden[1] [ALS, VA]
Galveston, Texas,
Nov. 14 1907.
My dear Helen,
Owing to a "lull" in "Southern hospitality" I am able to snatch a few moments to write a letter. I have been here for more than a week, and shall remain for another. I came only to see my friend, Mr. Howes, but *his* friends have refused to be ignored and it has been a rather strenuous experience of "attentions" and "entertaining."

Galveston is interesting, the weather has been glorious, mostly, the bathing in the surf is great, and, in short, I've had a pretty good time.

I stopped over on the way down and visited some of my old battlefields. Expect to go back by steamer as far as Key West, thence by rail up through Florida, South and North Carolina and Virginia.

I hope you are comfortable and prosperous—if only one, comfortable.

When I left I had neglected to subscribe for the American for you, but Carrie writes me that she attended to it.

My host has come in and has something "on hand"; so I close, with best wishes for you and Harry. Write me to Washington.
Affectionately,
Your Dad.

1. Helen Bierce's first marriage to Samuel Ballard was short-lived. Harry D. Cowden was her second husband, and Francis Isgrigg her third.

[142]   To S. O. Howes [ALS, HL]

[The Army and Navy Club
Washington, D.C.]

My dear Howes,

Thank you for the bathing togs, which came to-day, as did also the express stuff. I got home yesterday noon.

We had fine weather all the time on the gulf, but a pretty rough sea a part of the time. The Lampasas is a washtub for speed; we were exactly 7½ hours getting to Key West and—incidentally—to starvation. I was there only ten hours or I should have perished of famine. But every hour of the sea life was delightful. I chummed with the captain and sat at his table, with that pretty girl between of whom you predicted that she would not lack attention. Did I feel it my duty to confirm your reputation as a prophet? O, well, it was no great trouble. She too disembarked at Key West. I fear she lives there. She says so, but I don't see how anybody can!

From Tampa my journey was devoid of interest. I found Florida the most uninteresting country that I ever saw. Nothing but scrubby pines and sand, except in the cities, where "tropical" plants are cultivated sedulously and, I think, with difficulty.

Miss Christiansen asks me to thank you very much for the shells.

I'm writing Pollard.

Please present my cordial regards to the most charming of her sex, and convey to her my sense of her kindness to the Yankee invader.

Sincerely yours,
Ambrose Bierce.
November 30, 1907.[1]

1. Vertically in the left margin, AB wrote "Dec. 1. Snowing."

[143]   To George Sterling [ALS, NYPL]

[The Army and Navy Club
Washington, D.C.]

Dear George

It is all very sad about Nora May.[1] Believe me, I sympathize deeply. And I'm truly sorry that I made her the subject of an ill pleasantry in returning her verses.[2] She may not have "loved" nor "sinned", but evidently the poor girl had "suffered" more than enough. I hope that she did not know my cold opinion of her poetry if it would have been disagreeable to her. Of course I was more affected by the passing of Katie, of whom I was fond. Even Eva Crawford's philosophical view of that has not consoled me. Now to trifles.

[...]
I detest the "limited edition" and "autograph copies" plan of publication, but for the sake of Howes, who has done a tremendous lot of work on my book, have assented to Blake's proposal in all things and hope to be able to laugh at this brilliant example of the "irony of fate." I've refused to profit in any way by the book. I want Howes to "break even" for his labor.

By the way, Pollard and I had a good time in Galveston, and on the way I took in some of my old battlefields. At Galveston they nearly killed us with hospitality—so nearly that Pollard fled. I returned via Key West and Florida.

[...]
I'm not doing much. My stuff in the Cosmo comes last, and when advertisements crowd some of it is left off. Most of it gets in later (for of course I don't replace it with more work) but it is sadly antiquated. My checks, though, are always up to date.
Sincerely* yours,
Ambrose Bierce.
December 28, 1907.

* I can almost say "sinecurely."

1. Nora May French (1881–1907), California poet. She committed suicide on 13 November while staying at GS's home in Carmel. A volume of her *Poems* (1910) appeared posthumously, published with GS's assistance.
2. AB refers to his comment on one of French's poems in an earlier letter to GS: "I'm returning Miss French's poem. It has clarity and some other desirable qualities, but does not quite 'hit' me. My guess is that she never loved, sorrowed, suffered nor sinned. It would be a God's-blessing to seduce her—can't you undertake it? The work drags a little, owing to the equal number of feet in lines rhyming alternately—a meter not very tolerable in a long poem" (AB to GS, 25 June 1907; ALS, NYPL).

[144]   To S. S. Chamberlain [TLS, BL]
The Army and Navy Club,
Washington, D. C.
My dear Mr. Chamberlain,
Two or three years ago, when I withdrew from Mr. Hearst's newspapers because you and those whom you controlled made it impossible for me to continue work on them and retain my self-respect, Mr. Hearst asked me to continue my work on the Cosmopolitan. In consenting I suggested a readjustment of my salary. He replied: "You have not heard me shrieking about it, have you?"

I now hear a shriek, but it sounds like your voice, not at all like his. I fancy the agony is a purely Chamberlainian phenomenon.

When you took charge of the Cosmopolitan I foresaw the inevitable and told you that it would be better for me to retire. To persuade me to stay you made me several definite promises (four pages monthly for my department, all the stories that I cared to write, and so forth) but you have consistently broken them all, as I expected you to. Do you really think that I will make any arrangement with *you* again?

I will work for Mr. Hearst's magazine for any *salary* that he may name to me directly—that is a matter that I have always left to him without suggestion. But the notion that I will consent to my compensation depending on your goodwill and "acceptance" of my work is, in the light of experience, humorous. I should not make enough to pay for my cigars. Your proposal is rejected.

As to the Cosmopolitan bearing the whole expense of me, that is merely a matter of bookkeeping and does not at all affect Mr. Hearst's fortunes. Really there are some things that I might be presumed to know.

Mr. Hearst is fully advised of the situation and can appraise the value of my work as well as you can. He has copies of the stuff that I have written for his magazine, and will have copies of what I shall write henceforth, if he cares to have me write any.

If you think (as I do) that he is not getting from me the worth of his money you can easily give him its full value by using what I write. Perhaps you had thought of that; you are not without ingenuity.

Sincerely yours,
Ambrose Bierce

March 22, 1908.

[145]   To S. O. Howes [ALS, HL]

Washington, D.C.
March 24, '08.

My dear Howes,

I got out of New York on Saturday, after ten days of "riotous living," during which I was a model of abstinence and all the virtues. If you don't think so ask Neale, who avows his intention to meet you in Galveston and do things to you. He is to leave New York on Thursday—don't know when God will let him reach Galveston.

He has a project on for publication of my "complete works"—semi-complete, I hope. He will doubtless expound it to you. I'm not sure but it will require the coöperation of you and Blake eventually. But that part of it is in the far future.

I should like to accompany you on that trip to Yucatan, but dare say you'll not take it. By the way, give my love to Penland, whom I remember with pleasure and gratitude.

[...]

I've had a rather disheartening experience with Scheff—but you may ask Neale

about that. Still, I retain some small vestiges of my faith in the existence of a rudimentary gratitude in the heart of man. Don't know about a German.
Sincerely yours,
Ambrose Bierce.

[146]   To William Randolph Hearst [TLS, BL]
The Army and Navy Club,
Washington, D. C.
Dear Mr. Hearst,
You have larger affairs on your hands than the simple matter of *me*. Don't bother about me at all. I don't care to work for your newspapers: the combination of Chamberlain, Brisbane and Block is too many for me. For that matter I don't care to work for any newspaper.

As to Chamberlain's proposal, it is altogether absurd and insincere. If he would not use my stories (for example) when he got them for nothing—I being on salary—is it likely that he would use "six a year at $200 a story?" He makes me weary. He may, as editor, blue-pencil and waste-basket me into oblivion, but that he should have power to starve me in addition is out of the question. When he is my editor I must of course correspond with him occasionally, but *negotiate* with him or accept any terms of payment that he will have the power to affect—nay, nay.

If you want me to work for your magazine I shall be pleased to do so for any salary that you may name, and I will perform an equivalent service, as I have always done. But *you* will have to see that you get the worth of your money; the Chamberlains, Maxwells and Blocks of your entourage will not let you get it if by cheating *you* they think they can worry *me*. If you don't really care for my work the matter is very simple. I have remained on the magazine because you did not accept my resignation and I supposed that you *wanted* me to remain—despite my unwillingness to be a man-of-all-work (which I never undertook to be) and despite your persistent misunderstanding of my jocularity as sarcasm and my chaffing as serious accusation. But if you do not care for my work you have only to accept the resignation which I beg you to consider that you have always in hand. (I am working on my memoirs and need a whole lot of time anyhow.)[1]

I have never believed you cognizant of the annoyances to which I have been subjected, for you have tried to stop those that I have brought to your attention—thereby incensing their authors and making my last state worse than my first—but have always felt that you had somehow the notion that I entertained a personal dislike of you—which is so far from the truth that my personal regard for you is all that has kept me in your service, "in daily contact with the things" (mostly Chamberlains and Blocks) "I loathe."

You promise to consult with Chamberlain about me. Good, but how would it do to consult with *me?* If you will give me some idle half hour I can tell you some things that you will find interesting and profitable to know. Not about my compensation— that does not need any talking over with me or anybody. Fix it to suit yourself and you will suit me—if it does not depend on your editors' "acceptance" of my stuff.

    I guess that's about all, unless you care to see me.
        Sincerely yours,
            Ambrose Bierce.
March 30, 1908.

    1. It is unknown what these "memoirs" might be or if he was serious about writing them. By this time, all of AB's Civil War sketches, and also "A Sole Survivor," had been written and published. Possibly AB was revising these items, for they all appear under the title "Bits of Autobiography" in *CW* 1.

[147]   To Herman Scheffauer [TLS, NYPL]
                                  The Army and Navy Club,
                                        Washington, D. C.
My dear Scheffauer,
            How do you know that what I heard from Mr. Neale were "blundering and distorted tales?" How do you know that they were not true and accurate reports, to which I objected because, as you say, I "esteem the prostrations of sycophantic fanatics" (preferable) "to the intelligent praise of friends", and so forth. If you think that of me you have no right to assume that Neale blundered or distorted: a mere report by him that you thought me in any way fallible would be enough to turn me against you. Your remarks on Neale are, therefore, unwarranted. Maybe this logic is too cold for you.

    What Neale told me (authorizing me to repeat it if I cared to) was accurately in line with what I heard from California from all but one of those of our mutual friends with whom I am in correspondence; and all who have so reported are of one opinion: that it is due to my having put George Sterling above you as a poet. I don't say that they are right; I only know that your altered opinion of my critical abilities, or rather your habitual expression of it, was coincident in point of time with publication of my judgment of Sterling's primacy among American poets. A man's motive is known only to himself, and frequently not to him; so the motive does not cut any figure in this case—the fact is enough.

    The friends that warned you against the precarious nature of my friendship were right. To hold my regard one must fulfil hard conditions—hard if one is not what one should be; easy if one is. I have, indeed, a habit of calmly considering the character of a man with whom I have fallen into any intimacy and, whether I have any grievance against him or not, informing him by letter that I no longer desire his acquaintance. This I do after deciding that he is not truthful, candid, without conceit, and so forth—in brief, honorable. If any one is conscious that he is not in all respects worthy of my friendship he would better not cultivate it, for assuredly no one can long conceal his true character from an observant student of it. Yes, my friendship is a precarious possession. It grows more so the longer I live, and the less I feel the need of a multitude of friends. So, if in your heart you are conscious of being any of the things which you accuse *me* of being, or anything else equally objectionable (to *me*) I can only advise you to drop me before I drop you.

Certainly you have an undoubted right to your opinion of my ability, my attainments and my standing. If you choose to publish a censorious judgment of these matters do so by all means: I don't think I ever cared a cent for what was printed about me, except as it supplied me with welcome material for my pen. One may presumably have a "sense of duty to the public", and the like. But convincing one person (one at a time) of one's friend's deficiencies is hardly worth while, and is to be judged differently. It comes under another rule. Particularly is this so when the person enlightened is the publisher of the person under consideration, and there are pending between the two delicate negotiations affectible by the conversation.

Maybe, as you say, my work lacks "soul," but my life does not, and a man's life is the man. Personally, I hold that sentiment has a place in the world, and that loyalty to a friend is not inferior as a characteristic to correctness of literary judgment. If there is a heaven I think it is more valued there. If Mr. Neale (your publisher as well as mine) had considered you a Homer, a Goethe or a Shakspeare a team of horses could not have drawn from me the expression of a lower estimate. And let me tell you that if you are going through life as a mere thinking machine, ignoring the generous promptings of the heart, sacrificing it to the brain, you will have a hard row to hoe, and the outcome, when you survey it from the vantage ground of age, will not please you. You seem to be beginning rather badly, as regards both your fortunes and your peace of mind.[1]

So, you think that I disrupted our former relations "with scarcely the shadow of an excuse." It is not, I hope, your wish to revive all that. I told you once that our reconciliation would make necessary certain explanations by you. We met and I did not demand them, nor make any allusion to our cause of quarrel. This seems to have been greater magnanimity than you understood, or you would not now revert to the matter. I have forgotten nothing, however, and if you care to discuss that old affair when we meet, if we meet, I am reluctantly willing. Of course we will not do so by letter. But I shall have to begin the conversation by an imperative demand for an apology. Under the circumstances, it would perhaps be better to let that matter rest as it is.

Speaking of insults (you say I insult you) what do you call this from your letter? "Of course it would be quite in order for you to repay Neale for his 'fidelity' to you by reporting to him my opinion concerning his respected self."

That is perhaps your notion of what would be natural. But you did not get the notion from study of my character, I'm very sure, nor from associating with men of honor. I saw Neale every day while in New York, and he does not know that I feel the slightest resentment toward you, nor do I know it myself. So far as he knows, or is likely to know (unless you will have it otherwise) you and I are the best of friends, or rather, I am the best of friends to you. And I guess that is so. I could no more hate you for your disposition and character than I could for your hump if you had one. You are as Nature has made you, and your defects, whether they are great or small, are your misfortunes. I would remove them if I could, but I know that I cannot, for one of them is inability to discern the others, even when they are pointed out.

I must commend your candor in one thing. You confirm Neale's words in saying that you commented on "my seeming lack of sympathy with certain modern masters," which you attribute to my not having read them. That is a conclusion to which a low order of mind in sympathy with the "modern masters" naturally jumps, but it is hardly worthy of a man of your brains. It is like your former lofty assumption that I had not read some ten or twelve philosophers, naming them, nearly all of whom I had read, and laughed at before you were born. In fact, one of your most conspicuous characteristics is the assumption that what a man who does not care to "talk shop" does not speak of, and vaunt his knowledge of, he does not know. I once thought this a boyish fault, but you are no longer a boy. Your "modern masters" are Ibsen and Shaw, with both of whose works and ways I am thoroughly familiar, and both of whom I think very small men—pets of the drawing-room and gods of the hour. No, I am not an "up to date" critic, thank God. I am not a literary critic at all, and never, or very seldom, have gone into that field except in pursuance of a personal object—to help a good writer (who is commonly a friend)—maybe you can recall such instances—or laugh at a fool. Surely you do not consider my work in the Cosmopolitan, (mere badinage and chaff, the only kind of stuff that the magazine wants from me, or will print) essays in literary criticism. It has never occurred to me to look upon myself as a literary critic; if you *must* prick my bubble please to observe that it contains more of your breath than of mine. Yet you have sometimes seemed to value, I thought, some of my notions about even poetry. Still it must be very comfortable to feel that it is purely "by your own efforts" that you have risen. I am very glad indeed that you do not suffer from the sense of obligation which some minds find it a delight to feel.

Your talent for assumption is shown in your disparaging allusion to Neale's action toward Pollard.[2] What do you really know about that? You have not seen the correspondence (I *have*) and your "taking sides" in a matter on which you have no light is infinitely discreditable. If Pollard knew it I think it would not augment his admiration of you, yet that has a wide margin for augmentation. Perhaps I am unfortunate in the matter of keeping friends; I know, and have abundant reason to know, that you are at least equally luckless in the matter of making them. I could put my finger on the very qualities in you that make you so, and the best service that I could do you would be to point them out and take the consequences. That is to say, it would serve you many years hence; at present you are like Carlyle's "mankind:" you "refuse to be served." You only consent to be enraged.

I bear you no ill will, shall watch your career in letters with friendly solicitude—have, in fact, just sent in to the Cosmopolitan a most appreciat[ive] paragraph about your book, which may or may not commend itself to the editor; most of what I write does not.[3] I hope to do a little, now and then, to further your success in letters. I wish you were different (and that is the harshest criticism that I ever uttered of you except to yourself) and wish it for your sake more than for mine. I am older than you and probably more "acquainted with grief"[4]—the grief of disappointment and disillusion. If in the future you are convinced that you have *become* different, and I am still living, my welcoming hand awaits you. And when I forgive I forgive all over, even the new offence.
    Sincerely yours,
    Ambrose Bierce.
March 31, 1908.

1. AB speaks prophetically. In Berlin in 1926, Scheffauer killed a woman companion, then committed suicide by slashing his wrists and throat and jumping from a high building. Ironically, GS (AB's other disciple) also died, by suicide, in 1926.
2. The reference is to a dispute between Percival Pollard and Walter Neale over the terms of the contract offered by Neale for Pollard's book *Their Day in Court* (1909). Pollard maintained that the contract did not specify a sufficient amount of royalty.
3. AB wrote a paragraph praising Scheffauer's poetry volume, *Looms of Life* (New York: Neale Publishing Co., 1908), in "Small Contributions" (*Cosmopolitan*, June 1908).
4. Isaiah 53:3.

[148] To Walter Neale [ALS, HL]
                [The Army and Navy Club
                Washington, D.C.]
My dear Neale,
  [. . .]
  I am glad that your project still seems practicable to you—that is, that you think not only that you can come out without a loss, but with a profit. I should be better

pleased to drop it than to fear that you'd lose by it; and if at any time hereafter you have reason to fear a loss please do not hesitate to say so and we will abandon it.

There is one part of your plan that I'm doubtful about—the size of the volumes. Your notion is to have them 400 or more pages octavo. I have been hard at work getting the stuff that I have into shape and planning for the ten volumes.[1] I can't find 4,000 octavo pages of my *best* work, unless I use too much of one kind. I have enough (of all sorts) to make 10,000 or 20,000, but I want to be severely critical, admitting nothing but what I think my best work. And I figure out about 3,000 pages instead of 4,000—that is the volumes to be of 300 pages, or thereabout. Your first "Can Such Things Be?" is a fattish book, but it has only 320 pages. The London edition of "In the Midst of Life" is about the same size, with only 244.

We will talk of this when we meet. I go to New York (to dinner) tomorrow, but expect to be back in time to take luncheon with you here on the 6th May. I hope you can come out to the house, for I want to show you my "program" and what I have for the books. I've a tentative plan for each volume.

[...]

        Sincerely yours,
                Ambrose Bierce.

April 28, 1908.

1. AB's *Collected Works* ultimately was published in twelve volumes.

[149]   To George Sterling [ALS, NYPL]

                                                  Washington, D.C.,
                                                  May 8, 1908.

Dear George,

[...]

Neale passed last evening at my tenement. He is full of hope about my "collected works". I'm less sanguine. I showed him your sonnets. He has been studying up on sonnets lately, and thought yours the greatest ever. He would like to bring out a book from you, and *some* eastern publisher ought to.[1]

I'm glad to hear that Dick prospers, that his paintings command at least a living price. My love to him.

I do not remember to have told you of my latest—and last—break with Scheff; maybe you learned it otherwise. Scheff is impossible—I deeply regret that I ever knew him. I regret also that I transiently forgot my Schopenhauer, who warns against condoning an infamy by a friend, for in similar circumstances he will surely repeat the offense. (I forget the words.) I wish I could talk to you on this matter—I can't write much of it. I enclose my correspondence with Scheff on my recent return from New York; please regard it as confidential and return it. I was again in New York a week or so ago, but did not see him, nor wish to. His notion that Neale is my "henchman" and sycophant is this far true: that I don't know Neale's opinion of me as a writer, except in so far as it may be inferred from his willingness to publish my books. His opinion of me as a man I infer only from the fact that we dine and booze together.

I fear that I shall *not* get to California the coming summer. Neale's project entails an appalling sum of work in compiling, revising, proof-reading and the like. I'd better do it at once, for I might happen to die and leave the project incomplete. N's plan is to publish only two volumes a year but it would be hardly fair to him not to prepare the entire set as soon as possible. There'll be ten volumes, including, we hope, the Howes book as the last.
[...]
Good night.

A. B.

1. Neale never issued a volume of GS's poems, although he did publish the poem *To Ambrose Bierce* as a pamphlet in 1910. The only eastern publisher to issue GS's poetry in his lifetime was Henry Holt, who published *Selected Poems* in 1923.

[150]   To William Randolph Hearst [TLS, BL]

The Army and Navy Club,
Washington, D. C.

My dear Mr. Hearst,

I am sorry that in a matter more nearly affecting my interests than Chamberlain's you declined to consult me as well as him. That was neither friendly nor just. You say that there is no one about the Cosmopolitan office who is the least bit unfriendly to me. How can you know that? You have of course nothing but somebody's word for it, whereas you have had repeated proofs of Mr. Chamberlain's unfriendliness extending over a period of years. I have submitted them myself and you have acted on them by "reversing" him. If he is unfriendly to me is it to be supposed that he would tell you so? Surely you know human nature better than that. Well, I will submit more evidence. Since he came to the magazine my name has been carefully left out of the list of contributors, in the advertisements. I think it has not appeared once, whereas the others have been persistently "boomed," even the poorest of them. This is not a complaint, for I care nothing about it; it is mentioned as evidence of unfairness, and is not subject to any other interpretation.

Mr. Chamberlain tells you that he "cannot use a great amount of any one person's contributions without depriving the magazine of variety"—and you apparently accept that as true. Now it so happens that I am the only contributor whose work has been *various*. I have written nearly all the kinds of stuff that I used to write for your newspapers. I could write them no better, for whether I am writing for a newspaper, a magazine, or a book I cannot help writing as well as I know how. No good writer *can* help it, and no honest man would if he could. But Chamberlain has, persistently and without consulting me, cut out of my department all but one kind of stuff—this stickler for "variety"! If you looked at the slaughtered stuff that I sent you know that this is true. But I fear you find it more trouble to be just than to take somebody's word for it—somebody's else than mine.

Chamberlain finds no difficulty in using "a great amount of one person's contributions" in the cases of his much beboomed contributors, Lewis[1] and Block. One of them has a story every month and the other has had dozens—enough to make a large book. I have succeeded in getting in *two* (not counting three or four little ones of a page or so each.) If I had as much in the magazine as either of these two favorites would you not have thought that I earned my salary. If not your appraisement of the value of my work differs from that of the editors who are always asking me for stories. Only one of my two stories was run by Chamberlain, yet he promised to use as many as I cared to write.

Are Lewis's and Block's yarns distinguished for "variety"? One writes of nothing but cowboys, the other of nothing but Jews—one story just like another. I don't say that their work is not better than mine; I scorn to say anything about it; but they have no variety, and Chamberlain's reason for excluding me is an obvious lie. No, not an obvious one, or you would have seen its falsehood, but a lie all the same.

Now, I have told you that I would accept for the magazine work any salary that you choose to name. I stand to that. But it must be a *salary,* guaranteed by *you* and not dependent on Chamberlain's or anybody else's good will to me or my work, or anybody's treatment of it. I would not write for you for a dollar a word if any part of my money depended on any of your present editors' "acceptances" of the work. I've had a bellyful of that in my time.

If you figure my pay on the basis of Chamberlain's proposal, as to rate and amount of work, you will find that (assuming him to act in good faith) it about cuts my present salary in half. That is all right if I get the half, and may, as you say, write for other magazines and the weekly papers, or your papers. (But if I do write for your papers I shall set my own price on the articles and your editors can take them or leave them.)

So—I am willing to do the work that Chamberlain outlines (if that is what you want) for a salary of $2500 a year, so long as I am not subjected to any of the ten thousand kinds of annoyance that editors know how to use against contributors whom they personally dislike; some of which you know have been used against me, for on my complaint you have put a stop to them—temporarily. But I warn you that your stuffed Machiavelli will again resort to them when your back is turned.

It is a little amusing, the "fear" of me that you say pervades that neck o' woods. Perhaps that was why you refused to see me, though truly I should not have trampled you with my hoofs nor gored you with my horns. I should have been restrained by what has kept me working for you all these years: certain pleasant memories of the lovable Will Hearst of the old Merchant Street days—in the Hon. William Randolph Hearst I never took much interest.

O well, I am sixty-six, but I still cherish the hope that you may, before I peg out, meet a gentleman who personally knows me. Meantime, I shall await your answer to that part of this letter that is relevant to yours. The other parts are just "thrown in" for the joy of battle, and because I have a habit of proving my assertions. No part of it is confidential: I am entirely willing that Chamberlain should know what I think of him. It is honey and sugar compared with what posterity will think of him when I've done with him.[2]

   Sincerely yours,
    Ambrose Bierce.
May 18, 1908.

 1. Alfred Henry Lewis (1847–1914), one of Hearst's star reporters and a prolific contributor to *Cosmopolitan*.
 2. When AB compiled *CW*, he took the opportunity to skewer both Chamberlain and Hearst. For the poem "A Playwright," originally from a "Prattle" column of 27 October 1897, AB changed the name "McEwen" (alluding to him as a great liar) to read "Sam Chamberlain" (*CW* 5). A poem attacking Chamberlain entitled "A King of Craft" was added to "Some Ante-Mortem Epitaphs" in *CW* 4. In *The Devil's Dictionary*, AB changed the name of the "victim" in the poem for the definition "Diary" (1882) from an unspecified "Sam" to "Hearst" (*CW* 7).

[151] To William Randolph Hearst [TLS, BL]
            The Army and Navy Club,
            Washington, D. C.
Dear Mr. Hearst,
 [...]
 I am sorry that you think that my letter was censorious of *you*. I blamed you for nothing but refusing to see *me*, as well as Chamberlain, about this matter; which I thought, and still think, unjust. That is not so terrible, and is quite different from "devoting much time" to "proving that you are wrong in everything that you ever said or did." I merely tried to prove my assertion that Chamberlain was unfair and unfriendly—a statement that you had controverted. But I despair of making you understand my letters, for you seem to have the fixed idea that they are ugly, whereas I never write that kind of letter. You are not alone in this error however, I have had to

drop many good friends because they persisted in finding in my letters some of the qualities that distinguish some of my public work. Nor am I the only sufferer from that sort of thing: the satirists, from Rabelais down, have had to endure it with what cheerfulness they could. Shakspeare says:

> A jest's prosperity lies in the ear
> Of him that hears it, never in the tongue
> Of him that makes it.[1]

I doubt not that if the ancestors of some of your Jews were told that Jesus Christ was a sharp-tongued fellow they found the Sermon on the Mount a most bitter and sarcastic discourse. By the way, I was once told that you took seriously a preposterously jocular proposal from me to discharge me with a year's salary—maybe it was a month's—as an offending housemaid is dismissed. But perhaps my informant lied.

So if I misunderstand "the Hon. William Randolph Hearst" (though I don't remember that I ever thought he did not *want* to do right) he should not cast a very heavy stone at me, seeing that he himself is not without the sin of reading character through colored glasses and from slight personal acquaintance with the readee.

    Sincerely yours,
        Ambrose Bierce.
May 23, 1908.

1. Shakespeare, *Love's Labor's Lost* 5.2.851–53.

[152]   To Walter Neale [TLS, BL]

    Washington, D. C.
    June 7, 1908.

My dear Neale,

    The programme that you outline is alluring, but, I fear, more ambitious than we shall be able to carry through, especially in the matter of introductions to the volumes. My acquaintance (personal) with noted European writers is small, and I fancy their acquaintance with my work is still smaller. Certainly I doubt if any of them would have enough enthusiasm to be willing to write introductions as a labor of love. For that matter, I should not expect American writers to do that. It is only for a very dear personal friend that I would do it myself. We will talk of this, and all else, when you come.[1]

I have said nothing to Pollard about it.

To the early issue of so elaborate a prospectus as you have in mind there are even more difficulties than you mention.[2] I am thinking hard how to overcome most of them, but the one about the table of contents of each volume is, I fear, insuperable. Of even the volumes that I have virtually made up I cannot make tables, for I'm unable to say if I shall not have to add to, or subtract from, them when you have computed their bulk. With reference to those still to be made up the difficulty is worse. One or two of the books, as now existing, contain as many as 240 titles, some of which will be dropped, others added.

Within a few weeks I shall be able to make a *general* table of contents (something like the merely experimental one enclosed) with an account of the character of each volume.

Your intention regarding the get-up of the work looks good to me. The volumes should of course be uniform in "outward and visible"[3] aspect, each designated by its number. As to covers I go in for rich simplicity.

[...]

    Sincerely yours,
        Ambrose Bierce.

[Enclosure:][4]

Vol. I.	Ashes of the Beacon
	The Land beyond the Blow
	For the Ahkoond
	John Smith, Liberator
Vol. II.	In the Midst of Life
Vol. III.	Can Such Things Be?
Vol. IV.	Shapes of Clay
Vol. V.	Black Beetles in Amber
Vol. VI.	The Devil's Dictionary
	Epigrams+
	Apocryphal Dialogues+
Vol. VII.	Grotesque and Humorous Tales+
	Little Johnny+
Vol. VIII.	The Monk and the Hangman's Daughter
	Fantastic Fables
Vol. IX.	The Howes Stuff—title undetermined* +
Vol. X.	Essays in Little+
	Miscellaneous+

*This is the stuff that Howes meant for a second volume, and which I am asking back. Maybe Blake will not surrender it; if not I have plenty to take its place. You see I don't figure on the book that Blake is surely going to publish.

+Unpublished in Book Form.

1. *CW* appeared with no introductions by other writers.
2. In late 1908 or early 1909, Neale issued a thirty-two-page prospectus—titled *The Collected Works of Ambrose Bierce: Ten Octavo Volumes: Edited and Annotated by the Author*. Most of the pamphlet—consisting of a general account of AB, interwoven with extracts from his work—was written by Neale; but AB wrote some of the descriptions of the individual volumes (pp. 13–32; a typescript of AB's portion survives in the Library of Congress).
3. *Book of Common Prayer*: "An outward and visible sign of an inward and spiritual grace."
4. Vol. 1 also eventually contained "Bits of Autobiography"; Vol. 8 became Vol. 6; Vol. 7 contained *The Devil's Dictionary;* Vol. 8 contained the "grotesque and humorous tales" (published as "Negligible Tales," "The Ocean Wave," "The Fourth Estate," and "The Parenticide Club") as well as the epigrams; the Little Johnny sketches appeared in Vol. 12 as "Kings of Beasts," along with the "Apocryphal Dialogues" (retitled "Two Administrations") and other miscellaneous items. Vols. 9 and 10 contained essays of various kinds, though it is not certain which (if any) is "the stuff that Howes meant for a second volume." The book "Blake [was] surely going to publish" was Howes' compilation, *The Shadow on the Dial* (ultimately published by A. M. Robertson), printed in *CW* as Vol. 11.

[153]   To George Sterling [ALS, NYPL]

Washington, D.C.

My dear George,
    I am sorry to learn that you have not been able to break your commercial chains, since you wish to, though I don't at all know that they are bad for you. I've railed at mine all my life, but don't remember that I ever made any good use of leisure when I had it—unless the mere "having a good time" is such. I remember once writing (of Ina Coolbrith, I think) that one's career, or usefulness, was about ended when one thought less about how best to do his work than about the hardship of having to do it.[1] I might have said the hardship of having so little leisure to do it. As I grow older I see more and more clearly the advantages of disadvantage, the splendid urge of adverse conditions, the uplifting effect of repression. And I'm ashamed to note how little *I* profited by them. I wasn't the right kind, that is all; but I indulge the hope that *you* are.
[...]
  Neale has in hand already three volumes of the "Collected Works", and will have two more in about a month; and all (I hope) this year. I'm revising all the stuff and cutting it about a good deal, taking from one book stuff for another, and so forth. If

Neale gets enough subscriptions he will put out all the ten volumes next year; if not I shall probably not be "here" to see the final one issued.

[...]

Glad you think better of my part in the Hunter-Hillquist "symposium".[2] *I* think I did very well considering, first, that I didn't care a damn about the matter; second, that I knew nothing of the men I was to meet, nor what we were to talk about, whereas they came cocked and primed for the fray; and, third, that the whole scheme was to make a Socialist holiday at my expense. Of all 'ists the Socialist is perhaps the damnedest fool for (in this country) he is merely the cat that pulls chestnuts from the fire for the Anarchist. His part of the business is to talk away the country's attention while the Anarchist places the bomb. In some countries Socialism is clean, but not in this. And everywhere the Socialist is a dreamer and futilitarian.

But I guess I'll call a halt on this letter, the product of an idle hour in garrulous old age.

But before closing I want to say, in re Scheff, that I bear him no ill-will for his talk about me to my publisher, and to several other publishers. My indisposition to further intimacy with him is based mainly on many ugly things that he has said of others—some of them girls and women—things that I know to be false and obviously told to magnify his own irresistible charms to the sex. Nor do I forget his ungenerous attitude when you and I were "under fire". Instead of coming forward (as Miller and others did) and taking a hand in the fray, he stood apart, making mouths: each letter of his contained new objections to your poem.[3] As a poet he *knew* it a great poem, but that did not matter; if he'd had a single generous and loyal impulse in him he would have pitched in anyhow. He is niggardly of praise, niggardly of acknowledgement, niggardly in everything. I have a letter from him (unnoticed) *explaining* the niggard dedication to me in his book. I guess he had been comparing it with yours, or somebody had called his attention to the difference. He said that Dr. Doyle had advised him to go slow in that direction—Dr. Doyle, author of the dedication in "The Shadow of Quong Lung"![4]—my dearest of friends and a most grateful pupil! But Doyle was dead.

If I may be pardoned for quoting one of my own epigrams I think it will illuminate the subject:

"To most persons a sense of obligation is insupportable. Beware upon whom you inflict it."[5]

These are some of my views of Scheff's character; I don't invite you to share them, nor care that you should. He has been a keen disappointment to me, but I have no right to complain, for it had not occurred to me in the years that I knew him in California to make any inquiry as to whether he was worthy of my friendly interest. I was a fool, and it serves me right. I now learn (in mitigation of his offences) that he comes of a family of German peasants. If you know the type you know that he is not responsible; for the German peasant alters not from generation to generation—

Such as Creation's dawn beheld he rolleth now.[6]

Enough of Scheff. I'm sorry you cannot—will not—come East. It would do you heaps of good.
Sincerely yours,
Ambrose Bierce.
July 11, 1908.

1. In "Prattle," *SF* (16 October 1892): 6.
2. "The Social Unrest" (with Morris Hillquit and Robert Hunter), *Cosmopolitan* 41, no. 3 (July 1906): 297–302. Hillquit (1869–1933) was one of the leading socialists of his day and the author of *History of Socialism* in the United States (1903). Hunter (1874–1942) was a social worker and the author of *Poverty* (1904).
3. Scheffauer wrote no public remark about "A Wine of Wizardry," whereas Joaquin Miller published an effusively praiseworthy article, "Classic, Homeric, Titanic; Asserts Poet of Sierras," *SF* (8 September 1907): 37.
4. The dedication of Doyle's *The Shadow of Quong Lung* (Philadelphia: J. B. Lippincott Co., 1900) reads: "TO / AMBROSE BIERCE / THE GENTLEST, THE BRAVEST, AND / THE KINDEST OF MEN, THIS / LITTLE BOOK / IS AFFECTIONATELY DEDICATED BY / HIS GRATEFUL PUPIL."
5. "Certain Fool Epigrams for Certain Foolish People," *New York American* (26 August 1903): 14; *SF* (3 September 1903): 16; rpt. in "Epigrams" (*CW* 8.380).
6. Byron, *Childe Harold's Pilgrimage* (1812–18), Canto 4, l. 1638 ("thou rollest" in Byron).

[154]   To George Sterling [ALS, NYPL]

Washington, D.C.
Dear George,
  [...]
Thank you for the article from "Town Talk". It suggests this question: How many times, and covering a period of how many years, must one's unexplainable obscurity be pointed out to constitute fame? Not knowing, I am almost disposed to consider myself the most famous of authors. I have pretty nearly ceased to be "discovered", but my notoriety as an obscurian may be said to be worldwide and apparently everlasting.[1]

The trouble, I fancy, is with our vocabulary—the lack of a word meaning something intermediate between "popular" and "obscure"—and the ignorance of writers as to the reading of readers. I seldom meet a person of education who is not acquainted with some of my work; my clipping bureaus' bills were so heavy that I had to discontinue my patronage; and Blake tells me that he sells my books at one hundred dollars a set. Rather amusing all this to one so widely unknown.

I sometimes wonder what you think of Scheff's new book. Does it perform the promise of the other? In the dedicatory poem it seems to me that it does, and in some others. As a good socialist you are bound to like *that* poem because of its political-economic views. I like it despite them.

"The dome of the Capitol roars
With the shouts of the Caesars of crime"[2]

is great poetry, but it is not true. I am rather familiar with what goes on in the Capitol—not through the muck-rakers, who pass a few days here "investigating", and then look into their pockets and write, but through years of personal observation and personal acquaintance with the men observed. There are no Caesars of crime, but about a dozen rascals, all told, mostly very small fellows; I can name them all. They are without power or influence enough to count in the scheme of legislation. The really dangerous and mischievous chaps are the demagogues, friends of the pee-pul. And they do all the "shouting". Compared with the Congress of our forefathers, the Congress of to-day is as a flock of angels to an executive body of the Western Federation of Miners.

[...]

I think "the present system" is not "frightful". It is all right—a natural outgrowth of human needs, limitations and capacities, instinct with possibilities of growth in goodness, elastic, and progressively better. Why don't you study humanity as you do the suns—not from the viewpoint of time, but from that of eternity. The middle ages were yesterday, Rome and Greece the day before. The individual man is nothing, as a single star is nothing. If this earth were to take fire you would smile to think how little it mattered in the scheme of the universe; all the wailing of the egoist mob would not affect you. Then why do you squirm at the minute catastrophe of a few thousands or millions of pismires crushed under the wheels of evolution. Must the new heavens and the new earth of prophecy and science come in *your* little instant of life, in order that you may not go howling and damning with Jack London up and down the earth that we happen to have? Nay, nay, read history and get the long, large view—to learn to think in centuries and cycles. Keep your eyes off your neighbors and fix them on the nations. What poetry we shall have when you get, and give us, The Testimony of the Races!

[...]

I peg away at compilation and revision. I'm cutting-about my stuff a good deal—changing things from one book to another, adding, subtracting and dividing. Five volumes are ready, and Neale is engaged in a "prospectus" which he says will make me blush. I'll send it to you when he has it ready.

Gertrude Atherton is sending me picture-postals of Berchtesgaden and other scenes of "The Monk and the Hangman's Daughter". She found all the places "exactly as described"—the lakes, mountains, St. Bartolomae, the cliff-meadow where the edelweiss grows, and so forth. The photographs are naturally very interesting to me.
  Good night.
        Ambrose Bierce.
August 14, 1908.

1. A reference to a section, "The Genius of Bierce," in an unsigned column by Theodore Bonnet, "The Spectator," *Town Talk* no. 829 (18 July 1908): 14. AB's frustration found expression in "The Discoverers," written at about this time: "My! how my fame rings out in every zone— / A thousand critics shouting: 'He's unknown!'" (*CW* 4.366).
2. From Herman Scheffauer, "Proem and Dedication to E. D." (ll. 24–25), *Looms of Life*, 10.

[155] To George Sterling [ALS, NYPL]
              New York,
              Nov. 6, 1908.
Dear George,
  Your letter has just been forwarded from Washington. I'm here for a few days only—"few days and full of trouble," as the Scripture hath it.[1] The "trouble" is mainly owling, dining and booze. I'll not attempt an answer to your letter till I get home.
  Congratulations for your new book. I'm going to put that controversy over "A Wine of Wizardry" (my side of it) into Vol. X of *my* book—if you don't mind, and shall want to quote the entire poem, my article on it, and my reply to my, and your, "critics". *Do* you mind? Of course it will be a long time before Vol. X will be published.[2]
[...]
  By the way, why do you speak of my "caning" you. I did not suppose that *you* had joined the innumerable caravan of those who find something sarcastic or malicious in my good natured raillery in careless controversy. If I choose to smile in ink at your inconsistency in weeping for the woes of individual "others"—meaning other *humans*—while you, of course, don't give a damn for the thousands of lives that you crush out every time you set down your foot, or eat a berry, why shouldn't I do so? One can't always remember to stick to trifles, even in writing a letter. Put on your skin, old man, I may want to poke about with my finger again.
[...]
    Sincerely yours,
      Ambrose Bierce.

1. Job 14:1.
2. Although "A Poet and His Poem" and "An Insurrection of the Peasantry" were included in *CW* 10, AB did not reprint "A Wine of Wizardry" in the volume.

[156]   To Herman Scheffauer [TLS, NYPL]

Washington,
D. C.

My dear Scheffauer,

If our "falling out" is "incomprehensible" to you I suggest that you read our recent correspondence in the matter.

I would further suggest that if there is a way to my favor open to you it lies (as noted in that correspondence) through the region of repentance, confession and reform. My objection to you is your character, as illustrated in every phase and incident of our acquaintance—in your letters, in what all who know you tell me of you, and, more clearly than all, in what you have told me of others. As to that last I will recall to your memory a few characteristic instances. For the purpose, apparently, of establishing your reputation as a lady-killer you did not hesitate to slander George Sterling's sister. On the way to Saybrook you told me a particularly foul story, explaining that Shatsie told it to you. That needed no refutation. What it called for was something that (the more shame to me) I did not administer. When we were last in New York you told me that a lady whom it is needless to name had complained of the conduct of Dr. Franklin, whom I had taken to her house. That I found to be false, and I hardly think you will reaffirm it. Generally speaking, you have villified pretty nearly everybody that you and I have known, and I do not doubt that you have performed, or will perform, the same office for me.

Even in this letter before me, asking a reconciliation, the same ruling passion is manifest, first, in abuse of Mr. Neale, morally, socially and intellectually your superior, and, second, in a singularly dastardly attempt to set me against my friend Ed. Clough by as puerile and transparent a device as could be found in all the history of secret stabbing. I might forgive the stroke, for like all your assassin methods it is ineffective, but your low opinion of my discernment is unpardonable.

Do you care for further light upon your personal character? Of course you know it as well as I; the trouble is that you think it unknown to others; you are such an intellectual babe as to believe that one's character is a thing that can be hidden. You believe, doubtless, that your faithless and ungenerous nature did not show when in the famous controversy over George's poem—when your two friends were being foully assailed by the vicious and ignorant—you stood aside and made mouths. You probably think that I am unaware of your ingratitude in withholding any public acknowledgment of my years of service to you—a niggardliness which you accounted for with a lie derogatory to our dead friend Dr. Doyle. You did not know that I had the disproof of that falsehood in what I suppose to be the last letter that he ever wrote. Has it ever occurred to you to contrast yourself in this matter with that generous soul, George Sterling? I fancy it has. I fancy it was the consciousness of the difference that prompted your impudent attempt to minify my friendly help of others, even in letters to *me*. The attempt was to convince yourself. You would feel better if you could do that—your mind is that kind of mind: the sense of obligation is painful to it. "Every little distinction I have ever achieved has been through hard work, and purely by my own efforts." *This* to *me!*

I can easily conceive your state of mind on reading this letter. Even a friendly controversy is inconceivable to you; a difference of opinion is to you an opportunity for insult, and it is nothing else; and when you are cornered you are like a rattlesnake pegged down by the tale—you strike at everything in sight. But let me warn you: I have now struck at you, for as an honest man I have the right; but if ever again you strike at me I shall punish you.

I have kept these things to myself. The men and women that you have slandered do not know that you have slandered them. The fact that some of them maintain friendly relations with you should show you that. I hope for your success in literature, and shall probably do something (in a different way from the old way) to promote it,—an attitude that I do not expect you to comprehend. But our personal relations are at an end. If you have no more self-respect than to reply to this letter, that will be most unwise. Continue in that "serenity" of which you boast, but let me alone now and henceforth.

I am very truly yours,
                Ambrose Bierce.
January 10, 1909.

[157]   To William Randolph Hearst [TLS, BL]

                          The Olympia,
                          Fourteenth and Euclid Sts.
                          Washington, D. C.
Dear Mr. Hearst,
                I thank you for your good opinion of my story.[1] And it amused me to observe that you are not without a vestigial influence in the magazine; for both Mr. von Utassy and Mr. Norcross have suddenly discovered that I am a great writer.[2] Such an awakening!

Now, seriously, the story is no better than others that I have written for the mag. nor nearly so good as "The Moonlit Road," January, 1907; yet that and most of the others met with even more contemptuous treatment than *it* did—lying in the office for months unpublished, against my protestations. Indeed, nearly all my work has been treated in the same way. There is, or should be, pages of it in the office now.

In the three months since you and I had a distinct and definite agreement (which was immediately, and on two other occasions, "ratified" by Mr. Norcross) nothing has been done to carry it out, except to give me Horace Taylor to illustrate the "Little Johnny" stuff.

Mr. Norcross, when here a month ago, said the trouble was caused by Mr. Casamajor's disobedience of his orders, and he would discharge him—which I did not suggest. But Mr. Casamajor (who once, in the presence of the whole office force, told me that I should have but three pages in any issue) is still "disobedient" and still "undischarged". As long as that worthy Jew peasant and anarchist of the Brisbin Walker régime[3] is within a mile of the office there will be trouble about my work. I venture to suggest that you promote him to The Evening Journal and replace him with a human being. You are wrong, though, in the inference that I whacked him for what he did to my last story. I simply stopped sending stories. Excepting my last letter to Chamberlain, I have never written about my work to any of the gang otherwise than in the most civil and conciliatory way. All to no purpose.

You have always said you liked my work, and I suppose you do or you would not employ me. But have you ever seen it commended ("featured," I think they call it) in the magazine's advertisements and announcements? Tom, Dick and Harry have been crowed over (ineffectually, of course) as the greatest writers of the age, but Ambrose Bierce is never deemed worthy of more than mention by name, and seldom by so much as that. I am pretty tired of playing second fiddle, or no fiddle at all, to the nobodies whom your yellow journalist editors choose to think great. Do you wonder if I am not an enthusiastic contributor?

You will call this a roast of *you*. Not at all: I don't believe that you know how the men that serve *you* serve *me*. The matter seems hopeless. There can be no peace and good work until I am treated up there with at least as much consideration as is due from the Creator of the Suns to a scullery maid polishing a new tin pan.

Our agreement was that I was to have for my department of "Small Contributions" an irreducible minimum of five (5) pages, and was to do one article per issue (which might be a story), in addition—and I'm willing to throw in a "Little Johnny". Please look over the magazine of the last three months and see if that agreement has been kept. If not, I suggest that you demand an explanation. Of course I cannot, in making an agreement, deal with editors whom you change every foggy morning. I can only negotiate with you, for you only are permanent.

When Mr. Norcross was here he said that I should virtually edit my own department. Nothing came of the promise, and I have no more knowledge of what is going into it than the man from Mars. If *you* are willing that I shall edit my own department, and can rid yourself of the notion, sedulously implanted by your Chamberlains, that I would wreck your magazine, I will at my own expense go to New York and do so, every month. I don't hanker for the job, but foresee that it will pretty soon have to be that or nothing. But, anyhow, if the agreement that we made still suits you please see that your wishes are respected. Then you will get all the stories that you can want. I have carried out my part of our understanding by sending oceans of copy and giving you a monopoly of my work.

I am going to New York to-morrow to see what those fellows have done, or are going to do, with my stuff, though I have repeatedly done this before, at no expense to you. I shall probably be for a few days at the Navarre hotel, and shall be glad to call on you if for any reason you should care to see me.
   Sincerely yours,
     Ambrose Bierce.
March 7, 1909.

1. Apparently "A Stranger" (*Cosmopolitan*, February 1909), rpt. as "The Stranger" (*CW* 3).
2. George d'Utassy was a Hearst executive in New York. C. P. Norcross was editor of *Cosmopolitan*.
3. John Brisben Walker was briefly editor of *Cosmopolitan* (1905).

[158] To George d'Utassy [TLS, BL]
           The Army and Navy Club,
             Washington, D. C.
My dear Mr. von Utassy,
    Enclosed find my last check from The Cosmopolitan, sent under a misapprehension. I am no longer in Mr. Hearst's service.
   Sincerely yours,
     Ambrose Bierce.
March 23, 1909.

[159] To S. O. Howes [ALS, PU]
             Washington,
              D.C.
My dear Howes,
    I've just finished many days' work of proof-reading, and find time to "answer" letters—even to read some of them. (I read yours when it came.)

No, I've heard nothing from Robertson, nor from the books that he was going to send to me "in a few days."[1] What a long time eternity will be for that fellow! Has he really published the book, or is he going to?

[...]
I'm not writing for "Life," nor for anything—the article that you saw was written for "The Cosmopolitan" and kindly surrendered, with some other stuff, by the editor when I "quit."[2] "Everybody's," however, has just paid me $280⁰⁰ for an article on our navy, which will doubtless be published—sometime.[3] I'm living on my capital to finish my books.

Miss Christiansen (who has "nussed" me through another "instance" of asthma) sends love.

My "Write It Right" book is proof-read.[4] Here is an "entry":

"*Forecasted* for *Forecast*. For this abominable word we are indebted to the weather bureau—at least it was not sent upon us until that affliction was with us. Let us hope that it may some day be losted from the language."

   Sincerely yours,
     Ambrose Bierce.
July 27, 1909.
Many thanks for your good opinion of my poem.

1. AB refers to shipment of the long-delayed *The Shadow on the Dial*.
2. AB refers to "The Passing of Satire," *Life* (8 July 1909): 65.
3. AB, "Have We a Navy?" *Everybody's Magazine* (October 1909): 517–20.
4. *Write It Right: A Little Blacklist of Literary Faults* (New York and Washington, D.C.: Neale Publishing Co., 1909). The book sold very well, compared to *CW*.

[160] To Harry Cowden[1] [ALS, SC]
                  Washington, D.C.
Dear Harry,

I hope that by this time you have good news from Bib and your boys. You don't say so, but I suppose they are to be in Carson until you join them.

I guess it isn't much use for you and me to argue the "Christian Science" matter.

If the right kind of physicians (your embracing the "Christian Science" faith does not encourage me to think that you would know the right kind from the wrong) told you that you had Bright's disease you probably had, and if you had you have it yet.

As to the not having taken "a particle of medicine since", it is doubtless to that that you owe your "cure" of whatever disease you had, or thought you had. Here's a little story:

I have a friend who keeps a half-sanitarium, half-asylum, where he treats from fifty to a hundred patients at a time, most of whom he sends away in a few weeks cured.[2] He is a noted alienist, and is frequently called as an expert witness in cases involving insanity. I used frequently to visit him and his family, and came to know a lot about his affairs. One day he expressed to me his bad opinion of medicines, only a half dozen of which (naming them) he thought had any value. I asked him how, then, he effected the cures that I knew he did effect—which of these medicines he used. He replied: "None of them. My patients come to me saturated with medicines. I work the drugs out of them and they get well."

Sometimes he had patients that he did not need to deceive, nor do anything to—just cut off the drugs and *told* them that drugs were what was the matter with them. He is still running his daffy-shop with great success in that "Christian Science" way. But he doesn't claim any divine origin for his method.

The application of this story is that I fancy you got well because you stopped the drug habit.

Now about the two men who were "cured of double hernia" by "Christian Science". The explanation is very simple—the same that explains nearly all that is "wonderful" in this world: the men lied.

It will be useless for you to retort that they were honorable and truthful men. Nobody knows anybody to be truthful about his diseases and their symptoms and what cured them. If veracity in that matter were a necessary part of honor there would be so few honorable persons that the adjective would go out of use.

Here is something that I dare say you haven't been told, namely, that physicians can hardly ever believe their patients concerning the symptoms that it is important for the physician to know. Mr. Medico has to guess as well as he can—the patient, even on his deathbed, and knowing he is, will lie to him. (By the way, any district-attorney of experience will tell you that an ante-mortem statement under oath is mighty untrustworthy testimony.)

"Christian Science" can no more cure hernia than it can close an auger hole in a board. Medicine is equally powerless.

I have heard "Christian Scientists" say that their treatment has cured a broken leg. Then it can mend a broken broomstick.

These foolish people have got hold of a truth and don't know what to do with it. They are like the Fletcherites,[3] the Socialists, the phrenologists, and all the other one-idea gangs: they think their little truth is the whole thing, and has no limitations. They think the few phenomena that they have observed are the most important of all in the vast complexity of phenomena known to wider observation and more intelligent interpretation than their own. I once knew a man who thought that all the evils of society could be abolished if we would all sleep with our heads to the north. A friend of mine no longer calls on me because I refused to listen for the third evening to his exposition of a vegetable diet as the only thing to save mankind from disease and sin. Another believes that all man really needs is the habit of deep breathing—oxygen is life, &c. And so it is with all 'ists and 'ers and 'arians and 'ites—none can see the small figure that his fad cuts in the immense body of things worth knowing, because he doesn't know the others. Religions, even, are founded on such unimportant "miracles" as the "Christian Scientists" think they perform, though they call them by another name. All religions are founded on, or all, at least, are "attested" by miracles—mostly just such miracles as these cures would be if they were true and effected as they are said to be. I guess Mrs. Eddy has come pretty near to founding one.[4] She is of the sort to do it, for those whom the masses follow into the several temples have nearly all been poor, ignorant persons, such as Jesus the carpenter, Mahomet the camel-driver, Joseph Smith the farmer, and so forth. Jesus, however, *was* a wonderful man. I guess he would weep if he met Mrs. Eddy.

Of course it pains me to know that you and Bib have taken up with that gang, but it is your own affair more than mine, and we will not let it estrange us—at least not unless you put into practice some of its dangerous and unlawful tenets. That I would not stand. But I guess you're not bigot enough for that. Indeed, I don't think you are very strongly "wedded" to this new idol. It is a novelty and you have not thought to examine it and see if it is not stuffed with sawdust. Your business has not required you to know the relative values of things outside it. With years, observation and thought will come the power to discriminate, and you'll not be at the mercy of every dog of doctrine that gets you by the ear.

There, I feel a bit better, and having unloaded my mind I'll quit while I'm in a good humor, and before a renewed sense of the hatefulness of fads comes back to
                                    Your Dad.
August 8 1909.

   1. AB's son-in-law, the husband of his daughter Helen.
   2. Dr. John W. Robertson's facility in Livermore.
   3. Horace Fletcher (1849–1919) of Lawrence, Massachusetts, had advocated the the slow and thorough mastication of food. Among his numerous publications are *Glutton or Epicure* (1899) and *Fletcherism: What It Is* (1913).
   4. Mary Baker Eddy (1821–1910) founded Christian Science with the publication of *Science and Health* (1875).

[161]   To S. O. Howes [ALS, HL]
                                    Washington,
                                    D.C.
Dear Howes,
            I have been waiting for strength enough to write. My last bout of asthma was worse than the other; for ten days and nights I did not lie down. I'm all right now,

but a bit weak. If I dared I should go away, but would rather take my chance of another illness here, where I can have good care, than elsewhere. I shall be safe; and next spring I shall go to California.

I'm glad to infer that the book is at least *promising* well. Robertson (see enclosed note) seems hopeful. Of course it is getting a lot of abuse, as I expected it to—though I did not expect *you* to come in for any of it. You see what it is to be caught in bad company. Thank you for your futile effort in my behalf—the only recollected instance of a friend standing forth in my defense when my own hands were tied. Of course one cannot reply to criticisms of one's own books.

Lord, what a liar that "Current Literature" fellow is![1] Fancy my being a leading spirit of the Bohemian Club—to which I have not belonged for more than thirty years, and in which I never did take much interest. And did you observe how, in order to convict me of imitating Poe, he attributes to Poe a work that Poe never did—"a grotesque satirical tale" depicting "the downfall of the American republic."[2] Do you know of any such tale by Poe? If I had left the tragic and supernatural out of my stories I would still have been an "imitator of Poe," for they would still have been stories; so what's the use? For your entertainment I'm enclosing the Hildegarde Hawthorne and the Harrison Gray Otis "reviews".[3] Otis is ungrateful: when he was generally accused of cowardice for resigning his commission in the midst of the Philippine war I defended him by pointing out that it required the highest kind of courage to leave the battlefield and come home to face his wife's poetry.[4]

As to Hildegarde, somebody probably told her that she was witty and could pee against the wind. You may return these things when you've had your smile. They trouble me not.

Neale does not object to publication (by another) of the left-over essays subject to his right to incorporate them in his "set" finally. But I'd want to see them first, and possibly add something to widen the book's interest.

[...]

During this month another volume of the "Collected Works" should reach you; also my little blacklist of literary errors, "Write It Right"—beastly title, chosen with a naked and unashamed commercial purpose.

Sincerely yours,
            Ambrose Bierce.
September 6, 1909.

1. A reference to an unsigned article, "The Underground Reputation of Ambrose Bierce," *Current Literature* 47 (September 1909): 279–81, triggered by the publication of *The Shadow on the Dial* and *CW* 1.
2. AB wrote such a tale ("Ashes of the Beacon" in *CW* 1), but Poe did not.
3. Hildegarde Hawthorne (1871–1952), "Bearer of Evil Tidings" [a review of *The Shadow on the*

Dial], *New York Times Saturday Review of Books* (14 August 1909): 491. Harrison Gray Otis (1837–1917) was owner and editor of the *Los Angeles Times*. His review has not been found.

4. Otis's wife was Eliza A. (Wetherby) Otis (1833–1904), author of *Echoes from Elf-Land* (1890) and *California, "Where Sets the Sun": Writings in Poetry and Prose* (1905), both published by the Times-Mirror Co. See "The Passing Show," *SF* (10 September 1899): 12: "In the entire fortnight immediately preceding August 16 Mrs. Otis did not publish a single poem so howlingly precious as the hymn to Yosemite; or if she did she neglected to arrange it in lines of counted syllables and it was printed in her distinguished husband's paper from the original draft as an editorial article. It is now clear why General Otis (H. G.) scabbarded his tulwar and abandoned the island of Luzon. The censorship set up by his despotic namesake excluded Mrs. Otis's poems from that unhappy land. He had to come home in order to read them, and may the Lord sustain him! In view of the facts it is obviously unjust to describe him as a battle-scarred veteran. Nothing could scare a man like that."

[162]   To George Sterling [ALS, NYPL]

Washington,
D.C.

Dear George,

Here are your fine verses—I have been too busy to write to you before. In truth, I've worked harder now for more than a year than I ever shall again—and the work will bring me nor gain nor glory. Well, I shall take a rest pretty soon, partly in California.

I thank you for the picture card. I have succumbed to the post-card fashion myself. As to some points in your letter.

I've no recollection of advising young authors to "leave all heart and sentiment out of their work". If I did the context would probably show that it was because their time might better be given to perfect themselves in form, against the day when their hearts would be less wild and their sentiments truer. You know it has always been my belief that one cannot be trusted to feel until one has learned to think—and few youngsters have learned to do that. Was it not Dr. Holmes who advised a young writer to cut out every passage that he thought particularly good? He'd be sure to think the heartful and sentimental passages the best, would he not? I suppose, though, that the Bashford person merely lied.[1] Please, send me his remarks if it's no trouble. Thank you for the sonnet in defense.[2]

If you mean to write really "vituperative" sonnets (why sonnets?) let me tell you *one* secret of success—name your victim and his offense. To do otherwise is to fire blank cartridges—to waste your words in air—to club a vacuum. At least your satire must be so personally applicable that there can be no mistake as to the victim's identity. Otherwise he is no victim—just a spectator, like all others. And that brings us to Watson.[3] His caddishness consisted, not in satirizing a woman, which is legitimate, but, first, in doing so without sufficient reason, and, second, in saying orally (on the safe side of the Atlantic) what he apparently did not dare say in the verses.

[. . .]
I'm enclosing something that will tickle you I hope—"The Ballade of the Goodly Fere".[4]

The author's father, who is something in the Mint in Philadelphia, sent me several of his son's poems that were not good; but at last came this—in manuscript, like the others. Before I could do anything with it—meanwhile wearing out the paper and the patience of my friends by reading it at them—the old man asked it back rather peremptorily. I reluctantly sent it, with a letter of high praise. The author had "placed" it in London, where it has made a heap of talk.

It has plenty of faults besides the monotonous rhyme scheme; but tell me what you think of it.

God willing, we shall eat Carmel mussels and abalones in May or June.

Sincerely yours,
Ambrose Bierce.

January 29, 1910.

1. Herbert Bashford (1871–1928), poet, dramatist, and reporter for the *San Francisco Bulletin* (1909–19).
2. AB refers to "To Ambrose Bierce," which GS was going to publish in *Town Talk*, but which did not appear there until 24 June 1916. The poem first appeared in GS's *The House of Orchids* (1911). See letter 171.
3. GS had given AB a book by Sir William Watson (1858–1935), *New Poems* (New York: John Lane Company, 1909). The book had created a scandal because the poem "The Woman with the Serpent's Tongue" viciously attacked Margot Asquith, wife of prime minister Herbert Asquith.
4. Ezra Pound (1885–1972), "The Ballade of the Goodly Fere," one of "Three Poems," *English Review* (October 1909); in Pound's *Exultations* (1909).

[163]   To S. O. Howes [ALS, HL]

Washington,
D.C.

My dear Howes,

I've been so hard-at-work finishing up my book (it's off my hands) and going over the papers of half a lifetime that my correspondence has had to wait. I'm trying to get my affairs into "shape" so that I can leave for the West early next month. Alas, Galveston can not be in my itinerary, which includes New York, Kingston (Jamaica) Colon and Panama. A sea voyage is what I need most; a long railway trip least.

Percy and wife were in Boston a few days ago. His book is getting a lot of reviewing and some reviling.[1] Neale gives me a look at the stuff, but of course I can not keep it for Percy. I can only send him lists of the notices, with dates.

Shackleton's naming an antarctic mountain after Sir Henry Lucy amuses me. I knew Lucy very well—a little toady who afterward toadied himself into a title. Doubtless you know he is the "Toby M. P.," of *Punch*.[2]

If while in California I should find Robertson willing to bring out a new and *greatly revised* edition of "The Shadow" would you approve? I'm ashamed of the carelessness with which I edited (or rather did *not* edit) that book. Some of the stuff I think I did not read at all. However, I don't think Robertson will do it.

Yes, I saw Mrs. Atherton's kind remarks about me in *The Bookman*—and am surprised that Peck permitted them.[3]

We, too, have had a rather cold winter, but now the crocuses and tulips are out and the trees greening.

Miss Christiansen (who sends love) is blooming, too, in the expectation of an increased salary. She, also, hopes to pass her summer vacation at her home in California.

In Harper's new *The Great English Story Writers* (I'm included—none of these compilations now are without me)[4] "O. Henry" has "The Hiding of Black Bill"—a good story. But it would not have been written if there had been no French tale by— I forget author and title, but a translation recently appeared in *Town Talk*, San Francisco.[5] O, no, I don't think "O. Henry" a plagiarist, but both tales are stories of crime and a suspected criminal. But at the end it turns out that the narrator is himself the criminal—something so new and striking in fiction that it could hardly have been independently evolved. Still, "O. Henry" may have been the first. I find that European fiction is frequently "enriched" by American.

Would you mind giving me again the name and address of your nephew who is a book sleuth? I lost the card. I think you said he could get things.

I hope Robertson has turned in something for you, but doubt if he will ever be much. I ceased long ago to expect my books to sell, though Neale is now publishing the third thousand of "Write It Right"—and my fingers are itching to "revise" it.

Kindly remind Mrs. Schoolfield that I still think of her with tenderness.

  Sincerely yours,
    Ambrose Bierce.
March 7, 1910.

1. Percival Pollard, *Their Day in Court* (New York and Washington, D.C.: Neale Publishing Co., 1909). It contains a chapter on AB.
2. Sir Henry William Lucy (1843–1924) was a British journalist who wrote a long-running column in *Punch* (1881–1916) under the pseudonym "Toby, M.P." In 1909 he helped explorer Sir Ernest Shackleton out of some financial difficulties, and in return Shackleton named Mt. Henry Lucy (in the Supporters Range in Antarctica) after him.
3. Gertrude Atherton, "The American Novel in England," *Bookman* (New York) 30, no. 6 (February 1910): 633–40. The article has a section on "Bierce and Stephen Crane." AB refers to Harry Thurston

Peck (1856–1914), a highly respected professor of classics at Columbia University and editor of the *Bookman* (1895–1907). Evidently AB was under the impression that Peck was still editor of the *Bookman*. AB had earlier taken Peck to task in regard to his harsh remarks on the late Robert G. Ingersoll; see "The Dead Lion (Again) and the Living Professor," *SF* (10 September 1899); rpt. as "A Dead Lion" (*CW* 10).

4. William James Dawson (1854–1928), *The Great English Short-Story Writers* (New York: Harper & Brothers, 1910), containing "An Occurrence at Owl Creek Bridge."

5. William Sidney Porter [O. Henry] (1862–1910), "The Hiding of Black Bill," in *Options* (1909). AB apparently felt that the story was derived from Maurice Leblanc's "The Strong-Box of the Humberts," an English translation of which had appeared in *Town Talk* no. 912 (19 February 1910): 9, 32–33. Both stories feature a narrator who proves to be the perpetrator of a crime. The best-known treatment of this theme is Agatha Christie's *The Murder of Roger Ackroyd* (1926).

[164] To George Sterling [ALS, NYPL]

Washington,
D.C.

Dear George,

My plan is to leave here before April first, pass a few days in New York and then sail for Colon. If I find the canal work on the Isthmus interesting I may skip a steamer from Panama to see it. I've no notion how long it will take to reach San Francisco, and know nothing of the steamers and their schedules on the Pacific side.

I shall of course want to see Grizzly first—that is to say, he will naturally expect me to. But if you can pull him down to Carmel about the time of my arrival (I shall write you the day of my sailing from New York) I would gladly come there. Carlt,[1] whom I can see at once on arriving, can tell me where he (Grizzly) is. I'm mighty glad he has been brought to see the error of his way in the matter of your wife.[2]

I don't think you rightly value "The Goodly Fere." Of course no ballad written to-day can be entirely good, for it must be an imitation;[3] it is now an unnatural form, whereas it was once a natural one. We are no longer a primitive people, and a primitive people's forms and methods are not ours. Nevertheless, this seems to me an admirable ballad, as it is given a modern to write ballads. And I think you overlook the best line: "The hounds of the crimson sky gave tongue."

The poem is complete as I sent it, and I think it stops right where and as it should—

"I ha' seen him eat o' the honey comb
Sin' they nailed him to the tree."

The current "Literary Digest" has some queer things about (and by) Pound, and "Current Literature" reprints the "Fere" with all the wrinkles ironed out of it—making a "capon priest" of it.[4]

Fo' de Lawd's sake! don't apologise for not subscribing to my "Works." If you did subscribe I should suspect that you were "no friend o' mine"—it would remove you from that gang and put you in a class by yourself. Surely you can not think I care who buys or does not buy my books. The man who expects anything more than lip-service from his friends is a very young man. There are, for example, a half-dozen Californians (all loud admirers of Ambrose Bierce) editing magazines and newspapers here in the East. Every man Jack of them has turned me down. They will do everything for me but enable me to live. Friends be damned!—strangers are the chaps for me.

By the way, did that fellow George Wharton James put me into his book?[5] I see is out, but have not been able to get it.

I've given away my beautiful sailing canoe and shall never again live a life on the ocean wave—unless you have boats at Carmel.

Sincerely yours,
Ambrose Bierce.

March 7, 1910.

1. AB's nephew (son of his brother Albert), Carleton Bierce. In his later years AB was close to him and to his wife, Lora.
2. The words "your wife" were crossed out, presumably by GS, when he was assisting Bertha Clark Pope in editing *The Letters of Ambrose Bierce* (1922).
3. GS went on to publish many fine ballads, many of which are uncollected.
4. An anonymous article discussing Pound ("Current Poetry") appeared in *Literary Digest* 40 (26 February 1910): 402–4. "The Ballade of the Goodly Fere" was reprinted in *Current Literature* 38 (March 1910): 342–43.
5. George Wharton James (1858–1923), *The California Birthday Book: Prose and Poetical Selections from the Writings of Living California Authors, with a Biographical Sketch of Each* (Los Angeles: Arroyo Guild Press, 1909). There is nothing by AB in the book.

[165]   To Walter Neale [ALS, HL]

Guerneville, Cal.,
May 24, 1910.

My dear Neale,

I arrived on Thursday the 19th, but this is the first opportunity that I have had to acknowledge your notes. I think it very generous of you to allow me (and others) that discount on the "Collected Works," first edition. Thank you very much. Your present policy in marketing the book should, and I believe will, make it go. For your sake more than my own I sincerely hope so. The apprehension of your losing money through your faith in me has made me miserable a long time.

I had a pleasant, but rather long voyage. Was three days in Panama and saw something of the canal work—the magnitude whereof transcends expression. If I had taken the right line of steamers from New York (the Panama Railroad's line) it would have cost me eighty dollars less. One pays for one's ignorance and carelessness.

On arrival at San Francisco I gathered up my nephew and his wife and came directly up here to my brother's shack on the mountainside. And, faith! it is a paradise. Right above a beautiful river (we have a canoe) with a half-dozen pretty villages in sight below, and the woods already filled with their summer population from the city. One meets groups of pretty girls in camping attire everywhere—some of whom say that I held them on my knee when they were little (I mean to again) though I fancy it may have been their grandmothers! Ah, my good, good friend, how I pity you in your office, slaving at your oar! (How is that for mixed metaphor?) May the new baby do much to smooth the asperities of the situation. And I pray that its pretty mother may now have passed out of the danger zone.

I don't know when I shall go down to the city, and to Carmel, and to Yosemite. Sterling will probably come up here.

"The Betrayal" awaited me,[1] but I inadvertently left it in Berkeley.

Write me sometimes.
    Sincerely yours,
        Ambrose Bierce.

Better address me at Berkeley.

1. Walter Neale and Elizabeth H. Hancock, *The Betrayal: A Novel* (New York and Washington, D.C.: Neale Publishing Co., 1910).

[166]   To Walter Neale [ALS, HL]
        2009 Francisco St.,
        Berkeley, Cal.
Dear Neale,
    I sent off the proofs yesterday. Had to send mine—the ones Miss Christiansen had, and which your editor desired returned, got badly marred. However, I transferred such of his marks as I approved to the others.

They are a pretty badly marked-up set of proofs. I made a number of changes, and your printers had done about as blundering work as I ever saw. Guess it will show up all right if the corrections indicated are made. We (I and Miss C) have put in a lot of work on it.

I am half-distracted with a lot of friends (and some "lion-hunters") hauling me this way and that. My regular situation is that I'm due in a half-dozen places at once.

Gee! it is no joke this returning to one's old home. I'd give much for a week of Washington, or that very quiet village, little old New York.

I trust "The Betrayal" keeps up its lick. Hope to send you a couple of "notices" of it pretty soon—good or bad.

My love to Mrs. Neale and the children.
    Sincerely yours,
           Ambrose Bierce.
July 15, 1910.

[167]   To George Sterling [ALS, NYPL]
                           The Laguna Vista,
                                  Oakland.
Dear George,
    Since your note (and check) came I have been philandering variously, and have only just now got within hailing distance of my stationery. Thank you for the trouble you took in the matter of the abalone things. I have a cheerful letter from Eva, by the way.

I return Hubbard's screed on Jack London, and think it altogether just, excepting that it is too tolerant, Hubbard too being tainted with sympathy for criminals.[1]

You will perceive that the fact of my being compelled by civility to endure London for two days and a night has not altered my views of him in the least.[2] As to Hubbard's own character I do not see that has to do with his criticism of London. If only the impeccable delivered judgment no judgment would ever be delivered. All men could do as they please, without reproof or dissent. I wish you would take your heart out of your head, old man. The best heart makes a bad head if housed there.

I hope you and Carrie will be in Oakland again soon. Meantime let me express my sense of your fine hospitality to a most unworthy vagabond.
                                Sincerely yours,
                                    Ambrose Bierce.
September 1, 1910.

1. No article by Elbert Hubbard on Jack London has been located for this period.
2. See letter 171, n. 2.

[168] To William E. Connelley [ALS, YU]

2009 Francisco St.,
Berkeley, Cal.

William E. Connolley Esq.,
 Dear Sir,
  Replying to your letter of Sept. 7th I have to say that I regret my inability to give you any information regarding the Hannah Maria Bierce who was the mother of the late Senator Plumb, of Kansas. I am reprehensibly ignorant of family matters, having lived apart from my relations from an early age. My parents (Marcus A. Bierce and Laura Sherwood Bierce) were from Connecticut, and lived in Portage county, Ohio, in the early days of "The Western Reserve". So far as I have known, all Bierces have been related to me, and there appear to be many of them all over the country; but genealogy is to me an uninteresting subject and I have "traced" none of them—contenting myself with the hope that all are good and happy.
  I am sincerely yours,
   Ambrose Bierce.

October 4, 1910.

[169] To Helen (Bierce) Cowden [ALS, BL]

[THE ARMY AND NAVY CLUB
WASHINGTON.]

My dear Helen,
  I mailed you a post-card in Chicago, where I had to pass six or seven hours. If I had known that Bloomington was so near (which I learned by a casual glance at a map just before leaving Chicago) I could perhaps have run out to you for an hour or two. I thought it in the southern part of the State!¹
  My departure from California was somewhat hurried and unexpected at the last, but I did steal a day to visit the Grand Cañon of the Colorado; and when you go West again *you* must do so too. You will not regret having its memory always with you.
  I had a good time, and saw the greatest three things on the continent—Yosemite, the Grand Cañon and the work on the Panama Canal. But the *best* thing that I saw was your cousin Lora. She is a dear girl.
  I went to St. Helena and arranged for a new, large and beautiful lot in the cemetery, where the sun will shine and the grass grow. Your fern is all that grows on the old one, and it is sickly. Even the trees are dying.

The new lot will have a beautiful tall-growing palm in each corner. The lot is 20 ft. by 20. The necessary work will be done at once, and George Fee will see that [it] is done right. I hope you approve.
    Affectionately,
           Dad.
Nov. 4, 1910.

1. Harry and Helen Cowden had settled in Bloomington, Ill., about 135 miles southwest of Chicago.

[170]   To Lora Bierce [MEG]
                                              Washington, D.C.
Dear Lora,
    Thank you very much for the work that you are doing for me in photography and china. I know it is great work. But take your time about it.

I hope you all had a good Thanksgiving at Upshack. (That is my name for Sloots' place. It will be understood by anyone that has walked to it from Montesano, carrying a basket of grub on a hot day.)

I trust Sterling got his waistcoat and trousers in time to appear at his uncle's dinner in other outer habiliments than a steelpen coat. Doubtless he would prefer the scant attire, but has to consider the law.

I am glad you like (or like to have) the books. You would have had all my books when published if I had supposed that you cared for them, or even knew about them. I am now encouraged to hope that some day you and Carlt and Sloots may be given the light to see the truth at the heart of my "views" (which I have expounded for half a century) and will cease to ally yourselves with what is most hateful to me, socially and politically. I shall then feel (in my grave) that perhaps, after all, I knew how to write. Meantime, run after your false fool gods until you are tired; I shall not believe that your hearts are really in the chase, for they are pretty good hearts, and those of your gods are nests of nastiness and heavens of hate.

Now I feel better, and shall drink a toddy to the tardy time when those whom I love shall not think me a perverted intelligence; when they shall not affirm my intellect and despise my work—confess my superior understanding and condemn all its fundamental conclusions. Then we will be a happy family—you and Carlt in the flesh and Sloots and I in our bones.

I don't hear a word from Helen, although I sent her two postcards on my way home and wrote her on arrival. This does not worry me—she is that kind of affectionate daughter. And she is a Christian Scientist. Doubtless a Socialist as well.

My health is excellent in this other and better world than California.
God bless you.
Ambrose.
November 29, 1910.

[171]   To George Sterling [ALS, NYPL]

Washington,
Feb'y 15, 1911.
Dear George,
As to the "form of address".[1] A man passing another was halted by the words: "You dirty dog!" Turning to the speaker, he bowed coldly and said: "Smith is my name, sir." My name is Bierce, and I find, on reflection, that I like best those who call me just that. If my christen name were George I'd want to be called *that;* but "Ambrose" is fit only for mouths of women—in which it sounds fairly well.

How are you my master? I never read one of your poems without learning something, though not, alas, how to make one.

Don't worry about "Lilith"; it will work out all right. As to the characters not seeming alive, I've always fancied the men and women of antiquity—particularly the kings, and great ones generally—should not be too flesh-and-bloody, like the "persons whom one meets." A little coldness and strangeness is very becoming to them. I like them to *stalk,* like the ghosts that they are—our modern passioning seems a bit anachronous in them. Maybe I'm wrong, but I'm sure you will understand and have some sympathy with the error.

[...]

I fancy your chance of getting that sixty dollars from Wood is about as good as *my* chance of getting even a "statement" from him. As I paid the entire expense of publication of my book (to save you—he seems to have "put up" nothing) borrowing most of the money to do so, I have thought myself entitled to at least a "statement of account". There are "lots" of the books in the hands of purchasers, but not a cent did I ever get. I'm sorry that I did not sue him when in California. If I ever get him on the witness stand that will be sufficient satisfaction.

Of course I could not but be pleased by your inclusion of that sonnet on me in your book. And, by the way, I'm including in my tenth volume my *Cosmopolitan* article on the "Wine" and my end of the controversy about it. All the volumes of the set are to be out by June, saith the publisher. He is certainly half-killing me with proofs—mountains of proofs!

If Upton Sinclair wants to pitch into me he need not fear: he shall have the fight all to himself—probably; for I hold no speech with such as he. He is a liar and a fool.

By the way, who told you that Jack London and I had an argument at the grove, and he "did me up"? It would be natural for you to think me "done up", as you thought me "done up" in that *Cosmopolitan* "symposium"; but in fact London and I had not a word of argument on Socialism, nor on anything. You could hardly fail to observe that I said as little to him as possible. *Town Talk*, too, had some false information about London and me, regarding our meeting at the grove.[2]

[. . .]

Yes, you'll doubtless have a recruit in Carlt for your Socialist menagerie—if he is not already a veteran exhibit. Your "party" is recruited from among sore-heads only. There are some twenty-five thousand of them (sore-heads) in this neck o' woods—all disloyal—all growling at the Government which feeds and clothes them twice as well as they could feed and clothe themselves in private employment. They move Heaven and Earth to get in, and they never resign—just "take it out" in abusing the Government. If I had my way nobody should remain in the civil service more than five years—at the end of that period all are disloyal. Not one of them cares a rap for the good of the service or the country—as we soldiers used to do on thirteen dollars a month (with starvation, disease and death thrown in.) Their grievance is that the Government does not undertake to maintain them in the style to which they choose to accustom themselves. They fix their standard of living just a little higher than they can afford, and would do so no matter what salary they got, as all salary-persons invariably do. Then they damn their employer for not enabling them to live up to it.

If they can do better "outside" why don't they go outside and do so; if they can't (which means that they are getting more than they are worth) what are they complaining about?

What this country needs—what every country needs occasionally—is a good hard bloody war to revive the vice of patriotism on which its existence as a nation depends. Meantime, you socialers, anarchists and other sentimentaliters and futilitarians will find the civil-service your best recruiting ground, for it is the Land of Reasonless Discontent. I yearn for the strong-handed Dictator who will swat you all on the mouths o' you till you are "heard to cease." Until then—How? (drinking.)

Yours sincerely,
Ambrose Bierce.

1. GS habitually addressed AB in letters as "Master."
2. Theodore Bonnet's unsigned column, "The Spectator," *Town Talk* no. 949 (5 November 1910): 12, included a section entitled "Bierce and London Reconciled," about their meeting at the Bohemian Club Jinks in the summer of 1910.

[172]   To Ruth Robertson[1]

The Army and Navy Club,
Washington, D.C.,
March 1, 1911.

My dear Ruth,

It is pleasant to know that the family Robertson is "seeing things" and enjoying them. I hate travel, but find it delightful when done by you, instead of me. Believe me, I have had great pleasure in following you by your trail of words, as in the sport known as the "paper chase."

And now about the little story. Your refusal to let your father amend it is no doubt dreadfully insubordinate, but I brave his wrath by approval. It is *your* work that I want to see, not anybody's else. I've a profound respect for your father's talent: as a littérateur, he is the best physician that I know; but he must not be coaching my pupil, or he and I (as Mark Twain said of Mrs. Astor) "will have a falling out."

The story is not a story. It is not narrative, and nothing occurs. It is a record of mental mutations—of spiritual vicissitudes—states of mind. That is the most difficult thing that you could have attempted. It can be done acceptably by genius and the skill that comes of practice, as can anything. You are not quite equal to it—yet. You have done it better than I could have done it at your age, but not altogether well; as doubtless you did not expect to do it. It would be better to confine yourself at present to simple narrative. Write of something done, not of something thought and felt, except incidentally. I'm sure it is in you to do great work, but in this writing trade, as in other matters, excellence is to be attained no otherwise than by beginning at the beginning—the simple at first, then the complex and difficult. You can not go up a mountain by a leap at the peak.

I'm retaining your little sketch till your return, for you can do nothing with it—nor can I. If it had been written—preferably typewritten—with wide lines and margins I could do something *to* it. Maybe when I get the time I shall; at present I am swamped with "proofs" and two volumes behind the printers. If I knew that I should *see* you and talk it over I should rewrite it and (original in hand) point out the reasons for each alteration—you would see them quickly enough when shown. Maybe you will all come this way.

You are *very* deficient in spelling. I hope that is not incurable, though some persons—clever ones, too—never do learn to spell correctly. You will have to learn it from your reading—noting carefully all but the most familiar words.

You have "pet" words—nearly all of us have. One of yours is "flickering." Addiction to certain words is an "upsetting sin" most difficult to overcome. Try to overcome it by cutting them out where they seem most felicitous.

By the way, your "hero," as you describe him, would not have been accessible to all those spiritual impressions—it is *you* to whom they come. And that confirms my judgment of your imagination. Imagination is nine parts of the writing trade. With enough of *that* all things are possible; but it is the other things that require the hard work, the incessant study, the tireless seeking, the indomitable will. It is no "pic-nic," this business of writing, believe me. Success comes by favor of the gods, yes; but O the days and nights that you must pass before their altars, prostrate and imploring! They are exacting—the gods; years and years of service you must give in the temple. If you are prepared to do this go on to your reward. If not, you can not too quickly throw away the pen and—well, marry, for example.

"Drink deep or taste not the Pierian spring."[2]

My vote is that you persevere.

With cordial regards to all good Robertsons—I think there are no others—I am most sincerely your friend,

Ambrose Bierce.

1. Text derived from *The Letters of Ambrose Bierce*, 172–74. Ruth was the daughter of Dr. John W. Robertson, AB's friend who ran the Livermore Sanitarium.
2. Alexander Pope, *An Essay on Criticism* (1711), l. 216.

[173]   To Colonel Archibald Gracie[1] [TLS, BL]
Washington, D. C.,
March 9, 1911.
My dear Colonel Gracie,
From the trouble that you took to consult me regarding certain phases of the battle of Chickamauga I infer that you are really desirous of the truth, and that your book is not to belong to that unhappily too large class of books written by "bad losers" for disparagement of antagonists. Sympathies and antipathies are disabilities in an historian that are hard to overcome. That you believe yourself devoid of this disability I do not doubt; yet your strange views of Thomas, Granger and Brannan,[2] and some of the events in which they figured, are (to me) so obviously erroneous that I find myself unable to account for them on the hypothesis of an entirely open mind. All defeated peoples are "bad losers"—history supplies no examples to the contrary, though there are always individual exceptions. (General D. H. Hill is an example of the "good loser," and, with reference to the battle of Chickamauga, the good winner. I assume your familiarity with his account of that action, and his fine

tribute of admiration to some of the men whom he fought—Thomas and others.[3]) The historians who have found, and will indubitably continue to find, general acceptance are those who have most generously affirmed the good faith and valor of their enemies. All this, however, you have of course considered. But consider it again.

My very humble personal relation to the events at and about the Snodgrass house I partly explained to you, and you can get the rest from the little unmilitary sketch in the book that I lent you for the purpose.[4] It seems to me that it gave me entirely adequate opportunities for observation. I passed almost the entire afternoon at and near the Snodgrass house, with nothing to do but look on, and, as a topographical officer, with some natural interest in, and knowledge of, "the lay of the land." Of my credibility as a witness you have of course no knowledge—no more than you can have of that of many others whom you quote, and must quote. But since you have asked for my views, I will set them down here a little more definitely than was possible in conversation, and you may take them for what they may seem to be worth.

I believe (and gave you some reasons for believing) that Granger did not arrive on the field until well along in the afternoon—I should say (with Hill—see *Battles and Leaders*)[5] not earlier than three o'clock.

I believe that Hazen was already in the Snodgrass field when Granger arrived, and had detached the Ninth Indiana, which was then on the ridge west of the Snodgrass house; that it was among the men of that regiment that an ineffectual attempt was made to place a section of Aleshire's battery. The facts that the section was commanded by my brother and that the Ninth Indiana was my regiment have given the incident unusual interest to me and tended to fix it in my mind.

There was at no time during the afternoon any organized body of troops occupying ground in the rear (north) of the Snodgrass house. Granger's were the only ones that even moved across it. We had no reserves—all our men were on the firing-line.

There is no hill, bald or otherwise, immediately to the north of the Snodgrass house. All is, and was then, open, level country for miles.

Hazen's fire was at no time directed toward what I think you call Horse-shoe Ridge. He faced due south and all his fire was in that direction.

The ridge immediately south of the Snodgrass house (I do not know if that is the one that you call Horse-shoe Ridge) was at no time, until after nightfall, occupied by the Confederates, nor was any other part of the ridges that our forces had held. Nobody was "driven" from this position; all retired in perfect order in the evening, there having been no fighting here for a long time—I should say an hour or two.

I do not share the belief of some of the officers of my regiment that the regiment was intentionally "sacrificed" by General Brannan. There was no occasion, no need, to "sacrifice" anybody, for, as said above, we were not at all pressed. I mingled freely, naturally, with the officers and men of my regiment for many months afterward, at

Chattanooga and elsewhere, yet never heard a hint of such a thing. Nor did I see anything in what you read me from your manuscript to fortify such a charge.

The commonly accepted account of the second day's battle on our right is true if my eyes were normal. We were defeated all right, cleanly and gallantly, but not as some of your "authorities" say.

Sincerely yours,
Ambrose Bierce.

1. Colonel (USA) Archibald Gracie (1858–1912) was the son of Brigadier General (CSA) Archibald Gracie, Jr. (1832–1864), who commanded a brigade in Preston's Division of Buckner's Corps in Longstreet's Left Wing at Chickamauga. His book, *The Truth about Chickamauga* (Boston: Houghton Mifflin, 1911), asserts that the Confederates decisively won the battle, the Union forces fleeing the field, but that the most "stupendous blunder of the war" was the failure of the Confederates to pursue the Union army and put a seal on the victory.

2. Major General George Henry Thomas (1816–1870), a Virginian and prewar captain who stayed loyal to the Union and was commander of the XIV Corps at Chickamauga. Major General (USV) Gordon Granger (1822–1876), commander of the Reserve Corps of the Army of the Cumberland at Chickamauga. Brigadier General (USV) John Milton Brannan (1819–1892), a prewar captain of artillery, commanded the 3rd Division of Thomas's XIV Corps at Chickamauga.

3. Lieutenant General (CSA) Daniel Harvey Hill (1821–1889), commander of the II Corps in Polk's Right Wing of the Army of Tennessee at Chickamauga. He later wrote an article, "Chickamauga: The Great Battle of the West," *Century Magazine* 11 (April 1887): 937–62.

4. Presumably "A Little of Chickamauga," one of the "Bits of Autobiography" in *CW* 1.

5. *Battles and Leaders of the Civil War*, ed. R. U. Johnson and C. C. Clough Buel (New York: Century Co., 1884–88; 4 vols.).

[174]   To Walter Neale [ALS, HL]

Washington,
D.C.

Dear Neale,

I shall proceed to make Vols. XI and XII at once. This will enable us to use the omitted copy that your printers have on hand—the "overplus". Some of it is already in type—all the "Apocryphal Dialogues" and a part of the "Little Johnny." I suggest that it be all set up at once and proofs sent to me, so that I can see how to "bestow" it. Some of it will have to go in Vol. X, and I think that for congruity a part of it should go in Vol. VIII—I can tell better when I see it.

I have turned up a lot of stuff that I had prepared before going to California, laid away and forgotten about. We shall have plenty from the twelve volumes without "Right [*sic*] It Right"—which probably ought not to be included anyhow.

We have the *legal* right to use much (not all) the contents of the Howes book, but it will be better to have his written consent, which he will doubtless cheerfully give. I am writing him about it.

The announcement about the plates being all cast is all right—I only feared that it was true. Truth always terrifies me!
Sincerely yours,
Ambrose Bierce.
March 22, 1911.

[175]   To Samuel Loveman[1] [ALS, USC]
Washington,
D.C.
Dear Mr. Loveman,
I'm sorry to know that you did not go to California; you would have had much pleasure there. And before another year there may be another earthquake.
On June 3 the Sterlings are to go to Sag Harbor, Long Island, for the Summer. George was brought up there. You will enjoy his latest book, I think.[2] It has no such notable poem as either "The Testimony of the Suns" or "A Wine of Wizardry", but it is all good work.
I trust your letter to the N.Y. Times Review[3] may enlighten the darkness of that sheet. I mean the intellectual darkness—nothing can help its moral darkness. Between it and me is an implacable feud. With every assault on me it sends to my publisher a guarded intimation that it would be to his advantage to advertise in its columns. That's what I mean by moral darkness—just the kind of twilight congenial to a pirate of the Spanish Main.
Thank you very much for the photograph, though I shall blot out the dog. I detest dogs.
This is my dull period—I've been pleasuring for weeks in New York, and there's always a reaction. New York is cocaine, opium, hashish.
Are we to have a book from you?[4]
Sincerely yours,
Ambrose Bierce.
May 28, 1911.

1. Samuel E. Loveman (1887–1976), poet and longtime friend of AB, GS, Hart Crane, and H. P. Lovecraft, was the author of *The Hermaphrodite* (1926) and editor of *Twenty-one Letters of Ambrose Bierce* (1922).
2. *The House of Orchids and Other Poems* (1911).
3. The letter was published as "Mr. Sterling and Minor Poets," *New York Times Book Review* (4 June 1911): 352. It claims that GS is by far the greatest living American poet.
4. Loveman sent AB a copy of his *Poems* (Cleveland: Privately published, 1911).

[176] To George Sterling [ALS, NYPL]

Washington,
D.C.

Dear George,

Thank you for that Times "review".[1] It is a trifle less malicious than usual—regarding *me*, that is all. My publisher, Neale, who was here last evening, is about "taking action" against that concern for infringement of his copyright in my little book, "Write It Right". The wretches have been serving it up to their readers for several weeks as the work of a woman named Learned.[2] Repeatedly she uses my very words—whole passages of them. They refused even to confess the misdeeds of their contributrix, and persist in their sin. So they will have to fight.

About Miss Connelly.[3] Her notion about my "austerity" is, I fear, hardly correct. I have never been hard on women whose hearts go with their admiration, and whose bodies follow their hearts—I don't mean that the latter was the case in this instance. Nor am I very exacting as to the morality of my men friends. I would not myself take another man's woman, any more than I would take his purse. Nor, I trust, would I seduce the daughter or sister of a friend, nor any maid whom it would at all damage—and as to *that* there is no hard-and-fast rule.

Yes, I am, I hope, "a friend of Carrie's" but do not consider myself a custodian of her husband's morals, nor a guardian of her conjugal peace.

A fine fellow, I, to be casting the first stone, or the one-hundredth, at a lovelorn woman, weak or strong! By the way, I should not believe in the love of a strong one, wife, widow or maid.

It looks as if I may get to Sag Harbor for a week or so in the middle of the month. It is really not a question of expense, but Neale has blocked out a lot of work for me. He wants two more volumes—even five more if I'll make 'em. Guess I'll give him two. In a week or so I shall be able to say whether I can go Sagharboring. If so, I think we should have a night in New York first, no? You could motor-boat up and back.

Sincerely yours,
Ambrose Bierce.

July 31, 1911.

1. Apparently an unsigned review (written by the poet John G. Neihardt) of GS's *The House of Orchids and Other Poems*, in the *New York Times Book Review* (25 June 1911): 400. The review speaks approvingly of AB's championing of GS. No review of AB's books appeared in the paper at this time.

2. Leila Sprague Learned published several articles on English usage in the *New York Times Book Review* in the summer of 1911: "Slipshod English" (11 June 1911, pp. 359, 377); "The Careless Use of English" (2 July 1911, p. 421); "Guide-Posts to Good English" (9 July 1911, p. 435); "More about 'Good English'" (16 July 1911, p. 447); "Adventures in Expression" (23 July 1911, p. 455).

3. The name was crossed out, presumably by GS (see letter 164, n. 2). GS had been carrying on an

affair with a woman named Vera Connelly. His several poems to her were later collected as *Poems to Vera* (1938). In 1911–12 GS's wife, Carrie, wrote AB several poignant letters stating that GS's affair with Vera was continuing and urging AB to intercede on her behalf. AB's replies do not survive.

[177]   To S. O. Howes [ALS, HL]

Washington, D.C.

Dear Howes,

I'm only a few days back from a month's outing—mostly at Sag Harbor, Long Island. And since returning I've been playing at asthma—beating the game! I saw Percy—he was kind enough to pass a night with me in New York on my way home. We dined and breakfasted together, and missed you.

It was a good time that I had in Long Island, autoing and motorboating most of the time, and getting a succession of skins "under the sun." George Sterling was of the party, all of whom were Californians, male and female. *Now* I'm going to work.

[. . .]

Sincerely yours,
        Ambrose Bierce.
Sept. 17, 1911.

[178]   To Charles Dexter Allen [ALS, UP]

Army & Navy Club,
Washington,
D.C.

Cha[s.] Dexter Allen, Esqr.,
    Dear Sir,
            The story of the book "The Dance of Death" is interesting, but too long to write.[1] If you are ever in Washington I shall be pleased to relate it to you orally.

I am not the author of the book—I'm only *one* of the authors. The "William Herman" of the title-page was William Herman Rulofson, who wrote none of it—merely "financed" it. My collaborator was Thomas A. Harcourt, his son-in-law. You'll find some verses about him in Vol. IV of my "Collected Works", entitled "T. A. H."[2]

"The Dance of Death" was a serious enough matter to Rulofson, who had a beautiful wife, very fond of the particular kind of dance condemned; to Harcourt and me it was merely an opportunity to "make mischief" and a "sensation".

Of course I should like to hear about the "coincidence" relating to your copy.

Sincerely yours,
        Ambrose Bierce.
September 27, 1911.

P.S.—Rulofson himself executed a dance of death by stepping off the roof of a building. Harcourt died of drink—taken as an alternative to a life of sorrow from "domestic infelicity."

A. B.

1. In early 1877, AB collaborated with his friend Thomas A. Harcourt to write a treatise purporting to condemn ballroom dancing as lascivious. The descriptions of the dance and its participants were themselves so lascivious that the book caused a scandal in San Francisco. William Herman Rulofson (Harcourt's father-in-law) financed the book, *The Dance of Death,* and lent his name to it as a pseudonym. AB never specified exactly which parts he wrote. In a letter to Walter Neale (18 December 1911; ALS, HL) he writes that the book "is not mainly mine. I only had a free hand in it."
2. *SC* 56; *CW* 4.67.

[179] To George Sterling [ALS, NYPL]

Washington,
D.C.

Dear George,

I was of course disappointed not to meet you in New York. I had no other purpose in stopping there than to see a little more of you and Carrie than I had done in Sag Harbor, and in circumstances that would enable me to give you as good a time as you gave me in Sag Harbor and Carmel. For I'm "at home" in New York. On arriving (on the Thursday) I went at once to the Navarre to look for you; and left my address—the Albemarle. You surely remember my telling you that if I were not at the former house I would be at the latter. Moreover, you had only to telephone to my publisher, Neale, who would of course know where I was.

I went every day to the Navarre (five days) and when told that you had inquired for me again left my address and the clerk made a note of it. Twice, too, I sought you vainly at the Waldorf-Astoria.

In view of all this, your explanation doesn't explain very much, at least not in a way consistent with a particularly strong desire to see me. You seem to have acted throughout on "assumptions"—and an assumption by you is usually regarded by me as the ninth wonder of the world, the immediately previous assumption being the eighth.

[...]

I'm glad you saw the Grand Cañon. If we see it together it will probably have to be in autumn instead of spring. The girls cannot leave Washington until the schools close—about June 20—and we shall want to get into Yosemite as soon afterward as possible—before the several cascades are shrunken. So we shall push for that place first, and take the Cañon on the return trip. How would you and Carrie like another fortnight or so in Yosemite, with as many of our former bunch as can "attend"? I'll write to Carlt or Lora about it.

My health has been pretty bad since my return to Washington—it always is when I come back from the seashore. Guess I'm convalicentious now.

I'm sorry that the gate of Washington is guarded against you and Carrie by an angel with a flaming sword—albeit the angel is most desirous of putting *you* on the free list.

                Sincerely yours,
                    Ambrose Bierce.
September 29, 1911.

[180]   To Walter Neale [ALS, HL]
                Washington, D.C.
Dear Neale,
    [...]

Those are great advertisements; they *ought* to bring results. But doubtless *The Evening Post* will serenely continue to republish from *The Nation* the dirty disparaging "reviews", as usual. Somebody (I don't recollect who) told me that they are written by Hildegarde Hawthorne.[1]

On *The North American Review* is a tremendously clever woman, Miss Cutting, who entertained me charmingly at her house near Bridgehampton, Long Island, last month, and found me so supportable that she asked me to dine with her at her New York City house. If that set goes to *her* we are fairly well assured, I have the vanity to think, of a kindly notice. It will probably go to the office-girl with the banged hair and the no-grammar.

[...]

A. G. Stephens (see enclosed clipping from Australian paper) is the chap who wrote you, through Howes, for my books—for review, I think. He's a big man in his "ain countree"—"The Red Pagan", formerly of *The Sydney Bulletin,* which for years made me famous (in New South Wales, at least) by incessant quotation and comment. There should be a few orders from Sydney for the "Collected Works" if they could be properly offered there.

You need not return the clipping—Pollard gave it me.
        Sincerely yours,
                Ambrose Bierce.
October 21, 1911.

1. The *Nation's* reviews of AB's books at this time were uniformly unfavorable, or at best mixed. These include reviews of *The Shadow on the Dial* (30 September 1909), *CW* 1–4 (9 March 1911), *CW* 5 (4 May 1911), *CW* 6–10 (31 August 1911), and *CW* 11 (28 November 1912). All the reviews were unsigned. As the *Nation* was at this time published by the New York Evening Post Company, some of these reviews presumably appeared also in the *New York Evening Post*.

[181]   To George Sterling [ALS, NYPL]

Washington,
D.C.

Dear George,
   It is good to know that you are again happy—that is to say, you are in Carmel. For your *future* happiness (if success and a certain rounding off of your corners would bring it, as I think) I could wish you in New York or thereabout. As the Scripture hath it: "It is not good for a man to be in Carmel"—*Revised Inversion.*[1] I note that at the late election California damned herself to a still lower degradation and is now unfit for a white man to live in. Initiative, referendum, recall, employers' liability, woman suffrage—yah![2]
   [...]
   You say: "The more I like a chap, the poorer opinion you seem to get of him." *I* would put it this way: "The more certainly a chap belongs to a class of persons whom I dislike, the more certain you are to dote upon him."
   But you are not to take too seriously my dislike of Hopper. I like him personally very well; he talks like a normal human being. It is only that damned book of his.[3] He was here and came out to my tenement a few evenings ago, finding me in bed and helpless from lumbago, as I was for weeks. I am now able to sit up and take notice, and there are even fears for my recovery. My enemies would say, as Byron said of Lady B., I am becoming "dangerously well again".
   Miss Christiansen sends greeting. Let me, however, give you (unbeknownst to her) a tip: Don't use coarse language in writing or speaking to her—not even for the purpose of saying that *I* consider coarse language characteristic of a socialist—which I do.
   Thank you for the "poem". Naturally, I read it first in the error that it was *yours.* Fancy my state of mind after the first stanza!
   As to harlots, there are not ten in a hundred that are such for any other reason than that they wanted to be. Their exculpatory stories are mostly lies of magnitude.
   Sloots writes me that he will perhaps "walk over" from the mine to Yosemite next summer. I can't get there much before July first, but if there is plenty of snow in the mountains next winter the valley should be visitable then. Later, I hope to beguest myself for a few days at the Pine Inn, Carmel. Tell it not to the Point Lobos mussel!
   My love to Carrie.

Sincerely yours,
Ambrose Bierce.
November 16, 1911.

1. "And the Lord God said, It is not good that a man should be alone." Genesis 2:18. AB regularly attributed various periodic misquotations of the Bible to such false editions as the *Revised Inversion,* the *Unauthorized Version,* and so on.
2. In a special election on 10 October, California voters passed several amendments, including those for woman suffrage, the initiative and referendum, and the recall of executive and judicial officers.
3. James Hopper and Fred R. Bechdolt, *9009* (New York: McClure Co., 1908), a novel condemning the barbaric treatment of convicts in American prisons.

[182] To Mrs. Percival Pollard [ALS, NYPL]

Army and Navy Club,
Washington,
D.C.

Dear Mrs. Pollard,

This is terrible news that you write me; not in years have I been so shocked and distressed. I had thought that Percy had nothing worse than a bad case of grippe.[1] Surely there must be some grounds of hope; it is difficult to believe that an intellect like his can be so suddenly extinguished—blown out like a candle! But an operation on the brain—that is certainly ominous and full of awful possibilities, and doubtless you have the doctors' judgment as to what it means, even in case of survival.

I know that you are hardly in a condition to write letters, but if you *can* from time to time let me have a line or two about my poor friend I shall be most grateful.

I suppose it would do no good for me to go to him, nor, probably, would I be permitted to see him; but if I could be of service to you even in the smallest way I should be so glad to go to you.

Meanwhile, you do not need the assurance of my deepest sympathy—you know that you have it. I wish that it could comfort you, poor girl.

Sincerely yours,
Ambrose Bierce.
December 17, 1911.

1. Percival Pollard died on 17 December 1911 of neuritis of the brain.

[183]   To Walter Neale [ALS, HL]

Washington,
D.C.

Dear Neale,

I am forwarding Vol. XI. Having no box of the right size, I have had to double some of the typoscript sheets, but all are properly paged and you can easily straighten them out and put them in their places.

The quantity of matter is a guess; if necessary I can easily add or subtract. The table of contents is to be made when we know just what is to go in.

You'll observe that I continue loyal to my first-thought title: "Antepenultimata"—indicating that the stuff does not profess to be "the last word" on any subject, nor even the next-to-the-last. The title will, I think, lure the curiosity of the unlearned.

The "Publisher's Note" is a suggestion—perhaps you will prefer to put it into your own words. I promised Robertson and Howes some kind of acknowledgment favorable to *their* book.[1]

Now for Vol. XII, which will not require much time in the compiling.

Will it be possible to finish the books—proof-reading and all, before June? We will not want to be bothered with proofs in California.

[...]

Sincerely yours,
Ambrose Bierce.

January 3, 1912.

1. *CW* 11 opens with a brief "Publishers' Note" acknowledging that the bulk of the contents derives from *The Shadow on the Dial*.

[184]   To Eleanor (Vore) Sickler [ALS, BL]

Washington, D.C.

Dear Nellie Sickler,

Instead of "remembering" you with a Christmas card, it would have been kinder to reply to your good letter of November 7. But my correspondence is very onerous (burdensome in extent, but most agreeable, generally, in character) and many letters must wait. My work, too, is exacting and, finally, I was seriously ill for months—for several weeks helpless in bed with lumbago. May you never know what lumbago is. *Now* my health is perfect, barring that incurable disorder, age. I shall be seventy next June—think o' that!

I have read with pleasure and approval the verses that you sent, and make a few suggestions—suggestions *only*—in "The Dreamer."

If you are not a great poet it is worth while to be "a pleasing versifier", as you modestly put it. Maybe you have a formidable rival in your daughter Marion, whose notion that we are all dreamers talking in our sleep is true poetry.

It is no trouble for me to look over your little verses—when I reach them on my file. All that I have seen have "something in them."

If I live and keep my health I shall visit California again next summer. It is not likely that I shall get to Los Angeles, for I am pretty fully "programmed", as I was before; but if I do I shall try to see you. It seems odd that I never *did* see you. If we do not meet next summer we doubtless never shall. Well, it is something to know that you are happy; nobody can be anything half so good as that. Happiness is an end; all other things are means.

Since you like to read pleasant things about me, I'm enclosing a few. They are printed by way of advertisement by my publisher, "but don't you care".

Hood's "Rhymester" is useful, as are nearly all works on rhetoric, prosody and composition, though all are defective and many contain errors.[1] Hood, by the way, was a dear friend of mine in London, ages and ages ago.

Maybe it will help you—in prose—if I send my little book "Write It Right"—so I shall.

Good night and God bless you.

Ambrose Bierce.

January 10, 1912.

1. Thomas Hood the Younger, *The Rhymester; or, The Rules of Rhyme: A Guide to English Versiification* (1882).

[185]   To George Sterling [ALS, NYPL]

Washington, D.C.
[25 April 1912]

Dear George,

I did not go to Bermuda; so I'm not "back". But I did go to Richmond, a city whose tragic and pathetic history, of which one is reminded by everything that one sees there, always gets on my nerves with a particular dejection. True, the history is some fifty years old, but it is always with me when I'm there, making solemn eyes at me.

You're right about "this season in the East." It has indeed been penitential. For the first time I am thoroughly disgusted and half-minded to stay in California when I go—a land where every prospect pleases, and only labor unions, progressives, suffragettes (and socialists) are vile. No, I don't think I could stand California, though I'm

still in the mind to visit it in June. I shall be sorry to miss Carrie at Carmel, but hope to have the two of you on some excursion or camping trip. We *want* to go to Yosemite, which the girls have not seen, but if there's no water there it may not be advisable. Guess we'll have to let you natives decide. How would the Big Trees do as a substitute?
[...]
I hope you are getting down to work and forgetting that girl. Girls is pizen, but not necessarily fatal. I've taken 'em in large doses all my life, and suffered pangs enough to equip a number of small Hells, but never has one of them paralyzed the inner working man. The organ that I feel with is accessible to them, but the one that I think with is immune. But I'm not a poet. Moreover, as I've not yet put off my armor I oughtn't to boast.

So—you've subscribed for the Collected Works. Good!—that is what you ought to have done a long time ago. It is what every personal friend of mine ought to have done, for all profess admiration of my work in literature. It is what I was fool enough to permit my publisher to think that many of them would do. How many do you guess have done so? I'll leave you guessing. God help the man with many friends, for *they* will not. My royalties on the sets sold to my friends are less than one-fourth of my outlay in free sets for other friends. Tell me not in cheerful numbers of the value and sincerity of friendships.[1]
[...]
        Sincerely yours,
        Ambrose Bierce.

1. A paraphrase of Longfellow's "Tell me not, in mournful numbers, / 'Life is but an empty dream!'" "A Song of Life" (1839), ll. 1–2.

[186] To Walter Neale [ALS, HL]

                Washington, D.C.
Dear Neale,
    Now that my part of the work on Vol. XI is done, it doesn't matter about your part; take your time about it.

Thank you for the opportunity to write for the mag.[1] I don't *want* to write for anything, but who knows how sharply the monkey may bite me after a few months of inactivity? The chance to whack my friend Gracie is tempting. (You observed, doubtless, that he waded ashore from the Titanic.)[2] Something, I suppose, will depend on what kind of magazine it turns out to be. I had a 20-years' experience in writing for publications that were hateful to me, and am only just beginning to recover my self-respect. You see I'm still a pretty good damyank,[3] and if your mag. should be run in

the spirit of that conspiracy of liars and slanderers, the Southern Historical Society, I'd "see it in Helfurst"—which, as I have elsewhere explained, is a town in Silesia. My advice would be that it should contain no reference to any event more than forty years old—at least no military event. There are (in this case) several reasons for that. One is that doubtless you'll be your own editor; and no man who has not been a soldier is (and few men who have been are) competent to "pass upon" war stuff. Nor is a civilian competent to select a military editor—any more than he is to choose a general. *Teste* Lincoln, or Teddy Roosevelt. And there you are! Suppose you make it an agricultural publication—I'm strong on spring wheat!
[...]
Sincerely yours,
Ambrose Bierce.
May 22, 1912.

1. Neale was planning to issue a magazine, *Neale's Monthly*. Its first issue dates to January 191 3.It contained reprints of AB's tales but no original work.
2. Gracie was one of about 700 survivors from the *Titanic*, the British luxury passenger liner that sank on 14–15 April 1912, en route to New York City from Southampton during its maiden voyage. He later wrote the book, *The Truth about the Titanic* (1912), before dying at the end of 1912.
3. Cf. "The Matter of Manner" (*Cosmopolitan*, April 1906; *CW* 10.63): "As it is, they are in much the same state of darkness as that of the Southern young woman before she went North and learned, to her astonishment, that the term 'damned Yankee' was two words—she had never heard either without the other."

[187]   To S. O. Howes [ALS, BL]
Washington,
D.C.
Dear Howes,
We (Miss Christiansen, Miss Shipman and I) expect to depart this life on Wednesday next. I shall be unable to see you—my work on Vol. XII (and, thank God, last) not permitting. Neale has been very good to me, and I must leave the work in such shape that a little accident such as my death will not matter to him and his profit.
We shall go via Cincinnati, Chicago and the Santa Fe route, "stopping" two days at the Grand Cañon. I think my folks have programmed us for Lake Tahoe on our arrival in San Francisco. I wish you were to be of the party. (I'd like to go *around* Chicago, but can't. I can already *smell* that convention when the wind is wrong.)[1]
Luck to you in your Houston venture—it will at least take you out of Gomorrah. Miss Christiansen sends you an affectionate good-bye.

My address in California will be, simply, Oakland.
I return the clipping. It is bully! As the women in California are now all suffragettes, I've made up my mind to retain my seat in the street car, keep my hat on when I meet 'em, and treat 'em in all ways as I do other Democrats, Republicans, Socialists, etc.*
Pray for me.
Good-bye.
Sincerely yours,
Ambrose Bierce.
June 14, 1912.

*It is sad to think of, but in the Titanic disaster of the near future the women will all drown.

1. The Republican National Convention took place in Chicago on 18–22 June 1912. After bitter partisan bickering, President Taft was nominated for a second term.

[188]   To Walter Neale [ALS, HL]
Oakland, Cal.
Dear Neale,
I've been here nearly a week, but so "programmed" and pulled about that I've had neither time nor heart to write. And we are expecting to set out for Lake Tahoe (see your map) tomorrow morning.
We had a pleasant journey until we were about leaving the Grand Cañon, where we had passed two days of delight. Then Miss Christiansen was handed a telegram that her father was dying. He has since died, but she got home in time to see him and be recognized. Of course she can not be with us at Tahoe, but the irrepressible Priscilla Shipman will be of the party. Also Mrs. Sterling, but the divel a George "of that ilk". My address will remain Oakland, Cal. Let me hear from you, but if Vol. XI comes out while I'm here don't send my copy—I'll see my niece's. I've not transportation for books.
I'm enclosing something for the "Little Johnny" stuff—"Kings of Beasts". Please let it go *at the last* of that stuff.¹ It was accidentally omitted.
Will there be room for a preface—two or three pages?—kind of a farewell word to the reader.²
Good-bye; I'm awfully sorry you're not with me in this land of the sun and the suffragette.
Kindly remember me to Mrs. Neale and the bairns.
Sincerely yours,
Ambrose Bierce.
July 2, 1912.

1. The concluding sketch, "The Tail End."
2. No such preface appeared in *CW* 12.

[189]   To the Editor of *Town Talk*[1]

Editor Town Talk, Sir:
In a single day of last week all the daily newspapers of San Francisco published long eulogistic articles on the genius and work of young Clark Ashton Smith, the poet of Auburn.[2] Some of them have repeated their raptures with further quotations from Mr. Smith's verses to justify the transports. That all these writers should be persuaded to see the light at once is obviously more than a coincidence, yet I think it does not imply the interested activity of a "press agent"—only the zeal of some fool friend more concerned for the glory of a discoverer than for the good of the discoveree. I call this "team work" and its instigation pretty "raw," and having myself a good opinion of Mr. Smith, his verses and his possibilities, am sorry to see him thrown to the lions of reaction from so many hands—one might almost say from several sides of the arena at once.

In nearly all these eulogies I find myself credited with praises that I never uttered. One paper has me affirming Mr. Smith's "extraordinary genius," another "declaring" that his poems are "no way inferior to those of Keats," and so forth. These falsehoods have doubtless a common origin in the mind of the fool friend herein before mentioned but to me unknown.

Several weeks ago I had from a correspondent a manuscript copy of Mr. Smith's "Ode to the Abyss." It seemed to me uncommonly good work and a promise of better work to come. So I commended it—in just what words I do not recollect, but if I said any of the things recently attributed to me I beg my correspondent to cover me with shame and confusion by quoting them from my letter—and filing the letter in proof.[3]

My correspondent is Mr. George Sterling.
    Sincerely yours,
        —Ambrose Bierce.

Oakland, August 6.

1. Published in *Town Talk* no. 1042 (10 August 1912): 10–11.
2. Clark Ashton Smith (1893–1961), prolific California poet and writer of fantasy tales. His *The Star-Treader and Other Poems* appeared in 1912, when Smith was nineteen, and created a sensation, causing Smith to be compared to Keats, Shelley, and Swinburne.
3. AB had written to GS: "Kindly convey to young Smith of Auburn my felicitations on his admirable 'Ode to the Abyss'—a large theme, treated with dignity and power. It has many striking pas-

sages—such, for example, as 'The Romes of ruined spheres.' I'm conscious of my sin against the rhetoricians in liking that, for it jolts the reader out of the Abyss and back to earth. Moreover it is a metaphor which belittles, instead of dignifying. But I like it" (8 August 1911; ALS, NYPL).

[190]   To George Sterling [ALS, NYPL]

Oakland
Sept. 9, 1912.

Dear George,
   I think I'd better return these verses that I've had so long, for possibly I may not go to Carmel. And I guess I'll add to them the ones, received today, which you asked me to hand to Mrs. Sterling. I'd rather not hand "The Golden Past"[1] to a woman, and I hope you'll never hand it to the public, though it would doubtless delight the followers of Upton Sinclair. The conclusion is a trifle too graphic; you might as well have used "the shorter and uglier word".
   For the other verses I have nothing but admiration.
   I did hand to your wife the two others that I got from her. I made no notes on them, not caring to have her know that I've the cheek to censor your work. Nobody, I believe, knows that—unless you have told it. I *may* have mentioned it to Karen Christiansen.
   As to that rifle, I fancy I'd not be able to do much with it. I've not fired a rifle for many years. And for anything I know my eyes may have gone bad with age.
   Lora has gone home.

Sincerely yours,
Ambrose Bierce.

1. "The Golden Past," a series of two sonnets about a "vanquished tyrant" chained naked in a dungeon while his "faithless queen" lies in bed with "his conqueror." It was first published in *Poetica Erotica*, vol. 2, ed. T. R. Smith (New York: Boni & Liveright, 1921–22), 317.

[191]   To Helen (Bierce) Cowden [ALS, YU]

Washington,
D.C.

Dear Helen,
   I asked Carrie to write to you only because I was too ill to do so. Happily my illness was briefer than I expected it to be, and I am now up and about.
   I had a tedious and tiresome journey from Chicago—the train late always and everywhere. But Washington looks good to me.
   I shall not again go to California. Our relatives and their friends there are only a small group in my "social circle", but they disappoint.[1] They are all 'ists of one kind and anoth-

er: socialists, suffragists—anarchists, too, I think. I have no ill-will toward them, but there is no community of feeling between them and me. I don't like their ways, nor they mine; indeed, they seem rather to resent my existence. You see I have a pretty good opinion of myself as a thinker, take myself pretty seriously, and can have no pleasure in the society of persons who think their fool leaders wiser than I. So I shall not again go where they are.

Carrie and I are going to-morrow evening to hear Phyllis Partington sing. Carrie sends love.

The autumn here is delightful; the city and the country are very beautiful.

My love to Harry and the boys.
  Affectionately,
    Dad.

November 6, 1910 [i.e. 1912].

The defeat of Teddy fills the soul of me with a great white peace.[2]

1. AB wrote this letter less than two months after writing his last surviving letter to GS (9 September 1912; the final letter, whose greeting purportedly read, "Great Poet and Damned Scoundrel" [Fatout, *Ambrose Bierce: The Devil's Lexicographer*, 316], has not been found). AB seems to have ceased relations with GS about this time, largely because of GS's socialist politics and his continued philandering.
2. Theodore Roosevelt, running on the Bull Moose ticket, and the Republican incumbent William Howard Taft lost the presidential election of 1912 to the Democrat Woodrow Wilson.

[192] To Blanche Partington [ALS, BL]
                Washington, D.C.
Dear Blanche,
  I have your second letter. As you say that it is "chiefly" to tell me about Phyllis, and to say that I am to go to hear her sing, and that I am not to make love to her, etc. I shall in *this* note answer that part of your letter. (It is so much easier to answer than the other part—and the other letter.)

Phyllis has been singing here for nearly a week. I have not seen her, heard her, nor heard from her. Phyllis does not interest me. A few years ago in New York I was rather nice and friendly to her. (It seemed to me that at that time she might possibly not have many friends in New York.) And I did not make love to her.

Ever since then she has treated me with marked discourtesy—at least ever since her visit, shortly afterward, to San Francisco. She did not even reply to a note of condolence on the death of your mother, nor has she even so much as let me know her address—has, in brief, ignored my existence.

All this is not very important; it is written only by way of excuse for not obeying your natural command to go and hear her, and your implied wish that I meet her personally.

I could have told you something of this when we spoke of her one evening, but I could not say it in her own home. Besides, I seem to recollect that we had other things to speak of—which, also, it might have been better if I (and you) could not have said. Don't you think so?

Another matter. What was Lora's "fall from grace"? I know of none. Was it more serious than taking two toddies instead of one. As you say the fall was "such a little one," perhaps she took one-and-a-half. If not that, *what* was it?

Be patient, Bird-of-Paradise—you know I am a pedestrian: your blind guide, peripatetic philosopher and "just friend,"[1]

A. B.

November 8, 1912.

1. Alexander Pope, *An Essay on Man*, Epistle 4, l. 390: "Thou wert my guide, philosopher, and friend."

[193]   To Walter Neale [MEG (transcript)]

Washington, D.C.

Dear Neale,

I am sorry that anything I may have written about corrections and alterations should have given you so much concern and prompted you to use so much of your valuable time in considering the matter. I fear you have understood me as complaining, or asking that corrections be made. I had no thought of doing either. Nor have I any expectation of a new edition in my lifetime; probably not in yours. You could not, of course, afford it. My notion has been to leave the books in such a shape that if ever there *be* a new edition in the far future there may be found in your office, and maybe in the possession of my "heirs and assigns," these marked volumes to assist in making it. Surely it can, in any event, do no harm to mark errors whenever found and by whomsoever made. I thought I told you that I should mark as many of the corrections *as are practicable* when the time comes—if ever it comes. (In my recent letters to you I conjectured the "time" by writing of "the edition of 1999".) Nor have I meant at any time to convey any reproach to you or your house for the delinquencies of those doing your work—whom you have yourself assisted me to cuss.

But when it comes to justifying and defending them—Well, I don't think you ought, and you must allow me the freedom to reply.

I know that the inevitability of mechanical errors (typographical and other) in printing is a popular belief. I have seen and heard it affirmed from childhood, and once accepted it without question; but I've had an even longer experience than yours, and long ago found that it is largely itself an error. Absolute perfection is of course rare, but a near approach to it is found in nearly every book (and all *new* books are "new editions") that I read. I have edited three weekly papers, and so nearly perfect was the proofreading that I seldom gave myself the trouble to read the proofs of even my own work. I venture to say that in issue after issue there were not three typographical errors. I made it a rule to read the entire paper after it was "out" (partly with a view of inspiring my foreman and proofreaders with a wholesome fear of me) and many times I found *nothing* to mark. For years and years I wrote from three to a half-dozen columns a week for Hearst's newspapers (dailies) and never read my proofs, nor found it needful. I doubt if there was an error once a month. For a long time I wrote several pages a month in his magazine, "The Cosmopolitan", and I think there was never an error except my own. I confess that in his newspapers the other fellows did not fare so well as I—the general run of the work was "dirty." But when there was an error in mine that I did not make myself I was heard from in a way to surprise and pain, and, incidentally to insure care for many months. Which seems to show that accuracy can be attained by determination to have it. With me it was: "I get it or quit."

When you think yourself on the defensive—which you never are with me—you have an amusing habit of saying the first thing that comes into your head. Witness what you said the other day about the Macmillan books, and what you once wrote me of a magazine in which words were divided at the end of a line without reference to syllables. Now, honest Injun, don't you think you write in the same impetuous, devil-may-care way when you say some of the things that you do say in this letter before me about the abundance of typographical errors in the books of "the more important American and British publishing houses"? I too read many of these books—and I do not find the errors. As to the latest edition of the King James Version of the Bible containing more than three thousand (3000!) errors, the statement takes away my breath. True, you say "it has been said." By whom?—*That* is important; a statement worth repeating should be worth authentication. Certainly it is not "said" by any one having knowledge of the matter. I have read that book from cover to cover three times and am in the habit of reading it now—it is a very interesting book. I have never found *one* typographical error in it. I doubt if there is one. If there is the finder can get quite a bit of money for his discovery, and I am prepared to tell him how.

The importance of all this is that if you hold that a high degree of accuracy—a near approach to perfection—in the mechanical part of the art of book-making is unattainable you will, of course, not try to attain it; that would be a waste of time, money and effort. Whereby your (our) house will suffer, as, begging your pardon, it does suffer. Please, do please, understand that criticism is not censure in its modern meaning of condemnation. It may come, as in this instance it does come, of a sincere and friendly desire to be helpful to a friend to whom I owe so much.

Now for some details. It is true that Miss Christiansen and I did all that we could in the way of proofreading, as I suppose authors and their friends usually do. But that should not count. We are not professional printers and proofreaders. No author is a good proofreader of his own work: he cannot divorce his attention from the *sense* of the work and get it upon the typography. His is merely, with regard to that, an auxiliary function; it should not and does not lessen the responsibility of the expert proofreader employed by the publisher. Moreover, as I have frequently pointed out to you, some of the bad work in the "C. W." (See, for "awful" examples, pages 291 and 317, Vol. VIII and page 352, Vol. XI) was done after the proofs had irrevocably passed from my hands. There are many other instances.

The error in the table of contents in Vol. I was *not* "of my making." I remember it perfectly.

As to my marking-in on page 17 (same volume) the folio number at the bottom of the page, it was done for uniformity, and I have done it in many other instances throughout the volume, your printers having put it in more frequently than they had left it out. So of the Roman numerals at the heads of chapters. Most of them were in small type, but many in large; so I marked out the large and marked in the small. So of the quotes preceding the large initials; I have tried to have them uniform. Surely uniformity is desirable.

Many errors I have not attempted to correct, for examples, successive pages of Italic commas in Roman text. I *think* these occur in Vol. XII, which is not now accessible to me; anyhow I promise to cite volume and pages [as] requested. Miss C. says they are in Vol. VII and pages 50 *et seq.*

You say I marked out the d in "admiral"—page 230, Vol I. I should say I did! I marked it out on three several proofs and wrote notes about it to editor and compositor. I did all that I could to get it out and keep it out, for Milton, from whom I quoted the word, did not put it in, nor mean to put it in; he made the word "ammiral," as he made many other words different from the common form, as a poet has the right to do.[1] You evidently do not remember but on two evenings at my shack, I and Miss Christiansen expounded to you our ludicrous failure to keep out that d.

You cite my marking for "smaller type" the chapter numeral on page 251, (Vol. I). Why not? On page 250, *facing* it, and in most of the other chapter numerals in the article, and in the volumes generally, the smaller type is used. Should they not be uniform? Perhaps I should have said "Small caps," instead of "smaller type," but I am not a printer and do not in a matter of this kind know the difference. But surely the compositor would understand. I fancy my technical knowledge is at least as good as that of most other writers; I know it is a heap better than that of any of your editors with whom I have had to do.

"Hyphen omitted on page 269." Sure! Should there not be a hyphen?

Your other "instances" are equally wide of the mark, for they are instances of correct marking. If you mean that they are trivial I ask you to remember that a greater man than either of us said: "Perfection is made up of trifles, but perfection is no trifle."[2] I have marked *everything* wrong that caught my eye, as you will see more plainly in the later volumes—broken letters, blurred letters, misplaced commas—all. It is for you, or your successor, to say how many of the marks should be regarded—how near an approach to perfection you care or he cares to make. That is not for me to say; my job is to mark errors. I am surprised that you should think it could be too thoroughly and conscientiously done.

What I undertake to do I try to do well. I mean to take to you all the volumes of the cloth edition that I have marked and transcribe all the marks into yours if you will let me—all the marks made in both my first and my second reading. The books so marked will not bite you, and I don't see how they could stir you to controversion. Surely you must see that in doing this work I am doing it for *you*. *I* shall never see *one* of the corrections in print.

You say that the reviews have commended the *typography* of the "C. W." None that have come to me; many have commended the *type* and the other features of the books. And no one of them has said half enough about the beauty of the books—half of what *I* think and habitually say. But the typography—if that means fine, clean printing—is just our weak point—that and the binding of the cloth edition.[3]

But from my point of view, which is not that of a complainant nor that of a censor, all this is irrelevant. I repeat (if I have already said it) that my purpose is merely a friendly one—to do what I can to enable you to better one of your products in the publication of which you have laid me under an obligation which I can not hope to discharge. If in doing what I can I offend I am very, very sorry.

        Sincerely yours,
                Ambrose Bierce.
January 8, 1913.

1. AB refers to his quotation of the phrase "the mast of some great ammiral" (from *Paradise Lost* 1.293–94) in the memoir "On a Mountain" (*CW* 1.230; *A Sole Survivor* 8).

2. The adage "Trifles make perfection, and perfection is no trifle" is attributed to Michelangelo.

3. Cf. AB to Walter Neale (18 October 1911; ALS, HL): "In the slight handling necessary, some of these volumes (owing to bad binding) have gone out of shape. If the whole edition is that way I think you will be justified in thrashing the binder—which will give me a mighty contentment."

[194]   To Walter Neale [ALS, HL]

Washington, D.C.

Dear Neale,

We *seem* to be making a mountain out of a molehill, with all this correspondence about the printing in the "C. W.," but I really must notice some things in your letter of the 21st. First, though, let me say that you err in supposing that I "take no pleasure" in this culmination of my life's work in literature because of such defects in the printing as I have pointed out for possible correction in the far future. They do not worry me at all. I think them more numerous and more important than you do, but if I am right, a good deal more injurious to you than to me. I am entirely cheerful about it, but wish that you were a little less sensitive to criticism of that merely mechanical part of your work that you do not do yourself.

I can not agree with you that it is difficult to say what is a "typographical error"; it seems to me a very simple matter, and very easily avoidable. The question of "a publisher's accountablity for the imperfections of his authors" seems to me not to enter into the matter at all. I don't hold you in any degree accountable for mine; my having marked some of them means nothing of the kind. As explained in a previous letter, I marked them only in the hope that they might be corrected in some future edition. My notion was that sometime you or your successors *might* want to make a new edition from new plates—that is, set up again the entire work. In that case my mistakes could be as well corrected as yours, or rather your printers'. I had no thought of your making any changes in *these* plates that could not be made easily and without expense, or with *little* expense.

But here is a graver matter. You imply that two of your "expert proof-readers" declined to go on with the work because I was hard to get on with. If either, or any, of them told you that he lied. In the first place, no expert proof-reader (in *any* sense of the term) has had anything to do with them. I *know* the work of an expert in proof-reading as infallibly as I know the degree of scholarship of a man whom I talk with. The expert marks a proof differently from another man—marks it according to a code which I know. I sometimes do not know whether (for one example of many) small caps should be substituted for large or large caps from another font; I am not an expert in type; but I know the technical mark for every error that a printer can make. No proof-reader that has had to do with the "C. W." has had this knowledge. Their markings have been intelligible mostly, but frequently clumsy and awkward—amateurish, so to say. I doubt not that you believe your proof-readers expert, but you must try to pardon me if I believe my own eyes.

In the first two or three volumes the proofs were marked by one whom I understood to be your editor—I think his name was Mac-something, perhaps MacQueen. I had several little controversies with him, always conducted politely and, as I supposed, without feeling. He began them. Several times he marked supposed errors by me and called my attention to them; so I explained to him that they were not errors. Once, or oftener, he "corrected" my Latin without knowing anything of Latin. I patiently and good humoredly cited authorities, though as to those particular expressions I was myself an authority. Once he pointed out my error in writing of the "stock" of a rifle— which I might be supposed as a soldier to know about. He thought the word meant the "butt" of the rifle. There were many other instances, which I'll not bore you with. If he "quit" it was probably because he did not care further to disclose his ignorance— which is dark, profound and general. There was never anything between us that you are, or he is, justified in calling a "dispute". Nor with any other of your editors or mechanics. You might as reasonably call *this* correspondence a "dispute" between you and me.

As to your second man, I know nothing about him; I had no correspondence with any other; and if you care to look over the proofs (in case they still exist) you will not find a single mark of mine on them that is in any degree uncivil, or that implies censure or temper. I "cussed" them to you only, and you cussed them too, as you habitually and not altogether unjustly, cuss all printers. The savage things that you have written and said to me about your workmen would make a small volume of delightful reading. But lo! all at once they are saints all, and I am apparently a very testy and impossible person! Well, I "aint".

You say you are "held accountable" for my "arbitrary ruling on the division of words at the ends of lines". Held by whom, to whom? And you add: "I know of no power that could force you to write down your art as you know it." This I do not understand, if it means anything. As to "the division of words at the ends of lines," no power is needful to force me to expound so simple a thing as that: my principle is merely not to divide a syllable. If all the editors, foremen, printers, and even publishers in the world ignored (as I think they mostly do) or disputed the correctness of that principle (as many of them do, or would) it would not move me. And I venture to say that if you would adopt it, and insist on it, it would commend your books to those who know and love the English language.

Your memory is at fault: you never "told" me that the proof-reading would be left to me and Miss Christiansen, and if you "wrote" me so I did not receive the letter—at least I have no recollection of it, and can not find it in any of your letters. I fear that if I had received a communication of that kind, either oral or written, I should not have gone on with the work—might even have fallen dead! Anyhow, it was *not* left to me and Miss Christiansen, for all proofs were marked by somebody else, both before and after we had them.

Of course I shall be glad if you will refer me to a letter of yours from which I would have reason to think that Miss C. and I were to be the *only* proof-readers, and will promptly confess that your memory is better than mine—as in some things I know it to be. I shall not ask her about it, for I don't want to draw her into this amusing controversy; she has trifles enough of her own to look after. And some day (age having removed me from the field of your resentment) you might waylay and murder her, which would make me turn in my grave and—smile at your error in assassinating the wrong person.

You did not need to show me that you are not the only publisher issuing books typographically imperfect; I read books, and have eyes. What I "would have otherwise" is your apparent conviction that what I called a near approach to perfection is unattainable and your apparent near approach to indifference about it. We disagree as to the importance of it, that is all—except what appears to me your needless "touchiness" and your rather headlong determination to make me see black as white. I guess you see it so, as a mother thinks her child altogether beautiful; but, as I said, I must use my own eyes.

I *hope* you have read this screed in a comfortable mood. The reception accorded to a letter depends altogether on the mood of the receiver. If one is grouchy, and imagines his correspondent writing with a frown, the letter will seem objectionable—impolite, unfriendly; if he imagines him writing with a smile it will seem pleasant and amiable. Please understand that this is written in my most rollicking and playful frame of mind. I have, in fact, taken two drinks of uncommonly good Jamaican rum since beginning it.

    Sincerely yours,
        Ambrose Bierce.
January 23, 1913.

[195]   To Helen (Bierce) Cowden [ALS, YU]

        Washington, D.C.
My dear Helen,
    I am transferring to you the ownership of the new lot in the St. Helena cemetery. George Fee, who has attended to everything there for me and has taken much trouble and charged nothing for his services, wanted to buy the old lot. I told him he should have it for nothing. I had forgotten that the deed was in your mother's name and that you were now the owner as her heir. But I know that you will be glad to perform the promise made by me.

If you have the original deed please write at the bottom of it:

"I hereby direct and empower the St. Helena Public Cemetery Association to transfer and set over to George W. Fee all my right, title and interest in and to the above described lot of land."

Sign it and send the deed so amended to me, and I will send it to my St. Helena lawyer (James A. Nowland—maybe you know him) who says that will be sufficient.

If you have *not* the deed, or can not find it, take the enclosed paper to a notary and have it duly "executed," and send me that.

I think it better to have the new lot transferred to you while I am living, though I shall continue to pay the superintendent's bills, as before.

By the way, I do not wish to lie there. That matter is all arranged, and you will not be bothered about the mortal part of
    Your Daddy.

January 27, 1913.

P.S.—

I don't know how your mother's name is given in the deed, nor whether in a paper of this kind she can now be legally described as "Mrs. A. G. Bierce". (Harry will know, or can ascertain; or the notary will tell you). So I enclose two forms, so that you may use either, or a different one, as you may be advised.
    Dad.

[196]   To H. L. Mencken [ALS, EPFL]
    Army and Navy Club,
    Washington, D.C.
My dear Mr. Mencken,
    A few days ago I bought the May number of the rather clever magazine with the unpleasant name—"The Smart Set"—and was delighted to find in it two things by you.[1] Maybe you write for it all the time; I don't know. Well, I like your work and want to tell you so; I had not known that you could write so devilish well. What particularly takes my attention and traps my approval is your view of the "white slavery" fad—partly no doubt because of its conformity to my own notion, expounded many times in conversation but never written because I have now no "organ" and don't write *anything*. Aside from that, your remarks are more than merely cleverly made—they charm.

I'm not supposing that you will care particularly for my commendation, but I can't withhold it without doing violence to conscience. Now it is "off my mind."

I hope you prosper in so far as prosperity is compatible with happiness.
    Sincerely yours,
    Ambrose Bierce.
April 21, 1913.

236   Selected Letters

1. H. L. Mencken (1880–1956), "Good Old Baltimore" and "Weep for the White Slave!" (a book review column), *Smart Set* (May 1913). Mencken had been the magazine's book reviewer since November 1908. In November 1914, he became its coeditor (with George Jean Nathan).

[197]   To Willard Huntington Wright[1] [MEG (transcript)]
                                            Army and Navy Club,
                                            Washington, D.C.
My dear Mr. Wright,
         I'm sorry to have bothered you about the Carmel article. I wanted to know if you saw Carmel about as I did—a colony of cranks and cry-babies deeply concerned for the posterity of criminals.
    Thank you for the kind invitation to write for the "S. S." I've not written a half-dozen articles in four years, except for my "Collected Works"—I'm making a solemnly humorous attempt to live on royalties. The attempt is somewhat handicapped by my addiction to the baleful habit of loafing away the summers in California. Maybe I shall take to story-writing again. If so I'll remember you.
    By the way, at what rate would you pay if they suited you? That sordid consideration is commonly the controlling one with me.
    I want to congratulate you on the work of our friend Mencken. It was only through the accidental purchase of the magazine for May that I learned how well the chap can write; for I don't know him very well and am not so familiar with "The Smart Set" as I expect to be.
    I am sincerely yours,
                        Ambrose Bierce.
May 9, 1913.

1. Willard Huntington Wright (1888–1939), editor of *Smart Set* (1913–14). Although a widely published literary and art critic, Wright attained greatest celebrity with a series of detective novels about Philo Vance written under the pseudonym "S. S. Van Dine." Wright had published a half-admiring, half-satirical article on GS's Bohemian set at Carmel, "Hotbed of Soulful Culture, Vortex of Erotic Erudition," *Los Angeles Times* (22 May 1910).

[198]   To H. L. Mencken [ALS, EPFL]
                                            Washington, D.C.
                                            [May 1913]
My dear Mencken,
              I thank you for the books; they have delighted me. Of course you had an easy fight with La Monte, who, however would have been no mean antagonist

if he had a leg to stand on and a footing for the leg. The *manner* of your fighting is altogether admirable.[1]

Perhaps it is your courtesy to an opponent, but it seems to [me] that your treatment of Socialism is better than its merits. I should myself not think of opposing a Socialist otherwise than by a cuff upon the mouth of him. I have never met one that was not in open and candid sympathy with crime. In the immemorial war between the law-abiding and the law-breaking class the Socialist is what we Damyanks used to call a "copperhead." Moreover, he is a cry-baby and a 'fraid-cat. Furthermore, he is commonly devoid of decency, and his female is that way too. Observe that the fellow in jail for sending indecent matter through the mails is invariably a Socialist.

But if I *did* reason with one I should wish to reason about as you do.

All the same, Socialism is going to get our goat.

Sincerely yours,
Ambrose Bierce.

1. *Men Versus the Man: A Correspondence Between Rives La Monte, Socialist, and H. L. Mencken, Individualist* (New York: Henry Holt, 1910). Carey McWilliams lists Mencken's *The Artist: A Drama without Words* (Boston: John W. Luce, 1912) as a book in AB's library.

[199]   To Amy L. Wells[1] [ALS, BL]

Dear Amy Wells,
          Your little Easter card was handed to me a few days ago. It has been sleeping in a mail box at my club—a box that I relinquished last year when I started for California. Thank you. But did you forget to frame it?

Thank you, too, for the Rockridge picture, and the clipping about the death of my friend Gen. Foote.[2] I too shall always remember that evening stroll at Rockridge—the sunset, the grass fire, twilight, and the rest of it. It looks as if I shall remember even the girl. Alas, that memory must be all!—that it can not again *be*. What's the use?

I eat blackberries every morning, and every berry reminds me of "the days that are no more".[3] Some day, it may be, a weary, world-worn old man will sit under a strange tree in a beautiful valley in the heart of the Andes, where art, letters, religion, politics, taxi-cabs, morals, dogs, suffragettes, socialists, and white folks have never been heard of, and dream of a bungalow (and its bungalaine) in a life so far away in miles and years that it will all be dim and unreal, and its voices—even hers—"like noises in a swound".[4] Would you like to be there? Well, put on your hat and meet me at Panama. That valley will be big enough for *two* graves.

A. B.

June 13, 1913.

1. Amy L. Wells was a friend in Oakland with whom AB had been corresponding since 1893.
2. Lucius H. Foote (1826–1913) came to California in 1853 and held a variety of judicial and diplomatic posts, including municipal judge (1856–60), collector of the port of Sacramento (1861–65), and consul to Chile (1878–81). He was also a poet. See GS's article, "The Poems of Lucius H. Foote: A Brief Appreciation," *Town Talk* no. 1086 (14 June 1913): 7.
3. Alfred, Lord Tennyson, *The Princess*, 4.25 (also 4.30, 35, 40). See also letter 91, n. 4.
4. Samuel Taylor Coleridge, *The Rime of the Ancient Mariner* (1798), l. 62.

[200]   Amy L. Wells [ALS, BL]

Washington, D.C.

Dear Amy Wells,

You are the queen of letter writers. But your letters are so "full of things" that I can not hope adequately to answer them without transgressing the decent limitations of correspondence.

No, I have not "surrendered my army and navy ties"; it is only that I prefer to get your letters at my tenement rather than my club—it saves an hour. When you come here we will dine on the roof of the club, "as usual".

I did not hear about the Sterling-Bechdolt scrap.[1] I never hear from Sterling and his entourage of social impossibles; there is not enough charitableness in this vale of tears to make them and me personally congenial, or even compatible.

How nice of you to remember my birthday;[2] all women seem to have a genius for anniversaries. If they did not remind me I should forget the day when I am said to have been flung down into this wild welter of earthly existence. I think women pass a considerable part of the time allowed them for repentance in sticking pins into the several parts of the earth's circle round the sun.

Comes now your acknowledgment of the book. I had it with me, both times, in Oakland, but was not then so shameless as I have now become.

Don't imperil your health in your pursuit of art; it is more important that you be well than that you draw. *All* that Ruskin wrote of art will be helpful to you, but the book on drawing and perspective is the one that I had in mind. You'll probably find it in any library.

Am I truly "going to South America"? Sure—my valley in the Andes awaits me. I see it in visions of the night.[3]

That is all, Amy Wells, until I hear from you again.

Meantime, God bless you.

Ambrose Bierce.

July 10 1913.

1. Evidently a dispute between GS and Frederick R. Bechdolt (1874–1950), author of numerous works on Western topics and associate of GS.

2. AB was born 24 June 1842.
3. "Visions of the Night" (the phrase is from Genesis 46:2 and Job 4:13) is the title of AB's essay on his bizarre dreams (in *CW* 10 and *A Sole Survivor*).

[201]   To Amy L. Wells [ALS, BL]
Washington,
D.C.
"O, Psyche, from the regions which
    Are Holy Land,"[1]

I send you this souvenir of Jerusalem. No, it did not come from another woman; so it has not the taint of treachery on it.
You probably thought me killed in the recent storm that you must have read about.[2] No, I was running before it in a steamer that did not dare to turn its side to it in order to land. And when I came back home I found my apartment flooded from a "busted" window, my rugs and mats a wreck and my bird half dead from fright. Then (of course never before nor since) I longed for the peace, the security and the other things of Holy Land: 6100.[3] Amy Wells dear, do you think it ever storms in South America?
I am just loafing my life away here in Washington, eschewing pen-and-ink (never again) and keeping my face clean and my nails evenly pared. Sometimes, by way of variation, I go to my club to look over the foreign magazines and reviews. (I observe that Scheffauer has in "The Fortnightly" an article on the death of satire[4]—I don't care how dead it is.) And every evening after dinner a slender sylph from Georgia, with the most delicious Southern drawl, comes down from the flat above and makes coffee for me. You'd adore her, naturally. That is the history of my life, as it flows along toward the brink of the Cataract. But

"I shall see, before I die,
The palms and temples of the south"—[5]

Maybe.
    Sincerely x 10,
        Ambrose Bierce.
August 5, 1913.

1. Poe, "To Helen," ll. 14–15.
2. On 30 July 1913, Washington, D.C., was hit by a severe electrical and wind storm, accompanied by rain and hail. Two people died, dozens were injured, property damage was extensive, and government operations were temporarily suspended.

3. Amy Wells's address was 6100 Colby Avenue, Oakland, CA.
4. Herman Scheffauer, "The Death of Satire," *Fortnightly Review* 99 (June 1913): 1188–99. The article discusses AB in part.
5. Tennyson, "You ask me, why, tho' ill at ease" (1833), ll. 27–28.

[202]   To Helen (Bierce) Cowden [ALS, UP]

Washington, D.C.

My dear Helen,
I fancy we are not very "good correspondents." But really we have nothing to write about. Nothing occurs to either of us. However, I have had an outing (or inning) in New York, whence I have just returned. I expected to meet Carrie there on her way back to Washington, but we missed each other. Her trip to Sag Harbor seems to have done her some good, but she does not look very well.

If I am to hear from you again for a long time you'll have to answer this letter pretty soon. I am going away. My plans are not very definite, but they include a journey into—possibly across—South America. I have arranged for a pretty long absence. If we have trouble with Mexico before I leave I shall probably go there instead—or at least first.

My health is excellent.

With love to Harry and the boys,
    Affectionately,
        Your Father.
Sept. 10, 1913.

[203]   To The Neale Publishing Co. [ALS, UL]

The Olympia,
Euclid St.,
Washington,
D.C.

The Neale Publishing Co.,
    Union Square,
        New York City.

            Gentlemen,
                I have sold and assigned to Carrie J. Christiansen, of this city, all my copyrights, and all my right title and interest in the contract (dated the first day of June, 1908) between you and me for publication of "The Collected Works of Ambrose Bierce", and in all royalties or other profits accruing therefrom, both present and future.

This is to notify you of the transaction, in accordance with the terms of said contract. Kindly acknowledge receipt of this notification and that it is satisfactory to you.
    Very truly yours,
            Ambrose Bierce.
September 19, 1913.

The assignment to Carrie J. Christiansen covers and includes all my other contracts with you, and all my interests in which your house is concerned.
    Ambrose Bierce.

[204]   To Eleanor (Vore) Sickler [ALS, BL]
                            Washington, D.C.
Dear Nellie Sickler,
            (I don't like your stately name Eleanor)—That is a good, friendly farewell letter, very pleasant to receive, but I fear you have still a misapprehension which I thought I had removed. The "indefinite region" to which I expect to go for "an indefinite time" (not, I hope, for *all* time) is Mexico and South America. My plan, so far as I have one, is to go through Mexico to one of the Pacific ports, if I can *get* through without being stood up against a wall and shot as an American. Thence I hope to sail for some port in South America. Thence go across the Andes and perhaps across the continent. Isn't all that "indefinite"? Naturally, it is possible—even probable—that I shall not return. These be "strange countries," in which things happen; that is why I am going. And I am seventy-one!
    I have not the heart greatly to regret the uncheerful view of this my adventure that you seem to take, for has it not given me your affectionate letter? If you had not taken it all so seriously I should not have known that you care so much for your old friend whom you have never seen. Truly, you must have a good and loyal heart. It has to be to harmonize with your face, as shown in the photograph that you send. The picture is a pleasing revelation. I can hardly trace in it the awkward little schoolgirl clasping her diploma. Well, whatever you may or may not accomplish in literature, you *look* the poet. And, thank God! you *don't* look the suffragette and reformer. You look like the woman who betters and brightens her world by example and a still tongue—by good deeds, not words, words, words. That is the kind of woman whom I do not loathe. Man, too, for that matter—unless, as in my own case, words are his trade.
    Again good-bye, dear, and may "whatever gods may be" bless you and all yours.
            Ambrose Bierce.
September 21, 1913.

[205]   To Amy L. Wells [ALS, BL]

Washington, D.C.

Dear Amy Wells,

I don't remember if I wrote you since returning from New York—probably not. But I *do* remember a long and charming letter from you. (And one enclosing some newspaper pictures of women, with a line or two of text relevant to nothing in the world, proving that you are as crazy as other women—just stark, staring mad in a most delightful and candid way.)

You see I am bold to say anything to (and about) you, for you can not retort. I shall be going away before another letter from you can reach me. But I'll be good and send you a postal—maybe a letter—from somewhere, telling you where a word from you will reach me—down on the Mexican border, probably. For I've not given up my rather indefinite itinerary: "Through Mexico and to South America." My Andean valley still beckons to me. And (this you must keep to yourself) I mean to see—perhaps do—some fighting in "our sister republic." Pardon an old soldier's folly, but really life is very dull everywhere else in this hemisphere.

[...]

O yes, I suppose I look like the late Mark Twain—I've been mistaken for him all my life, sometimes most amusingly. By the way, you are "down" for a portrait of me, as I really am, by Miss Campbell, if it comes before I leave. It is from, or partly from—I had to give her a sitting for my nose—a photograph which I think you have. She doesn't like it very well, for I made her stick to the ugly truth, but *I* like it and hope that you will.

Before "visiting" Mexico (if I can get in) I am going over my old battlefields of a half-century ago—Chickamauga, Chattanooga, Murfreesboro, Franklin, Nashville, Shiloh, and so forth. I'd like to take you along, to show you just how and where I saved the Union for the workingman and the suffragette, the socialist, anarchist and eugenist, the Christian Scientist and the Puritan. Perhaps you can fancy the battle-scarred (or bottlescarred) veteran posing all by himself on the scenes of his prowess in arms! Isn't it a touching picture?

Seriously, dear Amy Wells, I am sorry to break the thread of connection between you and me. Despite "misunderstandings" (or were they flashes of understanding) our friendship has meant a good deal to me. I guess you are pretty dear to me, as I hope, if God so wills it that I do not return, my memory will be to you.

So—good-bye, and "whatever gods may be" bless you forever.

Ambrose Bierce.

September 21, 1913.

[206]   To Lora Bierce[1]

The Olympia,
Euclid Street,
Washington, D.C.,
October 1, 1913.

Dear Lora,

I go away tomorrow for a long time, so this is only to say good-bye. I think there is nothing else worth saying; *therefore* you will naturally expect a long letter. What an intolerable world this would be if we said nothing but what is worth saying! And did nothing foolish—like going into Mexico and South America.

I'm hoping that you will go to the mine soon. You must hunger and thirst for the mountains—Carlt likewise. So do I. Civilization be dinged!—it is the mountains and the desert for me.

Good-bye—if you hear of my being stood up against a Mexican stone wall and shot to rags please know that I think that a pretty good way to depart this life. It beats old age, disease, or falling down the cellar stairs. To be a Gringo in Mexico—ah, that is euthanasia![2]

With love to Carlt, affectionately yours,
Ambrose.

1. Text derived from *The Letters of Ambrose Bierce*, 196–97.
2. Cf. Carlos Fuentes's *The Old Gringo* (1985), a historical novel about AB's voyage to and death in Mexico.

[207]   To Helen (Bierce) Cowden [ALS, SC]

[THE MENGER
SAN ANTONIO, TEXAS]
Oct. 30, 1913.

My dear Daughter,

I have your letter and telegram—doubtless you already know why I did not have them before. I did not suppose that you cared particularly to see me, or I should have gone your way. It does not greatly matter; I can see you on my return—if I return.

It would not be prudent to tell you of my plans; this country is full of spies and watchers, and I've no confidence in even the U.S. mails. I mean to go into Mexico; that is all that you need to know. There is good fighting all along the border and everywhere. Maybe I shall see some of it—as an "innocent bystander."

I visited all my old battlefields—Chickamauga, Chattanooga, Stone's River, Franklin, Nashville and Shiloh—arriving here on Monday last pretty well worn out.

Shall stay a few days longer. After that I shall be out of reach of letters, so can not hear from you.
    My love to Harry and the boys. God bless and keep you all.
        Your Dad.

[208]   To Helen (Bierce) Cowden [ALS, YU]
        [THE MENGER
        SAN ANTONIO, TEXAS]
        Nov. 4 1913.
Dear Helen,
        I am still detained here—partly by ill health, for I arrived a week ago pretty well run down. But I'm now nearly well, and shall leave in a few days for Laredo and I don't know where else. This is a pleasant city, I have a charming hotel, and many persons have been exceedingly kind to me, but I'm eager to be off about my affairs. I can give you no address, so can not hope to hear from you soon. I could have heard from you if I had known that I was to be here so long. Carrie writes me every day, and I've had a letter from your uncle Grizzly. Carlt and Lora are still expecting to go to the mine in Calaveras county.
    I hope you are all well and happy. My future is uncertain (there can not be much of it, anyhow) but I am a bit better satisfied with myself than when idling away my life in Washington to no purpose.
    Affectionately,
        Your Father.

[209]   To Blanche Partington [ALS, BL]
        Chihuahua, Mexico,
        December 26, 1913.
My dear Blanche,
        I have been regretting my harshness to you in my letter from San Antonio, Texas—or was it from Laredo? I wrote in anger, having just read your letter forwarded from Washington, and was doubtless unjust. My anger was caused partly by your destruction of Miss Soulé Campbell's new portrait of me,[1] which I had had made more to please you than for any other reason. You had *asked* me for a picture.
    But also you asked me in the letter to "confess" that I cared for human sympathy, sentiment and friendship. This to *me* who have always valued those things more than anything else in life!—who have the dearest and best friends of any man in the world, I think,—sweet souls who have the insight to take me at my own appraisement (or,

perhaps you would say, to *pretend* to). You don't know any of them; it would be better for you if you did. Evidently you share the current notion that because I don't like fools and rogues I am a kind of monster—a misanthrope without sentiment and without heart. I can not help your entertaining that view, but you might have kept it to yourself. The "popular" notion of me I care nothing about, but when it is thrown at me by one whom I supposed immune to it by reason of years of friendly observation it naturally disgusts me. Still, I ought to have made allowance for the pressure of your social environment and for (pardon me) your limitations.

I was also impatient of your foolish notion that in the matter of my proposed visit to "the Andes" I was posing. I do not know why you think the Andes particularly spectacular—probably because you have not traveled much. To me they are no different in grandioseness from the Rockies or the Coast Range—merely a geographical expression used because I did not care to be more specific. The particular region that I had in mind has lured me all my life—more now than before, because it is, not more distant from, but more inaccessible to, many of the things of which as an old man I am mortally tired. What "interpretation" you put upon my letters regarding that spot you have not seen fit to inform me, which before rebuking me (I am not hospitable to rebuke) you should have done. I suppose you have a *habit* of "interpretation". You worship a god who (omniscent and omnipotent) has been unable to make his message clear to his children and has to have a million paid interpreters, and you are one of them. (Pardon me; you invited me to "convert you from the error of your ways.") So little do I know of your "interpretation" that I was not even aware that I had written you of my intention to go to "the Andes." If I did, as of course I did, I must also have told you that I intended to go by the way of Mexico, which I am doing, though it looks now as if "the Andes" would have to wait.

My enemies are fond of saying that I cannot keep my friends. They are right to this extent: many of my friends I *do* not keep. I can endure many vices and weaknesses in a friend, but one thing I can not and will not endure—the attribution of nasty little vices and weaknesses to *me*. When a friend offends in that way he (or she) sooner or later receives a formal note from me renouncing the advantage of further acquaintance. You and my foolish relatives are the only persons who have hitherto been exempt. *You* have offended seventy-and-seven times and I have overlooked it, but in the letter that angered me you passed the limit and (I say it with no feeling but regret) you go into the discard. No pleasure can come of a relation that is not inclusive of respect. If I am what you think me I am unworthy of your friendship; if I am not you are unworthy of mine. You will be spared henceforth the necessity of being either "ashamed" or proud of me, for I hereby withdraw your right to be either.

It is true that the latter half of your letter was apologetic, but that was insincere, for if one perceives that a letter is offensive, before it is posted, one can put it into the waste-basket.

So—I bid you farewell.
    Sincerely yours,
        Ambrose Bierce.

I do not know how, nor when, you are to get this letter; there are no mails, and sometimes no trains to take anything to El Paso. Moreover, I have forgotten your address and shall send this to the care of Lora. And Lora may have gone to the mountains. As to me, I leave here tomorrow for an unknown destination.

1. Presumably the portrait mentioned in letter 205, not the one by Campbell used on the frontispiece to *CW* 1.

BIBLIOGRAPHY

Bierce, Ambrose. *Black Beetles in Amber*. San Francisco and New York: Western Authors Publishing Co. 1892.
———. *The Collected Fables of Ambrose* Bierce, edited by S. T. Joshi. Columbus: Ohio State University Press, 2000.
———. *Collected Works*. New York and Washington, D.C.: Neale Publishing Co., 1909–1912. 12 vols.
———. *The Fall of the Republic and Other Political Satires*, edited by S. T. Joshi and David E. Schultz. Knoxville: University of Tennessee Press, 2000.
———. *Shapes of Clay*. San Francisco: W. E. Wood, 1903.
———. *A Sole Survivor: Bits of Autobiography*, edited by S. T. Joshi and David E. Schultz. Knoxville: University of Tennessee Press, 1998.
———. *The Unabridged Devil's Dictionary*, edited by David E. Schultz and S. T. Joshi. Athens: University of Georgia Press, 2000.
De Castro [Danziger], Adolphe. *Portrait of Ambrose Bierce*. New York: Century Co., 1929.
Gale, Robert L. *An Ambrose Bierce Companion*. Westport, Conn.: Greenwood Press, 2001.
Fatout, Paul. *Ambrose Bierce: The Devil's Lexicographer*. Norman: University of Oklahoma Press, 1951.
Grenander, M. E. "Ambrose Bierce and Charles Warren Stoddard: Some Unpublished Correspondence." *Huntington Library Quarterly* 23, no. 3 (May 1960): 261–92.
———. "Seven Ambrose Bierce Letters." *Yale University Library Gazette* 32 (July 1957): 12–18.
Joshi, S. T., and David E. Schultz. *Ambrose Bierce: An Annotated Bibliography of Primary Sources*. Westport, Conn.: Greenwood Press, 1999.
Litman, Simon. "Letters of Ambrose Bierce." In *Ray Frank Litman: A Memoir*, 85–114. New York: American Jewish Historical Society, 1957.
McWilliams, Carey. *Ambrose Bierce: A Biography*. New York: Albert & Charles Boni, 1929.
———. "Ambrose Bierce and His First Love." *Bookman* 75, no. 3 (June–July 1932): 254–59.

———. "A Collection of Bierce Letters." *University of California Chronicle* 34 (January 1932): 30–48.

Neale, Walter. *Life of Ambrose Bierce*. New York: Walter Neale, 1929; rpt. New York: AMS Press, 1969.

Pope, Bertha Clark, ed. *The Letters of Ambrose Bierce*. San Francisco: Book Club of California, 1922; rpt. New York: Gordian Press, 1967.

Ridgly, J. V. "Ambrose Bierce to H. L. Mencken." *Book Club of California Quarterly News Letter* 26 (Fall 1961): 27–33.

Scholnick, Robert J. "'My Humble Muse': Some New Bierce Letters." *Markham Review* 5 (Summer 1976): 71–75.

Slade, Joseph W. "'Putting You in the Papers': Ambrose Bierce's Letters to Edwin Markham." *Prospects* 1 (1975): 335–68.

Williams, Stanley T. "Ambrose Bierce and Bret Harte." *American Literature* 17 (1945–46): 179–80.

INDEX

Aldrich, Thomas Bailey, 56
Allen, Charles Dexter, 215
Alta California, 9n5, 13n1, 125n1
American Anthology, An (Stedman), 66n1
"American Kipling, The" (Cowley-Brown), 63n3
American News Company, 117
anarchism, 186
Anderson, Mr., 95
Anderson, W. P., 143
Andreyeva, Maria, 152n7
"Another Way," 67n1
"Antepenultimata," 220
Anti-Philistine, 63n3, 104
"Apocryphal Dialogues," 185n3, 212
"Applicant, The," 30n2
Argonaut, xvii, 42, 158
Arnold, Matthew, 130n1
"Ashes of the Beacon," 143, 150n2, 197n2
Asquith, Margot, 199n3
Astor, Mrs. John Jacob, 209
Atherton, Gertrude, 38, 62, 189, 200
Atlantic Monthly, 126
Austin, Mary, 139, 146, 147, 154

"Back, Back to Nature" (Scheffauer), 120n2
"Backslider, A," 152n3
"Ballade of the Goodly Fere, The" (Pound), xx, 199, 201
Ballard, Samuel, 170n1
Barkhaus, Henry, 107
Barnes, W. H. L., 96
Barr, Robert, 36, 67, 125
Barrow, Isaac, 85n5
Bartlett, William C., 5
Bashford, Herbert, 198
Battlefields and Ghosts, 114n1

Battles and Leaders of the Civil War (Johnson-Buel), 211
Bechdolt, Fred R., 219n3, 238
Becon, Thomas, 59n2
Belford's Magazine, 39
Berkove, Lawrence I., xxivn2, 63n2
Betrayal, The (Neale-Hancock), 203, 204
"Beyond the Wall," 161n3
Bible, 229
Bierce, Albert, xvi, xix, 16, 17, 81, 150, 201, 206, 218, 244
Bierce, Ambrose: and Black Hills, xvi, 19–20; on Christmas, 59; in England, 7–16, 36–37; on ethics, 56–57, 60, 63, 75–76, 111, 112, 130, 175–78, 190–91, 244–46; as fiction writer, xix, 21, 29, 30–31, 35–36, 58, 59, 68, 112–13, 116, 128, 142–44, 147–48, 162–63, 167–69, 174, 191–92; health of, 45, 52, 60, 79, 196–97, 226; as journalist, xvi–xviii, xix–xx, 7, 10–11, 17–18, 25, 31, 35, 42, 50, 51, 52, 58, 62, 67, 68, 86, 110, 119, 135, 136, 140, 146, 149–50, 152, 155, 156, 157, 160–62, 166, 172–73, 174–75, 180–83, 191–93, 194, 217, 236; as letter writer, xxi–xxiii, 132–33, 220, 240; as literary mentor, 23–27, 42, 43–44, 55, 64–65, 73, 78, 80–81, 82, 87–88, 108, 109, 120–21, 199, 209–10; and misanthropy, xv, xvi, xviii, xxi, 49; on New York City, 72, 100–101, 148, 164, 173, 179, 180, 189, 213, 216, 227; pets of, 64; as poet, xix, 39–40, 65–66, 67, 78, 86–87, 90–92, 94–97, 106–7, 169–70; on poetry, 30, 43–44, 49, 55, 84–85, 101–2, 119–20, 122–24, 138, 188, 221, 225, 226; on publishers, 7, 14, 28, 33, 37–40, 59, 64, 86, 88, 104, 113, 116,

249

117–18, 139, 157, 165; relations with family, xvi, xxii, 16–17, 18–19, 21, 28, 77, 78, 80, 205, 206, 234–35, 240; on San Francisco earthquake, 149, 150, 153–54, 158, 169–70; as satirist, xviii, 90–91, 94–96, 100, 198; sociopolitical views of, 23–25, 81, 82–84, 114–15, 186, 188, 208, 237; as soldier, xvi, 1–2, 20, 88, 114, 210–12, 242, 243; travels of, 13, 52, 53, 56, 72, 109, 114, 124–26, 129, 151, 164, 170, 171, 173, 189, 201, 202–5, 214–15, 216–17, 221–22, 223–24, 240, 241, 242, 243–46; on typographical errors, 228–34; on Washington, D.C., 50–52, 68–69, 99, 239; and women, xxii, 23, 29, 60–62, 93, 111–12, 124, 132, 214, 222

Bierce, Carleton, xvi, xix, 81, 201, 203, 206, 208, 217, 243, 244
Bierce, Day, xvii, 18, 22n2, 77n1
Bierce, Hannah Maria, 205
Bierce, Helen. *See* Cowden, Helen (Bierce)
Bierce, Laura (Sherwood), xvi, xvii, 16, 17, 205, 217
Bierce, Leigh, xvii, xxii, 13n2, 18, 21, 33, 37, 50, 63, 66, 74, 75, 77, 78, 147n3, 148n2
Bierce, Lora, xvi, xxiii, 203, 205, 206, 226, 228, 243, 244, 246
Bierce, Marcus Aurelius, xvi, 16, 205
Bierce, Mary Ellen ("Mollie"), xvi, 6, 8, 13, 14, 15, 17, 18, 140n5, 235
Bigelow, Henry Derby "Harry," 29
"Bits of Autobiography," xvi, 175n1, 185n3
"Bivouac of the Dead, A," 114n1
Black Beetles in Amber, 29n1, 32, 39–40, 66, 90, 91, 96, 97nn5, 6, 7, 8, 98n14, 169
Blake, James D., 169, 172, 173, 185
Block, Rudolph, 86, 161, 174, 181
Blythe, S. G., 68
Boalt, John H., 19

Bohemia, 60, 77
Bohemian Club (San Francisco), 9, 93, 95, 105, 197, 208n2
Bonnet, Theodore, 130n2, 189n1, 208n2
Bookman, 200
Boothroyd, Dyson, 20
Bowman, James F., 9
Brannan, John Milton, 210, 211
Brentano's, 118
"Bride, The," 67n1
Brisbane, Arthur, 164, 174
Browning, Robert, 85
Bryce, James, 159, 165n1
Bunner, H. C., 98n17
Burke, Edmund, 27
Burns, Robert, 30
Byron, George Gordon, Lord, 40, 90, 91, 123, 125n1, 133, 187n6, 218

Cade, Jack, 83
Cahill, Edward F., 68n2
California Birthday Book, The (James), 202n5
Californians, The (Atherton), 62
Call of the Wild, The (London), 105n2
Campbell, F. Soulé, 242, 244
Can Such Things Be?, xix, 39n2, 59, 62, 89n2, 148n2, 179
Carlyle, Thomas, 143, 178
Carmany, John H., 4, 5
Carrington, Carroll, xviii, 42, 54
Casamajor, George H., 149, 192
Cassell & Co., 38–39
"Certain Fool Epigrams for Certain Foolish People," 187n5
Chamberlain, Samuel S., 24, 159, 161, 162, 163, 164, 165, 172, 174–75, 180–82, 192, 193
Chapman, George, 123
Chatto & Windus, 12, 14, 38
Chaucer, Geoffrey, 85n3
"Chickamauga," 105n4
Chickamauga, Battle of, 210–12
Christian Science, 158, 194–96, 206
Christiansen, Carrie, 110n3, 111, 130, 141,

Index 251

170, 171, 194, 200, 203, 218, 223, 224, 226, 227, 230, 233–34, 240–41, 244
Christie, Agatha, 201n6
Civil War, xvi, xix, 1–3, 88, 109, 114, 210–12, 242, 243
Cleveland, Grover, 98n16
Clough, Edward H., xviii, 85, 190
Cobwebs from an Empty Skull, 13n2, 170n2
Coleridge, Samuel Taylor, 82, 123, 127, 143, 238n4
Collected Works of Ambrose Bierce, xvi, xx, 173, 178–79, 180, 182n2, 183–86, 188, 197, 202, 203, 207, 212, 215, 217, 220, 222, 223, 224, 228–34, 236, 240
"Confederate Flags, The," 98n16
Connolley, William E., xvi, 205
Connolly, Vera, 214, 222
Conversations with Eckermann (Goethe), 73, 93
Coolbrith, Ina, 158, 185
Cosgrave, John O'Hara, 37, 42, 104, 142
Cosmopolitan, xix, xx, 42n2, 68, 86n2, 126n1, 135, 143, 146, 147nn2, 3, 4, 149–50, 153n1, 155, 156, 157, 158, 159, 160–61, 163, 165n1, 166, 172, 173, 177, 178, 180–82, 187n2, 191–93, 194, 207, 208, 229
Cotton, Lella, 60n3, 72, 73, 124n6
Cowden, Harry D., 170, 194, 206n1, 227, 235, 240, 244
Cowden, Helen (Bierce), xvii, 18, 21, 28, 46, 78, 79, 80, 81, 170, 194–96, 205, 206, 226, 234, 240, 243, 244
Cowley-Brown, John Stapledon, 62, 67, 104, 142
Crawford, Eva, 124, 139, 150, 171, 204
"Creation," 67n1
Criterion, 62
Critic, 104, 127
Cummins, Ella Sterling, 22
Current Literature, 197, 201
Cutting, Miss, 217
Cymbeline (Shakespeare), 71
"Cynic's Dictionary, The," 127

Cynic's Dictionary, The (Thompson), 141n1, 151
Cynic's Word Book, The, 113n2, 141n1, 152, 154
Czolgosz, Leon, 82n3

Daily Chronicle (London), 36
Damien, Father, 75
"Damned Thing, The," 58n1, 106n4
Dance of Death, The, 100n1, 215
Danziger, Gustav Adolphe, xviii, xxv, 28, 31, 34, 54, 70, 74
Davenport, Homer, 148, 151
Davis, Robert H., xix, 86, 128, 151, 167
Davis, Samuel Post, 73, 126, 148
Dawson, Emma Frances, xviii, 54, 158
Dawson, William James, 201n4
Day, Mrs., 13, 14
"Dead Lion, A," 26n2
"Dead Lion (Again) and the Living Professor, The," 201n3
"Death of Grant, The," 67n1
"Death of Satire, The" (Scheffauer), 240n4
Debs, Eugene V., 83
de Castro, Adolphe. *See* Danziger, Gustav Adolphe
"Dedication: To Ambrose Bierce" (Sterling), 85n8
Devil's Dictionary, The, 9n2, 103n7, 113, 127, 141, 151, 163, 182, 185n3
De Young, Meichel Henry, 95
"Diagnosis," 97n4
Dickens, Charles, 50n2, 59
"Dies Irae," 106–7
Dills, Abe, 20
"Discoverers, The," 189n1
"Disjunctus," 102n3
"Diversions of an Idler," 150n2
Dix, John A., 108n1
Dorsey, Stephen, 96
Doubleday, Page & Co., 141, 152, 154, 157, 163n2
Doyle, Sir Arthur Conan, 162–63
Doyle, C. W., xviii, xxii, xxiii, xxv, 41n2,

46, 47, 48, 49, 51, 52, 54, 59, 60, 73, 75, 81, 88, 93, 101, 103, 104, 107, 186, 191
"Dream of Fear, A" (Sterling), 153
"Dreamer, The" (Sickler), 220
Dunciad, The (Pope), 40, 90
d'Utassy, George, 191, 193

Eckermann, Johann Peter, 73, 94n5
Eddy, Mary Baker, 196
Elder, Paul, 93, 98
English Bards and Scotch Reviewers (Byron), 40, 90
English Composition (Nichol), 27
Epictetus, 60, 63
Essay on Criticism, An (Pope), 27
Everybody's Magazine, 38n1, 142–43, 194
"Eyes of the Panther, The," 58n3

"Fables and Anecdotes," 97n13
"Fables of Zambri, the Parsee, The," 12
Fadiman, Clifton, xv
Fairchild, Lee, 96
Fairchild, Lucius, 96, 101
"Fall of the Republic, The," 144n3
Fall of the Republic and Other Satires, The, 40n1, 59n4, 166n1
Fantastic Fables, 59n4, 63, 144n2
Fatout, Paul, xvii
Fee, George, 206, 234
Field, Stephen J., 96
Fiend's Delight, The, 8n3, 37, 169
Figaro (Chicago), 36, 39
Figaro (London), 9n1, 15nn1, 3
Figaro Fiction (Pollard), 37n2
Fletcher, Horace, 196n3
Foote, Lucius H., 237
Forman, Allan, 95
Fortnightly Review, 239
Foss, Sam Walter, 30
Frank, Esther, 45, 53
Frank, Ray, xviii, xxi, 42, 45, 52, 53, 56
Franklin, Dr., 190
Frayser, Isabel, 148
French, Nora May, 171

Fuentes, Carlos, 243n2
Fun, 9n1, 11, 12n1, 13n2, 15n3, 86n2

Garfield, James A., 102n3
Gates, Mary Eleanor, 111n3
"Genesis," 97n6
Gladstone, William Ewart, 36
Goethe, Johann Wolfgang von, 73, 84, 93, 130, 176
"Goethe Was a Prophet as Well as a Poet," 74n3
Golden Era, 9n7
"Goldenb Past, The" (Sterling), 226
Goosequill, 104
Gorky, Maxim, 151, 153, 160
Gould, Jay, 96
Gracie, Archibald, xvi, 210, 222
Grand Army of the Republic, 98n15
Granger, Gordon, 210, 211
Grant, Ulysses S., 96
Great English Short-Story Writers, The (Dawson), 200
Greely, Adolphus Washington, 76
Grenander, Mary Elizabeth, xxv
"Grizzly Papers," 4n1, 5
Guiteau, Charles J., 101

Hancock, Elizabeth H., 203n1
Harcourt, Thomas A., 215–16
Harper's Magazine, 126
Harris, Joel Chandler, 152
Harrison, William Greer, 93, 95
Hart, Jerome A., 42
Harte, Bret, xvi, 3–4, 5, 7, 89n5
Harte, Walter Blackburn, 30, 36, 62
Harvey, George, 144
"Have We a Navy?," 144n4, 194n3
Havens, Frank C., 159n2
Hawthorne, Hildegarde, 197, 217
Hazen, Jean, 55, 60
Hazen, William B., 3n2, 20, 211
Healy, Henry, 20
Hearst, William Randolph, xvii, xix–xx, xxi, 24n5, 37, 48, 50n1, 58, 62, 67, 91, 119, 135, 136, 142, 146, 148n2, 149–50,

153, 156, 157, 164, 172, 173, 193, 229; letters to, 155, 160, 161, 174, 180, 182, 191
Heine, Heinrich, 90, 91, 133
Henley, W. E., 88n2, 130n2
Hershberg, Belle, 43n2, 55, 56
Hershberg, Harriet, 41n2, 43n2, 50, 55
"Hiding of Black Bill, The" (O. Henry), 200
Hill, Daniel Harvey, 210–11
Hillquit, Morris, 186
Holmes, Oliver Wendell, 198
Homer, 123–24, 138, 176
Homestead, Pa., 23
Hood, Thomas, the Younger, 7, 8, 10, 11, 14, 221
Hopper, James, 139, 218
Hotten, John Camden, 7, 12, 38, 169
House of Orchids and Other Poems, The (Sterling), 213n2, 214n1
How to Know the Starry Heavens (Irving), 131
Howells, William Dean, 48
Howes, S. O., 67, 68, 140, 141, 152, 154, 157, 164, 165, 166, 170, 171, 172, 173, 180, 184–85, 193, 196, 199, 212, 215, 217, 220, 223
Hubbard, Elbert, 77, 204
Hugo, Victor, 93
"Human Liver, The," 24
Hume, Hugh, 29, 37
Hunter, Robert, 186
Huntington, Collis P., xix, 50n1, 70

Ibsen, Henrik, 177
Idler, 36
Ihmsen, Max F., 160, 161
Iliad (Homer), 123, 138
Imaginary Conversations (Landor), 27
"In Memory of Dr. C. W. Doyle" (Scheffauer), 104n2
In the Days of the Comet (Wells), 147n4
In the Midst of Life, xix, 38n5, 59n4, 163, 179
Indianapolis Journal, 21n3

Ingalls, John James, 56n1, 96
Ingersoll, Robert G., 25, 201n3
"Insurrection of the Peasantry, An," xx, 190n2
"Invocation," 67, 78
Irving, Edward, 131
Isgrigg, Francis, 170n1

James, George Wharton, 202
Jesus Christ, 183, 196
"John Mortonson's Funeral," 147n3, 148n2
Johnson, Samuel, 119
Jorgensen, Christian A., 158
Josephare, Lionel, 147
"Jury in Ancient America, The," 150n2

Kahn, Julius, 74
Kames, Henry Home, Lord, 27
Kaufman, Charles H., 22, 112–13
Keats, John, 123, 127, 143, 147n1, 225
Keller, G. Frederick, 107
Khayyam, Omar, 94
"King of Craft, A," 182n2
"Kings of Beasts," 224
Kipling, Rudyard, 67, 88n2
Kirk, William F., 137n3

Lamb, Charles, 152n1
La Monte, Robert Rives, 236
Land of Little Rain, The (Austin), 140n7, 146
Landor, Walter Savage, 27, 146n2
Lang, Andrew, 123
Langton, William, 34, 39
Lantern (London), 15n3
"Last Chanty, The" (Kipling), 88n2
"Laus Lucis," 97n8
Learned, Leila Sprague, 214
Leblanc, Maurice, 201n6
Lentala of the South (Morrow), 167n2
"Letter from a Btrugumian," 102n2
Letters of Ambrose Bierce, The, xvii, xxv, 210n1, 243
Lewis, Alfred Henry, 181

Lezinsky, David Lesser, 33
Life, 194
Lilith (Sterling), 127, 207
Lincoln, Abraham, 49, 223
Literary Digest, 201
"Little Bobbie" (Kirk), 136
"Little Johnny," 86, 135n1, 136, 185n3, 192, 212, 224
"Little of Chickamauga, A," 212n4
Livermore Sanitarium, 60n1, 210n1
Livingstone, David, 97n2
London, Jack, 82n1, 84–85, 104, 110, 131, 145, 147, 165–66, 188, 204, 208
London Sketch-Book, 15n3
Longfellow, Henry Wadsworth, 47n1, 222n1
Longinus, 27
"Look into the Gulf, A" (Markham), 55n2
Looms of Life (Scheffauer), 178n3
Lovecraft, H. P., xxii, xxiii
Loveman, Samuel, 213
Lucian, 27
Lucy, Sir Henry, 200

Mackay, Robert, 120, 131, 143, 151
Macmillan & Co., 64, 229
Man: His Mark, A (Morrow), 76
"Man with the Hoe, The" (Markham), xviii, 39n3, 65, 66n3
"Marjorie Daw" (Aldrich), 56
Markham, Edwin, xviii–xix, 39, 55, 64, 66, 67, 73, 78, 81, 84, 85, 147, 151, 153
Martin, C. F., 54n3
Martin, Mabel, 54, 59, 60–62, 125
Massaniello, 83
"Matter of Manner, The," 223n3
Maxwell, Perriton, 155, 156, 161, 162, 174
McAlister, May Elizabeth, 77
McClure's, 64, 65
McCracken, Josephine Clifford, 89
McEwen, Arthur, 90, 95
McKinley, William, 81
McLoughlin & Steele, 19–20

McWilliams, Carey, xxiii, xxv, 3nn1, 4, 237n1
"Memorial Day, 1901" (Sterling), 79n2, 81–82
"Men Who Make Our Books, The" (Vore), 64n1
Mencken, H. L., xix, xxi, xxiii–xxiv, 235, 236
"Merciful Governor, A," 97n7
Michelangelo, 231n2
Millard, Bailey, 42, 65, 85, 135, 137, 143, 146, 149, 155
Miller, Joaquin, xvi, 8, 10, 14, 16, 33, 49, 127, 146, 148, 154, 161n5, 186
Milton, John, 101, 230
Moffett, Samuel Erasmus, 151
Monk and the Hangman's Daughter, The (Voss-Bierce-Danziger), xviii, 28, 31–32, 59n3, 70–72, 89n2, 189
"Montefiore," 67n1
Moody, William Vaughn, 88n2, 160n1
Mooney, C. P., 143
"Moonlit Road, The," 191
Morehouse, H. V., 95
Morris, Madge, 38
Morrow, W. C., xviii, xxiii, 35, 75–76, 93n1, 166
Mortimer, James, 14
Mulford, Prentice, 9, 14
Munsey, Frank A., 86n1
Munsey's Magazine, xix
Murphy, Daniel, 165
"My Favorite Murder," 106n4

Nathan, George Jean, 236n1
Nation, 217
Neale, Walter, xx, 89n2, 105n1, 147, 159, 173, 175, 176, 177, 178, 180, 183, 185, 188, 190, 197, 199, 202, 203, 212, 214, 216n1, 217, 220, 222, 224, 228
Neale Publishing Company, 88, 240
Neale's Monthly, 223n1
Neihardt, John G., 214n1
New England Magazine, 31n2, 36
New York American, 69n2, 102n2, 123,

132n1, 135n1, 136, 143, 144n3, 146, 155
New York Evening Post, 217
New York Journal, xix, 48, 50, 51, 65, 67, 68, 73, 78, 144n2, 192
New York Times Book Review, 213, 214
Newcomb, James Pearson, 9
Newman, John Philip, 95
Nichol, John, 27
Nietzsche, Friedrich, 109, 119
9009 (Hopper-Bechdolt), 219n3
Noble, Frank L. H. "Cosy," 24
Norcross, C. P., 191, 192
North American Review, 25, 217
Northern Indianan, xvi
Notre-Dame de Paris (Hugo), 93
Nowland, James A., 235
Nuggets and Dust, 9nn1, 5, 12n3, 125n1, 170n2

O. Henry, 200
Oakland Saturday Press, 39, 42n1
Oakland Times, 33, 85n12
"Occurrence at Owl Creek Bridge, An," 48n2
"Ode in Time of Hesitation" (Moody), 88n2
"Ode to the Abyss" (Smith), 225
Odyssey (Homer), 119, 123, 138
Old Gringo, The (Fuentes), 243n2
"On a Mountain," 231n1
"One Summer Night," 147n3
"Oscar Wilde," 122n5
"Other Lodgers, The," 161n3
Otis, Eliza A. (Wetherby), 198n4
Otis, Harrison Gray, 197
Our Bourgeois Literature (Sinclair), 139n1
Outlook (London), 67
Overland Monthly, xvi, 3–4, 8n3, 89n5

Papyrus, 121–22
Partington, Blanche, xviii, xxiii, 23, 24, 26, 28, 29, 30, 33, 37, 41, 81, 84, 113, 227, 244

Partington, Gertrude, 24n1
Partington, John H. E., 24, 25, 37
Partington, Phyllis, 38, 132, 164, 227
Partington, Richard, 24, 105, 179
"Passages from the 'Best-Selling' Books," 120n1
"Passing of Satire, The," 194n2
"Passing of Tennyson, The" (Miller), 50n3, 161n5
"Passing Show, The" (column), xx, 65, 74n5, 91, 114n1, 120n1, 123, 147n2, 149, 154n3, 155, 167n1, 198n4
"Passing Show, The" (poem), 67
Peck, Harry Thurston, 200
Peterson, Kate, 105, 126, 139, 171
Philosophical Enquiry into the Origin of Our Ideas of the Sublime and Beautiful, A (Burke), 27
"Pickett's Charge" (Scheffauer), 89n3
"Piratical Ballad, A," 93n2
"Playwright, A," 97n5, 182n2
Poe, Edgar Allan, 105n3, 123, 138, 140n3, 151, 197, 239n1
Poems (French), 172n1
Poems (Loveman), 213n4
Poems to Vera (Sterling), 215n1
"Poesy" (Sterling), 121
"Poet and His Poem, A," 160, 165n3, 190n2
Pollard, Percival, xviii, xxi, 36, 38, 58, 62, 81–82, 121–22, 130, 132, 138, 140, 141, 157, 166, 171, 172, 177–78, 183, 199, 215, 219
Pollard, Mrs. Percival, 219
Pope, Alexander, 9n4, 18n2, 27, 40, 44n2, 90, 91, 122n3, 123, 138, 210n2, 228n1
Pope, Bertha Clark, xvii, 202n2
Portrait of Ambrose Bierce (de Castro), xxv, 32n1, 72n1, 75n1
Pound, Ezra, xx, 199, 201
"Prattle," xvii, 30n3, 31nn1, 3, 4, 32n2, 37nn2, 3, 45n1, 48n2, 50nn1, 3, 56n2, 58, 62, 63n2, 66n3, 67, 91, 94nn4, 5, 98n17, 102n3, 108n1, 110, 122n5, 182n2, 187n1

"Presentiment," 67n1
Princess, The (Tennyson), 101
Puck, 96
Pulitzer, Joseph, xx, 160
Punch, 200
Putnam's Sons, G. P., 59, 62–63

Rabelais, François, 183
Realf, Richard, 33, 44
"Realm of the Unreal, The," 106n4
Rearden, Timothy H., 6
"Recessional" (Kipling), 67, 88n2
"Republic, The" (Scheffauer), 74n5
"Resumed Identity, A," 161n3
Rhymester, The (Hood), 221
Riley, James Whitcomb, 29, 30, 154
Road, The (London), 166n2
Robertson, A. M., 88, 90–91, 92, 93, 94, 95, 96, 97, 139, 145, 147, 193, 197, 200, 220
Robertson, John W., 60, 196n2, 210n1
Robertson, Louis Alexander, 104
Robertson, Ruth, 209
Roman, Anton, 4n1
Roosevelt, Theodore, 121, 223, 227
Rubáiyát (Khayyam), 94
Rulofson, William Herman, 100n1, 215–16
Ruskin, John, 238
Russell, Edmund, 29
Russell, George T., 98n18

St. Louis Mirror, 132
Sampson, Henry, 11–12, 13, 14
San Francisco Chronicle, 97n10
San Francisco Examiner, xvii, 24, 31, 36n1, 39, 42, 49, 50, 51, 54, 58, 68, 73, 127, 135n1, 146, 165nn1, 2
San Francisco News Letter and California Advertiser, xvi, 8n3, 12, 98n18
Scheffauer, Herman, xviii, xix, xx, xxi, xxiii, xxv, 78, 104, 105, 116, 125, 126, 137, 145, 148, 164, 173–74, 175, 179–80, 186–87, 188, 239; letters to, 43, 69, 72, 77, 79, 86, 88, 90, 92, 94,

98, 100, 103, 106, 109, 111, 113, 114, 118, 122, 124, 129, 132, 165, 175, 190
Schoolfield, Mrs., 200
Schopenhauer, Arthur, 136, 179
Schulte, F. J., 32, 35, 39, 72
Schwab, Charles M., 83
Sea Wolf, The (London), 131
Selected Poems (Sterling), 180n1
Semiramis, 55
Shackleton, Sir Ernest, 200
Shadow of Quong Lung, The (Doyle), 186
Shadow on the Dial, The, 67n1, 140, 152, 154, 157n1, 165, 180, 184–85, 193, 197, 200, 212, 218n1, 220n1
Shakespeare, William, 54n1, 71, 101, 152n5, 176, 183
Shapes of Clay, xix, 66n2, 67n1, 87n1, 90–92, 94–97, 98–100, 104, 106–7, 113–14, 116, 117–18, 139, 145, 150, 169
Shaw, George Bernard, 165, 177
Shaw, Mary, 132
Shearer, Flora, 150
Shelley, Percy Bysshe, 80n1
Shepard, Morgan, 93, 98
Shipman, Priscilla, 110n3, 111, 223, 224
"Short Story, The," 48n2
Sickler, Eleanor (Vore), 63, 220, 241
Sickles, Daniel Edgar, 88
Sinclair, Upton, 137, 207, 226
"Small Contributions," 147n2, 153n1, 156, 160n1, 165n4, 178n3, 192
Smart Set, 235, 236
Smith, Algernon, 12
Smith, Clark Ashton, 225
"Social Unrest" (Bierce-Hunter-Hillquit), 187n2, 208
Socialism, 83, 146n1, 147, 186, 206, 208, 218, 237
"Sole Survivor, A," 38n4, 175n1
"Some Ante-Mortem Epitaphs," 98nn11, 12, 182n2
"Some Uncanny Tales," 147n3
"Son of the Gods, A," 106n4
Son of the Wolf, The (London), 110
"Song of the Sword" (Henley), 88n2

Southern Historical Society, 223
Spencer, Herbert, 27
"Staley Fleming's Hallucination," 147n3
Stanford, Leland, 95
Stanley, Henry M., 94
Star-Treader and Other Poems, The (Smith), 225n2
Stedman, Edmund Clarence, 65, 67
Steele, E. L. G., 17, 40, 41, 100n1, 112
Steele, Mrs. E. L. G., 41, 112
Steele, Edward, 41
Stephens, A. G., 217
Sterling, Carrie, 79n3, 85, 105, 145, 147, 201, 204, 214, 216, 217, 218, 222, 224, 226
Sterling, George, xvii, xix, xx, xxii, xxiii, 32n1, 89n1, 102, 103n9, 106, 107, 108, 109, 119, 128, 134, 143, 165, 166, 167, 168, 175, 178n1, 190, 206, 213, 214, 215, 224, 225, 238; letters to: 78, 80, 82, 87, 99, 104, 110, 115, 117, 120, 123, 125, 126, 131, 135, 137, 145, 146, 147, 149, 150, 153, 158, 159, 162, 164, 171, 179, 185, 187, 189, 198, 201, 204, 207, 216, 218, 221, 226
Sterling, James Davenport, 138
Sterling, Marian, 79n3, 81, 85, 111, 122, 134, 138–39, 190
Stevenson, Robert Louis, 77n2, 94n2, 105n3, 158
Stoddard, Charles Warren, xvi, xvii, 7–16, 139, 148, 151
Stokes, Frederick A., Co., 86
Stone & Kimball, Messrs., 39, 40
Stoneman, George, 95
Story of the Files, The (Cummins), 22n1
Stott, A. W., 72
"Stranger, The," 193n1
Success, 120, 131
Summer Cruising in the South Seas (Stoddard), 13n1, 14
"Sweet By and By, The," 25
Swinburne, Algernon Charles, 73, 158
Sydney Bulletin, 217
Syle, Louis Du Pont, 100

"T. A. H.," 67n1, 215
Taft, William Howard, 224n1, 227n2
Tales of Soldiers and Civilians, xvii, xix, 18n1, 21n1, 34n4, 38n5, 59, 85n12, 100n1, 112, 116, 128, 167, 168, 169
Tapley, Mark, 49
"Ta-ra-ra-boom-de-ay," 25
Taylor, Ann, 77n4
Tennyson, Alfred, Lord, 49, 101, 137n1, 238n3, 240n5
"Terrible and Tragic in Fiction, The" (London), 104
Testimony of the Suns, The (Sterling), 85n1, 121, 127n3, 132nn2, 4, 147, 151, 165n3, 213
Thackeray, William Makepeace, 120n3
Their Day in Court (Pollard), xviii, 200n1
"Theosophistry," 97n8
Thomas, Belle, 15
Thomas, George Henry, 210, 211
Thompson, Harry, 141n1
"Three and One Are One," 169n1
Through the Magic Door (Doyle), 163
"Thumb-Nail Sketch, A," 38n3
Titanic, 222, 224
"To a Lily" (Sterling), 121
"To a Professional Eulogist," 97n9
"To Ambrose Bierce" (Sterling), 85n7, 152n4, 180n1
"To Ina Coolbrith" (Sterling), 159n5
"To the Colorado Desert" (Morris), 38n6
Tolstoi, Leo, 24
Torrence, Ridgley, 127
"Town Crier, The," xvi, 3
Town Talk, 138, 151, 152n4, 187, 200, 208, 225
Town Topics, 58, 62
Treasure Island (Stevenson), 94n2
Truth about Chickamauga, The (Gracie), 212n1
Tufts, James, 35
Tully, Mr., 110
Twain, Mark, xvi–xvii, 11, 12, 13, 144, 151, 209, 242

"Two Administrations," 27n2, 185n3
"Underground Reputation of Ambrose Bierce, The," 197n1
"Unfinished Story, The" (Morrow), 36n2
United States Book Company, 33, 39
"Unwilling Convert, An," 51n2
"Views of One, The," 132n1, 135n1, 146n1
"Visions of the Night," 239n3
Vore, Eleanor. *See* Sickler, Eleanor (Vore)
Vore, Elizabeth, 64n1
Voss, Richard, xviii, 29n2

Walker, John Brisben, 192
Walsh, Lily, xviii, 41, 45–48, 50, 54
Walsh, Myles, 41n2, 48, 50, 58, 79, 136
"War Topics," 63n2
Warner, Charles Dudley, 12n1
Washington Post, 78, 81
Wasp, xvii, 22, 29, 94n5, 107, 122n5, 127
"Watcher by the Dead, A," 106n4
Waterhouse, Alfred James, 49
Watson, William, 198
Wave, 30n2, 33, 37, 42, 104
Way & Williams, 59
Webster, Noah, 1
Wells, Amy L., 237, 238, 239, 242
Wells, H. G., 147
What Is Art? (Tolstoi), 26n1

Whitaker, Herman, 84
"White Rose, A" (Sterling), 121
Whitman, Walt, 8, 154
Whymper, Frederick, 16
Wilcox, Ella Wheeler, 164
Wilde, Oscar, 122
Wilkinson, Warring, 41, 45
Williams, Jo, 2
Wilson, Woodrow, 227n2
"Wine of Wizardry, A" (Sterling), xx, 116n2, 120, 121, 126, 128, 131, 135, 137, 143, 147, 164, 165, 186, 189, 190, 207
Wine of Wizardry and Other Poems, A (Sterling), 154n1, 159n5, 213
"With a Book," 85n13
Wood, W. E., 87n1, 98–99, 100, 106, 116, 117, 118, 139, 150, 207
Worcester, Joseph Emerson, 1
Wright, Clara, xvi, xxv, 1
Wright, Fatima, xvi, 1, 2
Wright, Oliver, 2
Wright, Willard Huntington, 236
Write It Right, 194, 197, 200, 212, 214, 221

Young, Edward, 15n4

Zeno of Citium, 60

www.ingramcontent.com/pod-product-compliance
Lightning Source LLC
Chambersburg PA
CBHW020943230426
43666CB00005B/151